Conferences and Conventions

D0080719

Books in the Series

Management of Events Operations by Julia Tum, Philippa Norton and J. Nevan Wright

Innovative Marketing Communications: Strategies for the Events Industry by Guy Masterman and Emma. H. Wood

Events Management 2e by Glenn A J Bowdin, Johnny Allen, William O'Toole, Rob Harris and Ian McDonnell

Events Design and Experience by Graham Berridge

Marketing and Selling Destinations and Venues: A Convention and Events Perspective by Tony Rogers and Rob Davidson

Human Resource Management for Events
Lynn Van der Wagen

Events Studies: Theory, Research and Policy for Planned Events by Donald Getz

Conferences and Conventions
A global industry

Second Edition

Tony Rogers

AMSTERDAM • BOSTON • HEIDELBERG • LONDON • NEW YORK • OXFORD
PARIS • SAN DIEGO • SAN FRANCISCO • SINGAPORE • SYDNEY • TOKYO

Butterworth-Heinemann is an imprint of Elsevier

Butterworth-Heinemann is an imprint of Elsevier
Linacre House, Jordan Hill, Oxford OX2 8DP, UK
30 Corporate Drive, Suite 400, Burlington, MA 01803, USA

First edition 2003
Second edition 2008

British Library Cataloguing in Publication Data
A catalogue record for this book is available from the British Library

Library of Congress Cataloging-in-Publication Data
A catalog record for this book is available from the Library of Congress

ISBN: 978-0-7506-8544-3

For information on all Butterworth-Heinemann publications
visit our web site at books.elsevier.com

Printed and bound in Slovenia
08 09 10   10 9 8 7 6 5 4 3 2 1

Working together to grow
libraries in developing countries

www.elsevier.com | www.bookaid.org | www.sabre.org

ELSEVIER   BOOK AID
            International   Sabre Foundation

Contents

Series editors

Glenn A J Bowdin is Principal Lecturer in Events Planning at the UK Centre for Events Management, Leeds Metropolitan University, where he has responsibility for managing events-related research. He is co-author of *Events Management*. His research interests include the area of service quality management, specifically focusing on the area of quality costing, and issues relating to the planning, management and evaluation of events. He is a member of the Editorial Boards for *Event Management* (an international journal) and *Journal of Convention & Event Tourism*, Chair of AEME (Association for Events management Education), Charter Member of the International EMBOK (Event Management Body of Knowledge) and Executive and a member of Meeting Professionals International (MPI).

Don Getz is a Professor in the Tourism and Hospitality Management Program, Haskayne School of Business, the University of Calgary. His ongoing research involves event-related issues (e.g. management, event tourism, events and culture) and special-interest tourism (e.g. wine). Recent books include *Event Management & Event Tourism* and *Explore Wine Tourism: Management, Development, Destinations*. He co-founded and is a member of the Editorial Board for *Event Management* (an international journal).

Conrad Lashley is Professor in Leisure Retailing and Director of the Centre for Leisure Retailing at Nottingham Business School, Nottingham Trent University. He is also series editor for the *Elsevier Butterworth Heinemann Series* on Hospitality Leisure and Tourism. His research interests have largely been concerned with service quality management and specifically employee empowerment in service delivery. He also has research interest and publications relating to hospitality management education. Recent books include *Organisation Behaviour for Leisure Services, 12 Steps to Study Success, Hospitality Retail Management*, and *Empowerment: HR Strategies for Service Excellence*. He has co-edited *Franchising Hospitality Services* and *In Search of Hospitality: Theoretical Perspectives and Debates*. He is the past Chair of the Council for Hospitality Management Education. He is a Chair of the British Institute of Innkeeping's panel judges for the NITA Training awards and is advisor to England's East Midlands Tourism network.

Series preface

The events industry, including festivals, meetings, conferences, exhibitions, incentives, sports and a range of other events, is rapidly developing and makes a significant contribution to business and leisure-related tourism. With increased regulation and the growth of government and corporate involvement in events, the environment has become much more complex. Event managers are now required to identify and service a wide range of stakeholders and to balance their needs and objectives. Though mainly operating at national levels, there has been significant growth of academic provision to meet the needs of events and related industries and the organisations that comprise them. The English-speaking nations, together with key Northern European countries, have developed programmes of study leading to the award of diploma, undergraduate and post-graduate awards. These courses focus on providing education and training for future event professionals and cover areas such as event planning and management, marketing, finance, human resource management and operations. Modules in events management are also included in many tourism, leisure, recreation and hospitality qualifications in universities and colleges.

The rapid growth of such courses has meant that there is a vast gap in the available literature on this topic for lecturers, students and professionals alike. To this end, the *Elsevier Butterworth Heinemann Events Management Series* has been created to meet these needs to create a planned and targeted set of publications in this area.

Aimed at academic and management development in events management and related studies, the *Events Management Series*

- provides a portfolio of titles which match management development needs through various stages;

- prioritises publication of texts where there are current gaps in the market or where current provision is unsatisfactory;
- develops a portfolio of both practical and stimulating texts;
- provides a basis for theoretical and research underpinning for programmes of study;
- is recognised as being of consistent high quality;
- will quickly become the series of first choice for both authors and users.

Forewords

Sue Stuart

Convention business is big business, and one of the most successful growth industries of our age.

All over the world more meetings are being held today than was ever thought possible. International congresses, exhibitions, trade shows, seminars, and conventions of all kinds are being organized.

The world has become a smaller place – horizons are widening and new cultures being absorbed daily. As a result, in every country competition to attract this valuable business has become keener.

Whilst the economic benefit to be derived from business tourism is important, meetings and conventions are about much more than simply generating delegate spend. They also play a vital role in business trade investment and professional development.

Conventions generate business activity and provide a focus for those who are interested in new investment and product promotion. Any community hosting these kinds of events has an edge on business development and an opportunity to benefit from the presence of high level decision-makers and potential investors right on their doorstep. Large events like conventions are designed to bring the best in any given field together in an environment where information can be shared and progress identified. When this happens, it creates a big boost to local knowledge and skills in any imaginable discipline.

This book provides excellent insight for individuals attracted to enter the fascinating and ever-evolving world of conferences and conventions. It also is an invaluable resource for lecturers and those already working in this truly dynamic and global industry.

Sue Stuart
Chair, British Association of Conference Destinations
Chief Executive, Edinburgh Convention Bureau

Jonathan Wilson

Many pundits predicted that the internet would kill off conferences, meetings and even exhibitions. After all, they argued, who will want to spend time and money travelling to a distant venue, to spend days being lectured at, when we could achieve the same result, more quickly and cheaply, just by logging on at a convenient time?

However, what these commentators forgot was that humans like meeting each other, that we enjoy sharing experiences, in person; and that we'd rather listen to, and participate, in a talk in the company of our peers than in isolation in front of a PC.

Which is why conferences and conventions will be with us for the foreseeable future, occupying an important part of the working and leisure lives of just about anyone, in any position, in every organization you can think of.

And for each conference or meeting there has to be an organizer, or (more likely) a team – with the ability, skill and experience

to plan, co-ordinate, supervise and manage a complex mixture of disciplines and suppliers.

Organizers have to learn their skills somewhere and a great starting point is this book which contains a wealth of information in a very accessible format. It will also be of considerable value to relatively experienced conference professionals – especially those who are moving their way up through the ranks of organizing companies – as it will fill many of the gaps that a reliance on learning by practical experience inevitably creates.

It is both an introduction to a vibrant industry and an invaluable guide for those working within it.

Jonathan Wilson
Chair, Association of British Professional Conference Organisers
Managing Director, Healthcare Events Ltd

Preface

I have been privileged to work for the past 18 years in the fascinating world of conferences and conventions. In that period there have been huge changes and developments in the way the industry is marketed, in the organization and presentation of meetings and conferences, in the competition for a share of the lucrative economic 'cake' that conferences and conventions represent, and in a multitude of other ways. And yet the essence remains the same: it is about bringing people together to communicate by sharing information and ideas, to motivate and inspire, to launch new products and disseminate the latest research, to negotiate in order to reach a consensus on the different challenges facing our world.

This book attempts to describe the many facets of this global industry and to provide both an insight into how it is structured and a broader picture of an industry in its totality. It can be dipped into for discrete pieces of information on specific aspects of the industry, or read in its entirety by those wanting a better understanding of the parameters and characteristics of this true twenty-first century industry. I hope very much that it will be of interest and practical use to students and lecturers, and to those working in the industry, as well as to those who may be looking to make a future career in the industry, to politicians (local and national), to journalists and consultants, and indeed to anyone seeking an overview of this dynamic, endearing, varied but still under-recognised sector of national and global economies.

The book would not have been possible without the unstinting help, advice and provision of data and material that I have received from literally hundreds of colleagues around the world. One of the delights of the conference industry, for me, is this very openness and willingness to share that I have experienced at every turn. To everyone who has helped in any way, I owe an enormous debt of gratitude. I trust they will understand if I do not mention them individually. To do so would certainly take up several pages but I am very afraid of missing someone out and unwittingly giving offence. But please be assured that my appreciation is heartfelt – I just hope that they each feel that the book justifies the efforts and contributions they have made.

SECOND EDITION

This second edition of the book represents a substantial re-writing. While I have retained the overall structure of the first edition, I have updated all of the factual and statistical information, replaced almost all of the case studies, and introduced a number of new topics (for example, virtual meetings technology; global event management companies; a more in-depth look at the international association convention sector; sustainability and 'green' meetings; procurement and ROI) which were not covered in the first edition or only referred to briefly. I hope, therefore, that it will prove to be a valuable resource both to new readers but also to those who may have purchased the first edition.

Each chapter follows a similar pattern with an introduction, learning outcomes, main theme, summary, review and discussion questions, and references. Many of the chapters include case studies to illustrate in more depth particular points made in the chapters. The case studies are positioned at the end of the book but their numbering relates to the chapter in which the topic is raised e.g. Case Study 2.2 refers to Chapter 2. There are also mini case studies embedded in the main text of several chapters.

In the text I have, for stylistic simplicity, used 'he' rather than '(s)he' where appropriate, but such uses should be interpreted as applying equally to both genders. Indeed, I should perhaps have used 'she' throughout as women are represented very strongly at all levels of the industry, probably outnumbering men in many sectors.

And, finally, I have used mainly UK terminology. I give below several common terms for which different words/phrases are used in North America and in certain other countries:

UK terms	North American equivalents
Accommodation	Housing
Exhibition	Exposition
Professional conference/ congress organizer (PCO)	Independent meeting planner
Delegates	Attendees

Tony Rogers
March 2007

Case studies

A global industry

The conference industry is a young, dynamic industry which is growing and maturing at a rapid rate. From origins in Europe and North America, it is now a truly international industry witnessing huge investments across all continents. Its youthfulness, however, does mean that it lacks some of the necessary characteristics of more established industries, such as well defined terminology, adequate market intelligence, appropriate education and training structures and clear entry routes. Conferences are part of the business tourism (or business events) sector, a major though often under-valued sector of the wider tourism industry.

This chapter looks at:

- the origins of the conference industry
- the foundations of a proper industry
- the industry's recent globalisation
- world rankings of leading cities and countries
- certain industry shortcomings
- industry parameters and definitions
- business tourism and leisure tourism
- the benefits of conference and business tourism.

It includes case studies on:

- City of Melbourne, Australia
- The Queen Elizabeth II Conference Centre, London, England
- Hyderabad International Convention Centre, India
- Abu Dhabi, United Arab Emirates
- Coral Beach Hotel and Resort, Paphos, Cyprus.

Learning outcomes

On completion of this chapter, you should be able to:

- Explain why and how the conference industry developed in the way it did
- Understand the international dimensions of the industry and appreciate which are the most successful cities and countries
- Discuss the features of the industry which illustrate the steps still required to achieve full maturation
- Understand the key benefits afforded by conference and business tourism, and what distinguishes it from leisure tourism.

THE ORIGINS OF THE CONFERENCE INDUSTRY

American Presidents hosting the latest Middle East Summit at Camp David in Maryland, the Royal College of Nursing holding its annual conference in Bournemouth, members of the International Congress and Convention Association gathering for their assembly and congress in Montevideo, shareholders of Microsoft or HSBC attending the company's annual general meeting, the sales force of GlaxoSmithKline coming together for a regular briefing or training event, or their high achievers jetting off for an incentive-cum-meeting trip to an exotic overseas destination.

The different events described above have one thing in common: they are all to do with bringing people together, face-to-face, to exchange ideas and information, to discuss and in some cases negotiate, to build friendships and closer business relationships, to encourage better performance by individuals and organizations. They are different facets of the same dynamic, international, economically vibrant conference industry. The terms used ('summit', 'meeting', 'conference', 'assembly', 'convention', 'congress', 'AGM', 'briefing', 'training', 'incentive') may vary, and the events themselves may have different formats and emphases, but the essential ingredients and objectives are the same.

Conferences are at the forefront of modern communications, whether this is for internal communications (sales meetings, training seminars, board retreats, major annual conferences, for example) or as a vehicle for communicating with key audiences (such as press briefings, product launches, annual general meetings, some technical conferences). Conferences is a generic term to describe a diverse mix of communications events.

The phrase 'conference industry' is of very recent origin, and is certainly not one that would have been heard until the second half of the twentieth century. Yet people's need to congregate and confer is one of the things that defines our humanity and, for a multitude of different reasons, meetings and gatherings of people have taken place since the early days of civilization. Shone (1998) traces the evolution of meetings since Roman times in Britain and Ireland, and the development of meeting rooms and meeting places to accommodate these, driven largely by the needs of trade and commerce.

One of the highest profile events in the past couple of hundred years, perhaps almost a launch event for our contemporary conference industry, was the Congress of Vienna held from September 1814 to June 1815. The Congress was called to re-establish the territorial divisions of Europe at the end of the Napoleonic Wars and representatives included all of the major world powers of the day (with the exception of Turkey). It is tempting to imagine what the 'delegate spend' must have been like, with delegates such as Alexander I, Emperor of Russia, Prince Karl August von Hardenberg from Prussia, and Viscount Castlereagh and the Duke of Wellington as the principal British representatives. Each representative would have been accompanied by a substantial delegation of support staff and partners, requiring accommodation, social programmes, lavish corporate entertainment, ground handling, not to mention state-of-the-art conference facilities. The Vienna Convention Bureau no doubt celebrated long and hard its success in attracting such a high-profile, high-spend event to the city!

As the nineteenth century progressed, universities increasingly provided facilities for the dissemination of information within academic circles, while the boom in spa towns and, in the UK, Victorian resorts with assembly rooms began to make available larger public spaces for entertainment and meetings. At the same time, the development of the railway network was accompanied by the construction of railway hotels alongside major stations. Many of these hotels had substantial function rooms available for hire.

Shone contends that the dawn of the twentieth century was accompanied by a change in the demand for meetings:

> *Though assemblies and congresses continued to be driven by trade and industry, there was a slow and gradual increase in activity which, rather than promoting products, or reporting a company's annual progress, looked to developing staff and sales. The precursors of the sales training meeting, the 'congress of commercials' (or commercial travellers) of the 1920s and 1930s, began to develop into something more modern and recognizable.*

The situation was somewhat different in North America during the latter half of the nineteenth century, particularly across the eastern seabord of the USA where various trade and professional associations, as well as religious groups, were being formed and, as they became more established, beginning to hold conventions for their memberships. Gartrell (1994) records that, in due course, a number of committees were also created to:

> *lure the growing convention business from these expanding and thriving associations'. As more and more cities became aware of the value of convention business, Gartrell suggests that it was 'inevitable that the solicitation of these conventions would be assigned to a full-time salesperson; and, while this might have happened in any one of many major cities, history records that it first happened in Detroit, Michigan, when a group of businessmen decided to place a full-time salesperson on the road to invite conventions to their city. Thus, in 1896, the first convention bureau was formed, and an industry emerged.*

Detroit was shortly followed by other US cities which established their own convention bureaux: Cleveland (1904), Atlantic City (1908), Denver and St Louis (1909), Louisville and Los Angeles (1910). Now many cities around the world have their own convention bureau, or convention and visitor bureau.

THE FOUNDATIONS OF A PROPER INDUSTRY

While the origins of today's conference industry lie in the political and religious congresses of earlier centuries, followed by business meetings and, in the USA, trade and professional association conventions, the development and recognition of a proper 'industry' is a much more recent phenomenon, in Europe especially, effectively dating from the middle to latter part of the twentieth century.

The foundation of trade associations is often a useful, objective way of marking the real formation of an industry. Some of the principal conference industry associations were founded as follows:

International Association of Exhibitions and Events (IAEE)	– 1928
Professional Convention Management Association (PCMA)	– 1957
Association Internationale des Palais de Congrès (AIPC)	– 1958
International Congress and Convention Association (ICCA)	– 1963
European Federation of Conference Towns (EFCT)	– 1964

International Association of Professional Congress Organizers (IAPCO)	– 1968
British Association of Conference Destinations (BACD)	– 1969
Meeting Professionals International (MPI)	– 1972
Meetings & Events Australia (MEA) (originally Meetings Industry Association of Australia – MIAA)	– 1975
Association of British Professional Conference Organizers (ABPCO)	– 1981
Meetings Industry Association (MIA) (UK)	– 1990

The Destination Marketing Association International (DMAI) (until 2005 known as the International Association of Convention and Visitor Bureaus – IACVB), on the other hand, with a predominantly North American membership, was founded as long ago as 1914.

Since the 1960s there has been a steadily increasing investment in the whole infrastructure that supports conferences, meetings and related events, an investment which accelerated into a rapid growth during the 1990s. The 1990s were almost certainly the decade which recorded the highest sustained investment to date in global conference infrastructure, but such investment has continued unabated into the new millennium. Tables 1.1 and 1.2 give details of newly-built and re-developed conference and convention facilities in just two countries, Australia and the United Kingdom, epitomising the huge scale of investment that has taken place over the past couple of decades. This list does not include other substantial investments in buildings which, though not purpose-built for the conventions industry, are capable of staging very large conferences, such as (in the UK) the Sheffield Arena (12 000 seats, £45 million), Birmingham's National Indoor Arena (13 000 seats, £51 million), Manchester's £42 million Bridgewater Hall and the 19 000-seat Nynex Arena, the Newcastle Arena (10 000 seats, £10.5 million) in Newcastle upon Tyne, and the Wales Millennium Centre, Cardiff (1900-seat auditorium, £104 million).

Case Study 1.1 traces the developments and investments made by the City of Melbourne in its convention 'product' over recent years, while Case Study 1.2 describes the ongoing enhancements to facilities and business development made by The Queen Elizabeth II Conference Centre, London.

But it is not just in Europe, Australasia and North America that major investments are being made. In the past 5–10 years, large-scale infrastructure projects have been undertaken throughout much of Asia and the Pacific rim, in the former East European

Name of Centre	Year of Opening	Cost (AU$m)
Adelaide Convention Centre	1987	Not available
	2001 extension completed	85
Sydney Convention & Exhibition Centre	1988	230
Canberra National Convention Centre	1989	Not available
Melbourne Exhibition & Convention Centre	1990 (1996 for Exhibition Centre)	254 (combined cost)
Melbourne Convention Centre	2009 completion of a new 5000-seat convention centre adjacent to existing facility	370
Brisbane Convention & Exhibition Centre	1994	200
	2009 completion of expansion programme	100
Cairns Convention Centre	1995 (Convention Centre extension opened in 1999);	Not available
	2005 major refurbishment completed	10
Convention Centre South – Sydney	1999	60
Federation Concert Hall and Convention Centre – Hobart	2000	16
Alice Springs Convention Centre	2003	14.2
Perth Convention & Exhibition Centre	2004	220
Darwin Convention Centre	2008 including a 1500-seat main auditorium	Part of a 1 billion waterfront development project

Source: PKFCA Research and author's research

Table 1.1
Investments in major Australian convention centres since mid-1980s

countries such as Hungary and the Czech Republic, in the Middle East, and in a number of African countries, particularly South Africa. Case Studies 1.3 and 1.4 give detailed examples of two such investments, one at venue level (Hyderabad International Convention Centre in India), and one at a national level (Abu Dhabi).

Name of Centre	Year of Opening/Completion	Cost (£m)
International Convention Centre (Birmingham)	1991	180
Plymouth Pavilions	1992	25
Cardiff International Arena	1993	25
Venue Cymru (formerly North Wales Conference Centre) – major expansion scheduled for completion in 2007	1994	6
	2007	10.5
Edinburgh International Conference Centre – a major expansion is planned for completion in 2009	1995	38
	2009	30
Belfast Waterfront Hall (Conference Centre and Concert Hall)	1997	32
Clyde Auditorium at the Scottish Exhibition and Conference Centre	1997	38
ExCel, London – plans for a £90 million extension are in the pipeline, for completion in 2009	2000	300
Manchester International Convention Centre	2001	24
The International Centre, Telford – major re-development	2002	12
Aberdeen Exhibition & Conference Centre – major re-development	2003	18
The Villa Marina, Isle of Man (major re-development)	2004	15
The Sage, Gateshead	2004	70
Bournemouth International Centre – major re-development	2005	22
Southport Theatre and Floral Hall complex – major re-development	2007	40
Arena and Convention Centre, Liverpool	2008	146

Table 1.2
Investments in major UK convention centres since 1990

There appear to be a number of reasons for these investments, many of which are paid for out of central government and other public sector funds:

- such countries and destinations are probably already active in the leisure tourism sector and have developed much of the infrastructure for this sector which is the same (airports and other communications facilities, 3-star/4-star/5-star hotels, attractions, trained staff, for example) as that required to attract international conference business. And, although additional investment in purpose-built conference and exhibition facilities may be a not insignificant cost, it is likely to be a relatively small additional amount compared with the total infrastructure investments already made
- such destinations quite rightly see conference business as complementary to leisure tourism business, in the same way that the longer-established destinations do
- conference and business tourism, being at the high quality, high yield end of the tourism spectrum, brings major economic benefits for developing as well as for developed countries. Such benefits include year-round jobs and foreign exchange earnings. There is also the potential for future inward investment from conference delegates who have liked and been impressed by what they have seen of a country while attending a conference there and return to set up a business operation, or persuade their own employers to do so
- there is undoubted prestige in being selected to host a major international conference and some less developed countries would see this as a way of gaining credibility and acceptance on the international political stage. There is perhaps an element of conferences and conference centres being developed as status symbols, signs of having 'arrived' as destinations to be taken seriously.

Such huge infrastructure investments are driven by a number of demand factors, both economic and social (analysed in further detail in Chapter 3). The challenge for those planning major new purpose-built convention centres (usually local authorities or municipalities and public sector organizations) is to anticipate future demand accurately. Lead time from the initial idea for a convention centre until its opening can be as much as 10 years. The process involves, inter alia, identification of a suitable site, design and planning stages, assembly of the funding package, construction of venue and related infrastructure, recruitment and training of staff, and advance promotion. In such a period, substantial changes in the wider marketplace may have occurred.

There is less of a risk for hotel and smaller venue developments, where the period between initial concept and completion is much shorter (typically 3–5 years), but the same principles apply. Many venues conceived, for example, in the boom times of the late 1980s found that they were opening in a very different market in the early 1990s, with the economy in full recession, and many of the venues struggled or foundered as a result. A similar economic cycle was experienced in the late 1990s and early years of the new millennium.

THE INDUSTRY'S RECENT GLOBALISATION

Conference and business tourism is a very important sector of the tourism industry, an industry which, in all its guises, is claimed to be the world's largest. Conference tourism is now a truly global industry, as evidenced by the examples of international investments described earlier in this chapter. But there is much other evidence to substantiate such a claim. Nowhere is its truth better demonstrated than in the evolution of one of the industry's major trade shows, the European Incentive and Business Travel and Meetings Exhibition (EIBTM), which is held in Barcelona in November each year. In 1988, 54 countries were represented as exhibitors at EIBTM (when the event was held in Geneva), a number which had almost doubled by 2005 to 95 countries. In the same period the number of visitors increased from 2850 in 1988 to 5689 in 2005, with 78 different countries supplying visitors to the show in 2005.

And yet, while competition is increasing from countries seeking to act as suppliers to the conference industry, the markets from which to win business still remain relatively few in number. 80 per cent of the visitors to EIBTM 2005 were drawn from just 8 countries (see Table 1.3).

There are a number of reasons for this:

- the national economies of many of the emerging nations are not yet sufficiently strong for their corporate sector organizations to be planning events overseas (sales meetings, product launches, incentive events, for example)
- the headquarters of many international associations and inter-governmental organizations are located in Western Europe and North America. Such headquarters are also where those organizing events on behalf of these bodies are based
- market intelligence is much better developed in respect of the 'buyers' (conference organizers) in the most experienced conventioneering countries. Quite sophisticated databases exist detailing the buying requirements and preferences of conference organizers in the more established North American and European markets. Such data do not yet exist, either in quantity or quality, for many of the newer markets.

Market	%	Market	%
Benelux	4.4	Spain	35.5
France	7.3	Scandinavia	2.5
Germany	9.8	Switzerland	1.9
Italy	6.5	UK	11.7

Source: Reed Travel Exhibitions

Table 1.3
Markets supplying visitors
to EIBTM 2005

WORLD RANKINGS OF LEADING CITIES AND COUNTRIES

The global nature of the conference industry is also very well illustrated by figures produced annually by the International Congress & Convention Association (ICCA), from its headquarters in Amsterdam, and by the Union of International Associations (UIA), which is based in Brussels. Such figures record the staging of international conferences and conventions by country and city. They enable trends to be monitored and give an indication of which countries and cities are gaining market share and which may be losing it.

International Congress & Convention Association (ICCA) Rankings

The International Congress & Convention Association (ICCA) began in 1972 to collect information on international association meetings. This association database now holds in-depth profiles with information on the location and other characteristics of around 11 000 international meetings, which have to conform to the following criteria for inclusion:

- be organized on a regular basis (one-time events are not included)
- rotate between at least 3 different countries
- be attended by at least 50 participants.

Some of the key characteristics and trends of the international association conference market, as elicited by ICCA in 2006, are summarized in the section on international association conferences in Chapter 2.

The database allows ICCA to provide rankings (by country and city) showing the market share achieved by individual countries and cities through securing and staging such international meetings. ICCA's figures for 2003–2005, shown in Table 1.4, reveal market share for the top 50 countries by number of events in that 3-year period (with rankings based on the country's performance in 2005). The table underlines the global nature of conferences, including as it does many countries which would not

	Country	2003	2004	2005
1	USA	445	435	376
2	Germany	264	323	320
3	Spain	273	304	275
4	United Kingdom	271	242	270
5	France	218	267	240
6	Netherlands	163	208	197
7	Italy	277	224	196
8	Australia	141	160	164
9	Austria	140	145	157
10	Switzerland	147	134	151
11	Brazil	85	114	145
12	Japan	156	147	142
13	Sweden	137	143	134
14	China	61	145	129
15	Singapore	78	105	125
16	Canada	128	144	123
17	Republic of Korea	74	118	108
18	Portugal	126	116	105
19	Finland	120	113	103
20	Hungary	75	94	97
21	Hong Kong	40	89	95
22	Greece	78	99	94
23	Belgium	79	99	92
24 =	Denmark	96	96	82
24 =	Thailand	82	85	82
26	Czech Republic	92	76	74
27	Poland	49	71	73
28 =	Norway	81	81	68
28 =	Turkey	53	59	68
30	Ireland	71	60	67
31	Mexico	77	74	65
32	South Africa	58	64	56
33	Malaysia	63	82	52
34	Taiwan	37	52	50
35	Chile	32	42	48
36	India	41	47	47
37	Argentina	28	40	37
38	Uruguay	15	10	34
39	Indonesia	24	22	31
40 =	Cuba	29	21	29
40 =	Slovenia	27	33	29
42	Russia	28	31	27
43	New Zealand	26	30	25
44	Philippines	29	21	23
45	Croatia	26	29	22
46	Iceland	16	18	20
47	Colombia	11	9	17
48	Cyprus	10	10	16
49 =	Egypt	12	11	15
49 =	Vietnam	12	13	15
	Total	4701	5155	5010

Source: 'International Association Meetings Market 1996–2005', International Congress & Convention Association (web site: www.icca.world.com)

Table 1.4
ICCA Rankings (Number of international association meetings per *country* 2003–2005)

have appeared at all, even just a few years ago, such as Croatia and Uruguay.

Although international conferences and conventions are tracked by country as shown in Table 1.4, the events are actually won by individual destinations (normally cities) through a bidding process, and ICCA's record of where events were held on a city basis in 2005 (see Table 1.5) provides a challenging test to

	City	2003	2004	2005
1	Vienna	98	108	129
2	Singapore	78	105	125
3	Barcelona	94	114	116
4	Berlin	80	105	100
5	Hong Kong	39	89	95
6	Paris	74	101	91
7	Amsterdam	52	67	82
8 =	Budapest	63	78	77
8 =	Seoul	43	71	77
10	Stockholm	69	68	72
11 =	Copenhagen	66	72	66
11 =	Lisbon	74	73	66
13	London	61	61	62
14 =	Beijing	23	76	61
14 =	Prague	79	68	61
16	Bangkok	57	60	56
17 =	Brussels	35	47	52
17 =	Madrid	56	55	52
17 =	Sydney	40	34	52
20 =	Dublin	53	45	50
20 =	Munich	24	32	50
22	Melbourne	39	34	48
23	Edinburgh	45	37	47
24 =	Athens	36	49	44
24 =	Istanbul	42	41	44
26	Rome	64	52	43
27	Taipei	25	43	42
28	Tokyo	28	28	40
29	Rio de Janeiro	34	36	39
30 =	Geneva	39	37	38
30 =	Kuala Lumpur	38	54	38
30 =	Santiago de Chile	26	28	38
33	Glasgow	33	31	35
34	Helsinki	65	47	34
35	Montreal	31	35	33
36	Cape Town	18	35	32
37 =	Sao Paulo	11	21	29
37 =	Shanghai	14	33	29
39	Vancouver	18	34	28

Table 1.5
ICCA Rankings – number of international association meetings per *city* 2003–2005

	City	2003	2004	2005
40 =	Gothenburg	28	23	25
40 =	Havana	25	20	25
40 =	Lyon	20	18	25
43 =	New York	21	22	23
43 =	Zurich	21	15	23
45 =	Buenos Aires	17	35	22
45 =	Montevideo	8	8	22
45 =	Oslo	34	39	22
45 =	Warsaw	18	20	22
49 =	Manchester	9	16	21
49 =	Toronto	17	26	21
49 =	Valencia	23	26	21
	Total	2105	2472	2545

Source: 'International Association Meetings Market 1996–2005', International Congress & Convention Association (web site: *www.icca.world.com*)

Table 1.5
Continued

anyone's knowledge of world geography. As well as highlighting the strength of international competition for convention business, the rankings also confirm that Europe's historical pre-eminence is being challenged by destinations in Asia (e.g. Singapore, Hong Kong, Seoul), Australia (e.g. Sydney, Melbourne) and South America (e.g. Rio de Janeiro, Santiago de Chile).

It should be noted that ICCA rankings are based purely on the *number* of meetings that meet the ICCA criteria, not their economic *value*. In other words, a destination would achieve a higher ranking than another destination because of a higher number of events held, even though such events might be considerably smaller in delegate numbers than a destination staging fewer events but with greater delegate numbers (and hence greater economic value).

Further information on ICCA statistics can be accessed at: www.iccaworld.com.

Union of International Associations (UIA) Statistics

Since 1949 the Union of International Associations has undertaken annual statistical studies on international meetings taking place worldwide. The statistics are based on information collected by the UIA Congress Department and selected according to very strict criteria. Meetings taken into consideration include those organized and/or sponsored by the international organizations (i.e. non-governmental organizations (NGOs) and intergovernmental organizations (IGOs)) which appear in the UIA's 'Yearbook of International Organizations' and 'International Congress Calendar' and whose details are subject to systematic collection on an annual basis by the UIA. Broadly these meetings comprise the 'sittings' of their principal organs (notably IGOs) and their congresses, conventions, symposia, and regional sessions grouping several countries. Other meetings of 'significant international character', especially those organized by national organizations and national branches of international associations, are included provided that they meet the following criteria:

- minimum number of participants: 300
- minimum number of foreigners: 40 per cent
- minimum number of nationalities: 5
- minimum duration: 3 days.

These more stringent criteria for inclusion account, in large measure, for the differences between the UIA and ICCA rankings.

The UIA figures for 2005 (published July 2006) include 8953 international meetings organized worldwide in 218 countries and 1468 distinct cities or destinations. The total number of meetings represents a decrease of 2.4 per cent on the 2004 figures, although the UIA is projecting that, once final figures are known (certain events are not formally registered until some months after they have taken place) the decrease could be as much as 7 to 8 per cent, equivalent to around 800 meetings. The results for 2005 suggest that the negative growth in international meeting activity, created by the collapse of meeting numbers in 2001–2002, is still not reversing as quickly as might be hoped. Approximately 15 per cent of the meetings surveyed by the UIA have a concurrent exhibition.

Some of the key findings of the 2005 figures, by continental region, highlighted by the UIA, are:

Africa • • •

Africa's share of the global market for international meetings has hovered around 5 per cent for some years. South Africa continues to be the most popular African country for meetings, and Cape Town the leading city. Kenya recorded strong growth in 2005, and occupied third place behind Egypt, with Morocco slipping into fourth position.

America • • •

America's share of the 2005 world market for international meetings was 20.4 per cent, almost identical to its position in 2004 but 1.6 per cent lower than its all-time high of 22 per cent achieved in 2000. In that year America hosted 2230 events; in 2005 it was 1824 events. The reduction has been throughout the continent with North America showing a 19 per cent fall and South America a fall of 17 per cent.

Asia • • •

Asia's market share in 2005 was 14.6 per cent, compared with 14.9 per cent in 2004. China retained the top position it assumed from Japan in 2003, despite hosting 13 per cent fewer meetings. South Korea recorded growth and occupied second position, with Singapore in third place and Japan fourth.

Australasia/Pacific • • •

The number of international meetings in the Australasia/Pacific region in 2005 was significantly down on 2004. The total of 264 meetings accounted for 2.9 per cent of the world market, with the long-term trends suggesting negative growth compared with its rapid increase during the latter half of the 1990s. At a country level only New Zealand is expected to show an increase in meetings for 2005.

Europe • • •

Europe hosted 5134 international meetings in 2005, 57.3 per cent of the total. This is expected to reveal a small reduction on the figures for 2004. Europe's halcyon days were in the 1950s: it hosted 80 per cent of the global meetings market in 1953. Since then Europe's market share has declined steadily, but it still remains significant and, at 57 per cent, is more than the rest of the world combined.

The UIA produces rankings by both country and city. Table 1.6 shows the leading countries covered by the UIA research.

Table 1.7 shows UIA rankings of leading cities. It should be remembered that it is the cities which are the actual 'destinations' for the meeting, conference or convention. Further information on UIA statistics can be accessed at: www.uia.org/statistics.

CERTAIN INDUSTRY SHORTCOMINGS

Limited market intelligence

It has been seen that, in comparison with many other industries, the conference industry is still a very young industry, barely 50 years of age in Europe and North America and even younger in most of the rest of the world. Although it is maturing at a very rapid rate, it is indisputable that one of the legacies of its relative immaturity is a lack of reliable statistics and regular research to provide a base of intelligence and information on trends and on the size and value of the industry (the ICCA and UIA statistics quoted in this chapter are something of an oasis in what has generally been a rather barren statistical landscape). This, in turn,

	Country	Number of meetings	Percentage of all meetings
1	USA	1039	11.61
2	France	590	6.59
3	Germany	410	4.58
4	UK	386	4.31
5	Italy	382	4.27
6	Spain	368	4.11
7	Netherlands	341	3.81
8	Austria	314	3.51
9	Switzerland	268	2.99
10	Belgium	242	2.70
11	China, Hong Kong & Macau	216	2.41
12	Canada	214	2.39
13	Australia	200	2.23
14	South Korea	185	2.07
15	Singapore	177	1.98
16	Sweden	170	1.90
17	Japan	168	1.88
18	Denmark	138	1.54
19	Greece	136	1.52
20	Portugal	125	1.40
21	Finland	119	1.33
22	Poland	118	1.32
23	Hungary	117	1.31
24	Turkey	109	1.22
25	Brazil	107	1.20
26	India	106	1.18
27	Czech Republic	103	1.15
28	South Africa	100	1.12
29	Norway	98	1.09
30	Russia	85	0.95
31=	Argentina	74	0.83
31=	Thailand	74	0.83
33	Mexico	73	0.82
34	Ireland	70	0.78
35	Malaysia	61	0.68
36	Egypt	48	0.54
37	Croatia	46	0.51
38	Chile	45	0.50
	Total Meetings (listed here)	7622	85.13

Table 1.6
UIA Rankings: Top International Meeting Countries in 2005

Source: 'International Meetings Statistics for the year 2005', Union of International Associations (*statistics@uia.be*)

	Country	Number of meetings	Percentage of all meetings
1	Paris	294	3.28
2	Vienna	245	2.74
3	Brussels	189	2.11
4	Singapore	177	1.98
5	Barcelona	162	1.81
6	Geneva	161	1.80
7	New York	129	1.44
8	London	128	1.43
9	Seoul	103	1.15
10=	Copenhagen	98	1.09
10=	Amsterdam	98	1.09
12	Budapest	96	1.07
13	Berlin	94	1.05
14	Rome	88	0.98
15	Stockholm	87	0.97
16	Maastricht	85	0.95
17	Istanbul	83	0.93
18	Beijing	82	0.92
19	Washington	81	0.90
20	Prague	78	0.87
21	Montreal	66	0.74
22	Lisbon	64	0.71
23	Munich	62	0.69
24	Sydney	60	0.67
25	Tokyo	56	0.63
26	Athens	55	0.61
27	Helsinki	53	0.59
28	Buenos Aires	51	0.57
29	Bangkok	50	0.56
30=	Kuala Lumpur	44	0.49
30=	Strasbourg	44	0.49
30=	Turin	44	0.49
33	Moscow	43	0.48
34=	Melbourne	42	0.47
34=	Dublin	42	0.47
36	Madrid	41	0.46
37=	Chicago	40	0.45
37=	San Francisco	40	0.45
37=	Shanghai	40	0.45
37=	Oslo	40	0.45
	Total Meetings (listed here)	3535	39.48

Source: 'International Meetings Statistics for the year 2005', Union of International Associations (*statistics@uia.be*)

Table 1.7
UIA Rankings: Top International Meeting Cities in 2005

has meant that governments have not taken the industry seriously as a major benefactor to national economies because it has been impossible to demonstrate clearly the economic impact that conferences can have (except in some of the so-called less developed countries which have very quickly realised its potential and invested accordingly).

However, new research activity and initiatives are now beginning which, over time, could contribute significantly to redressing the gaps in market intelligence. Among the most important is work to determine how a new statistical instrument, the Tourism Satellite Account (TSA), can be used to identify the economic contribution made by the conference and meetings industry. Davidson and Rogers (2006) describe the TSA as follows:

'A Tourism Satellite Account (TSA) provides a means of separating and examining both tourism supply and tourism demand within the general framework of the System of National Accounts approved by the United Nations. The term 'Satellite Account' was developed by the United Nations to measure the size of economic activities that are not defined either as industries in national accounts or as a cluster of them. Tourism, for example, impacts heavily on industries such as transportation, accommodation, food and beverage services, recreation and entertainment and travel agencies. Calvin Jones and David James (2005) state that:

> Tourism is a unique phenomenon as it is defined by the consumer or the visitor. Visitors buy goods and services both tourism and non-tourism alike. The key from a measurement standpoint is associating their purchases to the total supply of these goods and services within a country. The TSA:
>
> - provides credible data on the impact of tourism and the associated employment
> - is a standard framework for organising statistical data on tourism
> - is a new international standard endorsed by the UN Statistical Commission
> - is a powerful instrument for designing economic policies related to tourism development
> - provides data on tourism's impact on a nation's balance of payments
> - provides information on tourism human resource characteristics.

Agreement was reached in 2004 between the World Tourism Organization (a specialised agency of the United Nations), the International Congress & Convention Association, Meeting Professionals International, and EIBTM (the international trade exhibition for the conventions and incentives sector) for the TSA to incorporate meeting industry data for the first time, allowing studies to be made into the relationship between expenditure on meetings and other economic measures such as Gross Domestic Product and job creation.

A project team led by the Sustainable Tourism Cooperative Research Centre, based in Australia, was commissioned to make recommendations on how the economic impacts of meetings and conventions should be properly measured. Its report 'Measuring the Economic Importance of the Meetings Industry' (published January 2007) recommends a standard methodology for measuring the value of the meetings industry based on a TSA. It seeks to:

- identify the basic data units for collection of statistics
- explore how these fit into existing TSA statistics
- develop survey instruments to capture meetings-related expenditure and costs
- identify the indicators/variables to be used for quarterly measurement of the performance of the meetings industry
- create guidelines for the collection of statistics adapted to the functioning of the TSA
- describe the roles of the stakeholders in the process to ensure credibility.

Other important research projects are now well established in a number of countries (see examples in Chapter 3) so that overall market intelligence is improving, but there is undoubtedly still some way to go before industry practitioners will feel that they have the information resources that meet their needs and accurately reflect the scope and importance of the industry.

Non-Standardised terminology

One of the reasons for the limited statistics on the size and value of the industry is the lack of an accepted and properly defined terminology. At a macro level, arguments still rage over whether the term 'business tourism' is an accurate or appropriate one to describe the sector encompassing conferences, exhibitions and incentive travel. The link with 'tourism' is thought to be confusing and overlaid with a number of negative perceptions ('candy floss' jobs of a seasonal and poorly paid nature, for example, and dominant associations with holidays and leisure tourism). While business tourism is the phrase now widely in use in Europe as the accepted generic term, in Australia the industry has adopted the term 'business events' to describe its essential focus.

The acronym 'MICE' (for Meetings, Incentives, Conferences, and Exhibitions or Events) is also still in widespread use around the world, despite its somewhat unfortunate connotations! In Canada this is adjusted to MC&IT: meetings, conventions and incentive travel.

At the micro level, words such as 'conference', 'congress', 'convention', 'meeting' even, are often used synonymously or indiscriminately. Other words are also used with similar but more specialised connotations, such as 'symposium', 'colloquium', 'assembly', 'conclave', 'summit', though it is probably only the last of these for which it might be easy to reach a consensus on its precise meaning (namely, a conference of high level officials, such as heads of government).

A first attempt was made by a number of industry professionals in 1990 to produce a 'Meetings Industry Glossary'. A finished version of the Glossary was published in 1993 under the auspices of the Convention Liaison Council (now the Convention Industry Council – see Chapter 8) and the Joint Industry Council (now the Joint Meetings Industry Council – see Chapter 8) as the 'International Meetings Industry Glossary'. This has now evolved into an electronic glossary maintained by the Convention Industry Council as part of its Accepted Practices Exchange (APEX) initiative (www.conventionindustry.org/glossary). The glossary's definitions for several key industry terms are shown below:

Conference • • •

1. Participatory meeting designed for discussion, fact finding, problem solving and consultation. 2. An event used by any organization to meet and exchange views, convey a message, open a debate or give publicity to some area of opinion on a specific issue. No tradition, continuity or periodicity is required to convene a conference. Although not generally limited in time, conferences are usually of short duration with specific objectives. Conferences are generally on a smaller scale than congresses.

Congress • • •

1. The regular coming together of large groups of individuals, generally to discuss a particular subject. A congress will often last several days and have several simultaneous sessions. The length of time between congresses is usually established in advance of the implementation stage, and can be either pluri-annual or annual. Most international or world congresses are of the former type while national congresses are more frequently held annually. 2. Meeting of an association of delegates or representatives from constituent organizations. 3. European term for convention.

Convention • • •

> *An event where the primary activity of the atten-dees is to attend educational sessions, participate in meetings/discussions, socialize, or attend other orga-nized events. There is a secondary exhibit (exhibition) component.*

Meeting • • •

> *An event where the primary activity of the attendees is to attend educational sessions, participate in meet-ings/discussions, socialize, or attend other organized events. There is no exhibit (exhibition) component to this event.*

The descriptions listed above help to shed some light on the nature of different kinds of 'communications' events, but it is perhaps not surprising that they have not as yet been adopted as succinct, easy-to-remember definitions in regular use within the twenty-first century conference and convention industry.

It could be argued that the variety of available vocabulary is more a reflection of the rich diversity of the English language than a symptom of an industry with myriad events, each with its own distinct characteristics. At one level, it may not really matter whether an event is called a 'conference' or a 'convention', and certainly there are as many misuses of these terms as there are correct interpretations, if indeed such a thing as a correct inter-pretation really exists. Yet at another level, some of these terms do have a specific connotation in one part of the world, and a different connotation in another part, giving rise to potential confusion and misunderstanding. For example, the word 'con-ference' in the UK is used generically to describe events both large and small, whereas in the USA a 'conference' is essentially a 'meeting' and certainly implies an event with limited numbers of delegates/attendees. The word 'convention' is used to describe a large event in the UK and North America, whereas many coun-tries in mainland Europe prefer the term 'congress' to describe a large 'conference'.

An initiative spearheaded by the Joint Meetings Industry Council (see Chapter 8) is recommending the adoption of the term 'The Meetings Industry' to describe the sector, but by 2006 this proposal had only attracted modest interest and no consistent support internationally.

Clearly it is vital that any potential confusion over terminology is minimised, enabling statistics and data to be collected and interpreted in a standardised way on a worldwide level, as befits a truly global industry. This will enable the real size and value of the conference industry to be established and monitored, and is critical to the national and international recognition and support which the industry now deserves and demands.

Underdeveloped educational framework

One of the other reasons for the lack of a standardized terminology is that, for many of those now working in the industry, it is their second or even third career. They have come into conference work from related disciplines such as hotel and catering, travel, sales and marketing, public administration, but also from what might appear superficially to be unrelated spheres of employment. Whereas many, if not most, other professions have a formal induction and training process for new entrants which provides opportunities for them to be educated in the use of the accepted, clearly defined terminology, such opportunities and structures do not yet exist within the conference industry (although this is now changing with the advent of university and college courses offering undergraduate and postgraduate programmes specific to the conference and conventions industry – see Chapter 7).

Professional qualifications specific to the industry have existed for some years in North America. Such qualifications are now emerging elsewhere (see Chapter 7) and it is likely that, within the next 5–10 years, an appropriate range of continuing professional development (CPD) programmes and related qualifications will have been established at both national and international levels. Such a development will provide overdue support and recognition for what is a highly sophisticated industry but, nonetheless, one in which many conference organizers have received no, or only minimal, formal training, or obtained recognised qualifications to prepare them for their event management responsibilities. It is also frequently the case that conference organizing is only a small part of a person's job, undertaken for just a limited period of time (see Chapter 2). These are again factors which help to explain the problems sometimes experienced with semantics and the lack of a clear, well understood terminology.

INDUSTRY PARAMETERS AND DEFINITIONS

Even if precise definitions are not yet in regular use, it is important, at the beginning of a book on the conference industry, to set out certain parameters for the measurement of conference events and facilities.

In the UK the organisers of the annual 'British Conference Venues Survey' and the 'UK Conference Market Survey', respectively the British Association of Conference Destinations and the Meetings Industry Association, have agreed to use the following definitions in undertaking their surveys:

A Conference: 'an out-of-office meeting of at least four hours' duration involving a minimum of 8 people'.

In Australia, the definition used in the 2005 'National Business Events Study' to describe a Business Event was: 'Any public or private activity consisting of a minimum of 15 persons with a common interest of vocation, held in a specific venue or venues, and hosted by an organization (or organizations). This may include (but not be limited to): conferences, conventions, symposia, congresses, incentive meetings, marketing events, special celebrations, seminars, courses, public or trade shows, exhibitions, company general meetings, corporate retreats, training programmes.'

Other research programmes use somewhat different definitions, while major conference hotel chains often base their own conference statistics on meetings involving two or more people.

An early definition of a conference venue was: 'a conference venue must be able to seat 20 or more participants theatre-style'. However, this is so hopelessly inadequate that it could even describe a large living room or den in a private house! In October 2002 leading industry bodies in the UK agreed to use the following definition of a conference venue: 'a conference venue must be an externally-let facility (i.e. not a company's own meeting rooms), and have a minimum of three meeting/conference rooms with a minimum seating capacity of 50 theatre-style in its largest room'.

The conference industry forms one sector within 'business tourism', itself a sub-sector of the overall tourism industry which comprises both leisure tourism and business tourism. Apart from conferences, the other main components of business tourism are: exhibitions and trade fairs, incentive travel, corporate events or corporate hospitality and individual business travel (also referred to as 'corporate travel').

Table 1.8 provides a matrix of the main segments of business tourism and highlights some of their key characteristics.

One useful definition of a business tourist is:

> *a traveller whose main purpose for travelling is to attend an activity or event associated with his/her business or interests.*

Conferences, exhibitions and trade fairs, incentive travel and corporate events (sometimes referred to as corporate hospitality) are the four business tourism segments which are the prime focus of marketing activity by venues and destinations, because decisions about where the events take place are open to influence. The organizers of the event may have great flexibility in deciding where it is to be held, and are able to use their own judgment or discretion over choice of location. For this reason these four business tourism segments are sometimes described as 'discretionary'.

Individual business travel or corporate travel relates to those whose work regularly involves travel within their own country or overseas, such as a lorry driver or sales representative, as well as

Segment	Corporate organization	National association	International association/inter-government	Public sector/government
Meetings	An out-of-office meeting of at least 4 hours' duration involving a minimum of 8 people. Includes sales meetings, training, board meetings and retreats, AGMs.	Board meetings, regional meetings, training events, information events.	Limited number of board-level meetings, typically lasting 1–2 days maximum. Also international meetings hosted by national associations.	Mainly organizing non-residential meetings of up to 1 day's duration. Also training courses which may last for several days, and information events.
Conferences	Typically of 1 or 2 days' duration with a formal programme that has been promoted in advance. Delegates are often compelled to attend.	Usually an annual confer-ence/congress/convention for members lasting 2–3 days.	An annual (or less frequent) congress or convention rotating around different countries or continents, with selection based on bids received from individual cities. Typically of 3–5 days' duration.	Mostly 1-day conferences (occasionally 2 days) attracting delegates from the local area or region.
Incentive Travel	A business tourism trip to motivate and reward employees and dealers, usually containing a conference element.	Not applicable.	Not applicable.	Not applicable.

Exhibitions	Product launches, attendance as an exhibitor at trade and consumer shows organized by specialist exhibition organizers or trade associations. Also attendance as a corporate visitor ('buyer') at trade shows.	May include the organization of an exhibition to run alongside its own conference; also participation in other industry trade shows as an exhibitor. Trade associations are also primary exhibition organizers.	May include the organization of an exhibition to run alongside its own conference; occasional participation in other industry trade shows as an exhibitor.	Information/regional trade events.
Corporate Events (also known as Corporate Hospitality)	Hosted entertainment at major sporting events, concerts, and other high profile functions, and/or participation in sporting or outdoor pursuits-type activities.	Not common, although some professional and trade associations may organize golf days or other sporting events for their members.	Not normally applicable.	Not applicable.

Table 1.8
'MICE' Matrix (illustrating the segments which make up the business tourism sector)

to people who may have to travel away from their normal place of employment from time to time (a management consultant, for example, or an engineer responsible for installing a new piece of equipment in a client's factory). In all such business travel, which represents a major portion of business tourism, the opportunities to influence where the individual travels to are minimal, and this segment is consequently referred to as 'non-discretionary'.

BUSINESS TOURISM AND LEISURE TOURISM

Reference has already been made to the broad division of tourism into the two sectors of business tourism and leisure tourism, although these two sectors share much common ground. As Davidson (1994) points out:

> business tourism, in particular, can involve a substantial leisure element. Incentive travel, for example, may consist entirely of leisure, sport and entertainment. But, even for conference delegates, visitors to trade fairs and individual business travellers, excursions to local restaurants and places of entertainment, or sightseeing tours, can be a way of relaxing at the end of the working day. Socialising in this way can be an important part of the business tourism experience for groups, as it gives delegates or colleagues the opportunity to unwind together and get to know each other on a less formal basis.

This is why bidding destinations sell the concept of 'destination' and place great emphasis on everything from leisure, cultural and entertainment assets to shopping, sports and dining options.
Davidson also makes clear that:

> the distinction between the two categories of tourism is further blurred by the presence of 'accompanying persons' alongside many business tourism events. Incentive travel often includes the husbands or wives of those selected for such trips. But also, it is not uncommon for those travelling to exotic destinations for conferences or trade fairs and exhibitions to take their spouses along and make a short holiday out of the trip. In such cases, the couple may prolong their stay in order to have the time to tour around the destination after the business part of the trip is over.

The phrase 'business extenders' has emerged in the UK to describe this phenonemon, and much marketing spend is now devoted to increasing the number of business extenders.
Business tourism and leisure tourism rely on the same, or a very similar, infrastructure for their success. Both sectors need

accommodation (hotels, guest houses), transport and communications (airports, railway stations, good road networks, coach and taxi services, modern telecommunications links), entertainment (shopping, bars and restaurants, night clubs/casinos, visitor attractions), as well as information and advisory services, emergency medical services and an attractive, welcoming, safe and secure environment.

The Coral Beach Hotel & Resort, Cyprus is a good example of a tourism product catering equally well for both the business and leisure tourism sectors by focusing on several niche markets: conferences and conventions, incentive trips, sports tourism, and leisure tourism for higher spending holidaymakers. Case study 1.5 gives a more in-depth analysis of the Coral Beach product and business strategy.

But conference and business tourism has additional infrastructure needs, such as appropriate venues, specialist contractors (audio-visual suppliers, exhibition contractors, interpreters, for example), and, perhaps most importantly, staff who are trained to be aware of and to respond to the particular needs of conference organizers and delegates. It is in the provision of this latter service that venues and destinations sometimes fail, a theme which is further developed in later chapters of this book.

THE BENEFITS OF CONFERENCE AND BUSINESS TOURISM

Although business tourism and leisure tourism rely on a similar infrastructure, the former brings with it a number of significant extra benefits which makes it particularly attractive to destinations.

Greater profitability

Conference and business tourism caters for the high quality, high cost and, therefore, high yield end of the market. In 2005, for example, conference visitors to the United Kingdom from overseas spent an average of £164 per day compared with an average of just £57 per day for all categories of visitors (source: International Passenger Survey 2005). The greater spending power of business tourists means increased economic benefits for the host destination and a greater return on its investment in infrastructure and marketing.

All-year-round activity

Conference and business tourism takes place throughout the year. Spring and Autumn are the peak seasons of the year for conferences (with most of the larger, high profile association and political party conferences taking place at these times in the UK), but many smaller conferences and meetings are also held during the Winter months. In the northern hemisphere, January, July and August are the months of least activity which, for many resort-type destinations, is an added benefit because it means that there is no clash between the demands of leisure and business tourism, but rather they are complementary.

The all-year-round nature of conference and business tourism also leads to the creation and sustenance of permanent jobs, as opposed to the seasonal, temporary jobs which are a frequent characteristic of the leisure tourism sector. This, in turn, ensures that 'careers' rather than simply 'jobs' can be offered to new entrants, even though clearly defined structures and opportunities for career progression are not yet fully established.

Future inward investment

Those organizing a conference or incentive travel trip will always be very keen to make sure that it is as successful as possible. One of the ways in which this can be achieved is by giving delegates and participants a pleasant, positive experience of the destination in which the event is being held. This usually means showing delegates the most attractive, scenic parts of the destination in the hope that, by creating a memorable experience for them, many will return.

Where this has been undertaken successfully, some delegates/attendees return as leisure visitors, often bringing their partners and families for a holiday or short break. Some may have been so impressed that they decide to re-locate their business to the destination or look to set up a subsidiary operation there. As Davidson (1994) says:

> a business visitor who leaves with a good impression of the conference, trade fair or incentive destination becomes an unpaid ambassador for that place...these are often influential people, whose opinions of the destination will be instrumental in determining its image in the minds of others who have not visited it.

It could be argued that a single meeting of influential business executives can do more to increase a destination's exposure than years of promotion by economic development officials.

Professional development

Maple (2006), as president of the International Association of Congress Centres (AIPC) and general manager of the Vancouver Convention and Exhibition Center, contends that:

> large events like conventions are designed to bring the best (people) in any given field together in an environment

where information can be shared and progress identified. When this happens, it creates a big boost to local knowledge and skills in any imaginable discipline. Medical conferences are a great example. When the top researchers and practitioners get together, they are looking at the very latest results and procedures in their respective fields. They are deciding what advances are most important and which areas are the most promising for the future; in short, everything you would like the local medical community to have access to. Now multiply that possibility by any number of different professions, trades or business sectors, and you begin to get the idea of what having meetings, conventions and exhibitions can do to promote the professional skills in a community.

'Green' tourism

Conference and business tourism has fewer negative impacts on the environment than mass leisure tourism. It is concerned with smaller numbers, but much higher spend. It is characterised by the use of coach transfers and public transport (or Shanks' pony) within a destination, minimising traffic congestion and environmental pollution.

Conference delegates are together as a group, so that it is possible to inform and educate them about the local community in which their conference is being held in order to maximize the enjoyment of their stay but also to minimize any disruption and possible inconvenience to the local resident population. It is very much harder to manage, in the same way, the impact of individual leisure travellers on a destination.

However, it would be naïve to claim that business tourism does not have its negative impacts, especially on the physical environment. These are well summarized by Swarbrooke and Horner (2001):

If we want to make business travel and tourism more sustainable, we have to recognize that there are characteristics of business tourism which make it particularly problematic in relation to the concept of sustainable tourism. First, most business tourists take more trips in a year than the average leisure tourist, thus making more demands on transport infrastructure and destination services. Business tourists tend to be very demanding and want high quality facilities, even in towns and cities in developing countries. While both of these are difficult to reconcile with the concept of sustainable tourism, the positive side of business tourism is the fact that business travellers tend to be higher spending than leisure tourists.

Improved Quality of Life

Convention centres and the kinds of activities they support play an important role in enhancing the overall quality of life in a community. Maple (2006) suggests that, to survive, communities need some kind of industrial activity:

> *preferably one that brings in money from outside the local economy*

But, she adds:

> *a lot of of these industries are less than completely benign, particularly from a community or environmental perspective. The convention business, on the other hand, does more than simply avoid damaging its host community. It actually thrives on the kind of qualities people typically want around them: things like an attractive environment and cultural attributes, and provides a sound economic reason to support and enhance these qualities to everyone's advantage.*

Summary

- the USA was the first country to recognize the potential economic benefits of conference business for a city or local destination. Detroit was the first US city to establish a convention and visitor bureau in 1896, followed by a number of other US cities in the early years of the twentieth century. Europe did not follow suit until the latter half of the twentieth century, and it was at this time also that conference tourism came to be recognised as an industry in its own right
- the final two decades of the twentieth century and the early years of the twenty-first century have witnessed spectacular investment in the infrastructure which supports both leisure and conference/business tourism. Such investments are taking place not only in the more established conference destinations of Western Europe and North America, but in every continent and region
- the conference industry is now a truly global industry, with over two hundred countries vying for a share of the lucrative international conferences and meetings.

A greater market share is now being won by countries in Eastern Europe and in the Asia/Pacific region in particular

- the conference industry is still young though maturing at a rapid rate. Symptomatic of the industry's youthfulness, yet contributing to its lack of proper recognition in commercial and political circles, is the lack of a comprehensive statistical base to measure its true size and value, although improvements are now in sight. Its relative immaturity is also shown in its use and misuse of terminology
- conference/business tourism and leisure tourism are closely intertwined, relying on similar infrastructure and support services. However, conference tourism also has a number of unique characteristics and advantages, which can bring additional benefits to those destinations successful in attracting conference business.

Review and discussion questions

1. Analyse the destination and/or venue case studies in this Chapter and identify the principal features which each have in common and which are contributing to their success as conference destinations or venues. Then compare these with a destination or venue which has been less successful and put forward reasons why it has fared less well in the international conference marketplace.
2. Summarize the main changes in international convention market share experienced by one continent over recent years, giving examples of national and city destinations, and drawing comparisons with another continent. Suggest strategies for increasing its market share.
3. Compare and contrast the conference industry with another young industry (for example, computing and information technology, the fitness and health food industry). Draw conclusions on which has progressed further, and give reasons why.
4. Choose a resort destination active in both the leisure and conference/business tourism sectors. Identify the best niche markets for both sectors (see also Chapters 2 and 3) and produce the 'ideal calendar' of business for a year which maximizes use of its facilities and generates the highest level of economic benefit.

Notes and references

1. Davidson, R (1994), *Business Travel*, Addison Wesley Longman Limited.
2. Davidson, R and Rogers, T (2006), *Marketing Destinations and Venues for Conferences, Conventions and Business Events*, Elsevier Butterworth-Heinemann.
3. Gartrell, R. B (second edition, 1994), *Destination Marketing for Convention and Visitor Bureaus*, published under the auspices of the International Association of Convention and Visitor Bureaus by Kendall/Hunt Publishing Company.
4. *International Association Meetings Market 1996–2005*, International Congress and Convention Association (2006).
5. International Meetings Statistics for the year 2005, Union of International Associations (2006).
6. Jones, C and James, D, *The Tourism Satellite Account (TSA): A Vision, Challenge and Reality*, published in 'Tourism' Issue 123, Quarter 2, 2005 (The Tourism Society).
7. Maple, B, article entitled *More than just money,* Conference + Meetings World magazine (June 2006).
8. Shone, Anton (1998), *The Business of Conferences*, Butterworth-Heinemann.
9. Swarbrooke, J and Horner, S (2001), *Business Travel and Tourism*, Butterworth-Heinemann.

Further reading

1. Davidson, R and Cope, B (2002), *Business Travel*, Pearson Education.
2. *Dictionary of Meeting Industry Terminology*, available from the International Association of Professional Congress Organizers (IAPCO) (see Chapter 8).

The structure of the conference industry

Introduction

The conference industry is highly complex, comprising of a multiplicity of buyer and supplier organizations and businesses. For many conference organizers ('the buyers'), the organization of conferences and similar events is only a part of their job, and often one for which they have received little formal training and may only have a temporary responsibility. Suppliers include conference venues and destinations, accommodation providers and transport companies, agencies and specialist contractors. Both buyers and suppliers are welded together and supported by national bodies and associations, trade media and educational institutions, each contributing to the overall structure of this fast developing, global industry.

This chapter looks at the roles and characteristics of:

- the buyers (corporate, association, public sector, entrepreneurs)
- the suppliers (venues, destinations, other suppliers)
- agencies and intermediaries
- other important organizations (trade associations, trade media, national tourism organizations, consultants, educational institutions).

It includes case studies on:

- Apimondia World Apiculture Congress (mini case study)
- International Federation of Library Associations and Institutions' annual conference

- MCI Group
- Challenge and Change for PCOs (mini case study).

Learning outcomes

On completion of this chapter, you should be able to:

- Describe the overall structure of the conference industry
- Understand the characteristics of the different kinds of 'buyer'
- Identify the myriad of organizations that make up the supply side of the conference industry
- Define the range of other organizations needed for the overall functioning and effectiveness of a twenty-first century industry
- Appreciate the dynamism of the industry and the changes which impact its future development.

THE BUYERS

In common with other industries, the conference industry comprises 'buyers' and 'suppliers'. The buyers in this case are conference organizers and meeting planners who buy or, more accurately, hire conference venues and related services in order to stage their events.

Most people working within the conference industry refer to two broad types of buyer: 'corporate' and 'association'. There are also 'public sector' buyers who may be regarded as a discrete group, rather than being subsumed within the 'association' category. There is also a category of risk-taking, entrepreneurial conference organizer who puts together a conference and hopes to be able to attract sufficient delegates for the event to be profitable. All of the above may also employ the services of various kinds of 'agency' or intermediary to assist them in the staging of their events.

The corporate buyer

Definitions • • •

The term 'corporate' is used to describe conference organizers (often called meeting planners, especially in North America) who work for corporate organizations. Corporate organizations are companies established primarily to generate a profit and thus provide a financial return for their owners, whether these are the proprietors of a family-run business or the shareholders of a large publicly-quoted company. They can be manufacturing or service companies.

Corporate organizations are to be found in most, if not all, industry sectors. The sectors which are particularly prominent in generating corporate conference business include:

- oil, gas and petrochemicals
- medical and pharmaceuticals
- computing/IT and telecommunications
- motor manufacturing and other manufacturing
- financial and professional services
- food, drink and tobacco
- travel and transport.

Identifying the corporate buyer • • •

Relatively few companies have a dedicated conference or event management department. Indeed, during times of economic recession, this is often an area where many companies opt to make savings by closing down their event management departments and putting the work out to agencies on an outsourced contract basis. In some cases, such companies contract the employees from their former event management departments to continue to organize their events, but the staff now work on a freelance or self-employed basis and thus cease to be a direct overhead to the company.

The larger corporate organizations are, of course, multidivision entities located on a number of different sites, often in a number of different countries. Staff involved in organizing meetings and conferences appear in a whole range of guises and job titles. Research carried out for the 'UK Conference Market Survey 2002' found that fewer than 1 in 5 of the 600 conference organizers interviewed (300 corporate, 300 association) had job titles or responsibilities directly associated with 'conferences or events'. Table 2.1 gives further details of this research.

In broad terms, most corporate events fall within the ambit of the following departments: sales and marketing, training and personnel/human resources, central administration including the company secretarial activities.

Staff involvement in organizing events often varies considerably. At one extreme, their task may simply be to obtain information on potential venues for an event, while at the other they can be given complete responsibility for planning and running the event. It is estimated that, in the UK at least, up to 80 per cent of corporate organizers have received little formal training in conference and meeting planning; such activities account for just a part of their overall responsibilities; and their responsibility for conference organizing may only be of a short-term nature.

Job Title/Responsibility	% of Interviewees
Administration (including secretaries and PAs)	25
Sales and Marketing	23
PR/Communications	18
Training/Human Resources	11
Conferences/Events	18
Other	5

Source: UK Conference Market Survey 2002

Table 2.1
Principal job titles/
responsibilities of
staff engaged in
conference organizing

In the USA the role of a meeting planner is more established, with better defined training and career structures.

Identifying the corporate buyer is, therefore, a major and continuous challenge for those organizations wishing to market their facilities and services to him. The transience of many corporate conference organizers also makes it difficult to provide an effective education and training framework for them, and thus develop their expertise and increase their professionalism. It is only when such support systems are in place that the role of the corporate conference organizer will achieve full recognition and occupy its proper place at the centre of companies' communications strategies.

Corporate buying patterns • • •

Decisions about the conference or meeting (choice of venue, budget, size of event, visiting speakers, programme content, and so forth) are taken by the corporate conference organizer or a line manager or the managing director, or by a group of such people in consultation. The decision-making process is relatively straightforward and more-or-less immediate.

Corporate events can be of many different types and sizes. The most common of these events are shown in Table 2.2.

It is worth drawing the distinction between internal and external events. In the former case, the participants are employees of the company (typically sales conferences, general management conferences, rallies for the staff, etc.). External events are a vital part of Customer Relationship Management (CRM) strategies (see Chapter 4) with companies trying to build a long-term relationship with their key clients. One way of doing this is to invite these clients to be part of the company's development process through attending events: such events can include

Annual general meeting (AGM)	Product launch
Board meeting/retreat	Sales conference
Corporate hospitality/entertainment	Training course/seminar
Exhibition/exposition	Technical conference
Incentive travel	Team-building event
Roadshow	Symposium

Table 2.2
Main types of corporate meetings/events

new product launches, or educational meetings explaining complex new products or upgrades (especially in the field of IT). Participation in these events enables account managers to get close to key clients over coffee breaks or in the bar. One of the benefits for companies in running these events is that they get real-time feedback and can measure the return on investment (ROI) in a way that is impossible with traditional internal sales conferences.

Venue preferences • • •

The majority of corporate conferences and meetings are held in hotels. Some take place in purpose-built conference centres and management training centres. Incentive events and corporate hospitality often make use of unusual venues. Civic venues and town halls tend to attract relatively few corporate events because of a perception that they may be staid and 'basic', which is often far from the reality. Some corporate meetings are held in university and academic venues, especially where such venues have invested in dedicated conference facilities with high quality, en suite accommodation/housing (as, indeed, an increasing number have done).

Lead times and seasonality • • •

Corporate events often have a fairly short 'lead time', especially compared with association conferences, with just a matter of weeks or a few months available to plan and stage them. In 2005 there was an average lead time of seven months for corporate meetings in the UK ('UK Conference Market Survey 2006'). The majority of these events involve relatively low delegate numbers (e.g. from 10 to 200). Delegates are told to participate by the company, they are often not given a choice.

Budgets • • •

Corporate conferences and events take place throughout the year, peaking in Spring and Autumn. In the northern hemisphere July and August are the months of least activity because of holidays, although the corporate hospitality sector is buoyant with its links to major sporting events such as tennis at Wimbledon or Paris, test match cricket, grand prix motor racing and international golf tournaments.

The budget for corporate conferences, expressed in terms of expenditure per delegate, is generally much higher than that for many 'association' conferences as it is the company which pays for delegate attendance, not the delegates themselves. The costs can be incorporated into a company's marketing or staff training budgets, for example, and the selection of an attractive, quality venue coupled with a professionally produced conference will reinforce the importance of the event in delegates' minds and contribute to the successful achievement of its objectives, whether these be motivational, information sharing, team building, or other.

However, research undertaken by Ian Flint & Associates (and published in *Business Travel World* magazine – July 2002) among major national and multinational companies in France, Germany, Italy, Spain and the UK found that, while such companies were claiming an estimated annual expenditure on meetings of between US\$2 million and US\$10 million, 67.5 per cent of them said that they did not know how much they spent overall on meeting planning. The same research found that the three countries spending most on meetings were (in order) the UK, Germany and France, while the highest spending sectors were pharmaceutical, IT and motor manufacturing.

Procurement • • •

There is a clear case for changing and introducing more effective management systems to, indeed professionalizing, the whole meeting venue booking process (or 'procurement' as this activity is now fashionably known), and unmistakable signs that this is happening through the influence of companies' central purchasing (or procurement) departments – procurement is explored in more detail in Chapter 9. Web-based tools are now available enabling major corporations to make significant savings by obtaining bulk purchase discounts, particularly from hotel groups. Details of such tools are available on a number of web sites, including www.starcite.com.

Return on investment • • •

Corporate conferences are now more intensive, business-related events than was the case during the 1980s and early 1990s, when they were often seen as something of a 'jolly'. Return on investment (ROI) (see also Chapter 9) is one of the buzz phrases across the industry, emphasizing the need to measure the effectiveness of all investments and activities, including those investments made in a company's workforce. Despite this, research suggests that around one-third of corporate conference organizers do not evaluate their events after they have taken place, a finding which calls into question their professionalism and the investment which the company is making in them as people who place a high value on the virtues of two-way communications.

Typical delegates • • •

A survey of 300 corporate organizations on behalf of the 'UK Conference Market Survey 2006' found that:

- The average age of a delegate attending a corporate event during 2005 was 38
- 64 per cent of corporate delegates are male, attending on average 3 events per year
- At least 60 per cent of organizers categorize their delegates as senior or middle management, or sales and marketing professionals. 16 per cent are also organizing events for accountants or accountancy-related positions (a figure which has fallen from 43 per cent in 2001), and 15 per cent for general administration
- 83 per cent of those corporate conference organizers interviewed are satisfied with the conference venues used most of the time
- The most frequent cause for complaint by organizers is food/catering-related, cited by 24 per cent of interviewees, with criticisms of the meeting content, speakers or event organization accounting for 18 per cent of the negative comments received.

In summary, therefore, the corporate sector of the conference industry is characterised by: events with fewer than 200 delegates, fairly short lead times, and high spend with costs being borne by the company. Conferences are one of the prime ways in which corporate organizations communicate with their employees and their customers, although the generic term 'conferences' may describe a variety of sizes and types of events. Conferences are a high profile communications vehicle conveying important messages about the company: it is vital, therefore, that conferences should be successful in meeting the objectives set for them. This can mean that the budget for the event will be a generous one, making it an attractive piece of business for venues and other suppliers.

The association buyer

Definitions • • •

The term 'association' organizer or buyer covers those representing a wide range of organizations, including:

- Professional or trade associations/institutions (whose members join because of their employment)
- voluntary associations and societies (whose members join primarily to further an interest or hobby)
- charities
- religious organizations
- political parties
- trade unions.

The acronym 'SMERF' groups (social, military, educational, religious and fraternal) is sometimes used in North America to describe those types of organizations which are not work-related.

Associations are formed and operate at different levels. Many are purely national and restrict their memberships and their activities to one particular country. But, and perhaps increasingly in our global, shrinking world, these national associations are establishing links and relationships at a continental level to form bodies with memberships and spheres of influence at this wider, regional level (e.g. the European Federation of… or the Asian Association of…). In other cases, truly international associations exist whose members are drawn from all corners of the world – these latter are described in more detail later in this chapter.

Very few, if any, associations are established mainly to generate a financial return. They are 'not-for-profit' organizations which exist to provide a service to their members and to the community at large. There is, however, an equal need for the conferences organized by associations, as with corporate conferences, to be run extremely professionally, not least because they are often in the public eye, through press and media exposure, in a way that corporate conferences are not. And, while the associations themselves may be 'not-for-profit', association conferences must cover their costs and, in some cases, be planned with the aim of generating a profit which can then be re-invested in the administrative and promotional costs of future conferences. Such profits also frequently become core income streams which assist in funding the general running of the association.

Association Management Companies (AMCs) • • •

There are also specialist association management companies which make a living by providing a professional 'secretariat' for associations which do not have the resources or management expertise to run their association themselves. Association management companies are paid a fee to administer the association, and their role frequently includes the organization of the association's meetings and conferences. Some of the conference sector's own trade and professional associations, such as The Society of Incentive and Travel Executives (SITE – see Chapter 8) are now run by association management companies. Association management companies typically have a meeting planning department which, in essence, operates like a PCO (see below) on behalf of the organizations they represent.

Association delegate characteristics • • •

Delegates attending association conferences share a number of common characteristics:

- they normally choose to attend the conference or other event run by the 'association', rather than being asked to attend by their employer. This is particularly true for professional associations which have an individual (rather than corporate) membership (i.e. it is the individual person who becomes the member, not their employing organization)
- they may be required to pay their own expenses to attend, which means that the conference organizer must keep the costs as low as possible if it is important to maximize delegate attendance. In certain cases, particularly where the delegate is attending as a representative of a group of colleagues or fellow workers, as with trade union conferences, the delegate receives a daily allowance to cover his/her costs while attending the conference
- a range of accommodation may be required, from guest house to 5-star hotel. At least one major association in the UK insists that a destination must have a caravan park before it can be considered to stage its conference!
- the number of delegates attending the main annual conference can be substantially higher than for corporate events. Indeed, association conferences can attract hundreds and sometimes thousands of delegates, and frequently receive high media attention
- The 'UK Conference Market Survey 2006' shows the average age of an association delegate as 40, with 55 per cent of delegates being male and attending an average of 1.7 events per year.

These general characteristics may apply across the association sector, but they should not be allowed to hide some important differences between different types of associations. For example, delegates attending an annual surgeons' conference would expect to stay in accommodation of at least 3-star hotel standard (a 1000-delegate conference with many delegates bringing spouses would require a destination with a substantial number of high quality hotels), whereas a charity or religious conference is likely to require more modest accommodation at the budget end of the spectrum.

Buying patterns • • •

The association decision-making process is different from that in the corporate sector. Even though many of the larger associations have dedicated conference organizers and, in some cases, event organizing units/departments, the decision on where the annual conference is to be held is normally taken by a committee elected by the membership. The conference organizer does much of the research and related groundwork, producing a shortlist of the most likely destinations and venues from which the committee will choose, and may even make recommendations. The selection committee scrutinises 'bid' proposals or tenders submitted by destinations or venues, in some cases compiled in conjunction with a professional conference organiser (PCO), outlining how they can help the association to stage a successful event (a similar form of bid document may also be provided to corporate buyers when seeking to attract corporate business).

Destination bid documents are likely to contain a formal invitation, often signed by the Mayor or other civic dignitary, a full description of the destination highlighting its attractions, access and communications details (e.g. road and rail links, the number of scheduled flights from the local airport), information on the support services available in the destination (transport operators, exhibition (exposition) contractors, interpreters, audiovisual companies, and so on), a list of the services provided by the convention and visitor bureau or conference desk, details of hotel and other accommodation and, of course, full details of the venue being proposed to stage the conference. The convention and visitor bureau/conference desk, acting on behalf of the destination, may be invited to make a formal presentation to the selection committee of the association, in competition with other destinations similarly shortlisted. A representative from the main conference venue being proposed may also contribute to the presentation, perhaps with a recommended PCO, and this 'joined up' approach illustrating how the key players within a destination can work together in harmony conveys positive messages to the association about such a destination's ability to host its event successfully.

Bid proposals may also be put forward by host committees (i.e. local chapters of an association) (see example of this in relation to international association conferences in Case Study 2.2 – the same principle applies to national association events). Such host committees have an important influence on site selection. It should also be noted that internal 'politics' can also have a major influence e.g. the President or Chairman's wife wants to meet in Florida!

On-Line bidding • • •

Davidson and Rogers (2006) describe the use of on-line bid documents developed by a number of cities:

> Glasgow (www.seeglasgow.com), Stockholm (www.congressstockholm.se) and Madrid (www. madridconventionbureau.com) are among cities to have developed on-line bid documents. Glasgow was the first city to win a congress (the International Crustaceans Congress) using an on-line bid. Stockholm's bid-on-line system was launched in 2001 and has been found to be very useful when there is a large group of people, spread all over the world, who are involved in the voting process.

Before the selection committee makes its final decision, it may undertake an inspection visit to the destination to assess at first hand its strengths and weaknesses. The whole decision-making process can, therefore, be very protracted, sometimes taking months to complete.

Lead times • • •

Lead times for association events are much longer than for corporate events. It is not uncommon for associations organizing a 1000-delegate conference to have booked venues several years ahead. In part, this is because there is a much more limited choice of venue, in part because there is significantly more work involved in staging a 1000-delegate conference than one for 100 delegates. Some of the larger, purpose-built conference/convention centres have provisional reservations 10 years ahead from association conference organizers.

Rotations • • •

National associations tend to follow one of several patterns or rotations in the staging of their main annual conference. The examples given below relate to the UK but similar rotations are likely to apply to most other countries with a significant 'national association' conference market:

• some associations adopt an alternate north-south rotation, holding the conference in the north of England or in Scotland one year, and then in the south of England the next, returning to the north in year three

- some associations operate a 3- or 4-year rotation, moving to different regions of the country in order to be seen to be fair to their members who are probably drawn from most parts of the country
- other associations appear to be quite immobile, opting to use the same destination year after year
- and, finally, certain associations look for somewhere different each year, following no clear geographical pattern.

For those destinations and venues seeking to win their business, it is clearly important to have an understanding of which pattern a particular association has adopted.

Partner programmes • • •

Association conferences may have both delegates and their partners attending, a characteristic much less frequently found with corporate events, unless they include an incentive element. The partners do not normally attend the business sessions of the conference but they will be fully involved in the social events which form part of the conference programme. Partner programmes are designed to entertain partners while the conference is in progress. Destinations often work with the conference organizer to help in the planning of partner (or spouse) programmes, as well as in co-ordinating tours and activities both pre- and post-conference. Such pre- and post-conference tours, and the participation by delegates' partners, both add significantly to the economic benefits generated by the conference, encouraging many destinations to examine and adopt best practice in maximizing their 'business extenders'.

Venue preferences • • •

Association conferences, because of their larger size, are often held in purpose-built conference or convention centres. Hotels are also popular (particularly so in the USA where major resort hotels can cater for large conventions, all under one roof), while some associations use town hall and civic venues, and others book university and college venues. Where hotels are used, the event may well take place over a weekend because the hotel is offering cheaper rates than for weekday bookings. The peak seasons for association conferences are Autumn and Spring, but some conferences take place over the Summer months and a limited number during the Winter.

Table 2.3 summarises the similarities and differences between corporate and association conferences.

Table 2.4 summarizes the key findings from the 'UK Conference Market Survey 2006' based on interviews with 300 corporate conference organizers and 300 association conference organizers.

Corporate Conferences	Association Conferences
Corporate buyers are employed by 'for profit' organizations	Association buyers are employed by 'not-for-profit' organizations
Corporate organizations are to be found in both the manufacturing and service sectors	Associations are to be found in the manufacturing, service and voluntary sectors
The event decision-making process is straightforward and more or less immediate	The event decision-making process is prolonged, often involving a committee
Events have a relatively short lead time (usually measured in weeks or months)	Major conferences have a relatively long lead time (often measured in years)
Corporate buyers may organize a wide range of events	Association buyers organize a more limited range of events
Delegate numbers are typically less than 200 (and frequently well under 100)	Delegate numbers are often several hundred and, for the larger associations, can be several thousands
Mainly held in hotels, purpose-built conference/convention centres and unusual venues	Mostly use purpose-built conference/convention centres, conference hotels, civic and academic venues
A higher budget per delegate, with the company paying	A lower budget per delegate, with the individual delegate sometimes paying. There are variations both by type of association and by country
Events are organized year-round	Major events primarily in the Spring and Autumn, with some in the Summer
Events typically last between 0.5–1.5 days	Major conference typically lasts 2–3 days
Accommodation normally in hotels (3-star and upwards)	Wide range of accommodation may be required, dependent on the type of association and whether participants are paying out of their own pockets or whether their employers are paying
Delegates' partners rarely attend	Delegates' partners quite frequently attend

Table 2.3
Comparisons between corporate and association conferences

The findings relate to events organized in 2005, with findings for 2004 shown in brackets.

International 'Association' Conferences • • •

The above characteristics of national associations apply equally to those associations which are primarily international in nature, as well as to international governmental organizations and to academic bodies planning international scientific conferences.

	Corporate Sector	Association Sector
Average number of events organized	9.9 (11.4)	14.1 (14.3)
Total number of events organized by sample	2970 (3420)	4230 (4290)
Percentage change on previous year	– 13%	– 1.4%
Percentage expecting to organize more events in 2006	7% (4%)	28% (22%)
Average number of delegates	140 (99)	123 (68) (regular meetings, not major annual meeting for which the figure is 357)
5 most popular types of event	Staff conference Management meeting Training Presentation/ communication Annual general meeting	Annual meeting Education Regular member communication Technical information updates Fund raising
Average duration of event, in days	1.1 (1.3)	1.3 (1.6)
Percentage residential	26% (43.5%)	21% (38.7%)
Most popular days of week	Wednesday Tuesday Thursday	Wednesday Thursday Tuesday
Most popular months*	1. March 2. October 3. April 4. February 5. September	June April May October September
Average lead times (months)	7.3 (5.7)	12.9 (12.4)
Average budgeted day delegate rates inc. Value Added Tax	£48.70 (£52.90)	£39.00 (£47.70)
Average budgeted 24-hour rates inc. Value Added Tax	£164.50 (£157.60)	£148.20 (£170.40)
Average spend per organization on events	£141,000 (£99,700)	£93,400 (£89,400)
Top 3 cities used in 2005	London – 65% Birmingham – 38% Manchester – 34%	London – 47% Birmingham – 27% Manchester – 21%

Table 2.4
Key findings from the 'UK Conference Market Survey 2006'

	Corporate Sector	Association Sector
Percentage of conferences held outside UK in 2005	7% (6.5%)	3% (3%)
Most popular venue type	City centre hotel – 80% 2 = Unusual venue – 26% 2 = Purpose-built convention centre – 26% 4. Dedicated conference centre – 22%	City centre hotel – 57% University/academic venue – 37% Purpose-built convention centre – 27% Dedicated conference centre – 23%
Top 5 factors influencing venue selection	Location – 96% Price/value for money – 79% Access – 70% Availability – 56% Quality of service – 54%	Location – 90% Price/value for money – 81% Access – 63% Availability – 51% Quality of service – 45%
Top 5 sources of help with venue selection	Own knowledge – 78% Internet/web site – 75% Word of mouth – 63% Venue finding agency – 34% Computer software – 24%	Own knowledge – 69% Word of mouth – 57% Internet/web site – 50% Brochures/library – 26% Directories/guides – 23%
Percentage who visit trade shows/exhibitions	46% (36%)	35% (29%)
Factors at venues needing improvement	Service/staff Food Facilities	Food Service Staff issues
Percentage always or nearly always asked for feedback from venues	60% (40%)	55% (45%)
Top 3 audio-visual items used	PC/data projection Sound system Stage set	Sound system 2 = Flipchart 2 = PC/data projection
Forms of communication most used in addition to face-to-face meetings	Teleconferencing – 81% Email/Intranet – 79% Web site/Internet– 71%	Email/Intranet – 72% Web site/Internet – 71% Teleconferencing – 44%
Regular/occasional use of the Internet to market their events	80%	89%
Booking venues via Internet regularly	54%	38%
Take registrations via web site	55% (38%)	72% (54%)
Delegate joining instructions sent via web site	54% (39%)	70% (66%)

Figures in parentheses relate to the previous year
*Associations' annual event

Table 2.4
Continued

Destinations bidding to stage major international conferences have to be extremely professional in their approach and be prepared to begin working for such an event many years before it is due to take place. It is not unusual to find lead times of 5 years or more, necessitating a great deal of research by those destinations seeking to host the conference, particularly in their cost calculations. It could be all too easy to offer certain hotel rates and venue hire charges to the association which, because of the effects of inflation and other possible changes in the macro-economic climate, bear little relation to what should be being charged when the event actually takes place.

Rotations • • •

International associations and international governmental organizations also operate rotational patterns or cycles in the staging of their events, often on a continental basis: for example, an international conference held in Europe one year may well not return to a European country for at least another 5 years. The Union of International Associations (UIA) and the International Congress and Convention Association (ICCA) both devote considerable resources to tracking where international conferences and congresses are held (see Chapter 1). In recent years there have been some moves by international associations to hold a greater proportion of their conferences in developing countries as a way of building up their memberships in such countries. ICCA reports in its 2006 survey that the proportion of international association meetings which rotates worldwide is decreasing, with 49 per cent of the meetings they track rotating on a worldwide basis, the lowest percentage in 10 years. A greater proportion of meetings is rotating on a continental basis (especially Asia/Pacific, Latin America, or Europe). The reasons for these changed patterns may include cost, travel time, a greater reluctance post '9/11' for delegates to be too far from home, or other factors.

Bidding • • •

Bids to host an international conference are often channelled through the national member representatives of that organization. For example, a small group of Canadian or French members of an international association will form a committee to plan and present a bid to the selection committee. They are likely to get support and assistance from the destination (i.e. a Canadian city or a French city) which they are putting forward to stage the conference, while the national tourism organization or national convention bureau may also play a part in helping to fund the bid and contributing to it in other material ways.

Those preparing to bid for an international association congress or convention must gain an understanding of the key factors which each association considers to be of particular importance when deciding on the destination for its event. These factors will vary to some extent between associations. For example, the International Congress and Convention Association (ICCA), whose annual congress moves around all continents of the world, has set out the following as prime destination selection criteria (article in 'Association Meetings International' magazine, November 2006):

- *Value for money for the association*: not necessarily the cheapest proposal, but the one that delivers ICCA's strategic objectives most efficiently
- *Value for money for the delegate*: are there hotels for different budgets? are there cost effective transport options for delegates to travel to the destination from different parts of the world?
- *Accessibility*: not just international access, but also how easy is it for delegates to travel around the city once they are there?
- *Capacity to attract*: is it a destination with real pulling power? how are the hosts going to help bring in more delegates?
- *Teamwork*: how strong is the local host committee? and is there genuine national backing with financial commitment? what would happen if the leader of the bid fell ill?
- *Suitability of meeting venue*: this may be self-apparent, but ensuring that the venue is appropriate is crucial to the success of the event
- *Quality and attractiveness of the social event venues*
- *Networking opportunities*: critical to the success of the congress, but there is also a need to evaluate how to maximize its impact
- *Association development opportunities*: opportunities to grow ICCA's membership, or reach out to new markets with ICCA's services. What will the local hosts do to help?
- *Creativity*: vitally important! How will holding the congress in this destination lead to a marvellous, 'mind-shifting' event that no delegate will forget? what fantastic new ideas are the local hosts throwing into the equation?

Mini-Case Study 2.1 outlines the collaboration required by a number of parties in winning the World Apiculture Congress for Ireland. It also exemplifies the long time between the initial identification and bidding for the event and its actual taking place.

Case Study 2.1   Apimondia World Apiculture Congress

The World Apiculture Congress is the biennial congress of the international association Apimondia. The congress attracts between 2000 and 4000 participants for a 6-day programme, and has a large trade exhibition running concurrently. Technical tours to all parts of the host country are arranged for delegates, and a high percentage of participants opt to extend their stay as 'business extenders'.

The Irish success in winning this important international event was the result of a strong collaboration between many parties. The Federation of Irish Beekeepers' Associations and the Ulster Beekeepers' Association were the official host organizations for the conference in Ireland. They submitted their bid to attract the event to Ireland in conjunction with Ovation Group (now MCI Dublin), working as the appointed Professional Conference Organizer. Great support was also received from the Irish government (in particular the Department of Agriculture) and Failte Ireland (the national tourism organization).

Case Study 2.2 gives details of the annual conference of the International Federation of Library Associations and Institutions, including the criteria it uses to assess locations wishing to host the

Year	Action
1997	Ovation Group identifies the Apimondia World Apiculture Congress as an interesting event for Ireland: good size, good season, good potential to win the business (it had never been held in Ireland before).
1997	A meeting takes place with representatives of the Federation of Irish Beekeepers' Associations (FIBKA), the national body for beekeeping in Ireland.
1998	FIBKA re-affiliates to Apimondia as Irish member. Ovation presents to FIBKA national council; decision taken to proceed with bid for Ireland for 2005 as a joint bid between FIBKA and the Ulster Beekeepers' Association, making it an all-Ireland event.
1998	Background work done: booking of the RDS Irish International Convention and Exhibition Centre (in Dublin) as the venue, and of hotels for accommodation. First draft budget prepared.
1999	Two representatives of FIBKA travel to Apimondia congress in Vancouver and meet the international board. First presentation of bid materials. Lobbying work begins.
2000	Lobbying work continues with international delegates from the Vancouver congress. Congress logo and promotional flier are designed.
2001	Bid materials are formally re-submitted. A 30-strong contingent travels to Durban, South Africa, to attend the congress, accompanied by the Irish Minister for Horticulture, and representatives of the CBI, Department of Agriculture and Bord Glas (the Horticulture Board, now amalgamated with Bord Bia, the Food Board). A formal presentation of the bid is made to voting delegates (including a 1-minute video introduction by the Taoiseach (Irish Prime Minister)). Ireland wins the bid for the 39th Apimondia International Apiculture Congress against competition from Argentina, Indonesia and Australia.
2002	Establishment of Irish organizing committee. Set-up of web site and further promotional work. Preparation of exhibitor/sponsor manual.

Year	Action
2003	40-strong group attend Apimondia congress in Slovenia (accompanied by Irish Minister for Horticulture). Ireland takes an exhibition stand, circulates 2000 copies of the first congress announcement, and hosts an Irish night with a performance by Bru Boru. A meeting is held with all sponsors and exhibitors, and with the organizing committee and PCO in Slovenia.
2004	Exhibition space is on sale, delegate registrations commence July 2004.
August 21–25 2005.	Congress takes place in Dublin. 3351 participants are registered from 128 countries, and the concurrent exhibition attracts 120 stands. The budget for the event is 2 million euros, and the estimated value to the Irish economy is 6 million euros. The Irish Post Office produces a postage stamp to commemorate the event.

conference and the proposal document which has to be prepared by potential hosts.

Other characteristics of international association conferences and conventions, according to ICCA (2006), include:

- the frequency may be annual, biennial, or even every 5 years. Approximately half of all international association meetings are annual. The proportion of biennial meetings (ie. taking place every 2 years) has dropped gradually from 29.6 per cent of all meetings in 1996 to 22.9 per cent in 2005. ICCA also contends that the proportion of meetings held less regularly (e.g. every three to 4 years) is decreasing while the number taking place once, or more than once a year, is increasing
- the destination is chosen by the international organization (the Board, the General Assembly, or a special committee). However, 'a growing minority of about 25–30 per cent of the decision-making processes no longer include an official bidding procedure. Instead the international association appoints a 'central initiator' who selects the location and venues based on pre-determined and strict criteria'
- where a national association or local host committee is involved in submitting a bid they will, if successful, choose the venue and other suppliers, often drawing on the services of a Professional Conference Organizer (PCO)
- increasingly international associations are appointing a 'core PCO', who is contracted to organize the event no matter where it is being held. In the past, PCOs were appointed from within the country where the convention or congress was to take place, because of their local knowledge and expertise. The benefits from working with a core PCO include the PCO's understanding of the association and its specific requirements,

built up over several years. Such understanding is deemed to be of greater value than the destination knowledge of a locally-appointed PCO

- the programme for the event is designed by a special programme committee, which can be part of the local organizing committee or be a separate international body
- September is the most popular month for international association meetings. The average length of meeting is 4.08 days, the shortest duration for 10 years (but perhaps replicating trends noted among corporate and national association events). ICCA also reports that the average registration fee per delegate per meeting fell from US$530 in 2004 to US$472 in 2005.

The public sector buyer

The public sector (sometimes referred to as 'government') has much in common with the association sector (and, indeed, for research purposes is often subsumed within data for the association sector), covering organizations such as local authorities/ municipalities, central government departments and agencies, educational bodies, and the health service. These organizations are all 'not-for-profit' organizations and are accountable for the ways in which they spend public funds. Although delegates from public sector organizations are not normally expected to pay their own expenses to participate in a conference, it is likely that the events will be run on fairly tight budgets, often using the less expensive venues such as civic facilities, universities and colleges, and hotels up to 3-star standard.

There is, even so, a discernible trend for such public sector organizations to book higher standard facilities. Delegates' expectations are rising constantly and, whereas sharing a room or staying in bedrooms which are not *en suite* might have been the norm some years ago, this is now much less acceptable. Such trends help to account for the major investments which university venues, in particular, are making to upgrade their accommodation stock to enable them to compete in this highly price-sensitive marketplace.

In the context of public sector and government organizations, it is worth noting the phrase 'per diem' (literally 'per day'). In the USA, 'per diem' is a daily allowance which public sector employees can spend on food, accommodation and other expenses when attending a meeting or conference. The phrase may also be encountered outside the USA if hotels are dealing with US armed services or embassy personnel stationed overseas. In the USA some large hotel chains have a Director of Sales specialising in this area, assisting the group's hotels and also their government clients when quoting for conferences at which delegates are on this 'per diem' allowance.

The entrepreneurial buyer

The fourth type of buyer is one who does not have a recognized descriptor: his role is essentially that of an entrepreneur operating within the conference sector. In other words, someone who identifies 'hot topics' in the business or academic world and then plans and produces a conference at which the topics can be presented, discussed and debated by high profile speakers and experts. The entrepreneur aims to sell places at the conference to anyone interested in paying to attend. Clearly, as with any entrepreneurial activity, there is a financial risk to be borne as the entrepreneur incurs various costs (e.g. deposit payment on the venue hired, promotional costs, possibly cancellation charges to the venue and to speakers if the event does not go ahead) with no guarantee that he can run the conference successfully and make a profit. However, it is also possible to make significant profits on such conferences with delegate fees for a one-day conference often being as much as £300–£500.

Entrepreneurial conferences are typically organized by publishing houses, trade associations, academic bodies, and independent conference producers/organizers. It can be seen from the brief description above that one of the pre-requisites for success in this area includes having a finger on the pulse of specific industrial and business sectors to understand what are the contemporary issues and challenges that might provide the material for a conference. It is also important to have access to quality databases of potential invitees to whom the conference can be promoted.

Tables 2.5 and 2.6 show a classification system developed by the British Association of Conference Destinations (BACD) for its 'Conference Buyer Database'. The system differentiates between corporate and association buyers (and also has a section for Agencies – see later in this chapter) by industry sector (based loosely on the Standard Industrial Classification). It also gives numbers of records held for each buyer category. A search on **Sector Type 04**, for example, would pull out all of the corporate organization contacts in the **Computing and Telecommunications Sectors**, while the inclusion of **Sector Type 24** would bring in all of the association contacts for the same industry sectors.

THE SUPPLIERS

The suppliers are those who make available for external hire the venues, destinations and many other specialist services without which today's conferences could not take place.

Suppliers to the conference industry have grown in quantity and diversity in tandem with the overall growth of the industry over the past 50 years. Relatively few of these suppliers are dedicated exclusively to the conference industry, however.

Corporate		Non-corporate		Sector Description
Sector Code	Nos.	Sector Code	Nos.	
01	170	21	26	Mining, energy (gas, electricity), water companies, petroleum, chemicals
02	333	22	455	Pharmaceuticals, medical, cosmetics, toiletries
03	155	23	26	Engineering
04	469	24	10	Computer manufacturing and services, information technology, telecommunications
05	367	25	49	Manufacturing/processing
06	152	26	37	Building and construction, civil engineering, surveying, architecture, estate agency, housing associations
07	562	27	39	Communications and media (radio, TV, newspapers, PR/marketing consultancy, advertising, publishing
08	244	28	13	Commerce: retail and wholesale distribution, import/export
09	808	29	79	Financial and professional services: banking, insurance, building societies, finance/credit companies, solicitors/legal, accountants, management consultants, training consultants
10	166	30	21	Service companies (e.g. couriers/logistics, security, cleaning)
11	1948	31	223	Leisure and entertainment, hotels and catering, transport, travel (including professional conference/event/exhibition organizers, venue finding agencies)
12	23	32	101	Agriculture, forestry, environment, animals
13	53	33	194	Education
14	13	34	724	Central and local government depts. and agencies (not covered above), public bodies, charities, religious groups
15	2998	35	293	Others
	8461		2290	Total

Source: British Association of Conference Destinations

Table 2.5
BACD Conference Buyer Database Sector Coding

Buyer Code	Numbers Held in the Database	Buyer Code Description
		Corporate
10	651	Others
11	707	Conference/event/incentive organizer
12	32	Exhibition (exposition) organizer
13	1691	Secretary/PA, administration manager/assistant
14	862	Training and personnel manager/assistant, training consultant
15	1913	Sales and marketing manager/executive, PR/manager/executive
16	1015	Company secretary, managing director, chief executive
	6871	**Total Corporate**
		Agency
20	243	Other (e.g. incentive travel house, business travel agency)
21	1650	Professional conference/event organizer, conference production company
22	154	Venue finding agency (only)
23	41	Exhibition (exposition) organizer (independent)
	2088	**Total Agency**
		Association
30	115	Others
31	1234	Professional or trade association/institution/society
32	425	Voluntary association/society, charity, religious group, political party
33	59	Trade union
34	497	Local or central government, educational body, health authority, other public agency
	2330	**Total Association**
	11,289	**Grand Total**

Source: British Association of Conference Destinations

Table 2.6
BACD Conference Buyer Database Buyer Coding

This summary divides the supply side of the conference industry into three main categories:

- venues
- destinations
- others.

While the examples given relate mainly to the British Isles, most countries with a well-developed conference product have a similar base of suppliers, although the numbers and proportions vary from country to country.

Venues

Within the British Isles alone there are around 3500 venues being promoted as suitable for conferences, meetings, and related events. It is impossible to give a precise number because new venues are regularly becoming available for external hire, while other venues discover that their facilities no longer meet the requirements necessary for twenty-first century conferences, and so they pull out of the market. There are discussions and research underway (Autumn 2006) in the UK about the establishment of a grading or classification system for conference venues, although nothing of this kind is yet in place. In theory, therefore, almost any type of building could be promoted as a conference venue.

A clearer idea of which are the leading conference venues would no doubt emerge if it were possible to ascertain what proportion of their turnover is accounted for by conference business. There are probably fewer than 1000 venues in the British Isles in which conference business contributes more than 40–50 per cent of their annual turnover.

What is certain, however, is that hotels comprise over half of all conference venues, being particularly important to the corporate market sector. The main types of hotel active in the conference market are:

- city centre hotels.
- hotels adjacent to the national and international communications infrastructure (airports, motorways and highways especially).
- rural or country house hotels.

In addition to the conferences which they stage as venues in their own right, hotels located close to large convention centres also benefit as providers of delegate accommodation/housing when a major conference comes to town. Additionally, the bigger association conferences often choose one hotel as their 'headquarters' hotel, and there can be significant public relations benefits with the hotel being featured in national, and sometimes international, television and media coverage.

The larger hotel chains have invested very heavily in the design and equipping of their conference and meeting facilities, recognising that the standard multi-purpose function room is no longer adequate for the needs of the contemporary conference organizer. Many have also branded their conference product (see Chapter 4) to assist in the promotion of these facilities and services, seeking to assure the buyer that he will receive the same level of service whichever hotel in the chain is used. Staff trained and dedicated to meeting the needs of conference organizers and delegates are to be found in all the major conference hotels (see Chapter 6).

Alongside hotels, other principal types of venue include:

- **purpose-built centres** (residential and non-residential) – specifically designed to host meetings and conferences, whether they are the larger events for hundreds or even thousands of delegates (venues such as the International Convention Centre in Birmingham (England), the Orlando (Orange County) Convention Center in Florida, Hong Kong Convention and Exhibition Centre, Durban International Convention Centre in South Africa, Melbourne Convention and Exhibion Centre (Australia)) or smaller, day and residential, events (venues such as Henley Management College, Oxfordshire, England, and Belmont Square Conference Centre in Rondebosch, Cape Town, South Africa).

It should be noted that, in the USA, the term 'convention center' is used to describe a building with exhibition (referred to as 'exhibit') halls and convention/meeting rooms but no residential (sleeping) facilities. The term 'conference center' is used to describe a building with meeting rooms, bedrooms but no exhibition (or exhibit) space.

- **college, university and other academic venues** – there are around 150 academic venues in the UK, many only available for residential conferences during student vacation periods (but still staging some non-residential events during term time). Germany has over 300 universities, such as Kiel and Karlsruhe, available for use as meeting and convention venues.

An increasing number of academic venues have been investing in the construction of conference facilities which are available throughout the year, providing accommodation equivalent to a good 3-star hotel standard. In the UK the University of Warwick, Lancaster University and the University of Strathclyde are three very good examples of such investments. The East Midlands Conference Centre, located on the campus of the University of

Nottingham, can seat up to 550 delegates in its main auditorium, complemented with exhibition/exposition or banqueting space and a range of syndicate rooms, and might equally be classed as a purpose-built conference centre.

- **civic venues** – council chambers and committee rooms, town halls, and other civic facilities which are available for external hire e.g. Brisbane City Hall, Portsmouth Guildhall, and Bremen's Stadthalle are just three examples of such facilities
- **unusual venues** – this is a somewhat ill-defined term to describe a very wide range of venues (sometimes described as 'unique' venues) which do not fit into the more common categories listed above. The attraction of unusual venues is that they can give an event a special appeal and can make it memorable for years afterwards. Some have very high quality meeting and conference facilities, others may be quite limited in this respect but the setting in which the event is being held compensates for such shortcomings in the eyes of the conference organizer (and, it is hoped, of the delegates). Unusual options include sporting venues (e.g. football and rugby stadia, racecourses, golf clubs), cultural and entertainment venues (museums, theatres, television studios, stately homes), tourist attractions (theme parks, historical sites, castles, heritage centres), transport venues (ferries, steam trains, canal barges), even a lighthouse or two! In the British Isles around one-fifth of the 3500 venues being promoted to the conference market can be classified as unusual venues.

Figure 2.1 provides an analysis of the different types of conference venue in the UK.

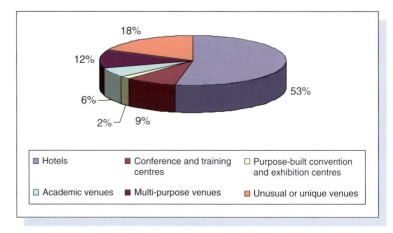

Figure 2.1
Analysis of the UK's conference venues by number and type. (Source: British Association of Conference Destinations)

Destinations

Conference organizers attach greater importance to 'location' than to any other single criterion when selecting their sites. Location may be expressed in terms of 'town', 'city', 'region of the country'. The widely accepted term to describe each of these is 'destination'. A destination may, of course, be an entire country (as a national destination), but within a country it is a discrete area with identifiable boundaries (usually!). Each conference destination must contain a range of venues, facilities, attractions, support services and appropriate infrastructure to help it to attract conference business.

Within the British Isles, the British Association of Conference Destinations represents almost all of the leading destinations active in serving the conference industry. Its 65 member destinations may be classified as follows:

- Cities – 23
- Towns – 15
- Counties/regions – 20
- Islands – 3
- Countries – 4.

A list of current BACD members is accessible on the BACD web site (www.bacd.org.uk). A consolidation of member destinations since the mid-1990s has led to mergers and a growth in organizations representing larger geographical areas i.e. counties/regions. At an international level, Destination Marketing Association International (DMAI – see Chapter 8) represents well over 600 destinations around the world.

Destination marketing organizations (DMOs), often trading as 'convention and visitor bureaux (CVBs)' or 'conference desks' (see Chapter 4), bring the destination to the marketplace, offering a 'one-stop-shop' enquiry point to the conference and event organizer. Their role is to promote the destination, highlighting all its strengths and facilities, generating and converting enquiries into confirmed business. They are also involved in product development: identifying weaknesses in venues and facilities and in general infrastructure and working to rectify such shortcomings. However, the role of CVBs is changing and evolving because of a range of factors and pressures, a point examined further in Chapters 4 and 9.

Other suppliers

The conference industry has to draw upon the services of many different supplier organizations in order to offer a complete service to its buyers. Those suppliers who fulfil a 'buying' role on behalf of corporate or association clients are described in the next section (Agencies). Examples of other key suppliers include the following:

- audio-visual contractors (supply and operation of specialist audio-visual equipment).
- telecommunications companies (videoconferencing/teleconferencing/satellite conferencing).
- transport operators (airlines, coach and rail companies, car hire, taxi firms, ferry companies).
- interpreters and translators (for international conferences).
- after-dinner speakers, entertainers, corporate events companies (e.g. companies running 'Murder Mystery' events, sporting and outdoor activities).
- speciality caterers (banquets, receptions, buffets).
- floral contractors (flower displays for conference platforms, registration areas, exhibition/exposition stands).
- exhibition/exposition contractors.
- companies which develop specialist computer software (e.g. venue-finding and event management programmes).

AGENCIES AND INTERMEDIARIES

'Agencies' is a generic term used to describe a range of different organizations which are both suppliers and buyers. They undertake a buying role on behalf of their clients, who may be companies or associations. They act as intermediaries or 'middlemen', and can be contracted to assist in the planning and running of a conference or similar event.

In the agency field in the UK, there are a number of agencies which are just 'one-man-bands', some of whom lack professionalism and the poor quality of service they provide has tainted the industry. The lack of a regulatory framework of the kind to be found among older-established professions is one of the issues still to be tackled by the conference industry.

Agencies come in a number of forms, and the nomenclature can be somewhat confusing, but below are listed the principal kinds of intermediaries operating within the conference and events industry.

Professional Conference Organizer

The Professional Conference Organizer, sometimes Professional Congress Organizer, is often referred to simply as a PCO (but may also be described as an event management company). In the USA the term PCO is not widely used and reference is more likely to be to an Independent Meeting Planner, while a Destination Management Company (DMC) may also fulfil some of this role (see description of a DMC below). Multi-management firm is another term used in the USA with a similar connotation i.e. a

Typical Portfolio of Services Offered by a Professional Conference Organizer (PCO)

- Venue selection, booking and liaison
- Reservation and management of delegate accommodation
- Event marketing, including the design of conference programmes and promotional materials, PR and media co-ordination, presentations to committees and boards
- Programme planning, speaker selection and briefing
- Provision of an administrative secretariat, handling delegate registrations, recruitment and briefing of conference staff, co-ordinating delegates' travel arrangements
- Organization of exhibitions/expositions, including sales and marketing functions
- Advising on and co-ordinating audio-visual services and the production of the event, including the provision of multilingual interpretation and translation services
- Planning the catering for an event, liaising with chefs, conference and banqueting staff, and independent catering companies
- Arranging social events, tour programmes and technical visits
- Arranging security cover and advising on health and safety issues
- Recording, transcribing and producing the proceedings of meetings for publication, arranging poster sessions, processing of abstracts
- Preparation of budgets, managing event income and expenditure, generating revenue through sponsorship, exhibitions/expositions and satellite meetings, handling VAT and insurance issues
- Preparation of contracts with venues and other suppliers.

Source: Association of British Professional Conference Organisers

Table 2.7
Typical portfolio of services offered by a professional conference organizer

company offering complete turnkey organizational support for a meeting, including administration and meeting management services.

Employed to assist in the organization of a conference, the PCO's role can include researching and recommending a suitable venue, helping to plan the conference programme including the social programme, marketing the conference and handling delegate registrations, booking accommodation/housing for delegates, planning an exhibition to run concurrently with the conference, producing a budget and handling all of the conference finances. The PCO is normally paid a management fee by the client organization, calculated on the basis of a registration fee per delegate (with a guaranteed minimum number of delegates) or on the estimated staff costs required to manage the event (number of staff needed × number of days × amount per day). PCOs may also charge a commission to the conference venue (usually 8–10 per cent of the value of the conference to the venue itself), as well as a commission on accommodation bookings and on other services provided, although the trend is for greater use of a management fee and less reliance on commissions.

Table 2.7 shows a typical portfolio of services offered by a professional conference organizer. Further insights into the work of a PCO are given in Chapter 5.

The industry is witnessing the rise and consolidation of the global event management company, with huge buying power. Case study 2.3 profiles one such company, MCI Group.

A survey carried out by the author among the members of the Association of British Professional Conference Organisers in December 2004 highlighted a number of significant changes in the traditional role and modus operandi of PCOs. Some of the key changes are summarized in Mini Case Study 2.4.

Case Study 2.4   Challenge and Change for PCOs

Financial

- PCOs are witnessing a number of challenges on the financial front: for example, the steady demise of commissions from venues, as clients book the venue direct over the internet, and their delegates also book their accommodation directly in the same way (only 25–40 per cent now book via the PCO, compared with 80 per cent 10 years ago)
- Convention bureaux are, in some cases, competing against PCOs for commissions from both venue and accommodation bookings, using such income to fund their ongoing destination marketing activity
- PCO contracts with hotels for bedrooms are being compromised by reduced rates nearer the time of the event available over the internet. The 'risk'-taking delegate can use the reduced rates on the web, therefore, and the hotel then becomes a competitor to the PCO, taking advantage of high room rates on contract to the PCO but not hesitating to sell rooms late direct to delegates – almost a monopoly situation made easy by the web
- The reduction in commission income has hastened the move to charging a management fee, but fee levels have either remained static over the past 6–7 years or even reduced

- Registration fees for delegates have moved very little in the past 10 years, while clients view a conference as a business venture from which they can make considerable amounts of money. Clients' profit expectations have risen substantially, and so the outcome can often be to reduce the conference budget either by not engaging a PCO in the first place or by reducing the PCO's fees.

Corporate Clients

- Within the corporate sector, in particular, PCOs are reporting a strengthening of relationships with clients, linked with a market consolidation. There are opportunities for a PCO/event management company to benefit from the fast-becoming standard practice, among corporates, of awarding all their business to one 'preferred' supplier (or 'vendor'), in return for savings and agreed service levels – this favours those PCOs with larger capacity, and therefore it is easier for such PCOs to continue winning major accounts and to grow more quickly than others – an opportunity for them but a threat to the smaller PCO
- In the association sector, there is a parallel development with the appointment of a Core PCO who will continue to work with a client and their event even when the event moves to a different part of the world
- This trend among corporates to consolidate their outsourcing to a smaller number of preferred suppliers is, in part, being driven by the influence of procurement departments who are seeking improved efficiencies in purchasing and a better, more transparent, control of costs (see Chapter 9)
- There is an expectation that the PCO will be proactive. In this context proactivity means exploring opportunities for outsourcing in order to achieve greater leverage or advantage for one's client. In other words, to suggest ways in which supplier costs and PCO costs can be reduced, where possible, through consolidated buying power, through greater efficiency or innovations in the PCO's systems. The PCO buys into the client's corporate objectives and puts his own second, the benefit being that he keeps the account which may be worth millions of euros, at least until it is put out to tender again! In effect the PCO is taking the longer term view, being seen to toe the line, to achieve proactive results so that other large accounts will come his way
- Return on investment (ROI) is one of the most popular mantras in contemporary corporate life, no more so than with respect to a company's events and conferences which are increasingly required to demonstrate tangible benefits to the company and a return on the expenditure made on them (see also Chapter 9)
- It was suggested that one of the less welcome trends has been a general dumbing down approach, as a result of the surge, often originating in North America, for automation-based quick

fix solutions in the venue search and selection process. This approach fails to understand that conferences are a very different animal from hotel bedroom reservations. It detracts from a service-driven profession which prides itself on the creative contribution of experienced, motivated and quite gifted people.

Impacts of Technology

- One of the impacts of technology has been to undermine the role of those PCOs whose focus is based on efficient administration – as the administration role itself changes (i.e. less paper-based, less centralised with the advent of web-based registration), then PCOs who are unable to offer more strategic or creative services may well find it harder and harder to get business
- One PCO described the benefits of technology as follows:

  Electronic communication has helped advance the PCO industry enormously. We no longer need to spend weeks keying in lists from other conferences to put together a comprehensive distribution list for the conference. We now receive mailing lists electronically and can send out electronic brochures or direct potential delegates to the conference web site immediately. I remember in 1994 we organised an International Neurotrauma Conference for 1200 delegates. The mailing list consisted of 25 000 contact names and addresses which we keyed into our database (this took one person a total of 50 days to key in!) and the postage was £25 000 (nearly 40 000 euros). Today we spend no time keying in contact names and the postage costs are around £5000 (or 8000 euros). The operational costs of stationery and postage are, therefore, now negligible in a conference budget. On-line registration has also helped the PCO cut overheads such as full time staff and, in turn, helped to keep the PCO's fees lower to be competitive.

- Another respondent described the PCO as a technology manager, or perhaps more accurately an information manager:

  A collector of more numerous small pieces of information via email. Email has made the job more complex and risky in managing information. Committee members feed in their opinions by email to the PCO who then needs to report back on the issue before any decision can be taken. Before, a good old committee meeting would have had a structured and more straightforward decision-making process – that process has now been complicated by email. Following on from this, often the motivation of the group is only by email and the pleasure of being out of the office to have a committee meeting is lost.

- The challenge is to remain at the cutting edge of technology but to marry this with human input: people still want to be treated nicely but the opportunity to nurture committees and clients is more remote with greater pressures on individuals to perform rather than to organize meetings
- Teleconferences demand different skills from face-to-face (F2F) events. They bring benefits in terms of logistics and saving time and money but often the committee members do not have the necessary documentation in front of them, placing greater reliance on the PCO to be not only a logistics expert but also a reliable and almost inexhaustible repository for things that have been said in the past.

A More Complex Role

- Conference organizing today is much more complex than it was in the mid- to late 1990s. The PCO has become a multinational legislation enforcer in areas such as risk and security. With security matters, and health and safety issues, there can be a whole chain of responsibility encompassing the venue, the PCO, sub-contractors, etc. but it is the PCO who plays a pivotal role in co-ordinating these various players and producing a coherent risk assessment and risk management strategy
- The PCO is required to be a financial and tax expert, and even develop strategies to prevent money laundering and minimise fraud from bogus conference delegates. More time has to be spent setting up accounts and addressing tax issues. As tax issues and regulations have become more complex, there is a greater reliance on outside consultants, who inevitably charge fees for their services. One ABPCO member commented:

    Rather than being seen as organizers, we are now looked upon as being a 'cheap' way of obtaining professional advice, such as being a VAT expert, an accountant, a legal adviser, handling contracts, an IT expert, webmaster, procurement officer, etc. For the organizational elements, they view the engagement of a PCO as a luxury, one which often they feel they can do without.

- Another member of ABPCO added:

    We offer advice in setting up the most appropriate financial vehicle for the conference and advice on all contracts between the conference and **third party suppliers**. *We never used to do this. Contracts from third party suppliers were almost non-existent 10 years ago – now they come complete with cancellation policies.*

Increasing Competition

- There is now much more competition than ever before – clearly, for the client, this is normally a good thing, but it can sometimes lead to a lower quality of service and a poorer quality event
- Venues are increasingly offering advice and practical support in organizing social and partner programmes, audio-visual entertainment, impinging on other PCO core activities and income streams
- The number of people involved with a conference today is more fragmented. One respondent gave the following example:

I was recently involved with a conference where the convention bureau was organizing the accommodation, an exhibition organizer had been appointed, the client's wife was organizing the social programme, the client was responsible for the scientific programme and we were responsible for the registration and abstract administration. We need to learn to be flexible.

she concluded.

Venue finding agency

As their name implies, such agencies offer a more limited service, restricted to researching and recommending a suitable venue for an event. Venue finding agencies typically put forward a shortlist of three potential venues to their client (or in some cases just one venue initially) and expect to receive a commission (paid to them by the venue chosen for the conference) of 8–10 per cent of the value of the booking to the venue. Venue finding agencies may also get involved in booking accommodation for delegates, and again would expect to charge commission to the hotels and other accommodation providers. The agency's services to the client are usually provided free of charge.

However, in the UK at least, many of the most successful venue finding agencies have expanded into the field of event management in order to develop a longer-term relationship with their clients. They have introduced client management team structures within the company, comprising an account manager, a venue finder, and an event planner, who often manage a handful of major accounts. This approach is attractive to major corporations and pharmaceutical companies who are constantly looking to obtain benefits from the economies of scale that the big agencies claim to deliver.

Conference production company

Such companies specialise in the actual staging of the conference: designing and building conference sets, providing lighting, sound systems, presentation technology (e.g. video/dvd, data projection, rear projection, overhead projection, satellite conferencing, webcasts) and special effects. Their expertise lies in audiovisual and communications technology, which they are required to match to the needs of different clients. They also need creative and theatrical skills, recognizing that conferences have to be professionally stage-managed and should be a memorable, striking experience for the delegates.

Shone (pages 91–103) describes in greater depth the technical equipment used by conference production companies and conference venues, but the technology is developing at such a rapid rate that it is highly likely that new equipment and presentation systems will be in use in three or four years' time which have not even been heard of at the time this text is being written (Spring 2007). Chapter 5 gives further information on the technology in use by conference organizers and conference production companies.

Incentive Travel and Incentive Travel Houses

All-expenses-paid travel, often to overseas destinations, is still regarded as one of the best incentives a company can use to motivate and reward its employees, distributors, and retailers. 'Incentive travel', as this has come to be known, was developed in the USA in the first half of the twentieth century, and is now an important industry segment in its own right. The official definition, according to the Society of Incentive and Travel Executives (SITE), is as follows:

> *Incentive Travel is a global management tool that uses an exceptional travel experience to motivate and/or recognize participants for increased levels of performance in support of organizational goals (SITE, 2006).*

A survey entitled 'Corporate Incentive Trends Survey' published in *Corporate Meetings and Incentives* magazine (November 2004) found that 42 per cent of respondents rated travel as the best motivator, ahead of cash (38 per cent) and merchandise (4 per cent).

Estimates of the incentive travel sector's global value suggest that it was worth some US$17 billion in 1990, which was expected to rise to US$56 billion by 2000. Figures provided by SITE estimate the value of spend by US companies on 'merchandise and travel' was US$26 billion in 1999, with the wider US meetings, convention and incentive industry being worth US$41.8 billion in the same year. Research commissioned by the British Tourist Authority et al put the value of incentive travel to the United Kingdom (both inbound and domestic markets) at £180 million in 1995. In 1999 the UK outbound incentive travel industry was worth £1.025 billion (including air travel costs), a figure which had reduced to £956 million by 2000 (source SITE UK & Ireland Chapter). However, generally research into the volume and value of incentive travel globally, or even by country, is extremely limited.

'The Meetings Market Report 2005', carried out by *Meetings & Conventions* magazine in the USA, indicated that the corporate sector spent c.US$32 billion on over one million meetings attended by almost 80 million participants. 28 per cent of the respondents to the survey said they organized incentives, an increase of almost 8 per cent over figures from 2003.

Companies operating in the automotive, financial services, pharmaceutical and information technology sectors are among the leading users of outbound (overseas) incentive travel from the United Kingdom. Research undertaken among 350 North American corporations by International Conference Research Inc in 2006 found that, among the top users of *international* award programmes, insurance corporations led the way by a substantial margin, followed by finance, direct selling, automotive manufacturers/dealers, and computer hardware/software manufacturers.

Incentive travel programmes should be tailored to the needs of each client company. An 'off-the-shelf' incentive programme is really a contradiction in terms. Incentive travel has been described as an 'extraordinary reward for extraordinary performance' (Paul Flackett, SITE member and Managing Director, IMEX Ltd). Incentive travel programmes are, therefore, designed to create an allure or dream which will make people want to produce that extra effort, achieve that exceptional performance, and strive to be the winners within a corporate organization. From the company's perspective, it is also about strengthening the loyalty of its best employees to the company, making them want to belong to the organization, and giving them reasons to perform even better in the future.

Attention is now being paid to developing incentive travel as a tool for motivating achievers across the board. David Hackett, then Chairman of UK incentive travel specialists TMO, elaborated this point as long ago as 1997 in the following terms ('Conference & Exhibition Factfinder' magazine, June 1997):

> *League tables are frequently created in order to offer rewards and create motivation at all levels. This can include lower targets to encourage first time qualifiers or*

graduated awards for top achievers to ensure they still strive to maximize their performance, even when they have qualified to participate in the travel programme. Individual benefits can include superior room allocation, upgraded flights and hosting allowances (for example, providing top achievers with budgets to host cocktail parties in their suites).

The 'Corporate Incentive Trends Survey' published in *Corporate Meetings and Incentives* magazine (November 2004) found that the primary goals of companies' major incentive programmes were:

- To increase sales across the board (66 per cent)
- To increase sales of a particular product or single product line (12 per cent)
- To grow product awareness (11 per cent)
- To draw market share from competitors (4 per cent)
- Other (7 per cent).

Incentive travel programmes increasingly have an educational element for the participants. This can involve visits to factories and businesses in the same industry sector as that of the award winners, team-building programmes, and a conference-type session with an award presentation ceremony and announcements of corporate plans, designed to encourage the incentive winners to reach future performance targets. Other trends in incentive travel programmes noted by Carolyn Dow, Director SITE European office, in a presentation to the UK Business Tourism Partnership Research Group (June 2001) were:

- Smaller groups
- Shorter lead times
- Shorter qualification periods
- More 'exotic' locations
- Active not passive programmes e.g. award winners engaging in outdoor pursuits activities rather than lounging by the hotel pool
- Many incentives now include a meeting – this is a way of delegates avoiding the need to be taxed on the benefit of the incentive trip. However, it also makes good business sense to build a more formal work-related element into the incentive programme.

The most popular incentive destinations for groups travelling from the UK, according to 'Meetings & Incentive Travel' magazine's 'Trends and Spend Survey 2005' (published May 2006) were Spain, France and Italy as short haul destinations and the USA, South Africa and the United Arab Emirates as long haul destinations. The 2004 Survey found that long haul trips lasted on average just over 4 days, with short haul trips lasting 3 days.

For corporations in the North American market (according to International Conference Research Inc), the top international incentive destinations in 2005 were, in order: Britain, Italy, Ireland, Spain and France. European Travel Commission research (2003) among US and Canadian corporations using incentive travel programmes found that the average number of participants on international trips outside North America was 116 with an average duration of 4–5 nights.

Incentive travel is probably more susceptible to the ups and downs of the national and global economies than most other segments of business tourism. In some cases, however, an economic downturn in a particular industry or country can actually encourage incentive travel schemes. The beauty of incentive schemes is that they are generally totally self-funding, with the travel award being paid for by the success of the incentive travel programme. If no one meets their sales targets, no one wins. It is, therefore, one of the best promotional tools.

Perhaps even more important than economic factors in the health of this business segment is the national/international political situation. The Gulf War in 1990, for example, virtually wiped out the American incentive travel market, even to Europe. Similarly, the events of September 11th 2001 in the USA caused a steep fall, particularly in American incentive travel business. No company directors want to put their best employees or associates on an aeroplane and risk losing them all (in fact, as standard policy, they would normally use several different flights to transport award winners to their incentive destination to minimize such risks). 'The Meetings Market Report 2005' showed that 77 per cent of incentive planners now rate the safety and security of a destination as very important in destination choice, above climate (73 per cent), availability of recreational facilities (70 per cent), and sightseeing, cultural and other extra-curricular attractions (66 per cent).

The specialised nature of the incentive sector has led to the growth of Incentive Travel Houses, as these 'agencies' are generally known. Incentive Travel Houses charge a fee to their clients for the work they undertake on their behalf. The definition of a Full Service Incentive Travel House is:

'Full Service Incentive Houses help corporations reach business goals by creating incentive programmes that utilize incentive class travel as an award. They also offer a staff service, marketing guidance in identification of objectives and construction of programme, programme administration and tracking motivational mailings and promotion and delivery of incentive class awards.'

Destination Management Company

Destination Management Companies (or DMCs) are specialist ground operators in the incentive travel field (who may also provide services to conference organizers, especially where a conference is being organized overseas). The definition of a DMC, given by the Society of Incentive and Travel Executives (SITE), is as follows:

'A DMC is a local service organization that provides consulting services, creative events and exemplary management of logistics based on an in-depth knowledge of the destination and the needs of the incentive and motivation markets.'

By comparison, ground operators have a more limited role, defined as:

'A ground operator provides transportation in a locale i.e. coaches, rental cars, rail, etc.'

DMCs, therefore, have detailed knowledge and expertise of a specific destination, be this a city, an island or other discrete region, and sometimes even a whole country. They also have access to unusual venues such as private houses and stately homes which are not normally open to the general public. They have considerable buying power which makes them very useful to Incentive Travel Houses situated in countries other than the one in which the incentive travel award is to be taken.

Incentive Travel Houses and DMCs, therefore, work very closely together. However, the relationship between an Incentive Travel House and a DMC can sometimes be fraught, often centring upon the definition of 'creativity' or the requirement to meet extremely tight deadlines and even tighter budgets. Incentive Travel Houses demand more and more creativity, wanting things that have never been tried before for their clients, but the budget or time available to achieve this may be insufficient, putting the DMC under great pressure to meet and satisfy such objectives.

When a company knows that it wants to hold an incentive event (or conference) in a particular destination, it can employ the services of a DMC to locate a venue, handle delegate accommodation, assist with transport arrangements, and put together itineraries and social programmes (for example, special interest visits, theme parties, unusual activities), even to provide 'pillow gifts' for award winners. DMCs are expected to develop tailor-made programmes within budget for their clients. They need to be creative and innovative and provide an experience which will give the participants an insight into a country or region which will be beyond the reach of the normal visitor or holidaymaker.

Most DMCs earn their income from commission, with the average commission figure being 15 per cent. It can be seen that there is significant overlap between the work of a PCO and that of a DMC, as well as the work of a convention and visitor bureau. Nowadays a DMC has to have some PCO, or at least venue finding, expertise.

The following web site gives details of DMCs around the world: www.conworld.net.

Corporate Events Company

Corporate events (also known as 'corporate hospitality') is one of the discrete segments of the business tourism industry which, while being separate from the conference sector, is often closely aligned to it. Corporate hospitality and corporate entertainment frequently involve the exploitation of major sporting and cultural events to strengthen the links between an organization, usually a corporate organization, and its clients or potential clients – for example, inviting clients to spend a day watching an international golf tournament, or being wined and dined at grand prix races at Monza or Indianapolis. Alternatively, activities may be arranged specifically for a client company, and typically involve drinks receptions, dinners and banquets, dances and discos. Wherever possible, such activities include a formal presentation or short speech to ensure that the company 'gets its message across'.

Specialist corporate hospitality/entertainment companies are usually hired to organize these events and programmes for their clients. Others may act in an entrepreneurial fashion (rather similar to conference entrepreneurs described earlier in this chapter), putting together corporate hospitality packages around major sporting or cultural events for sale to interested parties.

Corporate hospitality/events companies are also involved in corporate team building exercises and activities, aimed at clients and/or employees. These activities include golf days, clay pigeon shooting, off-road driving, go-karting, 'paint ball', and many, many more. In recent years there has been a noticeable trend towards the active, participatory kinds of corporate events, rather than the more traditional, passive, spectator type of hospitality.

Business Travel Agency

This is a form of travel agency, but one which seeks particularly to cater for the needs of business customers rather than the general public and which will not normally have a presence on the local High Street. The main thrust of their work is usually business travel: booking air, rail, coach, and ferry tickets, as well as making hotel reservations, to meet the needs of people travelling nationally and internationally for business purposes. But many of the larger business travel agencies also get involved in sourcing venues for conferences and similar business events, and may contribute in other ways to the planning and organization of such events.

Some of the larger business travel agencies have staff physically located in the offices of their major corporate clients. Such arrangements are referred to as 'agency implants'.

Exhibition Organizer

Exhibitions are, of course, a major business tourism segment in their own right, but any clear divide between exhibitions and conferences which may have existed in the past has now been greatly eroded, especially as far as business-to-business exhibitions are concerned (less so for consumer exhibitions catering for the general public). Many exhibitions have a conference programme running alongside as a way of adding value to the exhibition and making it even more worthwhile for business people to visit. Similarly, many of the larger conferences and conventions have an exhibition running in parallel: for the exhibitors, the conference delegates are seen as important customers or potential customers, and for the conference organizer the exhibition is an important source of revenue which helps to offset the costs of the conference.

While some conference organizers undertake the organization of their exhibition themselves, others prefer to employ the services of a specialist exhibition organizing company. In the UK there are approximately 100 exhibition organizing companies represented by the Association of Event Organizers (AEO).

When contracting a specialist exhibition organizer, conference planners either pay them a management fee for their work, or negotiate a payment based on the size of the exhibition itself (for example, the net exhibition area in square metres, where 'net' means the floor coverage taken up by stands alone, thus excluding aisle space and other space in the exhibition area). A further alternative is for the exhibition to be contracted out for a set period to an exhibition organizer in return for a fee paid to the owner of the exhibition (i.e. the conference organizer).

Agreements or contracts may well include incentives or bonuses linked to the sale of space or cost savings achieved by the exhibition organizer, although this latter approach could encourage the cutting of corners and result in an exhibition of unacceptable quality.

The larger exhibition organizing companies can bring added value to an event through their own network of contacts or simply via bulk purchasing power which would not be accessible to a conference organizer working independently. Exhibition organizers may already have links with airlines, hotel groups, stand and electrical contractors, carpet and furniture suppliers, as well as knowledge of the exhibition venue and specialist technical expertise. The services of such trade contacts can be made available to their conference organizer client at preferential rates, while first-hand knowledge and experience can be another invaluable asset.

There is a very broad spectrum of relationships possible between conference and exhibition organizer, from just buying into certain specialist expertise to handling specific aspects of the exhibition (visitor badging and registrations, stand erection, for example), right through to contracting out the organization of an exhibition in its entirety. The reasons for such variations on the part of the conference organizer include: in-house staff resources (number of staff available and their experience and expertise), the need for a guaranteed financial return from the exhibition (minimize risk by opting for a known income, even if this is less than it might have been possible to achieve), the overall profile of the event and the need to ensure its success, the benefits of having a well-known exhibition organizer working alongside thus giving confidence to potential exhibitors that the exhibition will be well organized and successful.

Some useful web sites for additional information on the exhibition sector include:

- www.iaem.org (International Association of Exhibitions and Events)
- www.ufi.org (UFI – The Global Association of the Exhibition Industry) (the initials UFI stand for Union des Foires Internationales, although the full name is no longer used)
- www.aeo.org.uk (services of the Association of Event Organisers (UK))
- www.beca.org.uk (web site of the British Exhibition Contractors Association)
- www.eeaa.com.au (web site of the Exhibition and Event Association of Australasia).

Other Agencies

There are other companies who undertake at least part of a conference organizing role for their clients, although this is not usually the main focus of their work. They include public relations and advertising consultancies (who will organize conferences and seminars, press briefings, product launches, for example), management consultancies (organizing 'retreats', meetings, training events), and training companies (running training, motivational, team-building events).

OTHER IMPORTANT ORGANIZATIONS

As an industry emerges and matures it requires other bodies and structures to help it to function professionally, to establish standards and codes of practice, to represent the industry to other industrial/business sectors as well as to government departments and public agencies. Within the conference industry, such bodies include, inter alia:

- trade and professional associations
- trade media
- national tourism organizations
- consultants
- educational institutions.

Trade and professional associations

Trade and professional associations are formed to serve the interests of their members. Their activities usually include lobbying and representation, establishing codes of practice, marketing and promotion, education and training, research and information.

Within the conference industry, some such associations are international in the composition of their membership, others are strictly national. Among the leading international associations are:

– Association Internationale des Palais de Congrès (AIPC) (International Association of Congress Centres)
– Destination Marketing Association International (DMAI)
– European Cities Marketing
– Eventia
– International Association of Professional Congress Organizers (IAPCO)
– International Congress & Convention Association (ICCA)
– Meeting Professionals International (MPI)
– Professional Convention Management Association (PCMA)
– Society of Incentive and Travel Executives (SITE)

Further details of the services and activities of these associations, as well as those of leading national associations, are given in Chapter 8.

Trade media

The conference industry trade media are primarily magazines published on a monthly, bi-monthly or quarterly basis. Increasingly electronic media are being developed in the form of conference/events industry web sites and e-newsletters (or e-zines). Both the paper-based and electronic media contain articles on new facilities and infrastructure developments, topical issues, how to stage successful events, destination reports, personnel changes, summaries of new books and reports, a correspondence section, and so on. They fulfil a very important role in keeping the industry abreast of the constant changes and developments taking place. Through their circulation to buyers, they also provide an important advertising and PR medium for suppliers wishing to promote their facilities/services to potential clients. Some of the magazines and media are international in content, emphasizing once again the global nature of the conference industry.

A list of the principal trade magazines is given in Appendix A.

National tourism organizations

Most countries in the world now have some form of national tourism organization, publicly funded, established for promotional activities to the international tourism industry. These bodies are primarily concerned with marketing, but some may also fulfil a lobbying and representational role. Within the conference sector of the tourism industry, a number of countries have established a national convention bureau specifically to market to this sector. There is no standard format for such national convention bureaus – indeed, it would be difficult to find two which operate in the same way with similar levels of funding and resources and providing the same kind of services. Examples of the roles of National Tourism Organizations are given in Chapter 4.

Some countries also have voluntary bodies established to provide a forum for networking, lobbying, joint working on key initiatives. These bodies play a vital role in furthering the interests of the business tourism sector. Examples include the UK's Business Tourism Partnership (www.businesstourismpartnership.com) and Australia's Business Events Council.

Consultants

Consultants play an important role in undertaking projects on a fee-paying basis for clients who are normally operating on the supply side of the conference industry. Typically, consultancy covers:

– the potential market for a proposed new conference centre
– the specification for a new conference centre or for a major refurbishment of an existing venue
– advice on marketing strategies for a destination or venue
– a feasibility study to establish and run a new convention and visitor bureau.

Consultancy can, however, cover any aspect of the industry. Consultancy is carried out either by specialist staff within the larger management consultancies (e.g. KPMG, Deloitte, Price WaterhouseCoopers, Pannell Kerr Forster) or by one of the smaller consultancies catering specifically for the tourism/ business tourism industry.

Educational institutions

The education and training of the conference industry's future workforce is vitally important in ensuring the continued growth and development of the industry. College and university institutions are now giving serious attention to conference and business tourism in their course programmes and syllabuses. A number of trade associations have developed educational programmes and certificated courses available to both members and, sometimes, non-members. Other training programmes within the wider tourism industry, such as 'Welcome Host' and 'Investors in People', also contribute significantly to the improvement of skills and expertise for those already working in the industry.

Further details of education and training opportunities are given in Chapter 7.

Summary

- the buying side of the conference industry includes corporate organizations, associations and government/public sector agencies, and conference entrepreneurs
- corporate organizations plan a wide variety of conferences, meetings and other events. Staff involved in the organization of these activities have many different job titles, but relatively few are employed as full-time event organizers. For the most part, corporate events attract less than 200 delegates and have comparatively short lead times. They have a higher average per capita expenditure than association conferences, with costs being borne by the companies themselves
- the term 'association' is used to describe a sector of the industry which encompasses professional and trade bodies, voluntary organizations, charities, political parties and other non-corporate entities. Association conferences are different in many respects from those held in the corporate sector, especially in their average size, duration, types of venues used, and accommodation/housing required. International association and inter-governmental conventions form a major segment of the 'association' market in their own right
- government/public sector organizations have many similar buying characteristics to associations, although delegate expectations are rising and some comparisons with the corporate sector may be drawn, particularly in respect of the types of venues used
- Conference entrepreneurs develop conferences in response to an identified demand as a purely commercial activity
- the supply side of the conference industry comprises venues, destinations, and myriad other companies offering specialist services, from audio-visual equipment supply to contract catering, from interpreting to coach hire
- the industry also features an important group of intermediary agencies which provide services ranging from conference management to venue finding, and from incentive travel planning to exhibition organizing
- this complex industry is reliant on a range of other institutions to enable it to operate professionally and develop in a structured way. Such institutions include trade associations, trade media, national tourism organizations, consultants, and educational bodies.

Review and discussion questions

1. Assess the benefits and disadvantages, for a corporate organization, of maintaining its own, in-house event department. Include an analysis of the pros and cons, for the company, of employing a business travel agency as an 'implant'.
2. Compile two incentive travel programmes to reward:
   i) a company's top sales executives
   ii) the same company's most productive 'blue collar' employees.
   Explain any differences in the programmes offered.
3. Identify and give reasons for the most appropriate types of conference/events business for the following venues:
   a) a 4-star city-centre hotel with 250 bedrooms and conference facilities seating up to 400 delegates. Choose a city which has an important manufacturing or service industy base.
   b) a multi-purpose heritage building in a resort location with a seating capacity of 1500.
   c) a residential conference centre with 6 conference rooms (the largest seating 80), accommodation of 3-star standard, situated in a rural location.
4. As an employee of a major trade association which holds an annual convention for approximately 1200 delegates, with an exhibition running alongside the convention, you have been asked to contract out the planning of the convention and exhibition. Describe the kinds of agencies you would consider and give reasons for your choices.

Notes and references

1. Davidson, R and Rogers, T (2006), *Marketing Destinations and Venues for Conferences*, Conventions and Business Events, Elsevier Butterworth-Heinemann.
2. Flint, Ian. article entitled *Buying Power*, published in 'Business Travel World' magazine (EMAP Communications) (July 2002).
3. International Congress and Convention Association (2006), *International Association Meetings Market 1996–2005*.
4. Shone, Anton. *The Business of Conferences*, published by Butterworth-Heinemann (1998).
5. *The UK Conference Market Survey 2006*, research carried out by The Right Solution on behalf of the Meetings Industry Association (July 2006).

6. *The UK Conference Market Survey 2002*, research carried out by The Right Solution on behalf of the Meetings Industry Association (2002).
7. *The Meetings Market Report 2005*, research carried out by 'Meetings & Conventions' magazine (2005).
8. *Trends and Spend Survey 2005*, published by 'Meetings & Incentive Travel' magazine (2006).

The economics of conferences and conventions

Introduction

Conferences are a vital economic benefactor for both local and national economies. Investment in conference facilities and infrastructure can bring substantial returns through the expenditure of organizers and delegates, with both direct and indirect benefits for the destinations in which conferences are held. While statistics and intelligence about the industry are not yet as well developed as those working in the industry would wish to see, sufficient information and research findings do exist to enable estimates of its value and potential to be made with confidence.

This chapter looks at:

- Conferences and conventions within the wider tourism context
- Factors affecting conference sector demand
- The inadequacy of the information base
- The size of the global conference industry
- The value of the industry, and measurement of economic impact
- Research findings, using the results of a range of national surveys.

It includes a case study on:

- Scottish Exhibition + Conference Centre, Glasgow.

On completion of this chapter, you should be able to:

- Appreciate the value of the conference industry in economic terms
- Explain the factors affecting the demand for conference activity
- Understand why existing datasets do not provide a comprehensive picture of the industry from an economic perspective
- Understand the concept of multipliers
- Appreciate the range and types of existing industry research.

CONFERENCES AND CONVENTIONS WITHIN THE WIDER TOURISM CONTEXT

It has already been seen that conference tourism is a segment of business tourism, itself a sector within the overall tourism industry comprising both business and leisure tourism. (The author has considerable sympathy with the view that conferences and conventions should not only be positioned as part of the tourism industry but should also be recognized as integral to a country's trade and economic development sectors.) All projections by economists confirm that the tourism industry was set to become the world's largest industry by the millennium or in this first decade thereafter. Figures issued by the United Nations World Tourism Organization (UNWTO) in January 2007 show that world tourism grew by 4.5 per cent in 2006 compared with the previous year, and international tourist arrivals reached 842 million, the highest ever. The UNWTO reports that destinations worldwide generated 100 million additional international tourist arrivals between 2002 and 2005. Further details at www.world-tourism.org/newsroom.

In Australia visitor arrivals totalled 5.2 million during 2004, an increase of 10 per cent on the 2003 figures. Tourism accounts for 5.7 per cent of total employment, contributing AU$73 billion to consumption spend per annum. It is worth more than 11 per cent of total exports.

Figures published by VisitBritain (the British national tourism organization) put the total value of tourism to the United Kingdom in 2005 at approximately £74 billion, supporting around 2.1 million jobs, some 8 per cent of total UK employment. This compares with a value of £40 billion in 1996 when the industry supported 1.7 million jobs, an employment growth approaching 25 per cent. (www.visitbritain.com)

Within the United Kingdom, estimates suggest that business tourism (business/corporate travel and conferences/exhibitions/incentives), worth in excess of £22 billion a year, accounts for between one-third and a quarter of the total value of tourism. Some £10.3 billion of business tourism revenues were contributed by the conference and meetings sector in 2005, according to the 'British Conference Venues Survey 2006'. If it were possible to produce aggregated figures for the conference industry on a global scale, the totals would certainly reach hundreds of billions of pounds.

There are a number of research projects now underway which help to build a more accurate and comprehensive picture of the size and value of the conference industry. This chapter will draw on these and on other sources, using material from Australia, Canada, Germany, Ireland, South Africa, Spain, the UK and the USA, to illustrate and emphasize that the conference industry is a major benefactor to both local and national economies, as a job creator and sustainer, as an income generator, and as a vehicle for attracting inward investment.

FACTORS AFFECTING CONFERENCE SECTOR DEMAND

The health of national and international economies

In line with most other industries, demand for conferences is driven to a large extent by the buoyancy of both national economies and the global economy. There is strong evidence to show that, during the recession of the early 1990s, during the crash of many Asian economies in the late 1990s, and again during the global recession in the early years of the twenty-first century, business activity levels declined with conferences being cancelled or, more typically, being run on much lower budgets. At such times companies trade down, reducing delegate numbers, cutting out the residential aspect of conferences, spending less on catering, and using lower quality venues (for example 3-star hotels rather than 4-star).

Similarly, fluctuations in the value of a country's currency can have both positive and negative effects on its conference industry: a weakening of the currency may assist it to win more international events as costs for incoming delegates and organizers will be lower and the country may be perceived as good value for money. However, it will be more difficult, and certainly more expensive, for delegates to travel abroad from that country to attend conferences and meetings because of the relative weakness of their national currency. The opposite situation applies when a currency is strong compared with other currencies.

However, one of the positive characteristics of the conference industry is its resilience, even in times of economic downturn. While there may be a trading down, many events still go ahead: public companies are required to hold an Annual General

Meeting for their shareholders, senior managers need to engage in management retreats to explore ways of reviving their business, new products are launched, staff have to be trained and motivated, sales forces need to be brought together for briefings, and many other types of 'conference' take place, albeit with reduced budgets.

The impact of crises, conflicts and emergency situations

'September 11th' (or '9/11') is a phrase now firmly embedded in the international vocabulary, describing an appalling act of terrorism in New York which had an immediate, catastrophic impact on travel around the world. It led to the cancellation or postponement of conferences and meetings scheduled to take place in the weeks and months following.

In the USA itself, conference delegates and business travellers refused to attend events held more than a short distance from their homes. A combination of '9/11' and economic recession led to 37 per cent of US associations experiencing a decline in attendance at their events in 2001 – this compares with a figure of just 9 per cent which had forecast a reduction in attendance a year earlier ('Meetings Market Survey 2002' published by 'Convene' magazine, March 2002).

Other crises (epidemics such as SARS, wars, agricultural disasters such as the 'Foot and Mouth' outbreak that affected the UK in 2001, for example) also have a negative impact on the demand for conferences in the countries and regions where they occur. Sometimes the impact is shortlived, sometimes it may be more prolonged.

Paradoxically, crises and disasters can also stimulate demand for meetings, training courses and international conferences. '9/11', for example, heightened awareness of the need for security and crisis management strategies as an integral part of overall conference management, generating seminars and training courses to address this educational and information need. Wars and threats of wars lead to international meetings and conferences in an attempt to find a peaceful solution to the causes of conflict.

Technological influences

Another factor affecting demand for conference facilities is the advent of satellite, video and teleconferencing technology, and the use of webcasts for broadcasting conferences over the internet. The 'UK Conference Market Survey 2006', for example, found that, among corporate organizations, video conferencing was used by 63 per cent of Survey respondents in 2005 compared with 51 per cent in 2004 (although a figure of 62 per cent was recorded in 2001, suggesting no major growth with this technology). Teleconferencing, on the other hand, was used by 81 per cent of corporations in 2005, up from 72 per cent in 2001 and webcasting by 19 per cent of companies in 2005 compared with just 9 per cent in 2004. Webcasting allows individuals to attend a conference as 'virtual' delegates by sitting at their computer screens and listening to speaker presentations through an electronic link, either in real time or post-event – the current expectation is that this technology will widen conference attendance by making an event affordable and accessible to a much greater, global audience, rather than reduce the numbers of delegates wishing to attend an event in person. This expectation is, to some extent, confirmed by the 'UK Conference Market Survey 2006' which revealed that only 18 per cent of organizers felt that these technologies were reducing the number of face-to-face meetings being held.

More venues have invested in the installation of video and teleconferencing facilities in an effort to win these new niche markets. Venues are also being required to provide wireless (wi-fi) technology: in the USA, for example, the '15th Annual Meetings Market Survey' published by Convene magazine (2006) found that 47 per cent of US associations requested wireless technology in convention centres and 59 per cent in hotels.

Social factors and working patterns

Social factors must have some effect on people's interest in conferencing, although no research has been undertaken to quantify these. Predictions that, for example, many more people would be working from or at home by the end of the last millennium have not proved to be entirely correct. However, if the 'office-in-the-home' should become a more common feature of everyday life in the future, its end result might well be an increased demand for conferences as people respond to their gregarious instincts by coming together in regular meetings.

Changes in a country's industrial and commercial structures can also have an impact on the demand for conference facilities. In the UK, for example, reductions in trade union membership since 1980 have led to trade unions merging which, in turn, has meant fewer trade union conferences (particularly affecting seaside conference destinations) but higher attendances than previously. Some resort destinations, the traditional hosts of many trade union conferences, have found that their conference venues are no longer big enough to accommodate their former clients.

Finally, it should be noted that fluctuations in conference demand are more noticeable in the corporate sector than in the association sector, often because of factors such as lead times. Corporate events, with relatively short lead times, can respond quickly to changing economic situations. Association conventions, with much longer lead times and frequently much larger delegate numbers, find it less easy to adapt but can also take a longer term view and avoid what may sometimes prove to be a panic reaction to a particular situation (while still retaining the ability to react to emergency situations such as that encountered after '9/11').

THE INADEQUACY OF THE INFORMATION BASE

Before looking at some of the available figures on conference tourism, it might be useful to understand why the information and intelligence base for the industry is incomplete.

The Economist Intelligence Unit, in a report entitled 'The European Conference and Meetings Market' published as long ago as 1994, listed four main reasons why not enough is known about business and conference tourism in quantifiable terms (with the author's comments on these shown in italics), reasons which are still largely valid in 2007:

1. fragmentation of industry sectors (in terms of both geography and markets). Each sector has its own trade association, and often more than one. International associations and organizations have varying degrees of representation in their member countries. *In part this seems to be a reflection of the tourism industry as a whole; in part it may also be due to the immaturity of the conference industry, with some rationalization of the industry's representative bodies beginning to take place because the market cannot sustain such a diversity of organizations. There is also a desire among the industry's leading associations to forge collaborative partnerships with like-minded bodies in order to achieve a more cohesive voice for the industry.*
2. lack of consensus on terminology and definitions. Segmentation of the market makes it difficult to produce a clear definition of each sector.
3. certain segments of business and commercial tourism are difficult to measure. *This is particularly true of 'business travel', but similar problems can arise with incentive travel and conferences.*
4. information about certain activities is sensitive and closely guarded. *This can apply to buyers and suppliers alike, with hotels enjoying special notoriety for their reluctance to release information on their bookings lest they give a competitive edge to other hotels in the vicinity.*

One or two practical examples may make clear why statistics and intelligence are far from comprehensive:

Many of the individuals and organizations which contribute to the conference industry do so as part of a wider role (see also Chapter 2). For example, a training manager will use the services/facilities of the conference industry to run a training course or seminar away from company premises, but may only do this once or twice a year. It would be inaccurate, therefore, to categorize him as a full-time conference/event organizer even though he is a buyer at certain times of the year. Public relations consultancies are often involved in organizing conferences, product launches or corporate events on behalf of their clients, but they remain first and foremost public relations consultancies and may also escape classification as 'conference organizers'.

Likewise, a hotel will hire out its function rooms to conference organizers, but may equally hire them out to someone staging weddings or other social events. In many cases the hotel will not differentiate in its record keeping between the different types of client or function, making it impossible to build up an accurate picture of the amount of conference business compared with other categories of business.

Despite such shortcomings in the industry's information base, much greater recognition is now being given globally to the importance of research, and further impetus will be given once the tourism satellite account is adopted (see Chapter 1). Examples of current research are given in this chapter and elsewhere in this book which, when aggregated, provide compelling evidence of the economic importance and vitality of this key industry sector at both national and international levels.

THE SIZE OF THE GLOBAL CONFERENCE INDUSTRY

At present there is little information available which adequately describes the size of the conference and convention industry. In the medium to longer term, programmes such as the adaptation of the tourism satellite account model to measure the economic importance of the meetings industry will, it is hoped, provide a more comprehensive dataset for use by any country or organization wishing to use such information. It is necessary, therefore, to use a variety of (mostly unrelated) data sources to help to construct the jigsaw. The following examples begin to give a feel for the size and scale of the industry:

- There are well over 200 countries now active in marketing their facilities and services to the conference and conventions industry. The Union of International Associations (UIA) has records of international conferences being staged in 218 countries in 2005
- The Destination Marketing Association International (DMAI) has 1300 professional members (individuals), and over 600 destination marketing organization members in more than 25 countries (2006)
- Meeting Professionals International (MPI) has 21 000 (individual) members in 68 national chapters and clubs (in 2006), a figure which had grown from 540 members at the time of

its first annual convention in 1976. MPI members comprise a 50/50 ratio of buyers and suppliers
- The International Congress and Convention Association (ICCA) has around 800 member organizations in 80 countries worldwide (2007)
- In the UK, there are an estimated 3500 conference venues, 15 000+ individuals with a conference organizing role, 530 000 people employed in 'business tourism' and, in 2005 (according to the 'British Conference Venues Survey') an estimated 1.58 million conferences and meetings staged, an average of 452 conferences per venue.

THE VALUE OF THE INDUSTRY

Measurements of economic impact

Assessments of the value of the conference industry to most countries are at best only estimates, based on information drawn from national and local surveys. Calculations of the value, or economic impact, of conferences measure the net change in the local (or national) economy resulting from the hosting of conferences and business events i.e. what difference have such events made to levels of expenditure, income and employment. These calculations must also take account of a number of factors, outlined by Cooper et al (1993), which apply to the tourism industry as a whole:

> Tourists spend their money on a wide variety of goods and services. They purchase accommodation, food and beverage, communications, entertainment services, goods from retail outlets and tour/travel services, to name just a few. This money may be seen as an injection of demand into the host economy: that is, demand which would otherwise not be present. However, the value of tourist expenditure represents only a partial picture of the economic impact. The full assessment of economic impact must take into account other aspects, including the following:
>
> - Indirect and induced effects
> - Leakages of expenditure out of the local economy
> - Displacement and opportunity costs.

Cooper et al refer to the 'cascading' effect of tourist expenditure, with the benefits of tourist spending being felt in hotels, restaurants, taxi firms, and shops and then permeating through the rest of the economy. From this total direct impact, however, must be subtracted the cost of 'imports necessary to supply those front-line goods and services ... for example, hotels purchase the services of builders, accountants, banks, food and beverage suppliers, and many others.' These suppliers, in turn, purchase goods and services from other suppliers, generating further rounds of economic activity, known as the indirect effect. 'The indirect effect will not involve all of the monies spent by tourists during the direct effect, since some of that money will leak out of circulation through imports, savings and taxation. Finally, during the direct and indirect rounds of expenditure, income will accrue to local residents in the form of wages, salaries, distributed profit, rent and interest. This addition to the local income will, in part, be re-spent in the local economy on goods and services, and this will generate yet further rounds of economic activity. It is only when all three levels of impact (direct *plus* indirect *plus* induced) are estimated that the full positive economic impact of tourism expenditure is fully assessed.'

Cooper et al also make reference to certain 'negative economic impacts' of tourist expenditure. These include opportunity costs and displacement effects. Opportunity costs refer to the use of resources such as labour and capital for the benefit of one industry rather than another. Decisions to invest limited capital resources in tourism infrastructure, for example, will have negative impacts on other industries which failed to attract that investment. 'Where tourism development substitutes one form of expenditure and economic activity for another, this is known as the displacement effect. Displacement can take place when tourism development is undertaken at the expense of another industry, and is generally referred to as the opportunity cost of the development. However, it is more commonly referred to when a new tourism project is seen to take away custom from an existing facility. For instance, if a destination finds that its all-inclusive hotels are running at high occupancy levels and returning a reasonable yield on investment, the construction of an additional all-inclusive hotel may simply reduce the occupancy levels of the existing establishments, and the destination may find that its overall tourism activity has not increased by as much as the new business from the development. This is displacement.'

Figure 3.1 illustrates the measurement of net economic impact arising from tourist expenditure in an area through the application of the tourism multiplier concept.

The use of multipliers

Measurement of the economic impact of tourist spending is effected by using multiplier analysis. Various types of multiplier exist, and it is important to use the correct multipliers for specific functions, such as those measuring the additional revenue or employment for an area arising from tourist expenditure. However, the formulas used to calculate the net impact of conferences and similar events are complex and resource-intensive to administer. For these reasons many industry professionals, required to

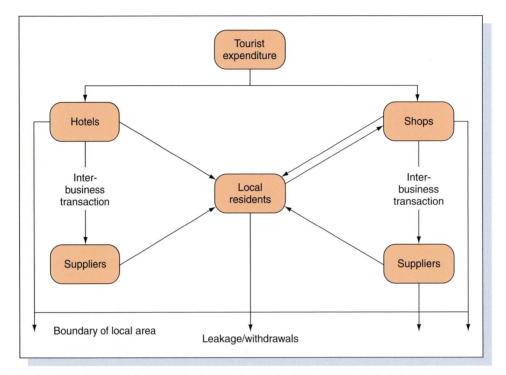

Figure 3.1 The tourism multiplier concept. (Source: Dr John Heeley, University of East Anglia.)

give account of the value of conference and business tourism to their city or area, tend to use the 'gross' figures rather than the 'net' impact figures i.e. the total gross expenditure calculated by multiplying:

- Number of delegates/attendees
- Delegate spending (which varies by origin and type of event – see Figure 3.2 and Table 3.1 as examples of such variations)
- Number of days' duration of the event
- Any additional days (i.e. for delegates staying on after the event or arriving early before the event starts)
- Additional members of the group (e.g. spouses/partners)
- Organizers' (and others') spending.

The totals arrived at only measure the direct expenditure to a destination and do not, therefore, take into account the negative effects (opportunity costs, displacement and leakages) referred to above. As an example of this practice, Visit London (the tourism marketing body for London) uses 'Conference and Convention Daily Spend Multipliers' to assess the value of business to England's capital city (see Figure 3.2).

LONDON CONVENTION DELEGATE SPEND MULTIPLIERS

a) Visitors to London from Key Overseas Markets, All Sectors (Residential)

Estimated daily expenditure rates by delegate/attendee are calculated as:

Market's total expenditure in London on convention & conference business
Market's total number of nights spent in London on convention & conference business

Overseas Markets Supplying Convention Attendees to London	Market Figures for 2005	Outcome in Spend Per Delegate Per Day
USA	£111,000,000 / 446,861	£248
FRANCE	£17,400,000 / 100,661	£173
GERMANY	£36,800,000 / 202,312	£182

The pre-eminent importance of the inbound US market for London is clear from the above figures.

b) All Other Domestic and Foreign Markets (Residential)

The average daily expenditure figures for UK conferences summarized in the 'Conference Delegate Expenditure Survey' (1998) are used for all other overseas markets and for domestic conference market sectors. These figures have been multiplied by appropriate percentages to allow for inflation in subsequent years. These result in spend figures as shown below:

YEAR	CORPORATE MARKET	NATIONAL ASSOCIATION MARKET	INTERNATIONAL ASSOCIATION MARKET	OTHER
	Spend per delegate per day	Spend per delegate per day	Spend per delegate per day	Spend per delegate per day
1998	£127 (Median)	£123 (Mean)	£182 (Mean)	£116 (Mean)
1999	£131	£127	£188	£120
2000	£133	£129	£191	£122
2001	£140	£136	£201	£128
2003	£146	£142	£210	£134

Figure 3.2 London convention delegate spend multipliers. (Source: International Passenger Survey.)

Average expenditure by delegate per trip and per day

An illustration of how and where different types of conference delegates spend money is shown in Table 3.1. The figures are based on a survey undertaken in 2006 by the national tourist boards of Britain and Ireland (VisitBritain – www.visitbritain.com), VisitScotland (www.conventionscotland.com), Visit Wales (www.meetings.visitwales.com) and Fáilte Ireland – www.irelandinspires.com). The survey involved 963 interviews with delegates at 29 conferences, complemented by 50 interviews with Professional Conference Organisers (PCOs). The figures

Expenditure Category	Corporate Day	Corporate Multi-Day	Domestic Association Day	Domestic Association Multi-Day	International Association	Other*
Registration fee	0%	0%	32%	16%	18%	10%
Overnight accommodation at the conference	0%	17%	0%	16%	23%	30%
Overnight accommodation before/after the conference	0%	2%	0%	4%	8%	1%
Local travel at conference destination	2%	2%	3%	2%	1%	1%
Food and drink at the conference	1%	5%	<1%	3%	5%	4%
Food and drink before/after the conference	2%	2%	6%	2%	3%	6%
Evening events/entertainment at the conference	0%	<1%	<1%	1%	1%	<1%
Evening events/entertainment before/after the conference	0%	1%	0%	1%	1%	1%
Shopping and gifts	11%	6%	<1%	2%	5%	8%
Day trips and/or pre- or post-conference tours	0%	<1%	<1%	<1%	<1%	<1%
Expenditure by people accompanying delegates	0%	0%	0%	1%	2%	2%
Total expenditure per day by the delegate	**16%**	**35%**	**41%**	**48%**	**66%**	**64%**
Total expenditure per day by the PCO	**84%**	**65%**	**59%**	**52%**	**34%**	**36%**
Total expenditure per day (£)	**£120**	**£459**	**£170**	**£461**	**£364**	**£305**

* Other = public sector and government bodies, charities, voluntary organizations, religious organizations, political parties and trade unions.
Source: Delegate Expenditure Survey 2006 produced by VisitBritain, VisitScotland, Visit Wales and Fáilte Ireland.

Table 3.1
UK and Ireland delegate expenditure survey: Average expenditure per delegate per day (%)

include estimates of expenditure by delegates themselves, by conference organisers on behalf of delegates, and expenditure by people accompanying delegates.

The figures shown in Table 3.1 provide a good basis for estimating the direct benefit of conference expenditure to an area, and some examples of how to apply the figures are given below:

I. A 45-delegate corporate meeting lasting 2 days: $45 \times 2 \times £459$ = total expenditure of £41 310
II. A 150-delegate international association meeting lasting 3 days: $150 \times 3 \times £364$ = total expenditure of £163 800
III. A 90-delegate domestic association meeting lasting 1 day: $90 \times £170$ = total expenditure of £15 300

The figures do not include any economic multiplier effects which may arise from any direct or indirect delegate spend.

The survey also provides some useful additional data on average duration of events, the frequency of accompanying persons participating with delegates, and the incidence of people staying pre- or post-conference. These findings are summarised in Table 3.2.

Davidson and Cope describe a similar approach to data collection in France, where 'the national association of conference towns, France Congrès, in 1998 developed a model which enables

Conference Type	Mean number of conference days	Incidence of People Accompanying Delegates	Incidence of People Staying Pre- or Post-Conference
Corporate day	1 day	2%	0%
Corporate multi-day	2.08 days	2%	6%
Domestic association day	1 day	1%	0%
Domestic association multi-day	2.90 days	7%	23%
International association	3.59 days	12%	31%
Others*	2.77 days	32%	10%

* Other = public sector and government bodies, charities, voluntary organizations, religious organizations, political parties and trade unions.
Source: Delegate Expenditure Survey 2006 produced by VisitBritain, VisitScotland, Visit Wales and Fáilte Ireland.

Table 3.2
UK and Ireland delegate expenditure survey additional data

	1999	2000	2001	2002	2003
Direct and indirect effects (euros)	558 000 000	670 000 000	626 000 000	644 000 000	596 000 000
Induced effects (euros)	853 000 000	1 020 000 000	958 000 000	985 000 000	912 000 000
Total economic impact	**1 411 000 000**	**1 690 000 000**	**1 584 000 000**	**1 629 000 000**	**1 508 000 000**
Jobs sustained	22 380	35 500	33 830	34 675	33 250
Number of delegate days	2 575 000	2 700 000	2 598 000	2 640 000	2 545 000
Number of delegate nights	1 911 150	2 300 000	2 150 550	2 193 560	2 117 300

Source: France Congrès
Notes:

- Direct economic impact = total of direct expenditure by conference centres in the local economy
- Indirect economic impact = expenditure by conference delegates with local services (e.g. hotels, restaurants, shops)
- Induced impact = multiplier effect generated by direct and indirect impacts.

Table 3.3
Economic impact of conference activity in france

conference centres to calculate the economic impact they have on the cities in which they are situated. Based on the calculation of delegates' spending, the use of the model produces estimates of the revenue created by conferences in each city and the number of jobs created or supported by them, taking into account the direct, indirect and induced economic impacts of such events (Gazette Officielle, 1998). When the first results were published in 2000, it was shown, for example, that, in Cannes, 10 per cent of the population were employed in that town's meetings industry.' Some 40 conference centres (but excluding Paris) now contribute to the study and Table 3.3 compares the impacts of conference activity over the 5-year period 1999 to 2003. Further details at www.france-congres.org.

Negative impacts of convention activity

Before looking at other current features and trends in the global conference industry, it is important to give consideration to the negative impacts of convention business on a destination.

Reference was made in Chapter 1 to the harmful effects of business tourism (part of which comprises conference tourism) on the environment because of the volume of trips undertaken and the demands of business tourists for high quality accommodation and facilities. There are also issues concerning CO_2 emissions by venues and the levels of waste generated by exhibitions (which are often staged alongside a conference). A number of steps are being taken to address these environmental factors (such as the development of quieter aircraft to reduce noise pollution, the work of the International Hotels Environment Initiative, the adoption of waste management and recycling strategies, more energy-efficient systems in conference venues, the use of email and electronic communications to reduce paper waste) but it is clear that much more needs to be done before the industry can claim genuine 'green' credentials (see also Chapter 9).

Not all expenditure on a conference is retained in a destination. As explained earlier in this chapter, some of the money leaks out through indirect and induced effects, opportunity costs affect other industry sectors in a negative way, and displacement simply moves existing business around without creating new, additional income for the locality. While these are not necessarily all negative impacts, they do mean that the positive impacts may not always be as great as portrayed.

Social disruption to the local community is inevitably caused when a major convention comes to town, especially where there is a need for high levels of security. This can mean that the area surrounding the convention centre is cordoned off during the convention and often for some days in advance, making it a no-go area for local residents and reducing trade for shops and other businesses in the vicinity. Similarly, restaurants may be full with delegates eating out, traffic may be congested and public transport overloaded. While most local communities now recognize that such inconveniences are a price worth paying because of the wider economic benefits, there is often still a minority of residents who voice criticisms.

RESEARCH FINDINGS

The following research findings have resulted from the application of economic impact studies and multiplier analysis to the conference and business events sector. In their totality they underline the importance of the sector at the high quality, high yield end of the tourism spectrum. The research also summarizes some of the current trends and characteristics of the industry.

Australia

In Australia the business events sector is recognised as a high-yield component of the tourism industry with direct connections to other key areas such as trade, foreign affairs, education, science, training and communications. It has great potential for further expansion. A study on Australia's meetings and exhibitions sector was undertaken by the Bureau of Tourism Research and was published in 1999 under the title of 'Meetings Make their Mark' – this study estimated that business events contributed AU$7 billion to the Australian economy. In the light of substantial developments to the sector in the early years of the new millennium, it was felt to be the time to undertake a comprehensive evaluation of the sector and to include other components such as incentive travel. The findings of this major research project were published in 2005 as the 'National Business Events Study', a report which runs to almost 150 pages. The extract below focuses on the methodology and scope of the research as well as highlighting key findings from the study.

The National Business Events Study (NBES) data were based on business activity in the 2002–2003 financial year. The key objectives for NBES were identified as:

- To provide an estimate of the sector in relation to its: Size and Economic contribution
- To provide increased knowledge on the decision-making processes of delegates/attendees in the Business Events sector and
- To provide key indicators for monitoring performance of the Business Events Sector in subsequent years.

For the purposes of the study, a business event was defined as:

Any public or private activity consisting of a minimum of 15 persons with a common interest of vocation, held in a specific venue or venues, and hosted by an organization (or organizations). This may include (but not be limited to): conferences, conventions, symposia, congresses, incentive meetings, marketing events, special celebrations, seminars, courses, public or trade shows, exhibitions, company general meetings, corporate retreats, training programmes.

The method used in the study was a quantitative survey approach based on a number of questionnaires designed to capture an understanding of business event activity within Australia. Each of the questionnaires was devised by the NBES Steering Committee, a committee comprising industry experts and researchers with relevant expertise. The method of questionnaire distribution varied with each component of the study with the delegate, trade visitor, exhibitor and venue questionnaires being administered on-line. This method of distribution was used because of its ability to reach large groups of potential respondents and its cost effectiveness. Other questionnaires, such as the incentive travel and the organiser surveys, were faxed, emailed or mailed.

The following components were identified by the steering committee as the key areas for research:

- Venues
- Meetings and conference delegates

- Meeting, conference and exhibition organisers
- Exhibitors
- Trade visitors
- Incentives.

All data collected in the study were confidential and were aggregated to avoid identification of any person, entity or event.

Key Findings • • •

An immense range of detailed information was collected through the study and is included in the published report. Key findings include the following:

- The overall estimated expenditure associated with business events in 2003 was in excess of AU$17 billion
- The direct contribution to employment was estimated to be 116 000 jobs
- 316 000 business events were held in the financial year 2002–2003 (284 000 of which were meetings and conferences)
- 28.4 million delegates attended these events. By event type the breakdown was:
  - Association: 8.3 million delegates
  - Corporate: 14.8 million delegates
  - Government: 5.3 million delegates.
- The busiest quarter for business events activity was October–December, which accounted for 29 per cent of all events
- The greatest influence on all respondents to attend a conference was the business or educational content of the conference programme; the opportunity to network was the second most important motive
- Meeting and conference delegates spent an estimated total of AU$11.5 billion in Australia in 2003, with AU$949 million being expenditure by international visitors and the remainder being associated with domestic delegates
- On average, each delegate spent AU$558 within Australia, although this varied substantially according to the type of delegate:
  - Local: AU$430
  - Intrastate: AU$892
  - Interstate: AU$2019
  - International: AU$3526.
- Average large exhibition organizer expenditure was AU$459 000 per event, and average revenue per event was AU$678 000
- An estimated total of 2.4 million trade visitors attended exhibitions in 2003, generating an estimated expenditure of AU$540 million

- Expenditure on incentive travel was estimated to be in excess of AU$585 million, with AU$46 million being domestic business and approximately AU$539 being international business representing new expenditure in Australia
- The average expenditure per incentive delegate, including some non-domestic airfares and personal expenditure, was:
  - Long haul delegates: AU$2560
  - Short haul delegates: AU$2180
  - Australian delegates: AU$1224.

Canada

The Canadian Tourism Commission (CTC) is an industry-led, market-driven and research-based Federal Crown corporation, whose ultimate goal is to grow tourism export revenues. The CTC works in partnership with industry and all levels of government to market Canada as a tourism destination of choice.

The CTC collates information from various sources (National Tourism Indicators, International Travel Survey, Canadian Economic Observer (Statistics Canada), and the UN World Tourism Organization) on the economic characteristics of meetings, conventions and incentive travel (MC&IT) visitors to Canada. A summary of the key data is given below:

MC&IT Market Visitors From the USA • • •

The USA is by far the most important source market for MC&IT visitors to Canada, contributing some 1.9 million overnight person trips in 2005, worth over CA$1.5 billion. This compares with 92 000 trips from the UK, the second largest international market, which were worth around CA$144 million in that year.

The damaging impact of the SARS epidemic and an unstable international political situation led to a decline in US MC&IT visitors in 2003. However, the following 2 years witnessed a strong recovery, with visitor numbers surpassing the previous highest year of the decade (2002), although expenditure was slightly lower, perhaps reflecting the shorter duration of trips and events, a trend noted elsewhere in this book. Attendance at meetings and conferences accounted for the highest proportion of visitors (over 1.1 million in 2005). Delegates at association conventions comprised a further 559 000 visitors, with the balance of 252 000 US visitors being made up of exhibition attendees, incentive travellers and other types of MC&IT visitors.

Table 3.4 highlights the key economic characteristics of MC&IT visitors from the USA for the 3-year period 2003–2005. Demographics:

- In 2005 66.8 per cent of U.S. MC&IT visitors were male and some 84 per cent were aged 35 and over.

	2003			2004				2005			
	Meetings	Conven-tions	Other	Total	Meetings	Conven-tions	Other	Total	Meetings	Conven-tions	Other	Total
Overnight person trips ('000)	998.2	481.6	229.2	1709.0	1154.5	581.8	254.1	1990.5	1152.5	559.0	252.1	1963.6
Overnight travel receipts (CA$M)	727.1	411.2	226.4	1364.7	827.4	517.3	238.7	1583.3	796.0	498.2	229.2	1523.4
Average trip duration (nights)	2.3	4.0	4.3	3.3	2.6	3.9	4.3	3.2	2.5	3.8	4.1	3.1
Expenditure per trip (CA$)	728.4	853.7	987.9	798.5	716.7	889.0	939.5	795.5	690.6	891.2	909.2	775.8
Expenditure per person per night (CA$)	272.8	211.8	228.3	243.8	272.0	230.3	219.4	248.3	275.6	233.0	220.8	251.2
Types of Expenditure (CA$M)												
Accommodation	294.7	178.3	93.4	566.4	353.5	244.1	99.8	697.4	345.9	222.3	96.0	664.2
Transportation	107.7	31.8	44.2	183.5	111.4	40.5	33.9	185.8	108.1	38.6	34.8	181.5
Food & beverage	137.4	71.8	44.4	253.5	169.0	95.2	45.3	309.5	165.8	86.7	36.4	288.9
Recreation & entertainment	31.1	20.1	13.4	64.6	31.1	27.5	12.5	71.2	28.9	28.3	13.5	70.8
Other	34.4	35.8	9.9	80.2	37.3	49.7	12.4	99.4	31.0	42.2	13.4	86.7

Source: Canadian Tourism Commission

Table 3.4
Characteristics of US MC&IT Visitors to Canada 2003–2005

Destinations:

- Ontario remains the most popular destination, followed by (in order) Quebec, British Columbia and Alberta.

Overseas MC&IT Market Visitors to Canada • • •

Apart from US-based MC&IT visitors to Canada, other overseas markets generate substantial MC&IT visitors. The leading markets are shown in Table 3.5 and again it is noticeable that, following a significant downturn in such visitors in 2003 for reasons explained above, recovery was strong in the following two years, with 2005 figures surpassing those achieved at the beginning of the decade. The total value of all overseas MC&IT visitors to Canada in 2005 was over CA$1 billion, with a growth of 30 per cent achieved between 2003 and 2005. This compares with a growth of just 15 per cent in the revenues generated by MC&IT visitors from the USA in that same period.

Destinations:

- Toronto remains the most popular destination, followed by (in order) Vancouver, Montreal, Edmonton and Ottawa-Hull.

Canada's position among other leading convention destinations in 2005 is shown in the ICCA and UIA rankings in Chapter 1.

Further information: www.Canada.travel.

Germany

Germany has some 11 000 meeting venues, according to information supplied by the German Convention Bureau (see Chapter 4). This figure is made up of more than 10 000 hotels, 420 conference centres and halls, 330 universities and 40 airports – these venues offer some 60 500 meeting rooms of varying sizes. In addition there are approximately 75 corporate venues and over 1500 unique or unusual venues.

Conference centres and halls have adapted to changing market needs over the years, for example by adding many smaller meeting rooms to their large auditorium facilities. About 700 venues, including all the convention centres, have a main auditorium with a minimum capacity of 500 delegates.

The meetings and convention industry has maintained its position as a significant contributor to the national economy, as illustrated by the following facts:

- Hotel bednights resulting from meetings and conventions are 30 per cent nationwide
- One overnight stay in three in Germany is generated by the meetings and convention industry

Overseas Market	2003				2004				2005			
	Trips ('000)	Spending (CA$M)	Spending per Trip (CA$)	Spending per Night (CA$)	Trips ('000)	Spending (CA$M)	Spending per Trip (CA$)	Spending per Night (CA$)	Trips ('000)	Spending (CA$M)	Spending per Trip (CA$)	Spending per Night (CA$)
United Kingdom	74.4	110.2	1482.4	147.5	77.1	106.0	1375.7	139.3	91.9	144.0	1566.6	157.5
Japan	45.6	56.6	1242.2	122.1	45.0	58.2	1294.0	254.4	56.4	72.4	1283.9	181.9
Germany	41.1	52.4	1275.1	141.7	55.1	69.0	1252.7	146.3	57.1	77.2	1351.3	146.3
Mexico	29.9	39.1	1309.5	75.4	31.7	34.3	1082.3	49.6	34.3	51.1	1487.8	84.3
France	39.2	47.7	1214.7	154.7	51.4	63.5	1236.1	158.7	42.7	59.1	1383.6	159.1
China	19.0	38.7	2041.3	154.9	24.1	41.3	1713.1	143.0	41.8	99.1	2373.2	158.2

Source: Canadian Tourism Commission

Table 3.5
Characteristics of leading overseas market MC&IT visitors to Canada 2003–2005

- More than one million conferences, meetings and seminars throughout Germany generate a total revenue of over 50 billion euros annually
- Approximately 60 per cent of these events relate to the corporate or for-profit sector, with the balance of 40 per cent arising from not-for-profit organizations such as associations, societies and institutions.

Ireland

While there is substantial conference and business tourism generated domestically across Ireland (both in the Republic and in Northern Ireland), the marketing activity by national bodies such as Tourism Ireland and Fáilte Ireland (see Chapter 4) is dedicated primarily to attracting business from overseas.

Table 3.6 shows that the number of overseas business tourists declined in the early years of this millennium from a peak achieved in 2000, but then showed healthy growth again in 2004 and 2005.

Table 3.7 illustrates the importance of Britain and of mainland Europe as markets supplying business tourists to Ireland, and distinguishes between discretionary business tourists (such as conference delegates and exhibition visitors) and non-discretionary (individual business or corporate travellers).

Table 3.8 compares the growth in the volume and value of discretionary business tourists to Ireland from 2004 to 2005. Substantial growth was achieved in all three segments, increasing the

Origin	1999	2000	2001	2002	2003	2004	2005
Britain	499	546	489	446	431	440	432
Mainland Europe	253	260	247	226	213	277	324
North America	96	103	75	73	68	68	69
Other Overseas	37	36	36	35	32	34	33
Total	885	945	847	780	744	819	857
Revenue from Overseas Business Tourism Visitors in millions of euros				443.4	400.3	423.0	456.6

Source of information: Central Statistics Office Ireland

Table 3.6
Overseas Business Tourism Visitors to Ireland (000s) and Revenue Generated

	Total	Britain	Mainland Europe	North America	Elsewhere
Association conference or convention	89	38	37	10	4
Corporate conference, seminar or company event	147	63	65	10	9
Trade fair or exhibition	27	16	9	2	0
Total discretionary business tourism visitors	**263**	**117**	**111**	**22**	**13**
Total discretionary business tourism visitors as % of total business visitors	31%	27%	34%	32%	39%
Other business visitors	594	315	213	47	20
Total business visitors	**857**	**432**	**324**	**69**	**33**

Source: Central Statistics Office/Failte Ireland Survey of Overseas Travellers

Table 3.7
Overseas Business Tourism Visits to Ireland in 2005 (000s) by Origin and Type

	2004 Nos. (000s)	2004 Per Capita Spend (euros)	2004 Revenue (millions of euros)	2005 Nos. (000s)	2005 Per Capita Spend (euros)	2005 Revenue (millions of euros)
International conference	77	936	72.1	89	959	85.4
Corporate meeting	116	742	86.1	147	761	111.8
Trade fair/exhibition	20	820	16.4	27	841	22.7
Total revenue	213		174.6		263	219.9
Discretionary business tourism as % of total business revenue			41%			48%

Source: Failte Ireland Survey of Overseas Travellers/TDI report on Ireland's International Conference, Corporate Meetings and Incentive Travel Sector 2004
Notes: As no estimate is available for spend at trade fairs/exhibitions, per capita spend is based on the average of conference and corporate meetings
Per capita spend 2005 is based on 2.5% inflation (Central Statistics Office)

Table 3.8
Volume and Value of Discretionary Overseas Business Tourism to Ireland 2004 and 2005

estimated revenue achieved by discretionary business tourism from 41 per cent to 49 per cent of total business tourism revenues. Further information: www.irelandinspires.com.

South Africa

Business tourism is still very much in its infancy in South Africa, but is already estimated to support around 250 000 jobs. The sector, including domestic and inbound business, is worth around R21 billion (approximately £1.5 billion or US$3 billion), according to Rick Taylor, one of the country's leading business tourism consultants. International conferences alone contribute R951 million (approximately £70 million or US$150 million) to South Africa's Gross Domestic Product, while creating 12 000 jobs. South Africa achieved 28th place in the UIA rankings in 2005 (see Chapter 1), and 32nd place in the ICCA rankings. The ICCA data also shows South Africa hosting some 44 per cent of Africa's total international meetings and conventions in 2005.

Spain

Since 1990 Spain Convention Bureau has produced an annual statistical analysis on conference tourism in Spain based on data collected by its member cities. The 2005 survey, to which 38 cities contributed, reveals that 13 969 conferences took place attracting a total of 2 798 388 delegates. This is the highest number ever recorded and continues the year-on-year growth in the number of conferences since 1995 (when just 3102 conferences were reported). The only exception to this was 2004 when there was a small reduction in the number of events compared with the previous year. The further increase in 2005 was across all types of events: association congresses, conferences and day meetings. Of the total of 13 969 events reported in 2005, 2374 were congresses, 3755 conferences, and 7718 were day meetings.

The sectors generating conferences are shown in Table 3.9.

Ranking	Sector	% (rounded)
1	Business/commerce	22
2	Medical/health	22
3	Cultural	14
4	Public sector	13
5	Others	10
6	Academic	8
7	Technology	6
8	Scientific	5

Table 3.9
Sectors generating conferences in Spain in 2005

Almost two-thirds (62 per cent) of all conferences and meetings take place in Autumn and Spring, with the most popular months being (in order) October, November, May and April. The month of least activity is August, when just over 1 per cent of all conferences take place. Over half (54 per cent) of all conferences have between 50 and 150 delegates, while only 3 per cent have over 1000 delegates participating. 58 per cent of events last for 2 days or less, 33 per cent for 2 to 4 days, and 9 per cent more than 4 days.

The average daily expenditure by delegates is estimated at 373 euros and the total direct economic impact of conferences in 2005 is estimated to be 3.2 billion euros.

The full survey report, for 2005 and for previous years, can be accessed on the Spain Convention Bureau web site: www.scb.es/ (see section on statistics).

United Kingdom

Information has already been given on the demand side of the UK conference industry (Chapter 2 – key findings of the 'UK Conference Market Survey 2006'). Supply side data are collected annually through research carried out among conference venues which is published as the 'British Conference Venues Survey'. The main results of the 2006 Survey, based on data provided by 347 venues across the UK, include:

- An estimated 1.58 million conferences and meetings (8 or more delegates) took place at UK venues during 2005 (compared with an estimated 1.47 million in 2004, and 1.4 million in 2001). Twenty-nine per cent of conferences involved delegates having an overnight stay at the venue or in the destination, a fall on the figure for 2004 when almost one in three (32 per cent) of conferences were residential
- Almost two-thirds (64 per cent) of all meetings and conferences took place in hotels while 11 per cent were held in conference/training centres and a similar proportion in unusual venues
- The average duration was 1.7 days although most conferences (58 per cent) lasted a day or less. This varied from 1.5 days for non-residential conferences to 2.2 days for residential conferences
- The average number of delegates was 49. 41 per cent of all conferences and meetings had 8–20 delegates, and a further 29 per cent had 21 to 50 delegates
- The peak months for conferences were September/October/November, followed by March/April/May/June. The quietest month was August
- Just over one third (35 per cent) of all conferences were booked through a professional conference organizer or venue finding

agency, compared with 33 per cent in 2004 and 31 per cent in 2003

- 30 per cent of the reporting venues had fewer than 5 meeting rooms, 37 per cent had between 5 to 10 meeting rooms, and 20 per cent had 11 to 20 rooms. The average number of rooms per venue was 14.9, although this figure fell to 9.2 if university venues were excluded. The average number of conferences per room in 2005 was 30.3, a figure that rises to 48.8 if universities are excluded
- Around a third (32 per cent) of venues had dedicated exhibition/exposition space available. Venues most likely to have such space included multi-purpose venues (64 per cent) and purpose-built venues (62 per cent)
- Venues were asked to estimate the average daily delegate rate achieved during 2005 (including Value Added Tax). Well over half (64 per cent) of venues achieved an average of between £26 and £50 while 18 per cent charged less than £26, and 17 per cent charged between £51 and £75. Overall the average daily delegate rate achieved was £43. The average 24-hour delegate rate achieved was £136
- Responses were received from different types of conference venue as follows: purpose-built conference centres – 3 per cent, multi-purpose venues – 9 per cent, educational establishments (mostly universities) – 10 per cent, hotels – 39 per cent, conference/training centres – 13 per cent, unusual/unique venues (e.g. castles, sporting venues) – 26 per cent.

Figure 3.3 gives an estimate for the value of the British conference market in 2005 and provides summary data on non-residential and residential conferences in that year.

The number of overseas business visitors travelling to the UK to attend a conference or large meeting in 2005 increased significantly to 996 000, up from 846 000 in 2004 and 633 000 in 2003, according to the 'International Passenger Survey 2006'. Their spend grew equally, rising from £393 million in 2003 to £541 million in 2004 and £666 million in 2005.

Case Study 3.1 provides an analysis of the economic benefits and impact of the Scottish Exhibition + Conference Centre, Glasgow, on the economies of Glasgow and of Scotland.

Food for Thought: an examination of the eating habits of a major convention can perhaps help to make real its benefits to a local economy (although maybe not to a delegate's stomach!). In 2006, the Conservative Party (a British political party) held its annual convention in Bournemouth, on England's south coast. In total, the convention attracted 8760 participants over 4 days/nights. They consumed:

- 24 650 cups of coffee
- 18 900 cups of tea

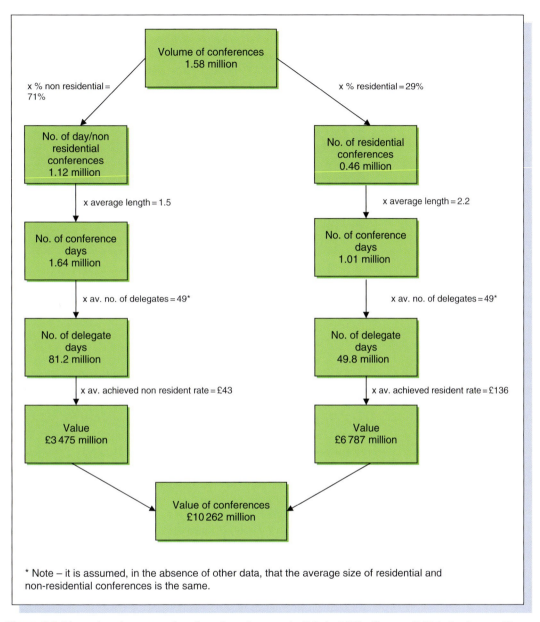

Figure 3.3 Measuring the economic value of conferences in Britain 2005. (Source: British Conference Venues Survey 2006.)

- 15 850 sandwiches
- 4700 cakes
- 8000 litres of water
- 2500 bottles of wine.

Bournemouth estimates that the convention generated approximately 50 000 bednights for the town's accommodation sector, with an economic benefit of around £10 million.

Figure 3.4
Catering for the 2006
Conservative party conference,
Bournemouth, England.
(Source: Bournemouth
International Centre.)

Figure 3.4 shows a small part of the Conservatives' consumption in Bournemouth.

United States of America

The Convention Industry Council (CIC) is the principal body in the USA gathering and publishing economic impact data. Key findings from its '2004 Economic Impact Study' (published September 2005), summarising the impact of meetings, conventions, exhibitions and the incentive travel industry in the USA, are:

- The industry is a 365-day-a-year business that operates in communities, large and small, across the country. Taken as a whole, it generated US$122.31 billion in total direct spending in 2004, making it the 29th largest contributor to the gross national product (i.e. more than the pharmaceutical and medicine manufacturing industry)
- The industry's spending and tax revenues ripple through every sector of the local economy, from restaurants and transport to retailing and other services, while supporting 1.7 million jobs in the USA. It generates more than 36 per cent of the hotel industry's estimated US$109.3 billion in operating revenue, and its delegates account for nearly 17 per cent of the air transport industry's operating income
- Association-sponsored events accounted for two-thirds, or US$81.94 billion, of the direct spending industry total. Corporate-sponsored events (including incentive travel) accounted for the remaining one-third, or US$40.37 billion

- The largest share of the convention and exhibition dollar (35 per cent) is spent in hotels and other facilities. The rest is widely distributed throughout local economies. After air transport (24 per cent), the biggest categories of delegate, exhibitor and sponsor spending were: restaurant and outside catering food and beverage outlets (14 per cent) and business services (12 per cent).

Convene, the magazine published by the Professional Convention Management Association (PCMA), undertakes an annual 'Meetings Market Survey'. The Survey covering 2005 was published in March 2006 and the findings, based on replies from 318 PCMA members (72 per cent of whom worked for US associations), show:

- One quarter of respondents report that their organization's total convention/meeting budget was US$2.5 million or more, and a half indicate that it was US$1 million or more. 30 per cent expect their budget to increase in 2006, with 55 per cent expecting no change
- More than two-thirds of respondents (69 per cent) report that the economic value of their largest meeting to the host destination was US$1 million or greater, while more than one quarter report the value at US$5 million or greater
- Association meeting planners and independent meeting professionals (PCOs) report that, on average, 50 per cent of the revenue from their largest 2005 event came from delegate registrations, while 27 per cent came from exhibition stand sales and 16 per cent from sponsorships and grants.

Meanwhile *Meetings & Conventions* magazine published its latest biennial survey of the US Meetings Market in August 2006,

	Number of Meetings	Meeting Attendance (in millions)	Total Expenditure (US$ billions)
Corporate	1 020 300	79.7	31.8
Association (Meetings and Conferences)	210 600	37.9	41.8
Conventions	12 700	18.9	33.6
Total	1 243 600	136.5	107.2

Source: *Meetings & Conventions* magazine (2006)

Table 3.10
Meetings & Conventions Magazine 2006 Survey of US Meetings Market

relating to events held in 2005 and based on responses from 460 corporate meeting planners and 276 association planners, with results extrapolated out to represent the 57 066 corporate and 13 017 association planners that make up the magazine's readership base. Table 3.10 shows the key economic results, with the industry worth an estimated US$107.2 billion. The survey also captured data on the meeting planners themselves and found that:

- Corporate planners had an average age of 45, and association planners an average age of 49
- Women predominate and account for an average 75 per cent of all meeting planners
- Planners typically had 10–11 years' experience in their roles.

Summary

- conferences are a segment of business tourism, which is itself a sector of the wider tourism industry. Estimates suggest that, within developed economies such as the United Kingdom, business tourism may account for between one-quarter and one-third of the total value of tourism. The conference segment of business tourism is worth hundreds of billions of pounds per annum on a global scale
- comprehensive statistics for the conference industry do not yet exist. There are many reasons for this, including the somewhat fragmented nature of the conference sector, the lack of consensus on terminology, and the sensitivity of certain commercial information
- measurements of the size of the conference industry are possible, even though these are based on partial rather than fully comprehensive surveys. They point to an industry which is active and vibrant
- calculations of the economic impact of conference business must take into account a number of negative economic impacts, such as opportunity costs and displacement costs, as well as the cascade of positive benefits, in order to arrive at an accurate assessment of net beneficial effects
- measurement of the economic impact of tourist spending is achieved by the use of multipliers. Multipliers can be used to measure income generated and employment supported, among other things
- national surveys and local studies confirm that conference tourism occupies one of the top places at the high yield end of the tourism spectrum. It provides substantial economic benefits for those countries which have embraced it vigorously and invested in the necessary infrastructure

to attract and retain conference business. It sustains jobs which are all-year-round and brings income through delegate expenditure which benefits many sections of local communities.

Review and discussion questions

1. If you were responsible for marketing an entire destination, what arguments would you put forward to the hotels you were representing to encourage them to disclose to you information on their client groups and bookings. What might be the benefits to them of so doing?
2. List the main arguments for and against the establishment of a comprehensive national database of conferences and similar events.
3. Develop your own questionnaire for measuring the economic impact of convention delegate expenditure on a specific destination.
4. You have been asked to make the economic case for public funds to be committed for the construction and marketing of a new convention centre. What arguments would you put forward? Illustrate your answer with data/statistics from comparable developments in other locations.
5. As a restaurant owner whose restaurant is situated close to a major convention centre, suggest the practical steps you might take to ensure that you gain maximum benefit from having this facility on your doorstep.

Notes and references

1. *British Conference Venues Survey* (2006), published by the British Association of Conference Destinations.
2. *Convene* magazine: '15th Annual Meetings Market Survey' (March 2006), Professional Convention Management Association.
3. Cooper, C, Fletcher, J, Gilbert, D and Wanhill, S (1993), *Tourism Principles and Practice*, Addison Wesley Longman Ltd.
4. Davidson, R and Cope, B (2002), *Business Travel*, Pearson Education.
5. Deery M, Jago L, Fredline L and Dwyer L (2005), *National Business Events Study*, Common Ground Publishing Pty Ltd.

6. *Delegate Expenditure Survey* (2006), published by VisitBritain, VisitScotland, Visit Wales and Fáilte Ireland.
7. Heeley, J, Tourism and Local Government, With Special Reference to the County of Norfolk, Volume 1, page 72, University of East Anglia (1980).
8. *International Passenger Survey* 2006, Office for National Statistics.
9. Rockett, G and Smillie, G, *The European Conference and Meetings Market*, The Economist Intelligence Unit (reprinted from Travel & Tourism Analyst – Issue 4 1994).
10. *Gazette Officielle du Tourisme* (No. 1419), 'France Congrès: un outil pour mesurer le poids économique de la filière congrès' (1998).
11. *Meetings Market Survey 2002*, researched and published by 'Convene' magazine (March 2002).
12. *The UK Conference Market Survey 2006*, research carried out by The Right Solution on behalf of the Meetings Industry Association (July 2006).

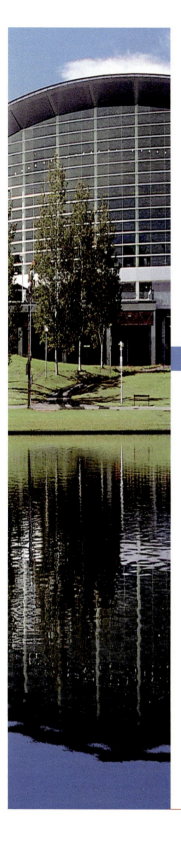

CHAPTER 4

Conference industry marketing activity

Introduction

Location has always been one of the key factors in decisions over the choice of conference venues. Its importance has led to the creation of marketing organizations whose prime focus is that of location or 'destination' promotion, operating at national, regional or city level. Following a summary of general marketing principles and their application to the conference industry, this chapter will look at the role of destination marketing organizations. It will also examine some of the other ways in which individual venues, or groups of venues, bring their product to the marketplace through branding and the establishment of consortia. The principles and practice of marketing conferences, conventions and other business events are covered in Chapter 5.

Specific sections in this chapter include:

- marketing principles (customer focus, marketing plan, market segmentation, marketing mix)
- relationship marketing and customer relationship management
- web marketing
- a definition of destination
- the branding of cities and other destinations
- destination marketing organizations
- conference venue marketing

- the branding of hotel venues
- overseas marketing.

It includes case studies on:

- Isle of Man branding strategy (mini case study)
- Edinburgh Convention Bureau
- Team San José.

Learning outcomes

On completion of this chapter, you should be able to:

- Describe the key principles of marketing and illustrate their application to the conference industry
- Explain how newer areas of marketing, such as web marketing/branding/customer relationship management, have been embraced by the conference industry
- Define the roles of different types of destination marketing organization
- Understand how individual venues have developed branded conference products.

MARKETING PRINCIPLES

Before looking at conference venue and destination marketing activities, it will be useful to summarize some of the general principles of marketing and how they apply to the conference and tourism industry.

Customer focus

There are many definitions of marketing. One of the more straightforward ones is that adopted by the (British) Chartered Institute of Marketing, which defines marketing as:

The management process responsible for indentifying, anticipating and satisfying customers' requirements efficiently and profitably.

This focus on customers' needs is the key to all successful marketing activity. There are alternative philosophies which are well described by Cooper et al (1993) and reproduced in Figure 4.1.

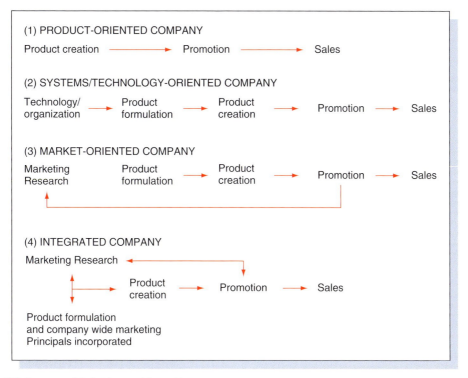

Figure 4.1 Four possible business philosophies.

'Examples 1 and 2 (in Figure 4.1) can be ineffective due to problems encountered in having the wrong product for the market, and therefore having to devote more resources to promotion and selling in order to achieve sales. In these examples it is normal to find companies which believe their products are acceptable, and all that is required for sales to occur is the identification of prime markets and methods of selling.' The emphasis is on the product, and in tourist promotional literature it is often characterised by photographs of empty bedrooms or conference rooms, of buildings and views of the destination. It is selling 'features' rather than the 'benefits' the consumer is seeking, and fails to show pictures of tourists and delegates enjoying themselves and receiving good service.

On the other hand, examples 3 and 4 in Figure 4.1 'offer the ideal approach to organizing business in today's tourism marketplace. They are driven by research which creates an understanding of the consumer, the business and the marketplace. The tourism industry is spending vast sums of money on developing new attractions, improving products, building hotels and investing in technology. The only way for the risk level to be kept to a minimum is through adoption of a marketing philosophy which provides products related to the needs of consumers.'

The establishment of a customer orientation which permeates through every department of a conference venue or conference marketing organization is essential to its success. This provides the basic building blocks upon which marketing strategies can be constructed. It will ensure that the physical product is suited to market needs: it will confirm, for example, that the multi-purpose hotel function room is less and less able to meet the increasingly sophisticated needs of today's conference planners. It will also ensure that the people servicing a venue have a proper understanding of the specific needs of the conference organizer and his delegates, and that they are equipped with the personal and technical skills to meet such needs in ways which will encourage the customer to return again and again.

Marketing plan

The practical steps involved in preparing to approach the marketplace include development of a Marketing Plan or Strategy, against which performance can be measured, and future marketing programmes fine-tuned in the light of experience. While there is no definitive standard of what should constitute a Marketing Plan, it is likely to contain most or all of the following sections:

1. Introduction setting out the organization's vision and mission and overall objectives.
2. An overview of the current market, highlighting opportunities and threats specific to the destination or venue.
3. An assessment of the destination or venue's strengths and weaknesses, in the form of a product audit, identifying specific competitive advantages.
4. Details of the marketing strategies to be implemented, outlining the markets to be reached, tactics and work programmes to achieve the strategies, with specific and measurable targets and timescales.
5. A comprehensive marketing calendar which summarises the key items from section 4 into a month-by-month activity plan, also showing where the lead responsibility for each activity lies.
6. A detailed budget.

The Plan may also include a PEST analysis, looking at the political, economic, social and technological changes which could affect the organization and the market.

The New Zealand city of Wellington's tourism marketing organization (known as 'Positively Wellington Tourism') set out its 'Marketing Vision 2004–2009' in the following terms (addressing its leisure as well as its business tourism interests and objectives), aiming to see:

- Wellington as one of the top three destinations visited in New Zealand by international visitors
- Wellington regarded by the international travel trade as a 'must-see' destination
- Wellington rated by at least 80 per cent of the domestic market as the 'hottest' city to visit in New Zealand
- A highly active marketing programme operating in Australia, with 200 000 visitors from Australia and Wellington regarded by Australians as a must-see destination
- The Wellington Visitor Information Centre fully integrated into the overall marketing function and delivery of Positively Wellington Tourism's marketing and product development programmes
- Wellington as New Zealand's leading events destination with a calendar of events that addresses low and shoulder season travel
- Wellington as a leading conference destination with a strong market presence in New Zealand and Australia
- Wellington leading e-commerce trading in the tourism industry with the most active RTO web site in New Zealand.

Later in this document (which has the overall title of 'Wellington Tourism Action Plan 2004–2009 – A Strategic Update'), Wellington identifies the target of 'mid-sized conferences (100 to 500 delegates) especially from Australia', as part of its aims to increase its international market share.

Writing and implementing a Marketing Plan, while important, are never sufficient. There also needs to be a regular and rigorous evaluation of the effectiveness of the Plan, measuring actual performance against the objectives and targets detailed in the Plan. This evaluation will, almost certainly, lead to some revision and re-writing of the Plan for the following year(s), as lessons are learnt and adjustments are made in the light of experience in putting the Plan into practice. It is also likely that, at some point, a major review of the Plan will be carried out, leading to the drafting of a new marketing strategy.

Table 4.1 shows the Table of Contents for the 'Business Plan and Marketing Opportunities 2007' of Jersey Conference Bureau (www.jerseyconferences.com). Jersey is the largest of the Channel Islands which are located between England and France. It comes under the sovereignty of the United Kingdom but has a large measure of independence from the UK, including its own States Government. Jersey Conference Bureau operates as a public private partnership between Jersey Tourism (the States Government-funded body) and conference industry suppliers. The Bureau is a sales and marketing body, working on behalf of

Contents	Page

Table 4.1
Jersey Conference Bureau Business Plan & Marketing Opportunities 2007 'Table of Contents'

the Island and its conference and incentive suppliers to encourage the development and growth of business tourism to the Island from the UK and from established markets in mainland Europe, as well as to explore potential growth markets further afield. Its mission is:

To place Jersey as a first choice destination for meeting, conference and incentive buyers by providing focus and co-ordination for the industry with the result to generate an increase in the meeting, conference and incentive business in Jersey.

Table 4.1 illustrates how the Bureau's 'Business Plan and Marketing Opportunities 2007' is structured and summarizes the principal activities for the year. The Plan itself includes detailed targets for each activity and sets out the proportions of the budget to be allocated to each one.

Market segmentation

An important part of the marketing planning process is the identification of appropriate market segments from which it is anticipated that business can be won. In broad terms, the conference and conventions sector (as we have seen in Chapter 2) is typically divided into the following segments:

- corporate meetings, conferences and events
- national association meetings and conventions
- international association conventions and congresses.

These broad categories can then be subjected to further segmentation in a variety of ways. For example, by industry sector, with the following sectors being particularly important:

- oil, gas and petrochemicals
- medical and pharmaceutical
- computing/IT and telecommunications
- motor manufacturing and other manufacturing
- financial and professional services
- food, drink and tobacco
- travel and transport.

Another important type of segmentation is that done by size of event: a venue might decide, for example, that it will target corporate meetings and conferences of between 50 to 100 delegates, even though it might have a room with a capacity of 200, because it lacks sufficient syndicate rooms for a 200-delegate conference to break down into five or six smaller groups. Similarly, there is probably little point in a destination with a 2000-capacity convention centre targeting events of this size if the destination's overall infrastructure does not have enough bedrooms of the right quality to accommodate a residential 2000-delegate convention.

  Segmentation can also be done by source or location of potential clients. It may be that very good transport links exist with particular cities or countries, facilitating travel to the destination from these areas. Such a criterion will be more relevant to corporate meetings and conferences where delegates may be travelling from only one or just a limited number of starting points. It will be less important within the association segment as delegates are normally travelling from a much wider range of locations to attend the convention or congress.

In the late 1990s, the Scottish Convention Bureau (now the Business Tourism Unit of VisitScotland – see later in this chapter) analysed the characteristics of the UK corporate meetings segment, and produced the findings (presented to the 1998 convention of the British Association of Conference Destinations) as shown in Table 4.2. This illustrates a variety of factors on which market segmentation can be based.

Similar research can be carried out for all market segments in order to identify the opportunities for marketing activity. Clearly, research must also be undertaken by a destination or venue into its own 'product' in order to build a comprehensive picture of its strengths and weaknesses so that appropriate target markets match the strengths of the destination or venue.

Characteristic	Research Findings
1. Scale	Large scale with 50 per cent of English and Welsh companies prepared to consider using meeting venues in Scotland
2. Seasonality	56 per cent of companies hold events between October and March
3. Size of events	70 per cent of the meetings held are for less than 50 delegates
4. Venue preference	Country hotel – 35 per cent City hotel – 31 per cent Conference centre – 8 per cent Academic venue – 2 per cent Unusual venue – 24 per cent
5. Destination role	80 per cent of companies choose place (destination) before deciding upon a venue
6. Key selection factors	Access (proximity to airport; time/cost of travel) Facilities Policy on rotation Business links with Scotland
7. Use of agencies	50 per cent use agencies to book venues and/or assist with aspects of conference management
8. Decision-making process	The company chairman or CEO has a key role in deciding final choice of venue/destination A wide variety of company departments has responsibility for meetings
9. Additionality/displacement	High risk of displacement
10. Competition	Extremely high

Source: Scottish Convention Bureau (1998) (now known as VisitScotland)

Table 4.2
Scottish Convention Bureau analysis of the UK corporate meetings segment

Marketing mix strategy

Once market research has been completed and target markets of current and potential customers have been identified (for example, corporate conferences for up to 100 delegates or professional association conferences for 500 to 1000, or in more specific niche and segment terms such as very high-spend pharmaceutical conferences for 20 to 40 delegates), an appropriate marketing mix strategy can be developed.

The marketing mix is frequently defined as comprising the four Ps: product, price, promotion and place (distribution). Other marketing gurus would extend these traditional four points to eight, to include packaging, planning, the prospect, and post-sale. In the marketing of a conference destination or venue, these terms signify:

- **Product** is the destination/venue and its facilities and resources. To conference organizers and meeting planners, it means a destination/venue which can handle the convention, meeting or exhibition requirements. It covers such issues as service, quality, branding, and those unique features which differentiate it from competitors (USPs or unique selling propositions).
- **Price** may cover a variety of issues including conference centre/venue hire charges and delegate rates, hotel or guest house accommodation costs, and transport costs. Pricing policies must take account of many factors including projected future demand and any seasonal fluctuations expected; the need to maximize yield (see Chapter 6); the perishable nature of the product (it is something that cannot be stored for future use, like a conference room that is unused on a particular day and brings in no revenue and that potential revenue is lost forever); the psychological impact on clients of raising or lowering prices; the activities of competitors; and the wider economic situation.
- **Packaging** relates to the way in which the product and price are offered in the market. Special delegate packages may be offered in conjunction with local tourist attractions or between conference venues and hotels. Most venues, both residential and non-residential, promote their own delegate packages: Tortworth Court Four Pillars Hotel, Gloucestershire, England, offers '24-hour' and 'day' delegate packages (see Table 4.3). Some convention centres make available their meeting rooms rent-free to certain types of not-for-profit organizations whose events meet specific economic benefit criteria. Conventions & Incentives New Zealand (CINZ) has developed its 'Conference Assistance Programme' (CAP) to assist the country to win more international association and international organization conferences. The CAP initiative helps a New Zealand (national)

TORTWORTH HALL FOUR PILLARS HOTEL – GLOUCESTERSHIRE, ENGLAND

24-Hour Delegate Rate.(£179 per person including Value Added Tax – October 2006) includes:

- Hire of main meeting room and equipment hire, to include LCD projector and screen, flip chart, conference tidy (stationery)
- Unlimited free Internet access for conference organisers
- Dedicated conference contact
- Overnight accommodation
- Full English breakfast and Continental buffet breakfast
- Unlimited tea, coffee and snacks served in the Conference Café. To include: fresh fruit, wrapped biscuits, nutria-grain bar, mini diet cokes
- Danish pastry (morning only), selection of muffins (afternoon only)
- Two course hot and cold seated buffet lunch
- Three course dinner with coffee
- Use of Peels Leisure Club: gym, sauna, steam room, spa pool and indoor heated swimming pool.

Day Delegate Rate (£69 per person including Value Added Tax – October 2006) includes:

- Hire of main meeting room and equipment hire, to include LCD projector and screen, flip chart, conference tidy (stationery)
- Unlimited tea, coffee and snacks served in the Conference Café. To include: fresh fruit, wrapped biscuits, nutria-grain bar, mini diet cokes
- Danish pastry (morning only), selection of muffins (afternoon only)
- Two course hot and cold seated buffet lunch
- Unlimited free Internet access for conference organiser
- Dedicated conference contact.

www.four-pillars.co.uk/tortworth

Table 4.3
24-Hour and Day Delegate Rates – Tortworth Hall Four Pillars Hotel, Gloucestershire, England

association or organization to bid for the international conference to which it is linked by undertaking an initial feasibility study on its behalf free of charge. It then assists with compilation of the bid in conjunction with a professional conference organizer and provides further support to the bidding process. Further details on the CAP initiative may be accessed at: www.conventionsnz.co.nz/cap.aspx.
- **Place (or distribution)** focuses on the activities used by a destination or venue to make its product available and accessible to prospective clients. Such distribution channels include trade

shows, destination or venue guides and brochures, CD-Roms or videos/DVDs, and web sites.

- **Planning** is the strategic process of analysing markets, assessing the competition, identifying programmes, and selecting appropriate marketing strategies.
- **Promotion** communicates information about the destination/ venue and its products to prospective clients. There is a need to inform and persuade current customers to remain loyal, potential future customers to experience the product, but also journalists and other key people (leading figures in the local community and politicians, for example) who may in some way influence business activity levels. Advertising, public relations, direct marketing, selling, and familiarization visits are some of the promotional activities undertaken.
- **Prospect** (or client/customer) is the sole reason for, and the object of, all the destination or venue's marketing endeavours. The 'Body Shop' retail company expressed the importance of the customer in its mission statement as follows:

> *A customer is the most important visitor on our premises. She is not dependent on us. We are dependent on her. She is not an interruption to our work. She is the purpose of it. She is not an outsider in our business. She is part of it. We are not doing her a favour by serving her. She is doing us a favour by giving us the opportunity to do so.*

It is this same customer orientation which is crucial to the success of all venues and destinations seeking to attract conference delegates.

- **Post-sale** processes address the continuing need to provide service to and for prospects and to ensure that the sense of expectation generated at the sales meeting is not just met but exceeded in the run-up to an event and, indeed, in the provision of service during and after it. Client retention is not always possible within the conference industry because of the buying patterns of certain organizations, especially within the association sector, but keeping satisfied clients is a much more cost-effective way of maintaining and building market share than having constantly to find and attract new clients. Recommendations by colleagues/peers of venues and destinations is frequently found to be a key way in which these are sourced, as a satisfied customer becomes an unpaid ambassador (or 'distribution channel') whose value should never be underestimated.

Other marketers suggest further Ps be added to the marketing mix, such as **People** – those who are between the product and the prospect, delivering the product/services to the client including convention bureau staff, venue personnel, destination management companies, professional conference organizers, restaurateurs, shop and visitor attraction staff.

There is clearly some overlap between these different marketing mix tools, but in total they provide the essential ingredients for bringing a conference venue or destination to the marketplace in a way that is professionally planned and likely to enjoy the greatest success.

RELATIONSHIP MARKETING AND CUSTOMER RELATIONSHIP MANAGEMENT

One of the key features of conference venue and destination marketing is the forging of relationships between suppliers and buyers, the building of trust between those offering facilities and services and those looking to make use of them to stage events. Gartrell (1991) suggests that:

> though a convention bureau is a sales organization, its premise of operation is the development of a relationship with planners that cultivates understanding and trust. Though such a relationship may not initially appear mutually supportive, the reality is that the bureau and planner have common goals and in essence need one another.

The meeting planner or conference organizer needs, for example, to carry out familiarization or inspection visits to a destination and its venues, to assess their appropriateness for specific events. The convention and visitor bureau is the ideal vehicle for the organization of such visits because it can provide a comprehensive overview, pull together all the necessary information, arrange a schedule of visits to venues and attractions and usually escort them as well, and then advise on the availability and accessibility of all the other components of a given conference package. DMCs and, to a lesser extent PCOs, may also be involved in this process in a similar way. For the individual conference organizer to plan such a visit using his own resources, possibly from hundreds or thousands of miles away, would require a huge investment in time and resources.

Trust and understanding are also of critical importance between the venue which is to stage the conference and the conference organizer. A chain of relationships is formed, initially between the venue sales manager and the conference organizer and then between the conference and banqueting manager/event co-ordinator and the organizer (see Chapter 6 for more detailed examples). All need to have confidence in each other: the conference organizer needs to trust the venue staff to deliver what has been promised within agreed budgets, and the venue staff need to feel comfortable that their client will keep his side of the deal (for example, in actual numbers of delegates attending, in the administration of the conference programme, and in the implementation of any specially planned arrangements). When such strong and trusting relationships exist, there is a much greater prospect of successful events and of future repeat business. When relationships are less strong, often because of high staff turnover in the venue, poor communications between client and venue, or because of insufficient planning time allocated by the conference organizer, problems are much more likely to occur.

In the author's experience, one of the real attractions of the conference industry is the many opportunities it affords for the development of relationships between buyers and suppliers, between buyers and buyers, and between suppliers and suppliers. It is very much a people industry and, while there may be fierce competition for business, this takes the form of friendly rivalry rather than cut-throat aggression. Formal and informal networks are established, and it is quite common for one destination to pass on information about a client or an event to the destination which will play host to them next. Similarly, buyers exchange their experiences of venues and destinations and peer recommendation is one of the most important ways in which future venues are sourced.

Relationship Marketing and Customer Relationship Management (and also Key Account Management) are the terms used to describe the establishment and nurturing of relationships with clients. Relationship Marketing focuses on the initial identification and building of contacts with potential clients, while Customer Relationship Management concentrates on the fostering and strengthening of such relationships.

The key to successful marketing lies in the ability to put oneself in the shoes of one's potential consumers or customers. In fact, marketing starts and finishes with the customer or target market. There is little point in developing a product unless there is a potential market for it. Similarly, there is no point in creating a great product unless potential customers can be informed effectively about it.

The customer (or consumer or client) is, in the words of Cris Canning of Hospitality Ink (a marketing firm specialising in the hospitality industry – www.HospitalityInk.com):

> the number one asset of a company – nothing happens until a sale is made. But a close second is the valuable information collected about those customers: knowledge is power. Enter the world of customer relationship management, or CRM. CRM is not about technology any more than hospitality is about throwing out a welcome mat. Rather it is a philosophy that should mobilise an entire organization toward serving the customer better. It is the 'architecture' behind a successful relationship

management programme that puts the customer first. This creates loyal customers who purchase more, cost less to sell to and who will refer at least five other customers over a lifetime. To be successful in using CRM, a venue or destination must already have a good sales process in place. If the processes, culture and skills are not in place, automating something that does not work will not enhance results.

Canning maintains that CRM is not a new principle:

the corner grocer of 100 years ago could remember all his customers and their buying habits. Now, with the aid of technology, greater quantities of that kind of information can be stored and sorted in very sophisticated ways. Modern CRM systems are designed to focus on integrating sales, customer service and marketing systems into one collaborative unit. Key features include:

- *Basic demographic and contact information.*
- *A single customer view combining all business and buying.*
- *Connectivity to include mobile phones and PDAs.*
- *Lead management.*
- *Campaign management.*
- *Data import/export.*
- *Third party support; and sometimes:*
- *Geographic information systems (GIS) tying geographic maps with data.*

Canning distinguishes between two levels of CRM: operational and analytical. Operational CRM creates a database of customers and the activities they have with the destination or venue. It represents the destination or venue's relationship with the customer and can be categorised by leads, potential clients, referrals, etc. Operational CRM systems can hold a wealth of information that can improve relationships and support customers. But, she suggests, this type of system alone will struggle to provide the deeper customer understanding required to add value to every interaction with each customer.

The sheer volume of customer information and increasingly complex interactions with customers have propelled 'data mining' to the forefront for making customer relationships profitable. Data mining uses a variety of data analysis and modelling techniques to discover patterns and relationships that may be used to make accurate predictions. The data mining process involves capture of data, 'scrubbing' it, pulling scattered entries into a single record and keeping it updated. Scrubbing data is the standardisation of crucial fields to ensure usability (otherwise an entry for "IBM" would not synchronise with one that said "I.B.M."). Some types of strategic concepts seem universal in the analytics of data mining:

- *Customer recognition (e.g. at a hotel it would include a customer's choice of room type and details of his other preferences)*
- *Data capture and maintenance (by each employee or department that touches the customer)*
- *Channel integration and consistency (each hotel property within a chain as well as the national sales office, for example, must contribute)*
- *Ranking and discrimination (which customers are A, B or C clients)*
- *Two-way personalised dialogues (so that no matter how the destination or venue contacts the client, or vice versa, this information is ready).*

One of the growing challenges facing CRM is the impact of data protection legislation which can restrict the amount of personal information to be kept on clients and, perhaps even more importantly, the uses to which such data may be put. It seems likely that this type of legislation will only increase in the future in order to protect the rights and the privacy of the individual. In the UK, for example, at the time of writing, the Data Protection Registrar (a Government agency) requires that those employed by a company/organization (as opposed to the private individual) have to be given the opportunity to 'opt out' of having their contact details held within a database. It is quite conceivable that this could change at some point to an 'opt in' regime i.e. such business contacts would have to give their assent to their contact details being stored in a database. Such a change would undoubtedly reduce the size of CRM databases and, depending upon the stringency of other aspects of any new legislation, have a potentially negative impact on CRM activity.

WEB MARKETING

The internet is now well established as a prime source of information and services for conference organizers and meeting planners. It is, therefore, vital for destinations, venues and other service suppliers within the sector to ensure that they have a winning web site. The ideas and tips for achieving this, set out below, are based on an article entitled 'Weaving the Web' which appeared in the July/August 2006 issue of

'Conference + Meetings World' magazine, written by a company, Dog Digital, which specialises in developing successful web site strategies (www.dogdigital.co.uk).

Site design

The graphic design element of a web site should be kept relatively clean and uncluttered. This does not mean that a site has to look plain or boring, but ensures that the focus is enabling users to find information, and the design should not overshadow structure or content. Good quality photography of a venue or destination, perhaps including a virtual tour, can also assist an organizer to assess suitability.

Use of technologies such as 'Macromedia Flash' to enhance a site can have a very positive impact, but it is important to note that a site built completely in 'Flash' is not open to search engines and should be avoided if search engine placement is important.

Site architecture/navigation

Finding key information on a site should not be an intellectual or time-consuming challenge. First level navigation should readily identify the major sections of the site and ensure users know where to find the information they require.

Site content

Content should be uppermost in any site. If the site is to promote a conference venue, all of the key features of the venue should be included, such as:

- Room details, dimensions and capacities
- Additional services: catering, technical, concierge services, security
- Technical specifications and floor plans in a downloadable format
- Contact details, including formal quotation form(s) or request for proposal (RFP) documentation.

Other useful content could include case studies providing independent testimonials from satisfied customers; event planning tools; destination information such as how to get there (with suitable maps in printable formats), and links to local hotels, restaurants and recreational facilities.

Site copy

One of the most frequently overlooked and badly executed features of a web site is the text. Copywriting for the web is a different discipline from print copywriting. Years of research and experience have shown that web site surfers generally do not read lengthy copy. The copy should be purpose-written, and kept to brief paragraphs and bullet lists. The tone should be appropriate to the business and understood by the target market. Jargon should be avoided, and the main copy should focus on what the venue or destination or supplier can do for conference organizers.

Content weighting

Many sites contain a wealth of useful information but unfortunately the site is not 'weighted'. The most important content in the site should be ranked accordingly. The site is, after all, about selling a venue or destination's services and facilities.

Domain choice

A good choice of domain name can make a big difference. A simple and intuitive domain ensures that prospective clients can find the site without too much trouble, be that in a search engine or simply by recollection from promotional literature. In particular, a well-chosen domain name containing keywords that should be found if used in a search will dramatically impact on the site's search engine ranking. Domain names are relatively inexpensive and making multiple domain name purchases can prove beneficial when used as part of a specific promotional campaign.

Search engine optimisation

This should be a key criterion for any web development brief. The site should be open to search engine spiders*, be optimized for keywords and be registered with all major search engines and directories. Attempting to establish or enhance a ranking retrospectively is much harder.

Multilingual

Consideration should be given to offering multilingual options on the site. These could be in the form of translated introductions or downloadable PDFs.

---

* Spiders, also known as 'bots', are the automated programs that search engines use to crawl the web and index its content. For example, Google's spider (or bot) is known as Googlebot (http://www.google.com/support/webmasters/bin/topic.py?topic = 8843) and it is the program used by Google to look at billions of pages on the web and automatically retrieve their content before adding Google's search index for use by the public.

A DEFINITION OF DESTINATION

'Location, location and location' is a commonly heard expression within the conference industry. When it comes to choosing a conference venue, the most important initial consideration for event organisers is its location. This factor often assumes greater importance than factors such as price, type of venue, quality of facilities, and proximity to tourist attractions, as confirmed by the 'UK Conference Market Survey 2006' research (see Chapter 2, Table 2.4). Buyers purchase location first and foremost.

Location can mean a number of different things: a town, a city, a county, a region, an island, a rural area, a city centre, even a country in the context of high profile international conventions. In some cases an organizer will express location in terms of 'proximity to an international airport', 'within a 20-mile radius of a certain town', 'somewhere between two named motorways'.

Where the reference is to a discrete area, the term most frequently and aptly used to describe this area is 'a destination'. Gartrell (1994) defines destinations as follows:

> From the perspective of the consumer, destinations are perceived as those geographic areas that have attributes, features, attractions, and services that appeal to the prospective user. How the consumer defines a geographic area varies greatly and may or may not include specific geographic boundaries.

The key phrase here is 'areas . . . that appeal to the prospective user'. The marketing of conference venues and destinations must be driven by what makes sense to the consumer, in this case the conference organizer and the delegates he is seeking to attract. It cannot be undertaken successfully by the artificial 'destinations' which are sometimes created to satisfy bureaucratic or political whims.

THE BRANDING OF CITIES AND OTHER DESTINATIONS

The branding of consumer products (cars, washing machines, for example) has played a major part in their promotion for many years. More recently, branding theory has been applied to the practice of marketing destinations and is now seen as a key component or tool in any successful promotion of cities, regions and countries. The city of Glasgow (winner of the ICCA 'Best Marketing Award 2006' for the launch of the 'Glasgow: Scotland with Style' brand) claims that

> a positive and unique image is the primary reason why visitors choose a city for a short break, the overriding reason why a convention organizer selects one destination

over another and the impetus behind an investor believing in the lifestyle values Glasgow offers. The management of that image, effectively positioning the city in a coherent, consistent way, is fundamental to ensuring future economic success.

The classical definition of a 'brand' is: 'A name, term, sign or design, or a combination of them, which is intended to identify the goods or services of one seller or group of sellers and to differentiate them from their competitors' (De Chernatony & McDonald, 1998).

However, this is very much a supply-side perspective – it is also necessary to consider the consumer's role in branding and to take account of the messages the consumer receives. A more modern definition of a brand which acknowledges this two-way process is the following:

'A brand is a simple thing: it is in effect a trademark which, through careful management, skilful promotion and wide use, comes into the minds of consumers, to embrace a particular and appealing set of values and attributes, both tangible and intangible' (Interbrand, 1990). A brand is a 'product or service made distinctive by its personality and its positioning. Its personality is a unique combination of tangible/physical attributes (i.e. what do I get?) and intangible/symbolic attributes (how do I feel?). Its positioning defines the point of reference with respect to the competitive set, and occupies a unique space in the consumer's mind' (Hankinson, 2001).

Brands work by:

facilitating and making the customer's choice process more effective. The objective of branding is to provoke a positive action in customers by facilitating the decision-making process. The development of a name, logo and the presentation of an attractive and (both physically and emotionally) feasible proposition for the brand validated by consumers and deliverers are basic branding procedures (Doyle, 1989).

To achieve really successful destination branding, the brand must come alive for visitors and delegates. Marketers must *'be in the business of delivering impactful experiences, not merely constructing a clever brand indentity on paper with slick slogans and brand logos' (Morgan et al., 2002).* Today many destinations have (or at least claim to have!) superb venues and hotels, easy accessibility, diverse visitor attractions, and a unique cultural heritage. But their future success in attracting visitors will depend on their ability to create a unique identity for themselves, to differentiate themselves from their competitors.

In this marketplace, what persuades potential tourists to visit (and revisit) one place instead of another is whether they have empathy with the destination and its values. The battle for customers in tomorrow's destination marketplace will be fought not over price but over hearts and minds – and this is where we move into the realm of branding (Morgan et al., 2002).

George Whitfield describes the importance of place branding in the following terms:

Branding is all about making the experience of a place as positive, memorable, different and exceptional as it can possibly be. A brand is a promise. To mean anything, a brand must be delivered and kept. The promise is not that visitors will find features of the destination physically present but that they will enjoy the experience of those physical attributes in a way that far exceeds their expectations. It is the experience, not the physical attributes and features, that fulfils a brand's promise. However spectacular the scenery, however famous the culture, however grand the built environment, the most important measure of any destination remains the reality of how visitors are treated and how they are made to feel. The most beautiful landscape in the world will not compensate for an inability to make a visitor or guest feel wanted, welcome and delighted.

Murdaugh (page 33) recommends that, from a destination perspective, the destination marketing organization (DMO) or convention & visitor bureau (CVB)

should craft a brand development programme that supports the destination through a fully coordinated and effective marketing communications plan. Branding steps should include the following, guided by research. First, define the unique selling points that separate your destination from the competition. Then produce and prioritise a series of crisp and clear motivational messages for consumers that address the positive visitor characteristics of the community. Next, craft a market "positioning statement" that describes the destination and separates it from other competitors in the eyes of the potential customer. Finally, consider creating a new theme line and graphic logo for the destination that supports the recently created positioning statement.

Whitfield reinforces this point:

> *Ultimately, it is always the people that assume the responsibility for delivering the brand promise and who are consequently essential to the brand's development. Physical attributes like great scenery, renowned culture, iconic monuments and the dramas of history all play a part but cannot, in and of themselves, present the real experience of a place. However stunning their vistas, mountains don't smile back and it is how the visitor is treated that defines and differentiates one city, region or country most powerfully from the next*

and, of course, to this list he might have added 'venue'.

The life cycle of a brand is such that it becomes fashionable after a successful launch, achieves peak sales as it becomes famous, but suffers from diminished appeal as it becomes too friendly. At this point, or just before it, the brand needs a revised image or the marketing of the brand needs re-inventing to keep the appeal of the brand fresh rather than over-familiar.

There is not space here to explore fully the theory and practice of destination branding, but it is worth emphasizing that,

> *whatever branding proposition is used, it must have the potential to last, to grow old and to evolve in a long-term branding campaign, so it is essential to get it right. However, the point of differentiation must reflect a promise which can be delivered and which matches expectations. Good destination branding is, therefore, original and different but its originality and difference needs to be sustainable, believable and relevant (Morgan et al., 2002).*

Case Study 4.1 describes the key elements of a branding strategy for the Isle of Man launched in 2006.

Case Study 4.1   Isle of Man branding strategy

The first phase of a branding strategy under the title of 'Freedom to Flourish' was launched by the Isle of Man in Summer 2006, designed to promote, protect and improve the Isle of Man. Developed after extensive research, the strategy is intended to:

- Protect the island's unique identity and heritage
- Ensure that everyone who lives on the island feels a part of its supportive community and able to reach their full potential

- Ensure that the island continues to have a strong economy by raising both the awareness and image of the Isle of Man internationally.

The branding strategy comprises four components:

- **Brand proposition:** the real benefit that the Isle of Man can offer – The Freedom to Flourish
- **Brand positioning:** what makes the Isle of Man different and able to stand out from its competitors? The Isle of Man is a land of possibility where people and business will find the right environment in which to reach their full potential, whatever they feel that might be
- **Brand values:** what are the beliefs and aspirations that define the Isle of Man? Independent thinking, resilience, resourcefulness, community loyalty
- **Brand personality:** what sort of a character do we project at our best? Spirited, authentic, encouraging/supportive, a combination of conventional and unconventional, colourful and multi-layered, secure, understated, salty, lyrical.

The branding book that accompanied the launch of 'Freedom to Flourish' includes sections on:

- Supporting messages: what's important to people outside the Isle of Man? What's important to people living on the Isle of Man?
- The brand explained
- Communicating with different audiences
- Freedom to flourish amplified
- Sensory exploration.

The implementation of the strategy is being overseen by the newly-established Positive National Identity Committee, a sub-committee of the Government's Council of Ministers. The Committee brings together politicians and civil servants to work with representatives of the Island's businesses and charities in identifying policies and activities to support and enhance the Island's national identity.

While the brand strategy is not exclusive to conferences or even to tourism, it does illustrate how a destination brand should be researched and developed, to provide a backcloth against which marketing specific to conferences and conventions can be implemented. Further details: www.gov.im/cso/flourish.

Davidson and Rogers (2006) describe a variation on the theme of destination branding in the form of the BestCities Global

Alliance (www.bestcities.net), a global collaboration comprising the convention bureaux of eight cities: Cape Town, Copenhagen, Dubai, Edinburgh, Melbourne, San Juan, Singapore and Vancouver. The Alliance was launched with the notion that convention bureaux could learn from strategies successfully practised in other industries: the airline industry, financial institutions and automotive manufacturing all provide examples of the formation of global alliances which have become an essential business strategy for the long term. The Vision for BestCities is 'to be recognised globally for being innovative and setting and delivering the world's best convention bureau practices for the meetings industry'. The BestCities Mission Statement says that it 'will deliver the world's best service experience for meeting planners and will help its partners earn more business as a result'.

The BestCities Alliance has been emulated by a group of leading international convention centres which have formed the 'All Corners of the World' partnership. The convention centres of Cairns, Cape Town, Dubai, Glasgow, Kuala Lumpur and Vancouver have established a marketing alliance under a common brand and, while it is not as formalised as the BestCities Alliance, nonetheless has a number of similar objectives. For further details visit: www.worldwideconventions.com.

DESTINATION MARKETING ORGANIZATIONS

Destination or 'place' marketing is undertaken at both a local level (city or county or even a region, for example) and a national level (by a national tourism organization). This section looks at a number of models of destination marketing organizations at both levels.

Local destination marketing

Convention and visitor bureaux • • •

Reference has already been made to the role of convention and visitor bureaux in the formation of the conference industry (Chapter 1) and in the provision of services to that industry (Chapter 2).

In structure, conference or convention bureaux (variations on the name are to be found) are usually formed and financed as partnerships between public and private sector bodies. In Britain this can include local authorities/councils, chambers of commerce, local enterprise companies/agencies, hotels, venues, and other private sector suppliers. The bureaux are established as not-for-profit organizations, controlled by a management board, to fulfil a strategic marketing role and to be the 'official' voice of the destination they represent. In most cases the bureau is established at arms' length from the local authority or authorities which it represents, but in others (Blackpool Conference Bureau or Kent Conference Bureau, for example) the bureau remains an integral part of the local authority structure.

Funding is derived from public sector contributions (usually the largest single source), private sector membership fees (members including venues of all kinds, accommodation providers, PCOs/DMCs, transport operators, audio-visual companies, and other kinds of suppliers), sponsorship, joint commercial activities with members, and, in some cases, commission which is charged to venue members on business placed. Some bureaux prefer to have a high membership fee which covers a full package of benefits and services to their members (with no or few hidden or extra charges). Other bureaux opt for a much lower membership fee which provides a core of benefits and then invite their members to buy into additional activities and services on a partnership basis. Both models have their strengths and weaknesses:

i) *High Membership Fee* – for the bureau, the high membership fee, which can amount to as much as £5000 per annum for large hotels, enables longer term planning to be undertaken with greater confidence, provided of course that the bureau can also achieve a high retention level amongst its membership. The bureau knows that it should receive a certain membership income in ensuing years and can plan its activities and expenditure accordingly. The high membership fee model also means that the bureau is not having to go back to its members on a regular basis to seek their financial support for particular activities during the year, which can be time-consuming for the bureau and a cause of irritation to its members. The weakness, or perhaps more accurately the challenge, of this funding model is the need to guarantee significant returns to members for their high investment in the bureau.

ii) *Lower Membership Fee* – this would typically be a membership fee of several hundred pounds (£500–£1000 is the normal range). For the bureau this can make it easier to 'sell' bureau membership to potential members because the initial outlay for them is much smaller. For bureau members there is greater flexibility in buying into those activities of the bureau (a stand at a trade exhibition or an entry in a piece of promotional print, for example) which are of most interest to them and which match their budgets. They do not have to buy into a full package of benefits, some of which they may not require. On the downside, there are significantly higher administrative costs with this model. It can also be argued with some justification that those members paying a lower membership fee may be less committed to the bureau than those who have paid a high fee and need to see the bureau succeed to justify their investment.

There is no right or wrong model. Each destination and the suppliers within it must agree what is appropriate for themselves and then develop and fine-tune the model in the light of experience. Bureaux are dynamic entities which must continue to evolve in the light of local circumstances, changes in market trends, the demands of clients, and a multitude of other factors (see also Chapter 9).

In the British Isles there are around 40 conference bureaux. Bureau is a generic term which, as has been seen, disguises a variety of models in terms of their staffing, funding and operations, although all share the same fundamental mission which, in the words of Gartrell (1994), is to:

> *solicit and service conventions and other related group business and to engage in visitor promotions which generate overnight stays for a destination, thereby enhancing and developing the economic fabric of the community.*

British conference bureaux have an average of three staff (typically a general manager, a sales executive, and an administrative assistant with IT skills), but the range is from just one member of staff up to 20. Case Study 4.2 describes the structure, resources, objectives and activities of Edinburgh Convention Bureau.

The concept of a convention and visitor bureau (CVB) is now widely adopted around the world. Bureaux in North America, for example, operate on a vastly different scale from the UK, largely because there is a longer tradition of CVBs (even relatively small towns have a CVB), with the world's first visitor and convention bureau, Detroit (or Metropolitan Detroit Convention and Visitor Bureau as it is now known) being established in 1896. In the USA bureaux are also funded differently, principally through a system of *hotel transient occupancy tax* (or bed tax) which means that hotel guests pay a tax which goes to the local city or town council, and can be added to the resources available to market the destination. In North America CVBs also play a prominent role at the centre of community life, being involved in a wide spectrum of community development issues which may impact on the future prosperity of the visitor industry. Case study 4.3 describes an innovative community partnership in the city of San José, California, in which the CVB plays a leading role. Team San José is a unique model which may highlight new forms of collaborative partnerships for other cities around the world.

The International Congress and Convention Association (ICCA) has a category of membership specifically for CVBs. Research is carried out into this category on a periodic basis. The 2002–2003 survey found that 60 per cent of these CVBs operated at a local city level, and 40 per cent at a national level (see later in this chapter for examples of a number of national bureaux). The research also found the average city convention bureau in Europe had eight staff, compared with an average of 14 in non-European bureaux. Net budgets for both averaged 1.8 million euros in 2003.

Convention and visitor bureaux provide a range of services, many free of charge, to conference organizers and meeting planners. They aim to offer a 'one-stop' enquiry point for their destination, with impartial advice and assistance (although there is increasing debate over whether their role should now be focused on steering customers towards the suppliers best able to meet their needs, rather than seeking to represent all of their suppliers in a comprehensive, unbiased way). Such CVB services are likely to include some or all of the following:

i) Pre-booking the event
- Literature and web site information
- Venue location and selection advice
- Availability checks
- Rate negotiation
- Provisional booking service
- Familiarization/inspection visits
- Preparation of bid documents
- Assistance with bid presentations to a selection committee/ board
- Assistance with civic hospitality requests.

ii) Preparing for the event
- Block accommodation booking service for delegates
- Co-ordination of the full range of support services including transportation, registration, translation, office support. In some cases these will be provided in conjunction with a professional conference organiser (PCO) or destination management company (DMC)
- Promotional and PR support to maximize delegate numbers and increase awareness of the event in the host destination
- Supply of delegate information
- Planning partner programmes, social programmes, and pre- and post-conference tours
- Arranging contact with local conference service companies and event organisers.

iii) During the event
- Provision of 'Welcome Desks' for delegates at major points of entry
- Civic welcome and recognition, and possible financial or in-kind support and subvention
- PR support
- Provision of tourist information.

iv) After the event
- Post-event evaluation and follow-up research
- Consultancy support to the destination which will next host the conference.

A typical portfolio of marketing activities for a British convention bureau will include some or all of the following, dependent upon staff and financial resources:

- **direct marketing** – particularly direct mail, but also telesales and, occasionally, with a sales person 'on the road'
- **web site and e-marketing** – promotion via a dedicated conference and business tourism web site and the use of electronic communications such as e-newsletters and email 'blasts'
- **print and audio-visual production** – compiling conference destination guides and other promotional print, as well as videos, DVDs/CD-Roms
- **exhibition attendance** – taking stands at trade shows such as International Confex, National Venue Show, EIBTM, IMEX
- **overseas trade missions** – participation in overseas roadshows and workshops, often organized by VisitBritain
- **familiarization visits** – organizing visits for groups of buyers and press representatives
- **receptions** – co-ordinating receptions, lunches, occasionally small workshops to which key clients, existing and potential, are invited
- **advertising** – in local and national press
- **public relations** – circulating information and releases to the media and often to influential community organizations
- **ambassador programmes** – identifying, recruiting, training and supporting key individuals in the local community (university academics, hospital professional staff, leading industrialists, members of the business community, trade unionists) as 'ambassadors' for the destination, assisting them to bid for and attract the annual conference of the professional institution or trade union to which they belong. Other variations of ambassador programmes aim to recognise and publicly acknowledge particular initiatives undertaken by companies and organizations designed to attract more conference business to the destination
- **supporting conference bids** – giving support to committees and associations bidding to bring a convention to their destination. This includes the provision of information for bid documents as well as personnel assistance with formal presentations to selection panels
- **financial assistance** – organizing civic receptions and other forms of financial or in-kind support to conferences which meet certain economic benefit criteria. Such support (often described as 'subvention') and criteria vary from destination to destination, and are usually only available to conferences in the 'not-for-profit' sector. Jersey Conference Bureau, for example, stipulates that, to attract subvention funding, a conference

(normally but not exclusively for an association or charitable organization), should:

- have a minimum duration of 2 nights
- have a minimum of 300 delegates
- ensure that, if the chosen venue is not owned by the States of Jersey, a maximum of 50 per cent of delegates stay in that venue.

Jersey's subvention policy includes funding for a maximum of 50 per cent of room hire charges, wine receptions (known in Jersey as 'vin d'honneurs') and air/sea tickets for site inspections. Every application for funding is scrutinised individually.

Conference offices and conference desks • • •

Conference offices (or conference desks) are normally established as part of a local authority's or a municipality's tourism marketing activity, where there is no convention bureau in operation. The staff, typically a conference officer with one assistant, are directly employed by the local authority/council and are usually located in a department involved with economic development or leisure services. In some cases they may share other staff resources (computer and administrative services, marketing, inward investment) available within the broader local authority structure.

Conference offices undertake many of the same marketing activities as convention bureaux, and offer similar services to conference and event organizers. The main differences between a conference office and convention bureau relate to structure and funding. A conference office does not have a formal membership, but it may co-ordinate the activities of a conference or tourism association within the destination, bringing together the main conference players to collaborate in joint marketing activities, for which financial or in-kind contributions are required. The conference office staff do not report to a management board but to managers and councillors within a local authority department and, where a conference association has been established, there is a need to report back to them as well on the success of the marketing programmes. The budget for the conference office is determined by the appropriate council committee, but is often supplemented by private sector contributions. Not infrequently, the conference officer may also have direct responsibility for the promotion of one or more civic buildings as conference venues. In the UK destinations such as Cambridge, Eastbourne, Newport and Swindon operate as a conference office or desk.

National destination marketing

The role of national conference destination marketing is undertaken by a variety of bodies which differ from country to country.

In some cases these bodies equate to a national convention bureau – and frequently contain the words 'convention bureau' in their name – and have many features in common with the city convention bureaux described earlier in this chapter. In other cases they are fully public sector organizations funded and administered within the central government structure.

The examples which follow, summarizing some of the leading national conference destination marketing organizations, highlight the variations which exist but also point to a number of common characteristics.

Australia: Team Australia • • •

Team Australia is an alliance of tourism leaders who combine the forces of Tourism Australia and Australia's leading convention bureaux (i.e. the 13 city and regional convention bureaux that are members of the Association of Australian Convention Bureaux (AACB)). It was formed (and formally launched in 1999) in the absence of a national convention bureau for Australia to assist in national marketing activity and position Australia as a Business Events destination.

Team Australia's objective is to encourage international corporations, associations and organizations to choose Australia as a destination for their meetings and events, and to do so through enhanced collaborative marketing for specific Business Events marketing projects. It involves branding Australia as a Business Events destination.

Team Australia was, therefore, formed to:

- Brand Australia as a Business Events destination
- Identify additional opportunities to grow the international market for Australia
- Identify the gaps in the current international marketing activities and resource activities to fill these gaps
- Improve dispersal of international business throughout Australia
- Increase the effectiveness of Australia's Business Events marketing efforts by collectively planning and resourcing projects
- Increase the resources being allocated to Australia's Business Events marketing efforts.

General management for projects is mainly undertaken by Tourism Australia's new division: Tourism Events Australia (www.event.australia.com). The most useful sources of additional information are probably the individual bureau members of AACB which may be contacted via the AACB web site: www.aacb.org.au. Further information on AACB itself is given in Chapter 8.

141

Canada: Canadian Tourism Commission • • •

The Canadian Tourism Commission (CTC) is a joint government-industry organization based in Vancouver that markets Canada as a four season destination to Canadian and international business and leisure travellers. The federal government of Canada created the CTC in 1995, replacing Tourism Canada, a government department, in response to the Canadian tourism industry's call for direct involvement in marketing Canada as a tourist destination. The CTC brings together people and resources from all levels of government – federal, provincial/territorial, and local – with the private sector and various local and regional tourism associations.

The Government of Canada contributes CA$83.7 million annually to the CTC. Private sector partners are expected to match this contribution, and have consistently done so, in some cases exceeding the Government contribution. The budget for the Meetings, Conventions and Incentive Travel (MC&IT) Program is approximately CA$8 million, of which CA$4.2 million is core CTC support and over CA$4 million is industry partnerships. A team of 12 in-market (on territory) MC&IT sales staff are dedicated to the US market (the largest for this sector), while in Europe, Asia and Latin America staff based in the CTC offices share their time also with the leisure market.

The MC&IT sector is one of the CTC's priority markets for several reasons:

- it provides an opportunity to attract a large number of visitors from a single organization
- it uses a wide variety of facilities and services and consequently gives a destination the opportunity to showcase the best it has to offer
- the year-round nature of the business enables Canadian venues and hotels to maximize occupancy levels throughout the year
- and the size, scope and number of organizations choosing Canada for meetings have meant that Canadian destinations have been able to expand their convention centres as well as the number and quality of hotel rooms.

The objectives of the CTC's MC&IT Program are:

- To continue to build awareness of Canada as a destination for convention, meeting and incentive travel buyers
- To influence consideration of Canada as a destination by building a relationship with qualified prospects
- To provide buyers with Canadian product information and the opportunity to move into the sales cycle
- To stimulate interest in lower-demand destinations during peak periods and shift demand for 'hot' destinations to shoulder seasons.

Target markets are:

- Corporate, association and incentive meeting/event planners
- Incentive houses
- Third-party planners (e.g. site selection companies, full service meeting planner companies)
- Sports associations
- The MC&IT industry itself.

European geographical market segments to be developed over the next few years include UK associations and incentives, French and German incentives.

Marketing activities include:

- *Multi-year strategic partnerships (U.S.)*: designed to cultivate sustainable demand for Canada as a first-tier meetings, conventions and incentive travel destination. Activities include national shows, regional education meetings with Canada as key sponsor themed against niche product awareness, board and committee representation, educational sponsorships, partnered research on customer and delegate behaviours, ongoing communications including re-engineering of advertising messages in organizations' publications to support in-market activities, qualification and maintenance of a national database detailing membership targets (noting both history and potential), with specific sales initiatives developed against those accounts.
- *Target marketing (U.S.)*: partner-led initiatives that expand and enhance the core programme and investment.
- *Direct mail/e-marketing*: customized direct marketing programmes using print and web-based media are designed to generate responses and requests for information on Canada's meeting destinations and to build the CTC MC&IT and partner databases.
- *Key account development*: creation and enhancement of working relationships with key meeting planners by the CTC's sales force and familiarization tours and site inspections under the 'Visit Canada Program'.
- *Trade shows and special events*: a Canadian presence at all major industry trade shows (such as ASAE, IT&ME, Affordable Meetings, MPI, PCMA, EIBTM) and hosting special marketplaces where Canadian suppliers are featured exclusively.
- *PR and media*: through activities linked to the CTC Leisure Marketing programmes, levering increased unpaid media exposure and public relations.

The CTC has sales staff located throughout the world with the aim of assisting meeting, convention and incentive planners in bringing their event to Canada. The staff can provide advice and suggestions on everything from customs to procedures, from site selection to conference facilities and to a wide variety of meeting and incentive services. If the organization meets the qualifying criteria, CTC sales staff can help to arrange familiarization tours to allow planners to experience Canada's destinations and facilities at first hand.

Further information: www.Canada.travel.

Finland: Finland Convention Bureau • • •

Finland Convention Bureau (FCB) is a not-for-profit marketing organization promoting Finland as a conference and incentive destination. The activities of the bureau are financed and sponsored by the Ministry of Trade and Industry, 16 major congress towns in various parts of the country and about 80 organizations representing the congress and travel industry (PCOs, conference centres, hotel chains, travel agencies, transport companies etc.).

The Bureau began operating in 1974 and at that time it was one of the first convention bureaux to set up in Europe. Until January 2002 the name of the Bureau was 'Helsinki-Finland Congress Bureau'. The Bureau has a staff of eight people.

The FCB:

• provides meeting planners with complimentary information on conference and incentive facilities and services in Finland
• assists organizers to find suitable venues, accommodation, and transport
• helps in preparing bid documents
• makes preliminary reservations
• provides promotional material, such as videos, slides and brochures.

The activities of the Bureau also include compiling information on international congresses and conventions taking place in Finland, undertaking studies and surveys, and preparing statistics.

The FCB works closely with international organizations of the meeting industry and is at the moment a member of European Cities Marketing, ICCA, MPI, UIA and SITE (see Chapter 8 for further details of these).

Publications: 'Meet in Finland' magazine, published three times a year.

Contact: Finland Convention Bureau, Fabianinkatu 4 B 11, Fin-00130 Helsinki, Finland.

Tel: +358-(0)9-668 9540, Fax: +358-(0)9-6689 5410; E-mail: info@ fcb.fi; Web site: www.fcb.fi.

France: Maison de la France and France Congrès • • •

Maison de la France began life as the 'Office Français du Tourisme' (French National Tourist Office) in 1925. The

French National Tourist Office became a 'Groupement d'Intérêt Economique' (G.I.E.) in 1987 and took the name of Maison de la France. Placed under the authority of the Ministry of Tourism, it represented a partnership between the State, the professionals in tourism, and the different sectors of the economy.

Maison de la France's mission is to promote the destination 'France' abroad for leisure tourism, conference & incentive travel, seminars, product launches and exhibitions. In 2005 France received 76 million foreign visitors generating tourism revenues of 34 billion euros.

As each market is special, Maison de la France helps its partners to promote their products and adapt them to each market. In order to cater effectively for a more demanding clientèle and to counter ever stronger international competition, Maison de la France has developed a network of 34 offices in 29 countries on five continents.

Promotional activity includes:

- Information to the public
- Press and P.R
- Commercial promotions: leisure tourism (with tour operators and agencies), conference & incentive agencies and corporates
- Publicity campaigns.

The Conference and Incentive Department of Maison de la France, operating as a national convention bureau, has three full-time staff at its head office in Paris; while its London office has three full-time staff and a trainee. There are also dedicated conference and incentive staff at the offices in the USA, Italy, Germany, Belgium and Spain. In addition, Maison de la France monitors 11 markets including Russia, China, Japan, South East Asia, and Brazil. The London office deals with the whole of England and helps the 160 members of the French Convention Bureau (which is their Conference & Incentive Club).

Maison de la France organizes one large event:

'Evènement France', which starts in Paris with the Bedouk MC&IT Exhibition. 200 conference and incentive agencies are invited by Maison de la France to meet French suppliers. Each delegation is then taken to different regions of France to participate in a 2½ day familiarization trip (team building, workshop, site visits, etc.).

Maison de la France has a large presence at trade shows such as International Confex, IMEX and EIBTM. Every year it hosts events such as the French Evening, a workshop for venue finders and French suppliers, and participates in the Eventia awards. Several familiarization trips are organized annually offering opportunities to meet suppliers specialising in conference and incentive travel from various regions of France.

In 2006, Maison de la France joined a consortium of 19 national tourist offices under the banner of 'Where the World is Your Oyster', and now participates in workshops totally dedicated to these destinations.

It produces a newsletter for the British market, with special offers and promotions, and one for the French market giving information on the British market, including updates on changes in conference and incentive agencies. Maison de la France maintains a very detailed agency database which is updated every year for the use of its partners. It also carries out research surveys and produces studies on the key conference/incentive sectors (automotive, pharmaceutical, IT, financial services).

Contact details: Maison de la France, 20 Avenue de L'Opéra, cedex 1, Paris, France. Tel: +33-1-42-96-70-95; Fax: +33-1-42-96-70-71; E-mail: tourisme.affaires@franceguide.com and for the French Convention Bureau: info.fcb.fr@franceguide.com Web site: www.franceguide.com/meetings

(As of May 2007, Maison de la France will be relocated in new offices in Paris. The web site detailed above will provide full contact information.)

Maison de la France, 178 Piccadilly, London, W1J 9AL. Tel: +44-(0)20-7399-3507; E-mail: info.fcb.uk@franceguide.com

In France there is also a body known as France Congrès. France Congrès was formed in 1965 when ten towns and cities joined forces to open an office in Paris in order to provide information, advice and promotional materials for corporate and association conference organizers. Membership of France Congrès now comprises 50 towns and cities in which the public and private sectors are working together to attract more conference and conventions business. The main activities of France Congrès now include:

- the provision of information on the products and services offered by its members
- research activity through studies and statistical reviews to enhance industry data
- initiatives to improve quality standards in conference centres and venues
- networking and the maximization of synergies with the industry's professional bodies
- representation to increase awareness of business tourism in both public and private sectors and to support its growth.

France Congrès operates in partnership with the Tourism Directorate, Maison de la France, DIACT (the French national and regional development agency), the Paris Visitors and Convention Bureau, ODIT France and other members of the business tourism industry (such as Traiteurs de France – the French Caterers' Association, SNCF French railways) to support the development of the industry.

Further information: www.france-congres.org.

Germany: German Convention Bureau • • •

The German Convention Bureau (GCB) markets Germany as a destination for conventions, meetings, events and incentives both on a national and international level. The GCB was founded in 1973. It is a not-for-profit organization and has around 200 members which include leading hotels, convention centres and destinations, car hire firms, event agencies and service providers to the German meetings and convention industry.

The GCB is an interface between organizers of meetings and conventions and suppliers from the German meetings and conference market. It offers advice and support for planning and organizing events, and provides contacts and addresses. The GCB was established to market Germany as a conference location and to provide impartial advice and suggestions to meeting planners concerning facilities, sites, accommodation, and programmes in Germany. It is based in Frankfurt with 13 staff and also has an overseas office in New York.

The GCB arranges conference services in Germany for clients around the world. It also works in close co-operation with German representatives of international associations and organizations and with meeting planners of associations, agencies and companies from abroad. Its web site features an online search facility for meeting venues, a newsletter, a Germany guide and more.

The GCB is also the strategic partner with IMEX, the 'Worldwide Exhibition for incentive travel, meetings and events', held in Frankfurt each Spring.

Contact details: German Convention Bureau e.V., Münchener Strasse 48, 60329 Frankfurt/Main, Germany. Tel: +49 (0)69 24 29 30 0: Fax: +49 (0)69 24 29 30 26; E-mail: info@gcb.de; Web site: www.germany-meetings.com.

Hong Kong: Hong Kong Tourism Board • • •

Conference destination marketing for Hong Kong is undertaken by a specialist team within the Hong Kong Tourism Board (HKTB). The Board plays an impartial role in representing all tourism products and services, including conference venues, hotels, tour operators, PCOs/DMCs, and retailers.

HKTB's specialist convention and incentives team is headquartered in Hong Kong but also has three dedicated overseas teams based in Los Angeles, Sydney and London. The work of the teams is divided into two sections, one to cover incentive travel and corporate meetings, the other to research for association events and exhibitions. HKTB has a further 16 offices worldwide which can assist in the planning and promotion of events to be held in Hong Kong.

The specialist team offers impartial advice and practical assistance to conference organizers at every stage of planning their events, including:

1. Production of bid documents.
2. Identification of suitable venues and selection of accommodation.
3. Co-ordination of inspections of conference facilities by decision makers.
4. Sourcing reliable service suppliers such as airlines, PCOs, exhibition contractors.
5. Suggestions for social, sightseeing or accompanying persons' programmes.
6. 'Value Plus' – an added value benefits package for all confirmed international association conventions and for exhibitions which, depending on group size, can include welcome packs for delegates, a discount card, lion dance, or police band to open or close a convention.
7. Ideas and contacts for gifts and convention materials suppliers.
8. Promotions to delegates to maximize attendance, and participation in planning committees.
9. Advising on customs and immigration procedures.

HKTB offers a wide range of promotional material, including 'Meeting Your Choice' video, 'Coming Conventions & Exhibitions' (details of confirmed events up to 2010), 'Venues' (a guide listing different types of venue with capacity details, etc), 'Conventions and Exhibitions' leaflet (giving facts and figures of Hong Kong's selling points), CD-Roms, presentation materials and shell posters.

Contact details: Business Development Unit, Hong Kong Tourism Board, 9-11/F. Citicorp Centre, 18 Whitfield Road, North Point, Hong Kong. Tel: +852-2807-6543; Fax: +852-2806-0303; Web site: www.DiscoverHongKong.com/eng/meetings.

London office: Hong Kong Tourism Board, 6 Grafton Street, London W1S 4EQ Tel: +44-207-533-7100; Fax: +44-207-533-7111; E-mail: *hchan@hktb.com.*

Ireland ● ● ●

Tourism Ireland

Tourism marketing structures in Ireland have undergone major change, leading to the creation of Tourism Ireland as a new organization marketing the island of Ireland overseas as a holiday destination in a new era.

Tourism Ireland was established under the framework of the Belfast Agreement of Good Friday 1998. As a company, its two goals are:

- to promote increased tourism to the island of Ireland
- to support the industry in Northern Ireland to reach its potential.

Jointly funded by the two governments, South and North on a 2:1 ratio, Tourism Ireland has been fully operational since the beginning of 2002 when it launched an extensive programme to market the entire island overseas as a tourism destination.

In addition to the company's primary strategic destination marketing role, Tourism Ireland also undertakes regional/product marketing and promotional activities on behalf of Fáilte Ireland (Irish Tourist Board) and the Northern Ireland Tourist Board through its 18 international market offices.

Product marketing includes conferences, meetings and incentive travel, necessitating close collaboration with the two existing bodies involved with MICE sector marketing, the Business Tourism Unit of the Northern Ireland Tourist Board and the Convention Bureau of Ireland, further details of which are given below.

Tourism Ireland may be contacted at:

i) Tourism Ireland, 5th Floor, Bishop's Square, Redmond's Hill, Dublin 2. Tel: +353 1 476 3400; Fax: +353 1 476 3666; E-mail: info@tourismireland.com.
ii) Tourism Ireland, 103 Wigmore Street, London W1U 1QS. Tel: +44 207 518 0800; Fax: +44 207 493 9065; E-mail: gbbt@tourismireland.com.

Northern Ireland Tourist Board Business Tourism Unit

The Business Tourism Unit of the Northern Ireland Tourist Board was established in 2004 (having previously operated as the Northern Ireland Conference Bureau since 1994). The Northern Ireland Tourist Board (NITB) is the statutory organization responsible for encouraging and developing tourism in Northern Ireland. NITB, in turn, is responsible to the Department of Enterprise, Trade and Investment for Northern Ireland (DETI). NITB has highlighted business tourism as one of its 'winning themes' within its Strategic Framework for Action 2004–2007.

The Business Tourism Unit (BTU), as part of the national tourist board, is wholly funded by the Government, although the industry in Northern Ireland pays to participate in marketing activities, generating additional operating income. The Unit has a team consisting of a manager, international sales person, domestic business tourism officer and administrative backup. With the establishment of Tourism Ireland, however, the Unit also has representation through 18 overseas market offices.

The BTU's main role is to provide strategic leadership and support the activities of the two city convention bureaux in Belfast and Derry and the regional tourism partnerships (RTPs) to attract conference, association and incentive business to Northern Ireland. In this regard, the Unit works to co-ordinate a positive market awareness of Northern Ireland, through exhibition participation, web site promotion, familiarization and inspection visits, assistance in kind and by providing a link to suppliers of conference services. The Northern Ireland presence at international exhibitions is as part of an all-Ireland stand. In September 2006 the first ever Northern Ireland 'Business Tourism Expo' was held which attracted 40 international buyers to Northern Ireland for business meetings and familiarization visits.

The Unit continues to work with conference organizers and meeting and incentive planners once they have made a formal decision to meet in Northern Ireland, ensuring that they have the necessary information and contacts to run a successful event. It advises organizers on the logistics of meeting in Northern Ireland and on the marketing of the destination to potential delegates.

Contact details: Business Tourism Unit, Northern Ireland Tourist Board, St Anne's Court, 59 North Street, Belfast BT1 1NB Tel: +44-(0)28-90-441676; Fax: +44-(0)28-90-441615; E-mail: businesstourism@nitb.com; Web site: www.discovernorthernireland.com/convention.

Business Tourism Unit, Fáilte Ireland

The Business Tourism Unit is a specialist section in the Product Marketing Department of Fáilte Ireland. It focuses on the marketing of conferences and incentive travel in partnership with the trade in Ireland. A Business Tourism Forum, made up of ten industry representatives, oversees the marketing activities undertaken by Fáilte Ireland and acts as an information exchange forum for trade specializing in these sectors.

The main marketing activities are:

- participation at overseas promotions such as Motivation (Chicago), EIBTM (Barcelona), and IMEX (Frankfurt) and co-ordinating Irish trade attendance
- production of marketing material
- organizing and supporting familiarization visits and site inspections by overseas incentive houses or conference organizers

- supporting conference ambassadors in their efforts to secure conferences for Ireland (*see below*)
- maintaining an all island web site (www.irelandinspires.com) to assist organizers with their planning of conferences and meetings in Ireland. The site contains an extensive database of available facilities.

A new business development plan is in place for the conference and incentive sectors with trade working groups for each to oversee implementation. It includes the roll-out of a new brand for business tourism in Ireland. A budget in excess of two million euros is allocated by Fáilte Ireland to business tourism marketing campaigns.

Increased funding has enabled the 'Conference Ambassador' partnership to be revived. This programme is aimed at encouraging Irish members of international associations or employees of multi-national companies to use their influence in attracting conferences and meetings to Ireland. It entails:

- a direct mail piece to targeted top executives in Irish-based international companies and senior Irish executives in companies located in Britain and the USA. Each mailing is followed by a telephone call and/or direct meeting
- presentations to leading Irish business associations to publicize the scheme i.e. Chambers of Commerce, marketing associations, etc.
- support to Conference Ambassadors includes help with organizing a national invitation and bid documents, support with site inspections, literature and promotional material, and garnering support from Government/State agencies where appropriate.

Contact details: Business Tourism Unit, Fáilte Ireland, Amiens Street, Dublin 1, Ireland. Tel: +353-1-884-7700; Fax: +353-1-855-6821; E-mail: businesstourism@failteireland.com; Web site: www.irelandinspires.com.

Japan: Japan Convention Bureau • • •

Convention and incentive travel promotion is the responsibility of the Japan Convention Bureau (JCB), a specialist department of the Japan National Tourist Organisation (JNTO). The JCB was first established in 1965 as a joint initiative with local public entities and other interested parties, and was merged with JNTO the following year.

In 1994 the Japanese Diet (parliament) approved a special law called the 'International Convention Promotion Law'. JNTO has subsequently restructured its Japan Convention Bureau to establish a cooperative relationship with government-designated

'International Convention Cities' which are keen to attract more international meetings and events.

The reorganized Japan Convention Bureau comprises two departments in JNTO's head office in Tokyo: International Marketing Department, and Promotion & Support Department, the latter being responsible for domestic marketing within Japan. Operating alongside these two departments are three overseas marketing offices, New York, Seoul and London, all staffed by convention specialists. Additionally, a Convention Manager has been appointed from the directorial/managerial staff of JNTO's 14 overseas offices to create a worldwide marketing network to promote Japan as an international convention destination.

In 1995, Japan Congress and Convention Bureau (JCCB) was established with the aim of promoting Japan as a location for international conventions and developing the convention industries in Japan. JCCB is composed of convention cities, convention bureaux, convention-related industries, the Ministry of Transport and JNTO. JNTO provides the Secretariat office and JCB the staff for JCCB's operation. There are currently 38 'International Convention Cities' in Japan. This list does not include Tokyo, even though Tokyo is one of Japan's leading international meeting destinations, partly because the city does not possess a convention bureau or specialist business tourism department but chiefly because the main aim of the Bureau's convention promotional activities is to achieve the decentralisation of international meeting traffic.

Japan Convention Bureau is not a membership organization but its activities are partly funded by annual contributions from the 38 International Convention Cities. These are set contributions, at two levels, depending on the size of the cities concerned.

Marketing activities include market research and the publication of statistics, participation in convention industry trade shows, organising sales missions to the USA and Europe, coordinating an annual study tour (familiarization visit), advertising, producing a detailed guide 'Convention Destination Japan', as well as newsletters and events calendars.

Contact details: Japan Convention Bureau, 2-10-1, Yuraku-cho, Chiyoda-ku, Tokyo 100, Japan. Tel: 03-3216-2905; Fax: 03-3216-1978; E-mail: convention@jnto.go.jp; Web site: www.jnto.go.jp/MI/eng/.

London office: Japan Convention Bureau, Heathcoat House, 20 Savile Row, London W1S 3PR (Tel: 44 207-439-3458; Fax: 44-207 734-4290; E-mail: chad@jnto.co.uk.)

Korea: Korea Convention Bureau ● ● ●

The Korea Convention Bureau (KCB) was established originally in 1979 as an International Meetings Department under the umbrella of the Korea National Tourism Organization.

Its principal responsibility is for national destination marketing, including bidding for events and implementing market surveys. The work of the KCB is complemented by that of the Korea Convention Event Industry Association (KCA), formed in 2003, which plays a major role in education and training, information and networking, and the management of industry databases.

In the 1990s the South Korean government recognized the importance of the convention industry and began to seek ways to support and enhance it. This led to the creation of a legal framework and the passing of the 'Law on Promoting the International Meeting Industry' in 1998. This law has subsequently been revised on several occasions to meet a variety of needs, identified as the industry itself has grown.

A 'screening committee' operates involving central government ministers, designed to encourage collaboration over the holding of conventions. At the same time, the Ministry of Culture and Tourism oversees a 'Convention Industry Promotional Committee' as well as an 'Advisory Committee for the Convention Industry', all of which function within this legal framework.

Certification of meeting planners has been in operation since 2003 and, by 2006, 290 qualified professionals (with the MPI designation Certified Meeting Planner – see Chapter 7) were working within the Korean convention sector. In addition there were over 160 registered PCOs.

By 2005, four cities had achieved the designation of 'convention cities': Seoul, Busan, Daegu and Jeju. This designation entitles them to priority support from central government through access to a 'Tourism Promotion Fund', set up to help cities develop their convention facilities and thus host more successful events which, in turn, lead to greater economic benefits and a stimulus to local economies. The 'Tourism Promotion Fund' was worth US$159,448 000 in 2004 and US$213,289 000 in 2005. Up to 10 per cent of this Fund can be used in support of the convention industry.

'Convention City' status also means reduced regulations for the cities' convention businesses.

Korea has seven purpose-built convention centres, with two more, in Daejeon and Songdo, due to open in 2007 and 2008 respectively.

Destination marketing is undertaken at both a local level (by CVBs) and at a national level by KCB. In 2006 five CVBs were operational: Seoul, Busan, Daegu, Jeju and Daejeon. Promotional activity includes web site marketing, PR, and video/CD production.

Korea's growing success in the international convention arena is demonstrated by the positions achieved in the UIA rankings (see Chapter 1 for full details): in 2005 it was 14th in the world's top 50 countries (staging 185 conventions compared with 124 in 2002). The UIA data also show Seoul in 9th position among the leading international cities.

Further information

Korea Convention Bureau, 40 Chungyechun Ro, Junggoo, Seoul, Korea Tel: 82-2-729-9551; Web site:

http://community.etourkorea.com/koreaconvention/.

Korea Convention Event Industry Association, 5th Floor, Seocho Joonang Plaza, 1687-2, Seocho Dong, Seocho Gu, Seoul, Korea. Tel: +82 2 3476 8325 7; Fax: +82 2 3476 8449; Web sites: www.conventionassociation.org, www.kceia.org.

Spain: Turespaña (Spain Tourism Board) and Spain Convention Bureau • • •

Turespaña is a central government-run body under the auspices of the Ministry of Industry, Tourism and Commerce. It does not, therefore, have a membership structure and its staff are mostly civil servants.

Meetings and Incentive Travel is one of the sectors or products on which Turespaña concentrates its resources (the others being Sun and Beach, Sports and Nature, and Cultural Tourism), although it has only had this involvement since 1994. Promotional activity is undertaken in conjunction with the 31 Spanish Tourist Offices overseas (20 in Europe, eight in America, one each in Japan, China and Singapore), which assist with the provision of local market research and intelligence. Each overseas office has a business travel specialist dedicated to Meetings and Incentive Travel.

Meetings and Incentive Travel sector promotional activities include organizing the participation of the Spanish public and private sectors in international exhibitions, organizing business workshops, and co-ordinating familiarization visits in partnership with local authorities, convention bureaux or regional governments. Publications include 'Spain Land of Congresses', a comprehensive guide giving full details of the main conference facilities and support services offered by individual cities. Turespaña has developed a major web site offering full information on Spain and its tourism facilities: www.spain.info.

Contact details: Turespaña, C/ José Lázaro Galdiano 6, 28036 Madrid, Spain. Tel: +34-91-343-35-00; Fax: +34-91-343-34-46; E-mail: info@tourspain.es.

The Spain Convention Bureau (SCB) is a not-for-profit body with 41 cities (as at November 2006) in membership, representing over 800 conference, meeting and incentive venues. SCB is part of the Spanish Federation of Towns and Provinces (FEMP). SCB's role includes developing the quality of Spain's conference and business tourism offer. It also produces research on the size and value of the sector (see Chapter 3), and engages in promotional activity in support of its member cities.

Further information: www.scb.es.

United Kingdom • • •

Within the United Kingdom, there are two national conference marketing organizations: VisitBritain, operating primarily
in overseas markets but also responsible for England marketing
through Meet England, and the British Association of Conference
Destinations (see Chapter 8), operating principally in the domestic marketplace. Scotland, Wales and Northern Ireland also have
their own national conference bureaux, subsumed within their
national tourist boards, while the islands of Guernsey, Jersey
and the Isle of Man also have independent conference marketing
organizations.

VisitBritain and Meet England

VisitBritain, a government agency (or 'non-Departmental public
body') responsible to the Department for Culture, Media and
Sport, is the official, non-profit-making body charged with the
promotion in overseas markets of Britain, and within Britain of
England, as a leisure and business tourism destination. It also has
a general responsibility for advising the Government on tourism
matters.

Facts & Figures:

- The grant-in-aid to promote Britain overseas during 2005–2006
  was £35.2 million
- The grant-in-aid to promote England domestically during
  2005–2006 was £12.4 million
- The grant-in-aid to promote England internationally during
  2005–2006 was £1 million
- The grant-in-aid included a capital element of £300 000 in
  2005–2006
- In addition VisitBritain generated £19.5m of non-government
  funding in 2005–2006.

It maintains a network of 35 overseas offices in 26 markets.

The Office for National Statistics produced figures from the
International Passenger Survey for 2005 showing the following
key results in relation to inbound business visits:

- 8.17 million business visits were made during 2005 contributing
  over £4 billion in spend
- 2005 overall business visits were up by 9 per cent and spend
  was up by 10 per cent on 2004 figures
- Business trade fair/exhibition visits were up by 21 per cent,
  with corresponding spend up by 9 per cent on 2004 figures
- Conference/Large Meeting visits were up by 17 per cent and
  spend was up by 23 per cent on 2004 figures

- With 1.08 million business visitors, Germany was the country with the highest number of business visitors visiting the UK, followed by France (1 million), the USA (0.80 million), and the Netherlands (0.65 million)
- Spending £799 million, the USA was the top country for business spend during 2005, followed by Germany (£316 million), France (£234 million), Italy (£183 million) and the Irish Republic (£183 million)
- London was the top destination for business visits with 3.18 million visits during 2005, contributing £2.18 billion in spend.

VisitBritain has a dedicated Business Visits and Events Department at its headquarters in London, with a staff complement of seven: Head of Business Visits and Events, two Managers (one for Meet England and one for Britain International) and four Marketing Executives (one for international associations and events, two for Britain International and one for Meet England). There are also a number of specialist Business Visits and Events personnel in key VisitBritain overseas offices around the world. Overseas office staff report directly to their own office/regional managers, although of necessity there is close and regular collaboration with the Business Visits and Events department in London.

The Business Visits and Events Department's activities include:

- encouraging international associations, corporate meetings and incentives to hold their events in Britain
- identifying and converting major sporting and cultural events to choose Britain as their destination
- initiating or supporting research into the conference, incentive and exhibition sectors and maintenance of appropriate databases
- publishing promotional print and directories, as well as advisory materials (including market intelligence) and information for the British trade
- supporting UK destination bids for international events
- co-ordination of workshops in Britain to which overseas buyers and decision-makers are invited, providing an opportunity for one-to-one meetings with the UK business visits and events industry
- co-ordination of British participation in overseas missions, trade fairs (such as 'EIBTM' (Barcelona) and 'IMEX' (Frankfurt) and presentations (participants include other UK national marketing organizations, namely VisitScotland, Visit London, Northern Ireland Conference Bureau and Visit Wales)
- developing Meet England campaigns (such as corporate hospitality, or city campaigns)
- co-ordinating press trips, familiarization trips and site inspections

- ensuring maximum publicity for business visits and events marketing opportunities offered by VisitBritain's overseas offices
- providing a business visits and events destination PR service to targeted business tourism and professional media worldwide, both directly and through the VisitBritain overseas offices
- promoting and maintaining a specific business visits and events web site www.visitbritain.com/business
- distributing e-communications to the UK business travel industry and a database of overseas buyers and intermediaries.

Contact details: VisitBritain, Business Visits and Events Department, Thames Tower, Black's Road, London W6 9EL. Tel: +44-(0)20-8846 9000; Fax: +44-(0)20-8563-3257; E-mail: *businesstourism @visitbritain.org*; Web site: www.visitbritain.com/business.

VisitScotland

VisitScotland is the national tourist board for Scotland and, as such, is the strategic lead body responsible for all aspects of destination marketing both in terms of business tourism and leisure tourism.

VisitScotland has a total of around 1130 staff (full-time and part-time), and operates with an annual budget of approx £66 million. Grant aid from the Scottish Executive provides around 60 per cent of this funding, with 10 per cent coming from local authorities (or municipalities) and the remainder from commercial income.

This budget is used to deliver the following core objectives across both the business and leisure tourism sectors:

- Attract visitors by building a successful Scottish tourism brand
- Engage and work in partnership with the tourism industry
- Enhance the visitor experience
- Provide strategic direction to the industry.

In 2005 it was decided by the Scottish Executive that Scotland would be best served by replacing the 14 former Area Tourism Boards with an integrated VisitScotland network. This national network, with 14 area offices, was set up to function as a single point of contact for tourism businesses and to act as one team for Scotland. In addition, there are four city convention bureaux (Glasgow, Edinburgh, Aberdeen and Dundee) charged with promoting their respective cities for conferences and business events.

It is the ambition of VisitScotland, working in partnership with the Scottish tourism industry, to increase the value of tourism to the Scottish economy by 50 per cent by 2015. In recognition of its growth potential, targets for business tourism are even more stretching, with 75 per cent growth projected over the same period. Scotland's national strategy and activities for promoting the country as a business tourism destination are overseen by VisitScotland's Business Tourism Unit (BTU), which was set up in 2003 and superseded the previous Scottish Convention Bureau.

Over the past few years, the BTU has emerged through a period of transition in which it has re-scoped its objectives and activities and increased its capacity to deliver. The principal objective of the BTU is to grow the volume and value of discretionary business tourism to Scotland. Specifically the BTU focuses on the following core markets:

- Association conventions
- Corporate conferences/meetings
- Incentive programmes.

Its programme of targeted marketing activities aims:

- to build strong brand awareness of Scotland as a business tourism destination
- to increase buyers' knowledge of Scotland's facilities for business events
- to provide routes to market for Scottish business tourism suppliers through a wide range of marketing opportunities
- to operate a free and impartial enquiry service for potential clients
- to undertake research to better understand and meet buyer requirements.

The BTU has a total staff of 16, including 9 based in the Edinburgh office, a dedicated representative in the VisitScotland London office, and regional managers throughout Scotland. The BTU also has overseas representation through BTU contractual relationships with sales and/or PR agencies (North America, Germany, Spain, Sweden, France), or through VisitBritain's office network.

The BTU's annual operating budget (including staffing) is approx £2.85m. The BTU's budget has doubled since the BTU's formation, as has the size of the team. Of this total, approx £430 000 is generated by the commercial activities of the BTU.

Contact details: VisitScotland Business Tourism, Ocean Point One, 94 Ocean Drive, Edinburgh EH6 6JH. Tel: 44-(0)131-472-2355; Fax: 44-(0)131-472-2009; E-mail: businesstourism@visitscotland.com; Web site: www.conventionscotland.com.

Visit Wales

On April 1st 2006 the Wales Tourist Board merged with the Welsh Assembly Government (WAG) and now forms part of the Tourism and Marketing Division within the Department of

	UK		Wales	
	Trips (m)	Spend (£m)	Trips (m)	Spend (£m)
Domestic visitors	22.5	5251	1.3	336
Overseas visitors	8.2	4055	0.2	68
TOTAL	30.7	9306	1.5	404

Source: UK Tourism Survey and International Passenger Survey.

Table 4.4
Wales' Share of Business
Tourism in the UK 2005

Enterprise Innovation and Networks (formerly the Economic Development Department of WAG), under the name of Visit Wales.

The merger has strengthened the Business Tourism Unit (first established in the early 1990s) which is part of the Events, Sponsorship and Business Tourism Division within Visit Wales Marketing. The Business Tourism Team now has three dedicated staff: Senior Marketing Executive, Sales & Marketing Executive and Marketing Assistant, plus the Head of Division.

An evaluation of the Visit Wales business tourism campaign for the financial year to the end of 2006 showed that an additional £30 million was spent in the Welsh economy as a direct result of the campaign.

Table 4.4 provides a summary of data from the International Passenger Survey and the UK Tourism Survey to show the value of business tourism to Wales over the 5-year period 2000–2005. It should be noted that these statistics do not include visits which have no residential element (ie. one-day conferences and meetings involving no overnight stay are excluded), and so they do not represent the total value and impact of business tourism in Wales.

Visit Wales Business Class Award Scheme

Visit Wales has developed a Business Class Award Scheme, which assesses meeting/conference facilities and bedroom accommodation for the business tourist.

Meeting spaces and bedrooms are graded separately and according to a list of specified criteria. The bedroom criteria range from having an uncluttered and adequate workspace and an express or early checkout through to having fax, e-mail access and voicemail in the bedroom. Meeting rooms, meanwhile, are judged on their soundproofing, pa systems, lighting, high speed internet access and video conference facilities among others. To be considered for the Award, serviced accommodation must first attain at least three stars in the Visit Wales or AA grading scheme. The scheme has three progressive levels – Silver, Gold and Platinum.

Marketing platforms

Visit Wales offers a number of marketing and promotional opportunities in support of the business tourism industry in Wales. These include:

- advertising opportunities in Visit Wales' Conference and Incentive Guides and on its web site (www.meetings.visit wales.com)
- a range of exhibition and workshop packages enabling attendance at events within a branded Welsh area, linked with pre-event marketing and post-event follow-up activities
- support to develop ambassador programmes designed to win association business for the country
- handling enquiries (250–500 per annum) and passing leads to local conference bureaus or to venues
- maintenance of a database of around 5000 buyer contacts
- direct mailing of publications, newsletter and promotional offers to database plus rentable lists
- familiarization trips for buyers and press
- liaison with dedicated marketing agency and PR agency in the UK, and with a US-based PR consultant.

In addition to the marketing activities listed, Visit Wales also supports the development of business tourism by:

- providing financial assistance to some of the local conference bureaux for joint marketing schemes
- undertaking research into the business tourism sector and providing statistics
- providing funding to upgrade hotels to business class standard.

Contact details: Visit Wales, Business Tourism Unit, Brunel House, 2 Fitzalan Road, Cardiff CF24 0UY. Tel: +44 (0)29 2047 5237; Fax: +44 (0)29 2047 5321;

E-mail: business-tourism@wales.gsi.gov.uk; Web sites: www. meetings.visitwales.com.

United States of America • • •

There is no national umbrella marketing organization in the USA responsible for promotion to the conference and conventions sector. Marketing activity is undertaken by individual cities/destinations, often working in partnership with their State tourism body. In other cases, the State tourism body takes the lead in promotions.

CONFERENCE VENUE MARKETING

It is very difficult for an individual conference venue to market itself effectively by operating on its own. Venues seeking to establish a market presence must contend with factors such as the scale of the competition (several thousand other venues in Britain alone), the substantial costs of marketing (both in human and financial resources), and the predisposition of buyers to buy location first.

It is for these reasons that most venues work in partnership with the destination in which they are located to generate awareness and enquiries from potential clients. The venues build links with the appropriate destination marketing organization, be this a convention and visitor bureau or conference office, an area or regional tourist board, and/or a national tourism organization. Many venues are also members of marketing consortia (groupings of similar properties interested in the same types of clients) which give them a higher market profile and through which they engage in collaborative marketing activities. Consortia can also provide tangible business benefits such as bulk purchasing discounts, networking, benchmarking and training. Belonging to a consortium can also give a venue credibility in the eyes of the buyer. Examples of major consortia operating in the conference industry include:

- **hotel groups** such as Hilton, Accor, Six Continents, Marriott, Starwood Hotels & Resorts, Thistle, and Sol Meliá. These are not strictly consortia as they are groups of hotels under common ownership and management systems. Most, if not all, have central reservations and marketing departments which undertake national and international marketing campaigns and which control the promotional activities of the individual properties to a greater or lesser degree. Even so, the majority of hotels within these chains are also allowed some discretion and budget to engage in their own marketing campaigns, for which the broad strategy and promotional materials are determined by head office. Over recent years, all of the large chains have developed their own branded conference product (see the next section in this chapter on the 'branding of hotel venues')
- **Best Western Hotels**. Best Western claims to be the world's largest global hotel brand, established for more than 50 years, with over 4100 independently owned and operated hotels in membership worldwide (covering 80 countries). It is a non-profit making organization whose sole purpose is to enhance the success and profitability of its member hotels. It has reservations centres in four countries with fully automated links to global distribution systems. Its recruitment brochure states that: *'Best Western brand markets to, and attracts, a bigger universe of customers than any single property on its own could ever hope to reach'*. For the conference and meetings market, 'Best Western

161

First Place' is the consortium's venue sourcing service. Best Western Hotels also offers joint marketing opportunities for its members, such as a presence at trade shows like 'International Confex'. For more information: www.bestwestern.com

- **Unique Venues** is a grouping of over 7000 non-traditional meeting facilities and function rooms in the USA, Canada and the United Kingdom: colleges, universities, museums, mansions, cinemas or movie theatres, conference centres, entertainment venues, cruise ships, restaurants, business centres and others. In this case, the common theme is the individuality or uniqueness of the venues involved, with a particular focus on their ambiance, memorability, flexibility, technology and affordability. Unique Venues has administrative offices in Colorado, Pennsylvania and South Carolina (USA). Further details can be accessed via: www.uniquevenues.org

- **Conference Centres of Excellence (CCE)** is Britain's largest consortium of dedicated, specialist conference and training venues, with some 41 venues in membership (as at March 2006). It was formed in 1992, with objectives to:

- undertake joint marketing through pooling marketing resources
- share PR activity designed to enhance the image of management centres in membership
- investigate opportunities to market the centres in mainland Europe
- share information and expertise.

One of the main aims of CCE has been to promote and market the unique benefits of conference venues that offer first-class facilities and professional standards (making comparison with other venues that do not dedicate staff or facilities to the business conference, meeting or training sector). Members are required to meet certain minimum criteria, which include 'actively seeking to attract conference, meeting or training events as their main Monday-Friday source of business'. Criteria are also laid down to cover the standard of conference rooms, bedrooms and other facilities provided. Members are also expected to participate in the Consortium's booking referral system and to promote its hotline 'One Call'. Would-be member venues are required to submit to inspection by the CCE's membership committee before being accepted into membership.

Whilst users of the CCE venues are guaranteed to receive excellent service in quality surroundings, the individual nature of the member properties offers contrasting atmospheres ranging from country houses in beautiful settings to purpose-built centres often attached to academia.

Further information: www.cceonline.co.uk (Tel: +44 (0)1306 886900).

Other examples of venue consortia include: Historic Conference Centres of Europe (www.hcce.com) and Leading Hotels of the World (www.lhw.com).

THE BRANDING OF HOTEL VENUES

In the early 1990s Forte Hotels (now broken up and sold off among other hotel groups) pioneered a branded conference product when it launched 'Venue Guarantee' as a standard package available at conference hotels across the Forte Group. Since then most, if not all, the major hotel chains have introduced their own conference brand, examples being: 'Hilton Meetings' and 'Hilton Conventions' (Hilton), 'Meeting Edge' (Marriott), 'The Academy' (Holiday Inn), 'Rendezvous@Novotel' (Accor) and 'Meeting Plan' (Thistle).

There are certain variations in each branded product, with some laying emphasis on high-specification, purpose-designed conference and meeting rooms, whereas others place the focus on bookability and the level of service. Overall, however, there is more common ground than distinctive features in these products, which are usually accompanied by a money-back guarantee if a hotel fails to deliver on any aspect of its quality-assured service. An example of a hotel group's conference brand is the 'MEETING@MACDONALDHOTELS&RESORTS' product shown in Figure 4.2.

Davidson and Rogers (2006) suggest that hotel chains' use of branding has

> brought them a considerable measure of brand equity in the form of the four major assets described by Aaker's (1991) model of consumer-based brand equity, as explored in Pike (2004):
>
> Brand loyalty – repeat and referral custom, arising from the desire for a reduced risk of an unsatisfactory experience.
>
> Brand awareness – the foundation of all sales activity. Awareness represents the strength of the brand's presence in the mind of the target. There is general agreement that planners' familiarity with hotels' meetings facilities' brands has increased through repeated exposure and strong associations.
>
> Perceived quality – there is little point in branding any product that is of poor or variable quality.
>
> Brand associations – A brand association is anything 'linked' in memory to a brand. These associations are a combination of functional and affective attributes, of which some will represent key buying criteria. 'What is most critical is that brand associations are strong, favorable and unique, in that order' (Keller 2003, quoted in Pike, 2004).

MEETING @
MACDONALD HOTELS & RESORTS

WHENEVER YOU BOOK WITH MEETING @ MACDONALD HOTELS & RESORTS YOU CAN BE CONFIDENT IN OUR COMMITMENT TO EFFICIENCY, FLEXIBILITY AND QUALITY OF SERVICE.

ENQUIRY HANDLING

Our dedicated Conference Direct team are committed to handling your enquiry within:

- 20 minutes response for single venue
- 60 minutes for multi venues

Should you contact the hotels direct, then we are committed to a response within 90 minutes.

A written proposal will be provided within 2 hours via email or fax, or 24 hours by post with an invitation to visit the hotel.

PRICING

Transparent pricing with no hidden extra costs.

ON THE DAY

Whether it's a conference, meeting or special event you can expect a Concierge service for the Organiser and a dedicated Meeting Host to be on hand at all times to aid in the smooth running of your day.

Your meeting room will be ready 30 minutes prior to scheduled arrival.

Refreshments are served on time, every time using only the freshest and finest ingredients.

AT THE END OF THE DAY

The Meeting Host will liase with the Organiser to gain their feedback which ensures we provide the highest standard of service and continually monitor and upgrade our product.

MEETING @
MACDONALD
HOTELS & RESORTS

Your full service solution

Conference Direct: **0845 604 4242**

meeting@macdonald-hotels.co.uk
www.macdonaldhotels.co.uk/business

Figure 4.2 Macdonald Hotels and Resorts' conference brand.

In an article entitled 'Emotional Intelligence' (*Conference + Meetings World magazine, October 2006*), Michael Wale, Starwood Hotels' senior vice-president and regional director of operations for North West Europe, writes:

> *To continue to grow and develop, Starwood must create differentiated world class hotel brands. We have moved away from price-based competition and bed wars and are focusing instead on emotionally relevant branding. Therefore, we have clearly defined each of our eight brands with meaningful positionings, to clarify to our guests, our suppliers and our associates (staff) what it feels like to be a Sheraton guest, what experience is part of the W Hotels ethos, etc. To create memorable and meaningful brands, guest service is the most powerful differentiator we have: we must sell on experience not a price point. We need to make the connection between branding and bonding with our guests, connecting with them and having an intellectual and emotional impact on them.*

A key objective behind branding is, therefore, to convey to the client that he can expect ethical practices and quality service and facilities at the same high standards, no matter whether the hotel is in Belfast or Bombay, Jakarta or Buenos Aires. It is to reassure customers that, having staged a successful conference at one hotel within the group, they can expect a similar outcome by using other hotels in the group. Branding is about building customer loyalty and increasing business retention because customers will have the confidence to keep their conferences and meetings within that particular group. Their own success is assured by the branded service and product which those hotels guarantee.

This approach has many strengths and, as all major chains have adopted branding, it seems to justify in financial returns the substantial investments required in venue and staff development. For customers it also has many attractions, yet it has one drawback: the very sameness of product can serve as a disincentive to its use. Conference organizers are constantly looking for somewhere new, somewhere a little different to make their event live long in the memory of their delegates. If delegates find that their surroundings and the type of service received are more or less identical at each conference, regardless of where it is being held, delegate perceptions of the event may not always be as favourable as the organizer would have wished.

An article entitled 'Brand Loyalty' in 'Business Travel World' magazine (January 2004) summarized 2003 research into conference hotel brands among buyers. It showed that recognition of the branded products had increased since earlier research in 2001 and that these brands did have some influence on where business was being placed. However, meeting planners and conference organizers did not rank 'buying into a brand as high as good service which included prompt and professional replies, knowledgeable staff, good quality food, good accommodation and good value', although Michael Wale of Starwood Hotels would presumably argue that successful brands and good service were one and the same.

In the author's experience, it is always important for an organizer to inspect a conference venue before booking because it is indeed the quality of staff and their service standards which is always one of the most decisive factors in venue selection and re-selection. No matter how strong the branding, and how good the staff training, the cloning of conference sales managers and banqueting co-ordinators has not yet been achieved (fortunately!). Individual personality and friendliness are often the crucial unique selling propositions (USPs), and these must be experienced at first hand.

OVERSEAS MARKETING

The promotion of destinations and venues to overseas markets is a huge subject which cannot be covered adequately in this book. The international marketplace is fiercely competitive and those organizations wishing to give themselves a realistic chance of success must take a long-term perspective, develop collaborative partnerships with other organizations (airlines, national tourist boards, and other marketing consortia), identify substantial financial and human resources, and follow through a detailed marketing plan similar to that outlined earlier in this chapter.

Friel (1997) notes that:

> It is instructive to observe that the former Soviet states of Eastern Europe chose tourism as the engine of economic recovery but the focus of their market positioning was not Russia but Moscow and St Petersburg; not the Czech Republic but Prague; not Hungary but Budapest.

He contends that it will be the city or 'urban region' which will be the future unit of analysis and the vehicle through which overseas markets will continue to be approached.

Bids to stage international association conventions are presented by cities, though positioned within a national framework – Cardiff, for example, is positioned within the context of Wales, and Helsinki is marketed under the umbrella of Finland. It is not a viable option for individual venues to market themselves overseas in isolation. It is even more important than in the domestic marketplace for venues, which are looking to attract overseas business, to work in partnership with their destination or to be marketed as part of an international chain or consortium.

No active steps into overseas markets should be taken without widespread consultation with experienced practitioners and the preparation of a detailed and costed marketing plan.

Summary

- the importance of location in decisions over the selection of conference venues has led to the creation of destination marketing organizations whose role is to promote the venues, facilities and attractions of a given area in order to generate increased conference business
- a focus on the needs of customers should drive all marketing activity, which has to be planned through the specific application of marketing principles and strategy to the conference and business tourism sector
- destination marketing is undertaken by convention bureaux and conference offices/desks which involve the public and private sectors in collaborative partnerships. The structures, funding and activities of such organizations vary from destination to destination, although two basic models are apparent
- the activities of city or local area convention bureaux are complemented in many countries by national tourism organizations
- some conference venues join marketing consortia, which comprise venues with similar characteristics, in order to develop a stronger profile in the marketplace
- many hotel chains have invested substantial resources in the development of a branded conference product as a means of reassuring and retaining their customers.

Review and discussion questions

1. Undertake a 'SWOT' analysis of two conference destinations, summarizing the strengths, weaknesses, opportunities and threats for each. Use the analysis to propose the most suitable target markets for both destinations.

2. Research the work of two convention and visitor bureaux. Compare and contrast their structures, funding, and marketing activities, commenting on the strengths and weaknesses of each.

3. Compose a Marketing Plan for a modern, 4-star conference hotel in your capital city. The hotel has six conference rooms, the largest seating up to 200 delegates, and two other rooms seating up to 100 each. It has 160 bedrooms and well-equipped leisure facilities. The hotel is privately owned. Three staff are involved in sales and marketing activities, and have a marketing budget of £10 000 (15 000 euros, US$20 000).

4. Undertake an in-depth appraisal of a venue marketing consortium. The appraisal should, ideally, include comments from venue members of the consortium on the value and benefits of membership.

5. Compare the branded conference products offered by two of the large hotel chains, noting both differences and similarities. To which kinds of conference organizers might these products appeal, and why?

Notes and references

1. Cooper, C, Fletcher, J, Gilbert, D and Wanhill, S (1993), *Tourism Principles and Practice* Longman.

2. 'DMO World': www.frontlinecommunication.co.uk/dmo world.

3. Davidson, R and Rogers, T (2006), *Marketing Destinations and Venues for Conferences, Conventions and Business Events*, Elsevier Butterworth-Heinemann.

4. De Chernatony, L, McDonald, M (1998), *Creating Powerful Brands*, Butterworth-Heinemann.

5. Doyle, P (1989), *Building Successful Brands: The Strategic Options*, Journal of Marketing Management 5(1).

6. Friel, E, *Compete & Conquer*, a presentation to the BACD annual convention (1997).

7. Gartrell, R (1994), *Destination Marketing for Convention and Visitor Bureaus*, Kendall/Hunt.

8. Gartrell, R (1991), *Strategic Partnerships for Convention Planning: The Role of Convention and Visitor Bureaus in Convention Management*, International Journal of Hospitality Management, 10(2).

9. 'Glasgow: Scotland with style – The City Brand' brochure (2006), Glasgow City Marketing Bureau.

10. Hankinson, G (2001 November), *Journal of Brand Management* 9(2).
11. Interbrand (1990), *Brands – An International Review*, Mercury Books.
12. Morgan, R, Pritchard, A, Pride, R (2002), *Destination Branding*, Butterworth-Heinemann.
13. Murdaugh, M (2005), *Fundamentals of Destination Management and Marketing*, Educational Institute of the American Hotel and Lodging Association AND the International Association of Convention & Visitor Bureaus.
14. Pike, S (2004), *Destination Marketing Organizations*, Elsevier.

Further reading

1. Muribi, M and Fojtik, C, *Marketing by Exhibiting in the Global Market*, published by Expressions International.

Conference management – an organizer's perspective

The conference industry is based upon events of different kinds (including conventions and congresses, meetings, seminars, product launches, management retreats) and of different sizes and durations, requiring sophisticated planning and administration to ensure their success. Events are organized by people with varying degrees of knowledge and experience, many finding themselves responsible for organizing conferences without much, if any, formal training. This chapter provides a framework for those who take up the challenge, and summarizes the main processes involved in planning and staging an event. In particular it looks at:

- a general introduction to conference organizing
- pre-conference planning and research
- budgeting and financial management
- sourcing and selecting a venue
- negotiating with venues
- programme planning
- event marketing

- conference management and production, and supporting technologies
- event evaluation.

It includes case studies on:

- British Educational Research Association's 'Invitation to Tender'
- A PCO philosophy in a changing world
- Using the internet to promote meetings (mini case study)
- Technology and virtual meetings and conferences.

Learning outcomes

On completion of this chapter, you should be able to:

- Discuss the strengths (and limitations) of conferences as a communications tool
- Describe the processes involved in organizing a successful conference or convention
- Understand the role of a professional conference organizer (PCO)
- Appreciate the opportunities provided by the new technologies and how/when these should best be used.

A GENERAL INTRODUCTION TO CONFERENCE ORGANIZING

The organization of a conference requires a similar strategic approach to that needed for planning and managing most other events. Clear objectives should be set from the beginning, a budget has to be established, a venue must be sourced and delegates' accommodation and travel arrangements made, a programme has to be prepared and the conference managed for its duration. Increasingly, health and safety, security, venue contracts and service guarantees are among a number of other aspects needing serious consideration, but there is not space to cover these adequately here. Then, after the conference is over, final administrative details have to be completed and some evaluation of the conference should take place. While there are different factors to take into account when organizing a conference for 500 delegates rather than one for 50, the essential components are the same.

Similar steps are required for the organization of other events, such as sporting events, concerts, celebrations and rallies, whether these are of national or international significance like the football World Cup Finals or the Olympic Games, or of more localised importance, such as an antiques fair or agricultural show.

Organizing conferences is a high-pressure activity, not recommended for those of a nervous disposition. Yet, well handled, it can be tremendously exhilarating and rewarding. It goes without saying that excellent organizational skills are a must, as are attention to detail and a willingness to work long and often irregular hours, especially in the immediate build-up period and during the event itself.

Conferences need to be planned with the precision of a military operation. Indeed, it is not surprising that a number of those now working successfully as conference organizers have come from a military background. Cotterell (1994) suggests that:

> *A conference for 200 people for two or three days is likely to take up to 250 hours or around six normal working weeks, even without counting the two or three 18-hour days which will be needed just prior to the event.*

But, in addition to hard work and attention to detail, conferences need a creativity and flair to be brought to them which will make them memorable occasions. They should live long in the memories of delegates, not only because of the benefits accruing from what has been shared and learned during the formal programme, but also for the opportunities they provide for informal networking and doing business, as well as socialising.

In some cases, companies and organizations will already have systems in place when the event is, for example, an annual event which runs along similar lines year after year. In other cases, it may be an entirely new event for which no previous organizational history or tradition exists. Both scenarios have their advantages and disadvantages:

- The regularly-held conference may operate smoothly with just some fine tuning and updating to established systems and procedures. It might, however, be failing to achieve its real potential as a conference, having become staid and predictable, and it may be that a completely fresh approach would be beneficial. The challenge for a new organizer will be to revolutionise the organization of the conference without alienating too many of the staff or members (if it is a membership organization) associated with the previous régime
- Where there is no previous event history, an organizer has the benefit of beginning with a clean sheet of paper. There are no set ways of doing things, no established contacts, no 'venues that we always use'. There is a freedom to bring something of his own identity to the event, to build up his own network of information and suppliers, and to ensure that the event management systems are put in place to his own design. But such freedom brings with it a responsibility which can appear daunting if the organizer has been thrust into the role

of running a conference with minimal training and experience. This, regrettably, is still the position in which far too many conference organizers find themselves.

This chapter attempts, therefore, to sketch out a framework for the successful organizing of conferences. A number of books have been written already on this subject and the chapter will make reference to some of these in summarizing the principles and steps needed to ensure that a conference is run effectively.

PRE-CONFERENCE PLANNING AND RESEARCH

The initial phase, of planning and research, is the one which lays the foundations for success. It is a crucial part of any event, and mistakes or oversights made at this stage can be difficult to remedy later on. It needs, therefore, to be approached thoroughly and systematically.

According to Carey (2000), it is also important to establish, at the outset:

> *the degree of autonomy that you, as the planner, are being given. Crucially, what degree of control do you have over the budget? A word of advice: Think strategically and claim as much authority as you think you can get away with. A conference organizer who has to check back to a superior (or, worse still, a committee) on the times of tea or the biscuit selection is doomed to preside over chaos and remain forever a bean counter.*

The initial planning phase is the time when the broad objectives for the conference must be set. These will vary from event to event. For example, the main objective for a meeting with a company's sales force may be to present new products, introduce a new incentive scheme, update them on sales performance and motivate them to reach higher targets, or inform them about a re-structuring of sales territories. The annual conference of American rose-growing societies (non-existent, as far as is known!) may have as its main aim to exchange information on new varieties of roses or to demonstrate the effectiveness of the latest pesticides, as well as maximizing attendance and generating a profit. Fisher (1998) quotes the example of objectives set for a real FMCG (Fast Moving Consumer Goods) conference:

- To debate future strategy
- To encourage delegates to get to know each other on a first-name basis
- To agree the general direction of the Group
- To have an enjoyable, memorable experience.

Objectives should be clear and measurable: for example, an objective for a sales conference which is simply 'To launch new product X' is hardly measurable, whereas 'To communicate the positioning, target audience, features, benefits and price structure of the new product X to all customer-facing staff' would be. However, it is also important not to have too many objectives, as this can lead to confusion on the part of delegates and speakers. Measuring return on investment (ROI) is increasingly an integral feature of any organizer's event management strategy, and will be explored more fully in Chapter 9.

These broad objectives need to be supplemented with detailed answers to questions about the *'who, what, when, where, why and how'* (Maitland, 1996) of the conference.

Who?

Pre-event planning needs to consider who the delegates will be, how many should be invited, and how many are expected to attend (essential for budgeting purposes). Is it appropriate for delegates' partners to be invited? Are there likely to be any special guests, including media representatives? Will there be any overseas delegates and, if so, is there a need to provide interpretation and translation facilities?

'Who?' also refers to the speakers who may be involved, either for presentations to plenary sessions or as leaders for workshops or 'breakout' sessions. Are there outside speakers to be invited, and will they require a fee as well as travel expenses?

'Who?' should also include the organizing team, which may be just one person or a dedicated group of people, some of whom could include intermediary agencies as described in Chapter 2. When there is a team involved, not all of them will necessarily participate from the initial planning stage right through to post-event evaluation, but their degree of involvement is something which will need to be thought through early on. The more complex the event and the numbers involved in organizing it, the more the need for some form of critical path analysis, mapping out the sequence of events in a logical order and within a realistic time-frame.

This is also the time to consider whether the conference should be organized in-house (using an organization's own staff resources and expertise) or outsourced to a professional conference (or congress) organizer (PCO). A PCO can undertake all aspects of the management of an event (see Chapter 2 for a list of typical PCO services) or simply be contracted to manage certain elements. If the decision is taken to outsource to a PCO, it is normal to prepare an 'Invitation to Tender' document which should include as much information as can be provided to enable those PCOs contacted to draw up a detailed and costed proposal for running the event. The 'Invitation to Tender' (also known as a Request for Proposal or RFP) will cover the types of information shown later in this chapter under 'Sourcing and Selecting a Venue', but should also describe the target audience and how to reach them, the likely final attendance numbers, how speakers are identified (i.e. whether by invitation or through the submission of papers) and the number of speakers and/or abstracts (i.e. summaries of specialist research or current work projects with which they are involved), the number of foreign languages for print materials and sessions, the level and nature of sponsorship required, whether there is to be an exhibition running alongside the conference, the spending power of the participants, past history of the event, and an indication of how many PCO companies have been invited to tender. Some of the above headings relate particularly to national and international association and scientific conventions, rather than to corporate sector conferences. Case study 5.1 gives an example of an Invitation to Tender prepared by the British Educational Research Association for the appointment of a PCO to manage its 2008, 2009 and 2010 annual conferences.

If it is decided to outsource the event to a PCO, care needs to be taken in the selection of the PCO. It is still the case in many countries that anyone can start operating as a PCO without the necessity of formal training, qualifications or previous experience (a further aspect of the immaturity of the industry referred to in Chapter 1). Choosing a PCO who is inexperienced or inefficient can obviously have disastrous consequences for the client, for the delegates, and for the venue whose reputation may be tarnished through no fault of its own. It is advisable to shortlist for consideration only those PCOs who are members of their professional association and who have had to prove their capabilities in the process (and/or who can provide strong testimonials from other satisfied clients). Professional bodies such as IAPCO and ABPCO (see Chapter 8) can give assurances for the professionalism of their members. Case Study 5.2 gives an insight into how one British PCO approaches his work and what he is aiming to achieve for his clients and for his own business.

What?

What kind of conference is being organized? Is it a corporate or association event? Is it a management retreat, training course, incentive event? A conference to update delegates on new developments in a scientific or medical field? A launch to dealers and trade media, or some other kind of event? Will delegates be listening and passive, or is there a high degree of participation, perhaps involving team building or outdoor activities?

What kind of message is the conference designed to convey? The organizer may have little or no control over this, as it may be something determined by senior managers or an organization's 'conference committee', but it is imperative that he understands this clearly.

When?

Timing is another major consideration. All too often inadequate time is allowed to plan and prepare for a conference. The conference organizer may simply be given the conference dates and asked to ensure that it happens. He may have made little input to the decision, even though his perspective is vital. The corporate sector, in particular, is notorious for allowing insufficient 'lead time'. Perhaps this is a reflection on the work that still needs to be done to raise the status of conference and event organizers to one which is on a par with an organization's senior management team. In the final analysis, it is a company's reputation, not simply that of the conference organizer, which is in jeopardy if an event is poorly run.

Some flexibility on dates can also be helpful in securing the best possible rates from the chosen venue. The venue may be able to offer more favourable rates if the dates selected assist in its maximization of yield (see Chapter 6).

Timing also needs to take into consideration the likely diary commitments of delegates. Are there any other events happening at the same time, or around that time, which might have an impact on delegate numbers? Is the conference occurring in a busy work period, or during holidays, or in winter months and, if so, what impact might any of these factors have?

Where?

Location needs to be determined at an early stage, whether this is expressed in rather broad terms such as a state/county or region of the country, or quite specifically such as New York, Nottingham, or 'within a 20-mile radius of Paris'. When deciding the ideal location, easy access to a motorway may be desirable (unless the event requires a venue off the beaten track). If many delegates are to use the train, location near a mainline station will be necessary, unless comprehensive local transport arrangements can be provided.

When events have an international dimension, with delegates arriving by plane, it is usually important to select a venue within reasonable travelling time of an international airport (often stipulated as 'no more than one or two hours' travel' from the gateway airport). Many hours sitting in a long-haul jet followed by several hours in transit around the country where the conference is to be held is not a recipe for a successful start to what will doubtless be a prestige event.

Does the location need to be a particular kind of venue to accommodate the event? Is there scope to explore an unusual venue, possibly to link in with the theme of the conference?

The choice of location may be taken out of the organizer's hands. He may be told to hold the event in a particular destination, or the conference may rotate around specific destinations/venues in a regular sequence. The organizer's role may simply be to draw up a shortlist of potential venues from which other people will make the final selection.

Why?

Maitland suggests that:

> The 'Why?' is almost certainly the most crucial question that needs to be asked at this stage. Don't ignore or underestimate it. You must be able to answer it well if you are going to proceed with your plans. Is 'because we always do it at this time of year' a good enough reason? It could be a huge waste of time and money if it is held for this reason alone. Are you staging it because it is the quickest and easiest way of putting across your important message to many people in a friendly and personal manner? That's a better motive. Consider carefully if a conference is really necessary. Are there less time-consuming and costly ways to achieve the same goals – perhaps a sales report, a promotional brochure or a press release?

How?

The format and duration of a conference are also very important factors, which will have an effect on some of the preceding considerations. Events requiring lots of syndicate rooms, as well as a main auditorium, plus exhibition space and catering areas will have a much more restricted range of options than events needing just one room with theatre-style seating for 75 people. Duration will also impact on venue availability, rates charged, accommodation requirements, and other factors. It may be appropriate to use videoconferencing technology or satellite conferencing, or to examine the benefits of webcasting (i.e. enabling delegates to attend 'virtually' via their computer screens as conference sessions are broadcast via the internet) to increase attendance levels.

'How?' should also take into account the way in which an event fits into a company's overall marketing or training programme. Where a membership organization is involved, such as a professional association or a trade union, how does a conference contribute to its communication links with members, and facilitate links between the members themselves? Are there ways in which these could be improved?

Fisher (1998) provides many useful tips on other practical aspects of managing an event, which there is not space to cover in this book. He describes the invitation process, the reception of delegates, travel and logistical arrangements, making the best use of refreshment and lunch breaks, handling overnight accommodation, the correct treatment of VIPs, the effective management of conference catering (traditionally the most common cause of problems and of delegate dissatisfaction), and organizing a conference overseas.

A conference organizer must also undertake a risk assessment for his event and develop contingency plans for dealing with crises that might occur. Swarbrooke and Horner (2001) give examples of some of the commonest problems:

- Keynote speakers who are unable to attend because of illness or travel problems
- Participants being seriously delayed or unable to attend at all due to transport difficulties or bad weather
- Overbooked hotels
- Fire alarms and bomb threats
- Failures of audio-visual equipment.

They contend, correctly, that:

> *all these risks are foreseeable and the organizer should have in place contingency plans to implement if they arise – what we might term the 'what if' approach. This may involve having an alternative schedule in reserve, or a suitable additional set of audio-visual equipment available. It is important that everyone on the team knows about these contingency plans.*

Risk assessment will also lead to taking out appropriate insurance cover for the event, and there are today a number of specialist event insurance providers operating at a global level.

BUDGETING AND FINANCIAL MANAGEMENT

Assembling a budget is fundamental to the planning of any event. Anticipated costs impose parameters or a framework when putting the budget together and these, combined with an organizer's previous experience and detailed quotes from potential suppliers, provide the building blocks on which the budget is constructed. Whether the conference is being organized for a corporate organization or for one in the 'not-for-profit' sector, financial management is equally important. There are, however, some key differences:

- within the corporate sector, the budget is set by the company. Budgets may be allocated per event or as an annual total budget which needs to be used effectively to finance a number of events. The budget is required to cover delegate expenses as well as the other costs associated with planning, promoting and staging the event

- within the not-for-profit sector (and with entrepreneurial conferences – see Chapter 2), conferences have to be income-generating with delegate fees being charged to defray costs. The events are designed to cover their own costs and perhaps make a profit which, in some cases, is used as a start-up fund to pay for the initial promotion and planning of the next event
- within the government and public sectors, either of the above approaches may apply.

Even so, the same principles hold good for all types of organization: budgets must be drawn up to show projected income and expenditure, systems need to be in place to manage income and expenditure flows and, at the conclusion of the event, a balance sheet should be prepared to show actual income against expenditure. This balance sheet then forms the basis for planning the next event, particularly if it is one in a sequence of conferences taking place on a regular basis.

Income streams will vary according to the nature of the organization and the event. With corporate events, the income source will be the company itself, but there may also be scope for attracting sponsorship for certain elements. With associations and other organizations in the not-for-profit sector, income will come primarily from delegate fees, although there may also be substantial opportunities to offset the costs of the conference through sponsorship and by running an associated exhibition. Trade union, political party and medical conferences and conventions, for example, often have concurrent exhibitions which attract exhibitors wishing to promote their products to the delegates. Opportunities also exist to attract sponsorship, as typified by pharmaceutical companies sponsoring aspects of medical conferences. McCabe et al (2000) also list income streams such as:

- grants – from government and/or other bodies
- merchandising – money from the sale of items appertaining to the event, such as educational materials, clothing (T-shirts, hats) and cassette or video tapes (CD-Roms, DVDs)
- advertising – money from the sale of advertising space, for example in the conference brochure, on clothing, and so on.

Many destinations are prepared to host a civic reception or banquet for delegates, as a form of welcome and expression of gratitude that the event is being held in their town or city. Some convention and visitor bureaux (CVBs) offer interest-free loans, particularly for events with a lead time of several years: the event organizer may incur expenses, especially promotional costs, well before any income is received from delegate fees. Loans are designed to assist with cash flow but will have to be re-paid once the event is over (and, if the conference has made a profit, the CVB may require a share of the profits).

Expenditure projections have to cover a whole host of items, but the main ones are usually:

- venue hire
- catering costs
- accommodation costs: delegates, partners, speakers/invited guests, organizers
- speakers' expenses: travel costs, fees, subsistence, possibly presentation materials
- delegate materials: written materials, CDs, badges, possibly gifts
- social and partner programme costs: entertainment, transport, other venue hire, food and beverage
- conference production costs: audio-visual equipment and technical staff to stage-manage the event plus, when appropriate, set construction
- promotional costs: leaflets and publicity material, press releases, possibly advertising and/or direct mail, e-marketing
- on-site staff (organizer) costs plus, in some cases, freelance event staff
- miscellaneous costs: event insurance, security, couriers, interpreters, taxes (both local/national taxes and tax on profits).

Maitland provides a cashflow forecast form (see Table 5.1) which can be computerised (spreadsheet software handles this very easily) or in paper format. This is a recognised way of keeping an overview of what is happening with the finances for an event, and helps to flag up any potential problem areas at an early stage.

Association and entrepreneurial conference organizers need to calculate the 'break-even' point for their events i.e. the point at which sufficient delegates have booked places to ensure that the conference does not run at a loss but, at the very least, covers its costs. McCabe et al (2000) state that:

> *break-even analysis is a tool that assists in the setting of prices. The basic concept is that at some level of sales (revenue), there will be sufficient income to cover the expenses of the convention or meeting (Getz, 1997, page 214). In calculating the break-even point, both fixed and variable costs are taken into consideration. The variable costs are relative to the volume of conference participants.*

Figure 5.1, based on McCabe et al, illustrates the break-even chart for an academic association conference for 250 delegates. Fixed

	Month			Month			Month			Month		
	Estimated	Actual	Variance	Estimated	Actual	Variance	Estimated	Actual	Variance	Estimated	Actual	Variance
A. INCOME												
Sponsors												
Delegates/Partners												
Other												
Total Income (A)												
B. EXPENDITURE												
Venue												
Accommodation/ Housing												
Speakers/partners												
Delegates/partners												
Publicity												
Outside assistance (e.g. PCO/DMC)												
Rehearsals & Production costs												
The programme												
Social programme Activities												
Other, incl. taxes and contingency												
Total Expenditure (B)												
Net Cashflow (A-B)												
Opening Balance												
Closing Balance												

Source: Maitland, I. (1996) (with some author's additions)

Table 5.1
Cashflow forecast form

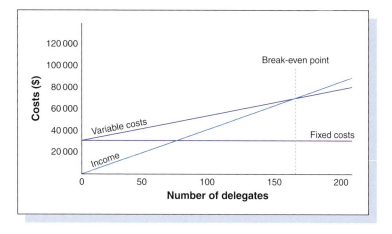

Figure 5.1
Break-even chart for a
conference of 250 delegates.
(*The Business and
management of Conventions*;
McCabe et al; John Wiley &
Sons Australia, Ltd; © 2007
reprinted with permission of
John Wiley & Sons Australia.)

costs include promotion and publicity, printing, brochures and
delegate bags. Variable costs include food and beverages. The
registration fee is $425.

It is now also possible to download, from web sites, work-
books and spreadsheets for tracking expenditure across a number of meetings/events. One such web site is located at
www.starcite.com.

The Convention Industry Council's 'International Manual'
(2005) examines budgeting from the perspective of organizing
events internationally. It suggests that *'budgeting for international
events is essentially the same process as budgeting for national and local
events, with the added complications caused by currency and tax issues'*.
It explains how movements in currency exchange rates (which
may float against one another, be fixed at a certain level, or even
float within fixed limits) can have a major impact on the bottom
line results of events, but the risks can be minimized with appropriate planning. Tax issues revolve more around implications for
delegates and the organizing company and whether it will be
necessary to pay income or company tax because an event has
been organized abroad. In some cases, the delegate is perceived
to have received a taxable benefit from the company, and the
company is potentially liable to pay any tax associated with providing a benefit to an employee. Local taxes in the form of sales
taxes (paid on hotel stays or the purchase of goods from shops)
or VAT (Value Added Tax) may also be payable by delegates.
Organizers need to take advice from financial professionals and
appropriate government agencies on tax, currency and similar
financial issues.

Fisher suggests an allocation of budget for a typical corporate conference, drawing a distinction between fixed costs and
variable costs, reproduced in Table 5.2.

Fixed Costs	Likely Percentage
1. Production, staging and outside speakers	
2. Invitation process, marketing, design	
3. Conference rooms	
4. Agency fees, initial recce	
5. Signage	
6. Security, car parking set-up	35%
7. Cabaret, entertainment	
8. Registration costs	
9. Conference office costs, telephones, faxes	
10. Wet weather back-up, if applicable	
(Item 1 could be as much as 25% of total costs)	
Variable Costs (Per Delegate)	
1. Meals, breaks	
2. Drinks at meals, breaks	
3. Accommodation (housing)	
4. Travel	
5. Delegate print	
6. Table/room gifts	50%
7. Porterage, car parking per delegate	
8. Partner programme	
9. Late bar drinks	
10. Insurances, VAT (Value Added Tax)	
Contingency	
1. 10% to cover all contingencies for direct costs	15%
2. Allowance for currency movements (if abroad)	
Total Budget	100%

Table 5.2
Budget allocations for a typical corporate conference

SOURCING AND SELECTING A VENUE

There are many sources of information and advice to assist with choosing the venue most suited to a particular event. These include directories and brochures, web sites and CD-Roms/DVDs, trade exhibitions, trade press, and specialist agencies.

Directories and brochures

There are a number of annual directories available which provide a very useful reference source, some of which are international in their coverage, others national, and updated annually. Examples of international directories include:

- 'Venue – The Worldwide Guide to Conference and Incentive Travel Facilities', published by Haymarket Business Publications
- 'Worldwide Convention Centres Directory', published by CAT Publications
- 'Recommended Business Meeting Venues Guide', as well as a series of Recommended Hotel Guides covering over 1200 privately owned and independently run hotels throughout the world – published by Johansens.

Most, if not all, international trade associations (see Chapter 8) produce member directories (also accessible in electronic format via their web sites) detailing their memberships and the services available through the trade association, which may include a venue finding and enquiry referral service. From a client (i.e. meeting planner) perspective, membership of a trade association by a venue or convention bureau can give a greater assurance of accredited standards and quality service.

At a national level, directories or brochures are produced by trade associations (BACD's 'British Conference Destinations Directory' has a well-established track record as a valuable reference guide), by national convention bureaux and tourist boards, by hotel chains, and by venue consortia of the kind listed in Chapter 4.

All venues produce some form of promotional brochure and conference organizers should keep up-to-date copies of such information for those venues they use on a regular basis. However, because of the number of available venues (between 3000 and 4000 in the British Isles alone), it would require a huge filing system to maintain a comprehensive set of brochures, many of which are designed in different shapes and sizes. It would also be a full-time occupation to keep these up-to-date.

A better use of limited filing and storage space would be to obtain a set of *destination guides*, produced by all conference destinations (CVBs) and mostly updated annually or biennially. These tend to be produced in A4 or quarto format, and describe (almost) all of the venues in a destination as well as summarizing attractions, communications, support services and other features.

Web sites and CD-Roms/DVDs

Computer software packages, listing conference venues, have been in existence since the early 1990s, although it is fair to say that the early versions struggled to achieve widespread acceptance among conference organizers. Nowadays, web sites and CD-Roms/DVDs have replaced the more traditional software format. Two of the leading Internet-based venue finding and enquiry systems are: www.venuedirectory.com and www.starcite.com. Sites such as these allow browsers to enter their own venue search criteria on line, and details of venues that match are supplied to them within a matter of seconds. Browsers can then look at detailed information on the venues, including photos, and may also be able to undertake a 'virtual' tour of the venue. There is also the facility to send a specific enquiry ('Request for Proposal' or 'RFP') to venues shortlisted. Similar information may be available in CD-Rom or DVD format, with meeting planners receiving updated versions several times a year.

Many of the directories and brochures referred to in the previous section above can also be accessed electronically through their respective web sites.

For those conference organizers who prefer to source their own venues, rather than use an intermediary organization, web sites and venue brochures/directories are a useful way of whittling down the options to a manageable shortlist. They do not, however, obviate the need to visit venues before making a final choice. Computer or printed images and text can help, but they do not replace the need to see a venue at first hand and meet the staff.

As Cotterell says, inspection visits:

> *are important because there is much that cannot be ascertained from a brochure. The experienced organizer will travel to a venue the way most delegates will, to experience at first hand any problems with finding it or reaching it. Judgements will be made on the overall first impressions, the attitude of the staff, the quality, colours, style and condition of furnishings, the ease of getting from one area to another, and so on. Many experienced organizers make a check-list of points they need to cover. It is sometimes easier to attend one of the group inspection visits organized by hotels, tourist boards, convention bureaux, trade associations and some trade magazines. These give an opportunity, often over a weekend, to inspect a variety of venues within a location in the company of other organizers, an aspect that can be a most valuable opportunity to add to one's own personal network.*

Trade exhibitions

There are a number of trade shows and exhibitions specifically designed for conference organizers and meeting planners, where the exhibitors include conference venues and destinations, conference service suppliers, intermediary agencies, transport companies and trade magazines. The benefit for conference organizers is that an exhibition enables them to make contact with potential suppliers, all under one roof – people it would be very expensive and time-consuming to contact individually away from the show. Exhibitions are a good way of updating information files, making personal contacts, finding out about new developments and facilities. Many exhibitions also have a seminar programme running alongside, covering topics of relevance to conference organizers in their everyday work.

Major industry exhibitions include:

1. *The Motivation Show*, the largest of the trade exhibitions in North America, held at McCormick Place in Chicago in September/October. Organised by Hall Erickson Inc. Further details: www.motivationshow.com.
2. *EIBTM* (European Incentive and Business Travel and Meetings Exhibition) – a truly international exhibition (see Chapter 1) held in Barcelona, Spain in November and organized by Reed Travel Exhibitions. Several thousand buyers are hosted to the show each year by the organizers, who provide complimentary flights and overnight hotel accommodation. Further details: www.eibtm.com.
3. *IMEX* – another highly international exhibition held at Messe Frankfurt, Germany in April or May each year, and also including a major programme for hosted buyers. *IMEX* incorporates a German trade show, *Meetings Made In Germany*. Further information: www.imex-frankfurt.com.
4. *International Confex* – the largest of the British shows which is held at Earls Court Exhibition Centre, London (usually late February/early March). Exhibitors are British and overseas companies and organizations. Organized by CMP Information Ltd. Further information: www.international-confex.com.
5. *AIME (Asia Incentives & Meetings Exhibition)* – held at the Melbourne Exhibition and Convention Centre, Australia in February (first staged in 1993). Organised by Reed Travel Exhibitions. Further details: www.aime.com.au.
6. *Incentive Travel & Conventions, Meetings Asia (IT&CMA)* – this show has been running since 1993, and has been held annually in Thailand (both Bangkok and Pattaya) since 2002. Previously it was held in Hong Kong from 1993 to 1996, and Malaysia from 1997 to 2001. It is organised by TTG Asia Media Pte Ltd. Further details: www.itcma.com.sg.

Trade press

Conference industry trade magazines are a valuable source of up-to-date news and features on conference venues and destinations, both national and international. As well as articles reviewing the facilities and attractions of specific areas, some magazines also include price comparisons between venues and case studies of events which illustrate how other organizers have staged events in particular locations.

Readers of trade magazines need to bear in mind that all of the magazines depend for their survival on attracting advertising support from conference venues and destinations, a fact which can sometimes influence editorial content. Despite this caveat, trade magazines are an important source of information and provide a service which does not exist elsewhere. They also contain many other articles, for example on trends and statistics and new legislation, which provide essential background for professional buyers.

Some of the industry trade magazines may be viewed in electronic format as well. From around 2005 onwards, specialist ezines have been produced for the conference and meetings industry which are only distributed electronically.

A list of the main trade magazines is given in Appendix A.

Agencies

Various agencies provide specialist venue finding services. These include venue finding agencies, professional conference organizers (PCOs), conference production companies, and destination management companies (DMCs) (see Chapter 2). Agency services are usually free to buyers (unless the agencies are also involved in the planning and organization of a conference), with commission being charged to the venues where business is placed.

Whichever source(s) of information organizers choose to use (one of the most popular sources, not listed above, is that of peer group recommendations i.e. recommendations of venues by colleagues or by other conference organizers), they will need to have at their finger tips the answers to questions about their event which will be posed by venue staff or intermediary agencies. They will require information on:

- The nature of the conference/event and its key objectives
- Duration of the event (including any build-up and break-down time for stage sets, exhibition stands, etc.)
- Proposed dates (and any possible flexibility with these to secure the best deal)
- Number of delegates/partners/exhibitors/speakers.
- Preferred location(s)
- Type of venue sought and space/meeting room requirements, with room layouts
- Technical and audio-visual equipment needed and whether a specialist conference production company is to be used

- Catering requirements, with any special arrangements (e.g. private dining, receptions, entertainment)
- Accommodation (numbers, types of bedroom)
- Social programme activities/requirements (where appropriate)
- Budget
- Deadline for receipt of information and details of the decision-making process.

(See also Case Study 5.1 with its example of a detailed Request for Proposal.)

Venue inspection checklist

Once a shortlist of potentially suitable venues has been produced, the next step is to inspect these venues by visiting in person. When undertaking an inspection visit, it is useful to go armed with a checklist of questions, such as:

- Is there the correct combination of rooms available for plenary sessions, syndicate groups, catering, possibly an accompanying exhibition?
- Is there good access for disabled delegates? Is the venue equipped in other ways to meet the many different disabilities that delegates (and speakers) may have (see also Chapter 9 section on accessibility)?
- What style of seating will be needed? U-shape, boardroom, theatre-style, classroom, hollow-square and herringbone are just some of the options (see Figure 5.2). For the purposes of calculations, a room which seats 100 delegates theatre-style will seat 50 classroom-style, 25 hollow-square/boardroom/ U-shape, and about 75 for dinner/lunch at round tables/top table with sprigs
- Do the meeting rooms have natural light? If so, can the room be blacked out satisfactorily?
- How noisy is the heating and air conditioning system?
- If the event is residential, how many bedrooms will be available at the venue, and how many of these are single/double/twin bedrooms? Is it important for all delegates to sleep under the same roof, or can they be accommodated in different hotels and transported to the conference venue?
- Does the venue have leisure facilities and, if so, are they available to delegates free of charge?
- What are the options for social activities in the vicinity, if there is time in the conference programme for these?
- Does the venue have a dedicated conference co-ordinator (or team) who can assist with the detailed planning and arrangements?

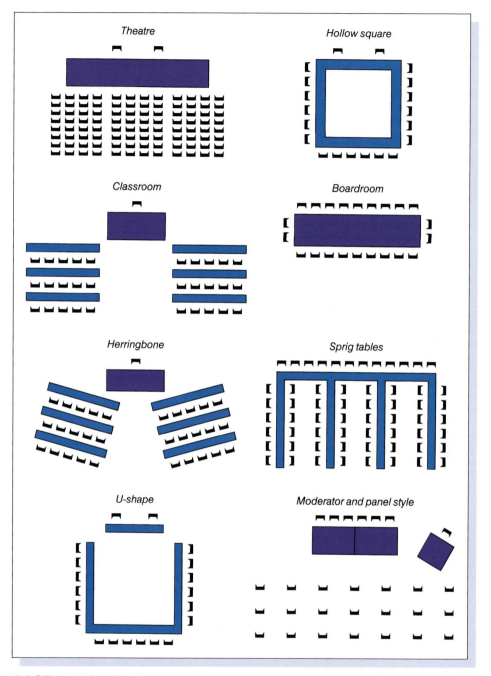

Figure 5.2 Different styles of seating.

- Are there other venue staff with whom you will be working and, if so, when will you be able to meet them? At what stage will the sales manager – usually the conference organizer's initial point of contact – pass on the booking details to colleagues, who then become the main points of reference?

- Are there in-house technical staff to operate audio-visual equipment? If so, is there an additional charge for using their services? If there are no such staff on site, what arrangements does the venue have with independent audio-visual companies, and what do they charge? What audio-visual equipment is needed during the event (normally this can be decided quite close to the event, unless the requirements are specialised or the event is a large one requiring substantial equipment and sophisticated production)?
- Can the venue offer any transport assistance for delegates travelling by public transport (e.g. collecting them by minibus from the airport or railway station)? How much car parking space does the venue have?
- Is there a high turnover of staff in the venue, which might create problems in the build-up? Does the venue team give the impression of being experienced, professional, easy-to-work-with?

Carey (1997) provides a series of checklists for conference organizers. An example of one of these, a 'Meeting Room Checklist', is given in Figure 5.3.

NEGOTIATING WITH VENUES

Once a shortlist of suitable venues has been produced and inspection visits made, the process of negotiating a final rate or package with the preferred venue takes place. Conference organizers should be aware of a venue's need to maximize yield from its bookings (as described in Chapter 6) but, nonetheless, there is almost always scope to negotiate on a venue's published delegate rates.

Carey suggests that:

> As a professional conference organizer, you are in a powerful position to negotiate a good deal with your chosen venue and it can be tempting to bully the management into ridiculously low room, food and beverage rates. This may make you feel good and impress your Finance Director but it will almost certainly jeopardize the vital relationship between you and the venue. As a rule, it is better to pay a reasonable rate for facilities and accommodation and then negotiate added value and service.

In short, good negotiation is about creating a win-win situation for both the event organizer and the venue, but also about building relationships and partnerships, and doing business with people who want to do business with you.

To attend a site inspection without a checklist is a recipe for extra work, as vital questions will remain unasked and important features remain uninspected. Every conference brings its own demands but if you investigate the following you will be halfway there.

A. Location
- Independent access[1]
- Freight access[1]
- Easy to find? (well signed?)
- Proximity to:[2]
  - Main entrance and car park
  - Meal areas and kitchens
  - Fresh air
  - Lifts
  - Toilets and cloakrooms
  - Telephones
  - Break-out rooms
- Disabled access

B. Fixtures
- Decor
- Wall and floor materials[3]
- Pillars/obstructions
- Room shape and partitions[4]
- Location of doors
- Where doors lead to[5]
- Fire exits[6]
- Natural light/views

- Chandeliers and mirrors[7]
- Stage area and access to it
- Registration area
- Light switches or regulators
- Power and telephone points[8]
- Temperature controls (location)[9]
- Blackout curtains
- Acoustics
- Ceiling height[10]

C. Non-fixtures
- Chairs (comfort factor)
- Tables (size and coverings)
- Table furniture[11]
- Signage

D. General
- Cleanliness
- Overall comfort
- Capacity
- Ambience
- Pre-function space
- Smell

Notes:
1. Direct on to concourse, foyer or street.
2. Explore for yourself.
3. Should be sound absorbent, not bright and not 'busy'.
4. Are partitions really soundproof?
5. Beware doors that open on to kitchens or garbage areas.
6. Are they blocked or locked?
7. Chandeliers can impede projection. Mirrors toss light from projectors and lecterns indiscriminately around a room.
8. You may need lots for PCs, modems and fax machines.
9. Are they in the room?
10. High enough for maximum screen height.
11. What is provided? e.g. Water, cordials, note pads, mints.

Did you hear about the organizer who checked the dimensions of the access doors with the venue (over the phone) and computed that the car would fit through them? Sadly, he was unaware until the day of the launch that the room he had booked wasn't on the ground floor!

Figure 5.3 Meeting room checklist.

Some flexibility on the part of the organizer can assist in the negotiation process, particularly if this can help to make a booking even more attractive in the eyes of the venue. The following points should also be borne in mind:

- Only negotiate with venue staff who have the authority to make decisions
- Underline and sell the stature and value of your event to the venue

- It is a good sign if the venue asks lots of questions about your event. Give them as much information as possible *before* discussing rates
- Be prepared by doing your homework on the venue's 'rack' (i.e. published) rates and having a copy of the venue's brochure on file before discussing a deal. Establish what the venue's tariffs are for other types of business
- Give the venue manager an indication of your budget (unless it is higher than their published rates!)
- If you can offer some flexibility on dates/timings, you are likely to get a better deal, bearing in mind that venues are seeking back-to-back bookings. If the event is to be held midweek, rates charged are likely to be higher than at weekends. Significant reductions can be achieved by holding an event at least partially over a weekend when occupancy levels, especially for hotels, are generally lower
- The scope for negotiation will also depend on the time of year (Autumn and Spring are the peak seasons for conferences, and so the busiest for the venues), the number of delegates, nature of the organization (lower rates may be available for not-for-profit organizations)
- Published rates do not cover the same package from venue to venue. It is, therefore, important to examine what the rates do actually include. The provision of audio-visual equipment is one of the areas where wide variations can exist
- While most venues (and certainly almost all hotels) promote a delegate package (expressed either as a non-residential or 8-hour or day delegate rate OR as a residential or 24-hour delegate rate), it is also possible to ask for room hire and catering charges separately, and sometimes these may be cheaper than an integrated package.

Cotterell puts forward a number of strategies to be used by conference buyers in the negotiation process, including.

- prepare – for example, know the prices charged by the venue to other clients (*if possible*), and know the prices charged by similar venues in the area
- be nice, but gain respect
- don't lie
- be flexible
- never reveal deadlines
- name drop
- hint at other business to be placed
- be patient
- disclaim responsibility (for the final decision)
- don't underestimate the sellers.

PROGRAMME PLANNING

It is of prime importance that the conference programme matches the overall objectives. The content, style and pace of the programme will, of course, vary from event to event. There is now a stronger business orientation to most conferences, plus a clear requirement for even large conferences to be more participatory, inviting delegate contributions to plenary presentations and, particularly, through a greater use of syndicate sessions. There is also a requirement for programmes to cater for different delegate needs: this may be less of a concern for corporate conferences where delegates' levels of experience and expertise can be checked and controlled, but a challenge for association conferences where delegates are self-selecting to a much greater extent and will have disparate levels of experience.

Research undertaken by McGill University (USA) over a 10-year period consistently showed that, for scientific international association conferences, programme content was the single most important determining factor in increasing delegate attendance (reported in *The PCO*, the newsletter of the International Association of Professional Congress Organizers, Autumn 2002). The research revealed that 48 per cent of delegates gave 'the programme' as the key reason for attending, followed by 26 per cent citing 'destination', 16 per cent stating that they 'always attend' and 10 per cent offering other reasons.

The choice of speakers, and leaders of syndicate or workshop sessions, is crucial to the success of the formal conference programme. In some cases, decisions about speakers may be imposed upon the organizer by senior managers or a conference committee. Where this is the case, the organizer's role is to ensure that speakers are properly briefed about the aims for the conference as well as for their own presentation, and that all of the technical and environmental factors (room layout, audio-visual facilities, introductory speeches) are carefully planned to create a successful 'performance'.

When the organizer has to source speakers himself, imagination and recommendation should be uppermost in his mind, probably in equal proportions. It is often stimulating for delegates to listen to a speaker with new ideas or controversial views, and a rousing opening session which generates discussion and debate may be just the spark needed to ensure a lively and productive conference. But few organizers will be willing to put their own reputations on the line by inviting relatively unknown speakers to the platform, unless they come recommended by others. Colleagues and peers are clearly an important source of such speaker recommendations. Other sources can include trade associations, editors of trade magazines, university or college departments, speaker bureaux, and professional conference organizers.

Some conferences are strictly business events with little or no free time. Others, particularly in the association sector, combine a business programme with a social programme. The social itinerary is another area where an organizer has an opportunity to display his creativity and really make the conference memorable. The social programme should allow delegates to mix informally and network (for many this is often the most worthwhile part of the event), but also to experience something of the destination in which the conference is being staged. It may be possible for social activities to extend, in a lighthearted way, the theme of the conference. Invaluable assistance in the design of social programmes is available from the local convention bureau or conference office, as well as from PCOs and, especially, DMCs. Examples of social events at BACD conferences in recent years have included:

- a tour of the Whisky Heritage Centre in Edinburgh followed by dinner, concluding with a late-evening guided tour of the narrow streets around Edinburgh Castle by a 'ghost' (Adam Lyal Deceased) – a truly haunting experience!
- a banquet in the splendour of Cardiff Castle featuring Welsh dancers and a male voice choir
- a Caribbean evening in Leicester, with delegates in Caribbean costume being entertained by steel bands and cabaret
- a torchlit drinks reception in the Roman baths in Bath, followed by a banquet in the Pump Room
- a formal whisky tasting, under instruction, at Glamis Castle near Dundee followed by a tour of the Castle and a sumptuous banquet
- a boat trip to the island of Sark (from a conference in Guernsey) with rides by horse-drawn carriage and bicycle (there are no cars on Sark), followed by dinner.

Each of these gave the event a unique character and made it an enjoyable and memorable experience.

EVENT MARKETING

Marketing is an essential part of the event management process. There is little point in devoting a great deal of time and resources to the organization of a conference, if few people bother to attend. The marketing should begin at the earliest possible stage, even if this only entails publicizing brief details of the event so that potential delegates have reserved the date in their diary.

Event marketing is not just about maximizing delegate numbers. It also creates a positive attitude towards the event for everyone concerned (speakers, delegates, venue and suppliers, trade media, etc.) and helps to raise its profile, both within its own industry sector but also within the conference sector.

Clearly the greater the budget for marketing, the more that can be done, but much can still be achieved without a huge promotional 'pot'. The following are some ideas that can be used or adapted to meet the needs of any organization:

- Ensure that the printed brochure/leaflet used to promote the event, containing the conference programme, is of the highest standard affordable. Increasingly the programme is also produced in electronic format as a 'PDF' which can be disseminated by e-mail to potential delegates, and/or be posted onto appropriate web sites. The programme sets the tone for the event and, if well done, goes a long way to creating interest in, and positive expectations from, the conference. It should contain:
  - An introduction (possibly in the form of an invitation/ welcome from the organization's Chief Executive or Chair)
  - The conference programme (in as much detail as is confirmed at this stage – a final programme can be circulated nearer the event to registered delegates)
  - Short biographies of speakers and contributors
  - Upbeat information on the venue (and destination) being used, ideally with some photographs
  - Details of any event sponsors
  - A booking form (either as part of the leaflet or as a separate insert).
- If the conference has been held previously, favourable quotations from delegates should be included in the promotional material and programme brochure. Peer group quotes are one of the most effective ways of generating interest
- A PR strategy should be prepared for the event (although not normally applicable to corporate conferences). This will include the issue of press releases to help create awareness of the conference and raise its profile as an event 'not-to-be-missed'. As well as giving key facts and figures about the conference, the releases should contain details of new or controversial issues and topics to be discussed at the conference, quotes from the organizers and keynote speaker(s) (where appropriate), and set out briefly what the conference is intended to achieve
- Direct marketing, including e-marketing, is one of the main marketing tools to be used, especially with association and entrepreneurial conferences, but is dependent on access to a good quality database of potential invitees
- Maximize use of the internet by developing a site for the event and/or incorporating full event details in other web sites. The web site may offer online registration facilities, including payment over the web, but the site must be secure and all data encrypted. Mini case study 5.3 describes best practice in the design and development of the internet to promote meetings
- Advertising may also be appropriate when promoting an entrepreneurial type of event, and sometimes when marketing to the association sector where delegates can choose whether or not to attend. Advertising should normally be used to complement other press and PR activity, rather than being used in isolation.

Case Study 5.3   Using the Internet to Promote Meetings

This mini case study is based on an article written by Corbin Ball (www.corbinball.com).

General tips on good web site design are given in Chapter 4. This mini case study focuses, therefore, on content:

- The key to a site being bookmarked is content – give viewers a reason to go there in the first place and then come back!
- Put the conference programme and agenda online and make it searchable by topic, speakers, dates, times, key words, etc.
- Include statistics of past meetings (charts and graphs of attendance and demographics, past exhibitor lists). Make them as visually interesting as possible – use graphs over tables
- Post the pre-registration list online – people may wish to contact others in advance, which can encourage attendance
- Have online pre-conference forums, electronic bulletin boards, and chat rooms. Establish a virtual community around the event
- Create a virtual exhibition section to increase traffic, promote the exhibition, increase exhibitor visibility, and generate revenues through sales of links to exhibitors' web sites
- Update your site frequently with press announcements and news releases about the event
- Put past keynote addresses and other speakers online (using streaming video and audio software programs that bring sound and motion pictures to your web site)
- Offer a registration discount for those registering via the web.
- Make the online registration form user-friendly, allowing for individual session sign-up
- Utilize an automated e-mail confirmation system giving immediate feedback that the registration has been received
- Use advance e-mail surveys to determine delegate expectations, interests and desires
- Have an 'ask the presenters' forum, or 'ask the conference chair' forum where prospective delegates can pose questions in advance.

CONFERENCE MANAGEMENT AND PRODUCTION

The general management of a conference requires, in Carey's words:

> common sense, forethought, meticulous planning and attention to detail, team work and sometimes crisis management.

Much of the administration can be enhanced by the use of event management software packages, which are designed to handle delegate registrations and correspondence, itinerary planning, accommodation arrangements, abstract management, speaker liaison, exhibition management, invoicing, report production, delegate evaluations and other aspects. Increasingly such products are also available as web-based tools which allow on-line registrations and other real-time applications.

Examples of such software packages and web-based services include:

- 'Events Pro' and 'Events Interactive' produced by Australian company Amlink. Further details from www.amlink.com.au
- 'Visual Impact System VI' from UK company Event Management Systems. Further details from www.eventmanagement systems.co.uk
- 'MeetingView', produced by US company Starcite. Further details from www.starcite.com
- 'Eventbookings.net', produced by UK company Eventbookings.com. Further details from www.eventbookings.com.

There is a very useful free e-newsletter detailing the latest developments in technology and web applications for meetings, hospitality and travel industry professionals, circulated free of charge every two months and compiled by Corbin Ball. It is entitled 'Corbin's Techtalk Newsletter' – anyone wishing to be added to the circulation list should email him at: corbin@corbinball.com.

It is useful to provide delegates, either in advance or at the registration desk, with a printed itinerary detailing the timing and location of individual sessions, particularly important when there are a number of sessions running concurrently or 'in parallel'. When this is the case, delegates will normally have been asked to pre-select the sessions of most interest to them and it is worth producing a reminder list of these sessions for them, perhaps with a list of the other delegates who have chosen the same sessions. Delegate badges can now have a microchip inserted to track whether delegates are attending the correct conference sessions or which stands they have visited in a major exhibition.

It should be remembered that a conference is an event which needs to be stage-managed and which requires a very professional approach to its production and presentation on the day. Through familiarity with television programmes and other broadcast media, delegates now expect the same high standards of presentation in their working environments. Poorly-produced slides or overheads, problems with projectors or microphones, ill-prepared chairmen, intrusive air conditioning, uncomfortable seating are just some of the all-too-frequently-voiced criticisms of conferences and all are less and less acceptable. What is more, all can and should be avoided with proper planning.

While the message is, of course, more important than the medium used to convey it, the message may get lost or misinterpreted if not presented in a way which holds delegates' attention. For this reason, the appropriate use of audio-visual technology should be discussed with speakers, who will usually have their own ideas about how best to make their presentations. If something more than just an overhead projector and flipchart, or data projector and computer, are to be used, an organizer should look at employing a specialist conference production company. The services of such companies are not cheap, but their costs can be built into the budget and will minimize the risk of embarrassing crises, as well as reassuring speakers that their presentations will not be plagued by technical hitches.

Wherever possible, speakers should participate in rehearsals, both to familiarize themselves with the room and technical equipment to be used, and also to run through the sequence of introductions and cues to be used with the session chairman.

Technology is now on the market which allows an entire conference to be recorded on video, audio and in text format, translated into any language and placed on a single CD to be played back on a computer by the delegate (or, of course, sold to those who were unable to attend the conference, both to extend the conference audience and to generate additional income streams for the organizers). Some products contain a complete 'virtual' environment, allowing delegates to walk between lecture theatres and meeting rooms as if present at the conference.

Case study 5.4 describes in detail the technologies available for virtual meetings. Chapter 9 explores whether virtual meetings will, one day, replace the need for face-to-face meetings and conventions.

EVENT EVALUATION

Once the conference is over, an evaluation of the event needs to take place as soon as possible. Ideally, delegates should complete assessments for each session as soon as it ends or shortly afterwards, either through a printed questionnaire or an on-line evaluation form. Delegate itineraries can include evaluation questionnaires (a sample from a BACD conference is shown at Figure 5.4) for each session, as well as an overall evaluation sheet for completion at the end of the conference. Feedback from delegates is essential in assessing the success of the conference. It is also very important as a means of gathering ideas for future events. It may be appropriate for delegate questionnaires to be completed anonymously to encourage honest comments, and some form of incentive can also increase the number of responses.

In some cases, of course, a fully objective appraisal of the conference will not be possible until months later, as the outcomes

BACD CONVENTION

CONVENTION SESSION 1 – EVALUATION SHEET

Session Title:

Session Date:

Presenter:

The following is a general questionnaire, some statements may not be applicable to this session. If so, please omit.

Please indicate the extent to which you agree or disagree with the following statements regarding this session. (4 = strongly agree, 1 = strongly disagree; circle one number only.)

	Strongly Agree			Strongly Disagree
The speaker demonstrated knowledge of the subject	4	3	2	1
The speaker was effective in communicating the subject matter	4	3	2	1
The subject matter was of relevance and interest	4	3	2	1
The visual aids/handouts formed a useful part of the presentation	4	3	2	1
The question and answer session was of benefit	4	3	2	1
I learnt new skills/gained new insight and understanding	4	3	2	1

- **My overall impression of the session was:**

_____
_____
_____
_____

- **Additional Comments:**

_____
_____
_____
_____

Source: British Association of Conference Destinations

Figure 5.4 Example of a conference evaluation questionnaire.

of the event are translated into improved sales, enhanced performances, a more effective sharing of information, or whatever objectives were set in the first place.

The organizer will also want to evaluate how, from his perspective, the conference was managed and to what extent it met the set objectives. Ideas for improving those aspects which did not work well should emerge, and the more successful elements can be developed further in the future.

An appraisal should also take place with the venue. In the author's experience, this is an area where many venues lose marks. Discussions between the venue and the client after the event seem to be the exception, whereas they should be the norm. Even when an event appears to have run smoothly, there will always be scope for further improvement. Venues should take the initiative in following up with clients to assess all aspects of their performance. Unfortunately, many do not seem to bother.

Finally, it is worthwhile preparing a post-conference/convention report: a detailed summary of every aspect of the event, from total attendance to room usage to food and beverage functions and more. It will take time to prepare such an in-depth document, but the rewards are worth the effort. It is both an invaluable reference tool for planning next year's conference (it is much easier reading through a detailed 4-page or 5-page summary document than having to work through bulky files), and a powerful negotiating tool since it contains accurate figures from the conference, including details of all revenue spent at the conference venue.

Summary

- the planning of a conference involves steps which are similar to those involved in the staging of many other events. It demands a logical approach and great attention to detail on the part of an organizer, but also affords scope for creativity and imagination
- at the outset, clear objectives for the conference should be set and as much information collected as possible about the participants, programme, timing, location and format. Financial aspects are another important part of the planning process: budgets need to be drawn up and, where appropriate, cashflow forecasts prepared
- the selection of a suitable venue is crucial to the success of any event, and time and resources should be allocated to ensuring that the right choice is made. Various forms of assistance in venue finding are available, including directories, brochures, computer software and web sites, exhibitions, magazines and specialist agencies. Once a shortlist of the most suitable venues has been completed, inspection

visits are made and negotiations take place between organizers and venues to determine an agreed package

- planning the detail of the conference programme should always take account of the objectives set for the event from the start. The choice of speakers is a critical factor in delegate perceptions of the event. Social programmes present an ideal opportunity for organizers to bring something distinctive and memorable to an event

- marketing the conference needs to begin at the earliest possible moment, ideally at the previous year's event if it is one in a regular sequence. Various promotional tools are available, designed to increase the profile of the conference as well as to maximize delegate numbers, and to distribute the message of the conference globally and over an extended period of time

- no conference ends with the closing session. Organizers should spend time evaluating the event through feedback from delegates and other interested parties. Ideas for improving future events will emerge from this evaluation process.

Review and discussion questions

1. From the perspective of an event organizer, compare and contrast the various information sources (directories, brochures, computer software and web sites, magazine features) for a chosen conference destination. Evaluate the strengths and weaknesses of each source.

2. Re-read the section on 'Negotiating with Venues' together with the sections on 'Yield Management' and 'Negotiating with Organizers' from Chapter 6. Describe the characteristics of a 'win win' negotiation which both organizer and venue would consider a success.

3. You have twelve months to plan a new medical association conference for 300 delegates (plus partners). There is no previous event history. Produce a schedule which details the actions and decisions required on a month-by-month basis in the planning and staging of the conference. The schedule should include a budget and cashflow forecasts. The conference committee has given you an initial promotional budget of £3000 and asked you to make a profit of £5000 which can be used as a start-up fund for the following year's conference. Demonstrate how this will be achieved.

4. A venue charges £50 per delegate as a non-residential or day delegate rate, to include room hire, lunch, and morning

and afternoon teas/coffees. Alternatively, these may be bought as separate items at a cost of £1000 for room hire, £18 per person for lunch, and £3-00 for each tea/coffee consumed. Calculate the best way of buying for 40, 70, 100 and 150 delegates.

Notes and references

1. Carey, T (1997), *Crisis or Conference!*, The Industrial Society.
2. Carey, T, *Planning The Planning*, an article in Meeting Planner magazine (Winter 2000 issue, Volume 4 Number 16).
3. Cotterell, P (1994), *Conferences – an organiser's guide*, Hodder & Stoughton.
4. Fisher, J. G (1998), How to run a successful conference, Kogan Page.
5. Getz, D (1997), *Event Management and Event Tourism* Cognizant Communication Corporation.
6. Maitland, I (1996), *How to Organize a Conference*, Gower Publishing Limited.
7. McCabe, V, Poole, B and Leiper, N (2000), *The Business and Management of Conventions* John Wiley and Sons.
8. Swarbrooke, J and Horner, S (2001), *Business Travel and Tourism*, Butterworth-Heinemann.
9. The Convention Industry Council International Manual (first edition) (2005).
10. *The UK Conference Market Survey 2006*, research undertaken by The Right Solution on behalf of the Meetings Industry Association (July 2006).

Further reading

1. *Professional Meeting Management*, edited by Polivka, Edward G., Professional Convention Management Association (fourth edition).
2. *Professional Meeting Management – A European Handbook*, edited by Tony Carey and published on behalf of the MPI Foundation (ISBN: 90-804834-1-9).
3. Seekings, D. and Farrer, J., How to Organise Successful Conferences and Meetings, Kogan Page (1999).
4. Appleby, P *Organising A Conference*, How To Books Ltd (2005).

5. Bowdin, G.A.J., McDonnell, I., Allen, J. & O'Toole, W. *Events Management*, Butterworth-Heinemann (2001).
6. Craven R E and Johnson L, The Complete Idiot's Guide to Meeting and Event Planning, Alpha (2006).
7. Friedman S, *Meeting & Event Planning for Dummies*, John Wiley & Sons (2003).
8. Goldblatt J J, Special events: best practices in modern event management, 2nd Ed., Van Nostrand Reinhold (1997).
9. Torrence, Sara R., *How to Run Scientific and Technical Meetings*, published by Van Nostrand Reinhold International (1996).
10. Hoyle L, Event Marketing: How to Successfully Promote Events, Festivals, Conventions, and Expositions, John Wiley & Sons (2002).
11. Allen, Judy, *The Business of Event Planning*, published by John Wiley & Sons (2002).
12. IAPCO documents (see www.iapco.org):
    - *How to Choose the Right PCO*
    - *First Steps in the Preparation of an International Meeting*
    - *First Steps for a Medical Meeting*
    - *Guidelines for Co-operation between the International Association, the National Organising Committee and the PCO*
    - *Guidelines for the International Scientific Programme Committee*
    - *Guidelines on Poster Presentations*
    - *Sponsorship Prospectus*
    - *Housing Guidelines.*

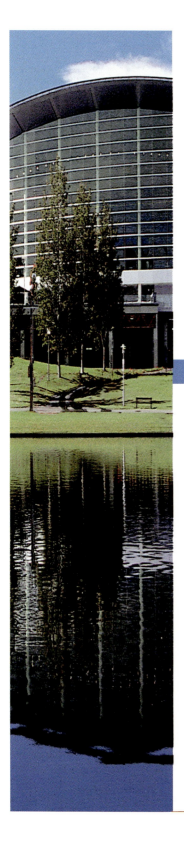

CHAPTER 6

Conference management – a venue perspective

Introduction

Organizing a successful conference is dependent upon many interlinking factors, not least of which is effective communications and teamwork between the conference organizer and the conference venue. Chapter 5 has looked at the management of the event from the standpoint of the organizer, whether this is the 'end user' or 'buyer' (corporation, association, public body, etc.) who has ownership of the event, or a PCO or intermediary organization acting on behalf of the end user. This chapter explores conference management from the perspective of the venue or 'supplier', and describes the team approach within a venue, and between venue and client, to deliver successful events.

The chapter looks at:

- Client-focused product innovations
- Professional inspection visits and showrounds
- Yield management and 'REVPAR'
- Negotiating with clients
- Venue case studies:
  - The Westin Turnberry Resort, Ayrshire, Scotland
  - Adelaide Convention Centre, Australia
  - Woodland Grange Training and Conference Centre, Warwickshire, England.

On completion of this chapter, you should be able to:

- Understand how conference venues seek to maximise and retain business
- Explain the meaning of esoteric terms such as 'yield management' and 'REVPAR'
- Describe best practice in conducting showrounds of venues and in negotiating with conference clients.

CLIENT-FOCUSED PRODUCT INNOVATIONS

In times of economic downturn, venues often find themselves facing strong competition for fewer events. In these situations it is those properties that 'put themselves in their clients' shoes that win the business'. This is not simply a question of providing discounted rates. Clients want, more than anything, to see their suppliers delivering services to the promised standards.

Some practical examples of the outworking of such a client-focused approach are given later in this chapter as seen through the eyes of several venues. Many venues are also investing heavily in their physical 'product' (bedrooms, meeting rooms, technology, for example) to give them a competitive edge and to underline their customer orientation. One practical example of this is Le Meridien's Cumberland Hotel in central London, launching its first 60 'Art & Tech' rooms as part of a £72 million refit and described in an article entitled 'Bed and Broadband' in *Business Travel World* magazine (June 2002). The 'Art & Tech' rooms aim to capitalise on two emerging trends for the hotel world in the 21st century: boutique-style design and the use of high technology to enhance the guest experience. The new rooms have 42-inch plasma televisions providing interactive services including fast internet connections and movies on demand; safes large enough to take laptops as well as provide battery recharging connections, and electronically-controlled beds to elevate guests' legs and torsos. In the article John Ryan, Le Meridien's senior vice president of worldwide sales, explained their philosophy as follows:

> *Over the past 15 years hotels have tended to invest in technology that was primarily geared to hotel operations rather than guests, such as electric door locks, comput-erised operations and yield management systems. In the 21st century we need to turn this around and focus on what the customer wants from new technology, especially as the hotel guests of today already have modern*

technology in their homes and offices. We need to look, therefore, at such things as better entertainment services and improved communication tools.

The same *Business Travel World* article reported that Marriott Hotels had unveiled new conference technology in many of its UK hotels, including the latest webcasting facilities and high-speed net access, video conferencing for meetings at different hotels, and e-mail kiosks and internet cafes for delegates to use during meeting breaks. Hyatt Hotels has introduced a computerised billing system for conference groups, providing a summary and detailed support information including room charges, functions, convention services, audio-visual and other charges – this system is designed to overcome the frustrations of meeting planners who found it time-consuming and frustrating to reconcile separate bills.

The International Convention Centre, Birmingham (England) has produced an interactive CD containing video clips, animated three-dimensional plans and images of the Centre which, once a booking is made and the customer is given a password, changes to a planning tool. It then provides order forms, checklists, high resolution images for literature and a searchable directory of hotels, restaurants, nightlife and attractions in the area. The CD is now complemented by on-line ordering for guests and for exhibitors: for example, guest attending banqueting functions at the Centre can pre-order and pay in advance for drinks; exhibitors can pre-order plasma screens or catering for their stands on-line. A demonstration of this service can be viewed at: www.theicc.co.uk/onlineordering.

Campbell (2000) outlines ways in which venues are seeking to meet the needs of the 'inner delegate'. He comments that:

Leisure clubs with swimming pools have always been rated highly by many organizers, but these too have been overtaken by progress. Today's increasingly essential facility is a spa, offering a full range of look-good and feel-good options. Facials are no longer just for women, nor massages just for men. Pampering delegates in strawberry-flavoured wraps with honey-infused oils against a background of soothing meditative music for the inner soul is no longer a freakish idea, but part of the esteem-enhancing, equilibrium-guaranteeing process of preparing top executives for the conference fray. Consequently, venues have to be up to speed with their holistic lifestyle features. Against this background of body awareness it is hardly surprising that more organizers are requesting a higher proportion of no smoking bedrooms for their guests, with 60 per cent no longer being unusual.

Campbell also waxes lyrical on conference seating:

> *Curiously, a seat is no longer a seat. Instead, it's a figure-contoured, posture-supporting, attention-assisting investment in delegate involvement. They are moulded to the delegate in a bid to keep him or her awake and alert. Old-fashioned banqueting chairs no longer pass the test, nor, for that matter, the minimalist and stylish scrap of aluminium and leather. Today's organizers want a 'smart' chair that reduces delegate snoozing!*

Smart venues are also investing in chairs with improved stack-ability and in flip top tables that can be cleared away in a fraction of the time of more traditional products. Many conference and meeting rooms are set up and cleared by women and the turn-round time is important. Lightweight, more manoeuvrable furniture makes the process easier.

The challenge for hotels and venues is often to distinguish between a fad among their clients and a long-term cultural change, and then to invest in product development accordingly. It may seem an obvious requirement but it is perhaps only in recent years that hotels have fully appreciated the importance of ensuring a good night's sleep for their guests. In 2003 Sofitel hotels launched their 'My Bed' concept, which allowed customers to choose the type of bedding they wanted. Starwood hotels introduced their 'Heavenly Bed' concept for their Westin brand, while Holiday Inn offered a 'Pillow Menu' of five different types of pillows plus an effective room blackout to aid rest.

One of the other important ways in which venues are introducing new products and services, in line with societal demands for eco-friendly practices, is in the development of energy-efficient and 'green' systems and facilities. Interestingly, among the top ten criticisms of hotel venues by conference booking agencies at *Conference & Incentive Travel* magazine's Agency Forum 2006 was 'lack of a sustainability policy' (*C&IT* magazine, October 2006). Progress in the greening of conference venues is explored further in Chapter 9.

PROFESSIONAL INSPECTION VISITS AND SHOWROUNDS

For conference and meeting venues, a key part of the sales and marketing process is the opportunity to show a potential client the benefits and attractions of their venue through a personal showround or inspection. In the author's experience, this is often an activity in which venues fail to do justice to themselves because the showround is conducted by inexperienced, untrained and ill-informed staff who fail to sell the benefits of their venue effectively and so fail to convince the customer that his event will be successful if held there. The guidelines below set out how such visits should be handled by the venue to maximize the chances of winning the business. They draw heavily (as does the later section on 'Negotiating with Clients') on venue training courses run by Peter Rand, one of the most respected trainers in the UK conference industry.

The showround provides an opportunity to:

- Build a rapport with the client which demonstrates an understanding of his needs
- Develop his confidence in the venue team
- Address detail, recognize and use confidence signals, remembering that clients cannot sample the actual service before an event.

Careful preparation and planning are vital. When the appointment for the showround is being made, the following should be covered:

- Decide on the appropriate level of hospitality to be offered and whether this should involve an overnight stay
- Check that the right staff and the correct facilities will be available on the proposed visit date
- Ensure the client's correct contact details are held, including mobile/cell phone number for emergency contact, and numbers of people visiting
- Clarify the client's travel arrangements (e.g. arrival time, time available to spend at the venue, method of transport being used).

A written acknowledgement of the appointment and arrangements should be sent, with reassurances of meeting any specific interests or concerns (e.g. availability of the chef), and enclosing full venue location details.

Before the visit takes place, internal communications within the venue should determine the appropriate venue personnel (numbers, job role, specialist knowledge) to meet the client. Full details of the client should be circulated, including the reason for the visit. Agreement will be needed on the appropriate layout for the conference rooms (subject to other commitments). And, finally, the person overseeing the showround should check that he has the authority and knowledge to cover any potential areas of negotiation, has got the necessary venue and destination product knowledge to hand, and has prepared a photo file of the venue (especially if the conference room(s) are not available or are set up for a different kind of event).

On the day of the visit, the 'welcome' from the venue Reception staff must show that the client is expected. Appropriate introductions should be made, refreshments offered, and the agenda for the visit re-confirmed. The venue representative(s) will need to:

- Discuss the enquiry in a logical way (chronologically)
- Clarify the client's needs, objectives, and priorities for the event
- Show an interest in the client's organization, products/services, and future development
- Use open questions, listen carefully to replies, check understanding where necessary
- Give the client a site plan of the venue, showing its general layout and indicating the route of the showround
- Show those parts of the venue relevant to the client
- Highlight the venue's benefits based on the client's needs (rather than just listing the 'features' of the venue)
- Introduce and involve appropriate personnel
- If appropriate, show the grounds and/or leisure facilities, and kitchens
- And, throughout the visit, invite questions, check understanding, make notes, indicate locations on the floor plan as they relate to different aspects of the client's event, and look/listen for buying signals.

At the conclusion of the visit, it is important to find a quiet corner with the client to summarize the event, check and overcome any concerns, clarify the next step(s), and agree a time for the next contact. The 'close' should include a re-affirmation of interest in staging the client's event. After the visit, there should be a written follow-up with the client, and the venue's sales follow-up system should be updated. In due course, feedback on the visit to the venue staff should be given.

YIELD MANAGEMENT AND 'REVPAR'

The 1990s saw the adoption of the theory and practice of yield management by conference venues, hotels especially. The application of yield management is seen most importantly towards the end of the marketing process, at the time when a customer (conference organizer) is negotiating a booking with his chosen or shortlisted venue.

Yield management aims to 'maximize revenue by adjusting prices to suit market demand' (Huyton and Peters, 1997). It:

> *emphasizes high rates on high demand days and high occupancy when demand is low. The focus of yield management is to maximize revenue every day, not for seasons or periods. It places the needs of the customer secondary to those of the hotel.*

Huyton and Peters suggest that:

> For many years prospective hotel guests have become used to bargaining for their room rates or at least expecting that a room, at the rate they normally pay, will be available. Hotels have been seen by their customers as simply providers of rooms and beds. The idea that they are organized establishments, whose sole purpose is to make money for the owners, appears not to be a part of hotel guests' thinking. For as many years as this attitude has been expressed by customers, the hotel industry has permitted it by acceding to guests' needs, wants and whims. The idea seems to have been that we should be grateful for who we can get to come and stay. Yield management has turned this aspect of hotel operation on its head. What the system now tells the customer is that there are certain rooms set aside at certain price categories and, once they are full, you will have to pay more.

Yield management principles apply not just to the sale of bedrooms. Hartley and Rand (1997) explain that:

> For a venue having conference, function and/or exhibition space, yield management systems, designed to increase the overall profitability of the venue, must include consideration of many factors beyond room inventory and room pricing. While the yield-related information needed to handle a bedroom booking can be assessed relatively quickly, conference function and exhibition space can be sold and used in many different ways and for many different purposes – combinations of which will produce significantly varying profit potential. Ultimately, yield will be determined by how you sell the total facilities available.

Hartley and Rand outline a 'Conference Capacity Strategy' which a venue's sales team should develop in order to maximize yield from conference business. The Strategy looks at business mix, market strength and competitive edge, profitability, lead times and refused business. They expound the factors and techniques involved in allocating capacity to particular enquiries, and give practical tips on how to secure the business. They contend that:

> Price, and the way the pricing issue is managed by the venue, are components of the 'package' that the venue constructs at this stage of the enquiry. The overall relevance and quality of the package will be determining factors in winning or losing the business.

They strongly discourage the frequently used terminology of '8-hour', '24-hour' or 'day delegate rates', preferring to use 'residential' and 'non-residential rates' as more appropriate terminology. They put forward what they describe as a:

> *Radical but still potentially flexible approach: the 'up to' tariff where the maximum rate is quoted as the published rate but it is still apparent that a reduced tariff may be available, dependent on the overall attractiveness of the booking to the venue.*

Figure 6.1 (taken from Hartley and Rand, 1997) illustrates the measurement of conference capacity yield in a venue over a period of one week, showing the potential and realized figures.

'Revenue per available room (REVPAR) is increasingly used as the definitive measure of a hotel's performance, replacing or complementing the measurement of occupancy and average rate. (*This information on REVPAR is taken from an article written by Pamela Carvell of Pampas Training (e-mail: pampasmark@aol.com)*

	Target (potential) (week)	Actual realized (week)
Accommodation		
Number of bedrooms		
(allocated to conference sector)	400 rooms	325 rooms
Accommodation rate	£70	£65
Conference space		
(capacity of 850* sq. mtrs)		
*inc. private dining facilities		
Revenue per sq. m	£93	£75

Conference sector bedroom yield

$$\frac{\text{Rooms sold}}{\text{Rooms available for sale}} \times \frac{\text{Average rate of rooms sold}}{\text{Average rate potential}} = \frac{325}{400} \times \frac{65}{70} = \frac{21125}{28\,000} = 75\%$$

Conference space – revenue earned

$$\frac{\text{Revenue per sq. m realized} \times 850}{\text{Potential revenue per sq. m} \times 850} = \frac{£75 \times 850}{£93 \times 850} = \frac{63\,750}{79\,050} = 81\%$$

Conference sector capacity yield

$$\frac{\text{Accommodation revenue realized} + \text{Conference space revenue realized}}{\text{Accommodation revenue potential} + \text{Conference space revenue potential}} \times 100$$

$$\frac{21125 + 63\,750}{28000 + 79050} \times 100 = \frac{84875}{107050} \times 100 = 79\%$$

Figure 6.1 The measurement of conference capacity yield in a venue over one week (Source: Yeoman and Ingold (1997) *Yield Management – Strategies for the Service Industries*)

and is reproduced with her permission). And yet, too often, too few people in a hotel fully understand the significance of this measurement. Similarly, too many people think that REVPAR and yield are the same measurement. Many hotels which claim to practise yield management are simply measuring REVPAR on a daily basis and staff are incapable of explaining to a guest why different rates are charged on different days for the same room.

Yield management and revenue management (as opposed to REVPAR) are one and the same thing. Essentially they are an approach to increasing profit by responding to what we know about the past, what we know about the present and what we think will happen in the future. In other words, we are trying to sell the right room at the right time, at the right price to the right person. You could say that this is nothing new, but on the other hand many hotels are focused on occupancy or average rate and make most decisions on a very short-term basis. Yield management is a systematic approach to simultaneously optimising both average rate and occupancy, the ultimate aim being 100 per cent yield i.e. 100 per cent occupancy at rack rate (the published rate).

Yield is derived from the basic economic theory of supply and demand. In times of high demand, high prices can be charged. Conversely, when demand is low, prices will be lowered. Also, when supply is limited, prices rise and when there is an over-supply, prices drop. We are trying to match supply and demand by establishing a customer's willingness to pay a certain price.

Yield management only really operates in hotels and airlines by virtue of the following:

- Capacity is relatively fixed
- Demand is derived from distinct market segments
- Inventory (bedroom and meeting room stock) is perishable (see below)
- The product is often sold well in advance of consumption
- Demand fluctuates significantly.

Whilst airlines started using yield management in the 1970s, hotels have only really been using it in a disciplined way since the mid-1990s. The common factor in both industries is that if a seat or bedroom is empty on one flight/night, it cannot be sold twice the next day to make up lost revenues (it is thus a 'perishable' product). This is unlike most other industries whereby sales shortfalls today can be made up at some time in the future. Also, other industries can increase and decrease manufacturing output to match fluctuations in demand, but a hotel cannot increase or decrease its number of bedrooms or meeting rooms to match demand.

Yield is measured as a percentage, being the actual room revenue as a percentage of total room revenue (see Figure 6.1). The closer it is to 100, the better the yield is, but a typical hotel will achieve around 60 per cent yield. A yield measurement enables comparisons between hotels of different standards and in different countries.

REVPAR is a monetary amount and is calculated by dividing the total room revenue by the total number of rooms. The psychological disadvantage of both these measurements is that they will be lower than the traditional measurements of occupancy and average rate. But, they are a truer reflection of a business's performance.

Yield management is about forecasting, discounting, managing inventories, overbooking, evaluating group (including conference) enquiries, redirecting demand and logical, rational pricing. Essentially the key to successful yield management is the ability to differentiate customers who are prepared to pay high prices from those who are prepared to change their travel plans to secure low prices, or make a commitment well in advance to secure the low price.'

NEGOTIATING WITH CLIENTS

The principles and practice of yield management provide the backcloth against which sales activity takes place, one key element of which is negotiating with the venue's conference clients. Some aspects of negotiating have already been touched on (see section on 'Professional Inspection Visits and Showrounds' above). However, there are a number of other factors which a venue will need to consider as part of this negotiation process, all of which link with the objectives of maximizing occupancy and yield, and help in determining whether a venue wants a particular piece of business and, if so, at what rate. Such factors include:

- Decisions on the correct business mix for the venue (identifying the most appropriate conference market segments (see Chapter 2) as well as other types of business if, for example, the venue is a hotel also seeking individual business travellers, leisure tourists, coach groups, etc.)
- Dates – accepting business that allows the venue to maximize bookings on 365 days a year, including factors such as whether the event is weekday or weekend or a combination of the two

- Timings of a meeting or conference – if, for example, the event does not start until the afternoon or evening, is there an opportunity to sell the meeting room(s) to another client for the first part of this day?
- Duration and seasonality
- Numbers of delegates, bedroom occupancy, and overall value of the piece of business
- Numbers of meeting rooms required, and the implications this might have for other potential business that might have to be refused
- Future opportunities for business from this client.

Before commencing negotiations, it is also important for the venue sales manager to prepare fully through an understanding of the market:

- Knowing the main sources of business for the venue
- Understanding market segmentation and the different types of conference clients with different types of events, objectives, budgets. What is the market position of the client?
- Keeping abreast of the current state of the conference market (strengths and weaknesses, trends) and of the general economy (local/national and increasingly international)
- Being aware of the venue's principal competitors
- Being fully informed of major events in the locality (sporting, cultural, business) which will have an impact on demand for bedrooms and possibly function rooms.

A venue needs to decide, prior to negotiation, what the ideal outcome would be, but also what a realistic outcome would be and, finally, what its fallback position should be.

Once negotiations start, it is important to establish at an early stage what are the important criteria (i.e. critical factors in determining how successful an event has been) for the client; what alternatives are available (both other venues being considered but also alternative dates and formats for the event to allow maximum flexibility); whether the buyer/organizer has any concessions to offer and, if so, what he might be expecting in return; and what concessions the venue can bring to the negotiating table which will cost little but be perceived as valuable by the client.

VENUE CASE STUDIES

This section of the chapter elaborates on points made in previous sections: it looks at the ways in which three different types of venue are structured and operated to enable them to compete effectively in winning and retaining conference business through the delivery of successful events. It examines an international hotel chain venue, a purpose-built convention centre and a residential training and conference centre.

Case Study 6.1 The Westin Turnberry Resort, Ayrshire, Scotland

The Westin Turnberry Resort is part of the Westin brand within the international Starwood Hotels and Resorts chain (www.westin.com/turnberry). A five-star resort hotel complete with a globally-renowned golf course, The Westin Turnberry is located on the Ayrshire coast of south-west Scotland, enjoying stunning views across to the Isle of Arran.

The following information was provided by the hotel's Sales Director:

The venue team/the responsibility chain for an event

There are various potential communication/booking chains that can be associated with an event. The enquiries can be marketing-generated and transmitted directly to the Resort Events team who will prepare the proposal and send it directly to the client, copying either the Turnberry-specific or Starwood Sales Manager responsible for that account or geographical area.

All enquiries, whether generated externally or from a Turnberry/Starwood source, are directed to the Resort Sales team (in Turnberry's case one manager and two executives). For each enquiry they will send directly to the client an e-proposal

Figure 6.2
The Westin Turnberry Resort
(Source: The Westin Turnberry
Resort)

which is effectively a stand-alone web site built for each enquiry which contains both specific pricing, availability and capacity topics related to the enquiry, as well as generic information and pricing for all incremental resort activities ranging from clay pigeon shooting to airport transfers. The Resort Sales team member who has sent the e-proposal receives an e-mail alert when the client is viewing the proposal so that a follow-up phone call can be made at THE most appropriate time.

Once the client negotiation has been completed, either by the Resort Sales team or the other Turnberry/Starwood sales function, a contract is prepared and sent out by the Resort Sales team. When the signed contract and deposit have been received, the event file is passed to the Resort Events team: an Event Manager is allocated to the group and the process for building event orders and internal communication is moved forward by an events professional.

In 2002 we refined our Events selling process to split a somewhat generic Events team into two teams, one of which focuses purely on sales and conversion (Resort Sales) and the other which focuses purely on event delivery and the required attention to detail (Resort Events).

Client relationship

The ideal client relationship is where the client clearly communicates his specific requirements and can highlight any problems or opportunities from experience of the same event in another venue. It is also highly beneficial for the client to be introduced to, and develop a relationship with, some of the key players who will deliver their event such as the Banqueting Manager, Executive Chef, Golf Director, Outdoor Activities Manager etc. We try, wherever possible, for large events to arrange a pre-convention meeting on the day before or the day of arrival – at this stage we can present to the client a detailed understanding of his event by all of the team involved. At this pre-convention meeting ('pre-con'), we can also better understand the finer details such as VIP arrivals, individual room amenities, time/pressure points etc.

We have had some good examples of where either a third party event organiser or inexperienced client has, through poor communication, impacted our ability to deliver an event to a Five Star standard. We emphasize to all our clients the important role that they play in the success of their event. With a very large event or series of small events, we can demonstrate better ability to deliver where the client has played an excellent communication role in the build-up to the event.

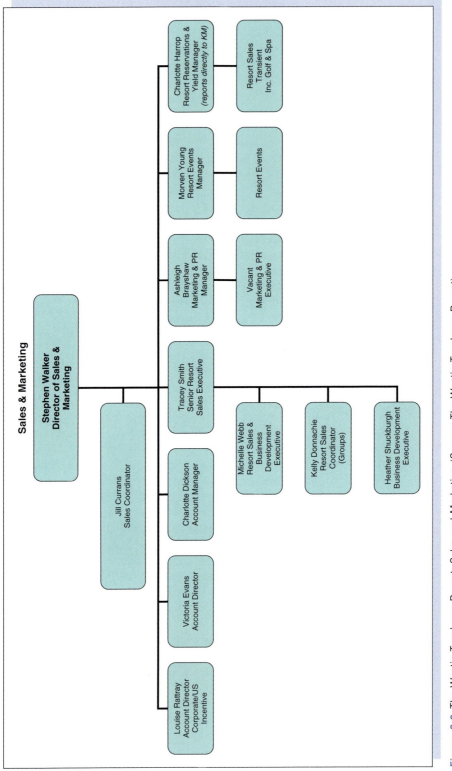

Figure 6.3 The Westin Turnberry Resort, Sales and Marketing (Source: The Westin Turnberry Resort)

Client advice

We have an excellent in-house service for social programmes, guided tours, audio visual etc. However, we also have a range of specialist suppliers we recommend for clients with a particularly detailed requirement.

Health & Safety

Our Resort Security/Health and Safety department will liaise directly with our clients on any questions about legislative requirements the organizer may have.

Training of the conference department

We value all members of our Events team as being an extension to our sales force. All of the team enjoy extensive training in Professional Sales Skills, Negotiation Skills to an advanced stage, Presentation Skills and the Financial/Profit aspect of group business. A Resort Sales Executive with us for 3 years may enjoy an investment of up to £12 000 in their training in this period. This training is available to all Sales and Events teams within Starwood.

The sales process in a resort property like Turnberry with such diverse products as spa treatments, golf, fishing, fine dining etc. requires a broad skill set and certain maturity as we seldom service two events that are identical.

Further information: www.westin.com/turnberry.

Case Study 6.2 Adelaide Convention Centre, Australia

The Adelaide Convention Centre has become an icon for tourism in South Australia, not just because of its landmark location on the banks of the picturesque River Torrens, but because of its reputation for quality and professionalism. It was the first purpose-built convention centre in Australia and for many years has set the benchmark for those that have followed.

The quantity and quality of business it has consistently attracted since opening in 1987 has dispelled the myth that regional, less well-known cities find it hard to attract world-class convention business. On the contrary, the Adelaide centre has drawn a diverse mix of events and clients, with a high rate (more than 60 per cént) of repeat business. On average, 300 000 people pass through its doors each year.

Figure 6.4
Adelaide Convention Centre
(Source: Adelaide Convention
Centre)

It boasts more than 10 000 square metres of pillarless floor space, with a catwalk height of 11 metres. This space can be divided into six soundproofed halls and provides an exhibition capacity of 585 booths. A plenary hall of 2000 square metres divides into five separate units and has a theatre-seating capacity of 3500 guests. Fourteen meeting rooms of various sizes complete the accommodation picture.

The workforce remains fairly stable at around 500, comprising about 150 permanent and contract staff, plus some 350 casuals. The number of casuals tends to fluctuate depending on business needs. Apart from the Adelaide office team, the centre is also represented internationally with representatives based in the UK and in North America.

The centre is the only meetings venue in Australia to offer all event-related products and services in-house, while its competitors outsource various parts of their products and services. 'It means we can effectively ensure the quality of the end product – from food to technology,' says Sales and Marketing Director, Sue Hocking. 'We regard this as a core competency and a true differentiator. It means our people – and our equipment – have to be good, very good. And they are.'

Margaret Terrell, Manager, Event Planning Services, says the philosophy that underpins all contact with clients – from conversations and correspondence through to final execution – is 'customer service that goes the extra mile'

'I don't think you can underestimate that in terms of client relationships, word-of-mouth marketing and future business. It's about making sure that our people know their job intimately, understand where it fits in the grand scheme of things and, if they themselves can't help, they know where to go to find out who can.'

Margaret explains how the system works, once Sales and Marketing have secured the business:

We handle our clients like treasures. The hand-over from Sales to Event Planning is as personal as it can possibly be, given geography. Often it's in our restaurant, Regattas, over coffee. That's when the client is introduced to the Event Planner and the Technical Planner who will guide them all the way through to the day of the event, or the day it begins.

We have a lot of repeat business and those clients tend to come straight back to their Event Planner, rather than to Sales, because we build the relationship with them.

We maintain contact with clients in a variety of ways throughout the lead-up – and sometimes that can be two years or more. Between us, we hammer out the details of the Event Agreement. This can take a lot of discussion and to-ing and fro-ing and there are often lots of changes as we progress. Big events, like conferences, tend to evolve and often the details change significantly between the initial 'sale' and the execution. This is done through meetings, via e-mail, on the telephone . . . whatever is the most appropriate and efficient communication for the client.

Our Technical people are highly knowledgeable and we have state-of-the-art equipment and facilities. The technicians work closely on the planning, too, and do some fantastic, creative things for clients who want something special or dramatic.

We look after clients in all sorts of other ways, too. We often invite them here to get them acquainted with the Centre – and with us. Sometimes it's dinner at Regattas, or even a night at the football. That does tend to depend on the client and the size of the event, or its regularity.

We offer clients a range of complimentary services, such as car parking for meetings and during their conference, free coffee and discounts at Regattas. Our Chief Executive hosts boardroom lunches for VIP clients with a State Government Minister in attendance; and international clients are invited to dinners or lunches with the Chief Executive or the Director Sales & Marketing when they are overseas.

During the planning process, we bring the Food and Beverage Manager who liaises with clients to design a menu – for example, around a particular theme, or with a focus on South Australian local produce. Many of our international clients love to do that because we have such a reputation here in South Australia for our wine, fresh produce and gourmet foods.

We're happy to work with professional conference organisers and often recommend a collection of local operators to interstate or overseas clients. We've done some spectacular and unusual things over the years to make client events really special.

Just before the event, we meet again with the client and introduce them to the dedicated representatives from every department that will touch their event – House Services, Food and Beverage, Customer Relations (reception), Technical Services, Security if required, and, of course, the floor staff. We run through absolutely everything so everyone is quite clear what's happening, what's desired, who's who and what has priority. But for the duration of the event, it's the Event Manager assigned to the client who really is at their 'beck and call'. And they're superbly trained to do that. Our people would do backflips for clients if that's what they wanted.

Every day, reports are completed by the event mangers and technical managers on all aspects of every event. That information, plus all the feedback gathered during and post-event, is stored electronically for future use. It's often particularly valuable for repeat clients and provides insights for the current team wanting to ensure that this year's service delivery is even better than last time.

Sue Hocking comments from a marketing perspective:

We're very particular about assessing all client feedback and the Chief Executive responds to every client with a personal letter. One of the most common comments we get is about the 'can do' attitude of our staff. It often surprises us because it's just the way we operate but it seems to be very refreshing for clients.

We reap a high return on our investment over many years in developing a true training culture in the organization. We are a Registered Training Organization, which means we have national accreditation, and we also work with external providers. In 2006, the Adelaide Convention Centre won the national training award for the Services Industry and were named 'South Australian Employer of the Year'.

Further information: www.adelaidecc.com.au.

Case Study 6.3 Woodland Grange Training and Conference Centre, Warwickshire, England

Woodland Grange Training and Conference Centre is located in rural Warwickshire, close to Royal Leamington Spa and in the centre of England. Following a £5 million development completed in 2006, the venue has 114 bedrooms, with 13 main conference rooms and 13 syndicate rooms, and substantially enhanced leisure and relaxation facilities, including a completely new leisure centre with internet café bar, games room, gymnasium and saunarium. In 2006 Woodland Grange handled over 1100 events (approximately 90 per week), ranging from 3 up to 200 participants, and accounting for almost 26 000 day delegates in total.

The Conference Centre team has approximately 70 contracted employees, with additional casual labour being employed from time to time dependent upon business levels.

The venue is a member of the British Association of Conference Destinations, the Meetings Industry Association and Conference Centres of Excellence.

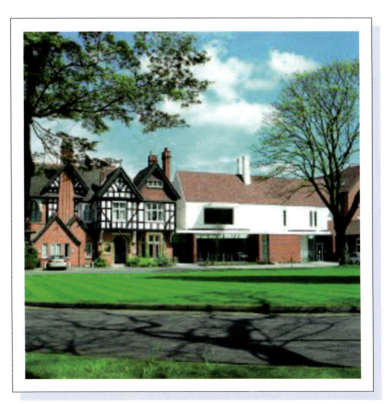

Figure 6.5
Woodland Grange Training and Conference Centre (Source: Woodland Grange Training and Conference Centre)

Key factors

Woodland Grange sees the successful delivery of conference services as the combination of the highest standards of facilities and service with a comprehensive, systematic process for understanding and managing client needs, from the building of an initial personal relationship through to the final invoice, follow-up and beyond.

The key elements are.

- robust and completely reliable procedural disciplines and systems
- an ongoing dialogue and excellent communications with the client
- facilities that are state-of-the-art in every respect, with maximum flexibility to respond to change
- the personal support of staff who are proven specialists in the conference activity
- absolute transparency in terms of charges and fees.

Internal disciplines

Communication of client details and requirements between the conference office and other operational departments is continually reinforced, through daily contact, 'head of department' meetings and live updates through the venue's networked event management software. This minimises vulnerability.

Continuously reviewed performance targets exist for the conference office staff in respect of speed of response to enquiries and pro-active follow-ups to maximise the opportunity.

The conference office also sets and communicates site-wide standards in terms of internal and external presentation. These include staff grooming and conduct, attire, the tidiness and cleanliness of public areas and toilets, and grounds maintenance.

Planning the event and building relationships

Woodland Grange understands that conference organizers now have more options than ever to optimize their event, particularly, but not exclusively, in terms of technology. '*With all the possibilities that are available, and the varying attitudes and interpretations of conference organizers, more than ever there needs to be a meeting of minds in advance of the event,*' says Woodland Grange's Director of Operations, David Vaughton: '*We positively encourage clients into this preliminary planning stage so that, on the day, to put it simply, neither side is surprised.*'

The close relationship that is formed is not allowed to fall away. Through a pro-active approach to client relationship management, contact is maintained beyond the event, a strategy that has helped produce high levels of repeat business. The close relationship is also a critical mechanism for encouraging feedback.

The right environment

The Centre seeks to create, for organizers and their guests, an environment which enables them to focus on the event, to respond to it positively, to be relaxed yet receptive and above all not to be distracted by anxieties, frustrations or interruptions.

The Centre seeks to create an ambience that is efficient without being cold or forbidding, including warm carpeting and wall coverings, comfortable relaxation areas and a welcoming new reception area.

Its training and conference rooms, including the three major new conference and linked syndicate rooms that are part of the latest investment, are designed to provide an ideal environment for learning and teaching. Great attention has been paid to acoustic design and materials, while all have plentiful natural daylight, with variable light reinforcement.

The venue also places great importance on providing an environment which is both safety-conscious and secure, with physical measures and processes that provide reassurance for the client.

Comprehensive support

Committed, informed on-day support is regarded as a critical element of the service. 'Whatever facilities we provide, the success of our service depends on providing properly experienced staff who genuinely understand the conference business,' said David Vaughton: '*It's an equally vital investment – not just having staff who know how to help, but having enough of them available. Ultimately, that's probably the single factor organizers value the most.*'

One of the areas of support that is most prized by clients is the existence of a fully experienced on-site technical team, which can not only address problems or concerns, but also help the organizer to optimize the options. This maximizes the value to the client of the leading edge IT in which the venue has invested. Woodland Grange also makes extensive provision for organizers who arrive with presentations that require last-minute change: it has an in-house 'open resource' centre allowing copying, print and design, with professional support on hand.

Transparency

Woodland Grange is determined to ensure that when the final invoice is received, the client is not disappointed by unexpected extra charges. The venue operates a policy of complete transparency, based on all-inclusive, clearly stated pricing packages.

Clear positioning and focus

Woodland Grange believes that its ability to offer a genuinely focused service for business events is a key factor in winning custom and achieving a consistently high level of client satisfaction. It believes that its specialisation provides major advantage over venues that do not offer focused provision: it has the ability to tune the event as precisely as possible to reflect the client's needs, and to reassure clients of consistent delivery time after time.

Further information: www.wgrange.com.

Summary

Venues must continuously invest in their physical product to maintain a competitive edge. They must also adopt a customer focus in their sales and marketing strategies and in their service delivery, while aiming to maximize return on investment through their approach to, inter alia, yield management and client negotiations.

Review and discussion questions

1. 'Investments in a venue's physical product (meeting rooms, audio-visual technology, furniture and décor, bedrooms, etc.) can compensate for any failings in service delivery by the venue's operational team.' Discuss and debate and illustrate with specific examples.
2. Compare and contrast the approaches of The Westin Turnberry Resort and Woodland Grange Training and Conference Centre to winning and retaining conference business. Look at their web sites and identify the key conference market segments for each venue.

Notes and references

1. Campbell, D, *Market-driven venues adapt to meetings needs*, an article in Catering Magazine, Issue 15 (December 2000), Croner CCH Group Ltd.
2. Carvell, P, *Managing yield to increase profits*, www.pampas training.co.uk/ezines/managingyield.htm.
3. Hartley, J and Rand, P, *Conference Sector Capacity Management* in Ian Yeoman and Anthony Ingold (eds) *Yield Management Strategies for Service Industries*, Cassell (1997).
4. Huyton, J and Peters, S, *Application of Yield Management to the Hotel Industry*. In *Yield Management: Strategies for the Service Industries*, Yeoman, I and Ingold, A, Cassell (1997).

Further reading

1. McCabe, V, Poole, B, Weeks, P, Leiper, N, *The Business and Management of Conventions*, Wiley (2000).
2. Davidson, R, Rogers, T, *Marketing Destinations and Venues for Conferences, Conventions and Business Events*, Elsevier Butterworth-Heinemann (2006).
3. Shone, Anton, *The Business of Conferences*, Butterworth-Heinemann (1998).
4. Prerequisites for a conference hotel, an advisory paper prepared by the International Association of Professional Congress Organizers (IAPCO).

A people industry

Introduction

The conference industry depends for its success and future profitability on attracting people with the highest-quality interpersonal and organizational skills. Such skills are equally important to both the buying and supply sides of the industry. Education and learning programmes, coupled with training and continuing professional development (CPD) courses specific to the conference sector, have emerged and are increasing in number and quality. Stimulating and rewarding careers can be enjoyed, although clear entry routes and progression paths do not yet exist in most countries. This chapter examines:

- the importance of people skills
- education and learning, training and CPD opportunities
- careers in the conference industry
- salary levels.

It includes case studies in the form of career profiles of personalities within the international conference industry. They are:

- a destination marketer /convention and visitor bureau chief executive – Rick Antonson
- a writer, consultant and trainer – Tony Carey
- a convention centre sales and marketing director – Jenny Salsbury
- an exhibition director and company chairman – Ray Bloom
- an industry academic, lecturer and writer – Rob Davidson
- a conference and incentive agency managing director – Patrick Delaney

- a chief executive officer of an international conference industry trade association – Martin Sirk
- an events and marketing executive with a national conference industry trade association, as an example of a recent entrant to the industry – Lucy Watkins
- a managing editor of a conference and incentive industry trade magazine – Martin Lewis.

Learning outcomes

On completion of this chapter, you should be able to:

- Identify the skills and personal qualities needed for a successful career in the conference industry
- Understand the opportunities available for continuing professional development
- Define the types of career opportunities available within the industry
- Appreciate how leading figures in the industry have reached their current positions, and what they see as the rewards and satisfactions of their jobs.

THE IMPORTANCE OF PEOPLE SKILLS

The conference industry is, by definition, about people. The word 'confer' implies a discussion or meeting involving two or more people. It follows, therefore, that those wishing to make their career in the industry need to be 'people' people. They need to have very good interpersonal skills and enjoy mixing with a very wide range of people. Diplomacy, flexibility, tact, patience, friendliness, approachability, a sense of humour, a team player, are just some of the skills needed for success. A variety of other skills is also required depending upon the actual position occupied.

The following job vacancy descriptions are based on actual advertisements and are quoted to highlight the types of skills needed for different posts:

> Conference Administrator: *Small, high-profile conference company seeks an administrator to organize prestigious events. Computer literate, well organized, meticulously accurate team player required. Competitive salary according to experience.*

Conference and Publicity Co-ordinator: *Are you a grad-uate with experience of organizing major high-profile conferences and publicity events? Do you have proven knowledge of media and public relations? Have you at least 2 years' experience of project management and budgetary control? If you fit this description, you could be responsible for the planning, marketing and co-ordination of events, an Annual Conference and Exhibition and pub-lic relations for... (a professional medical association). You will lead a small dynamic team and, in addition to the stated skills, will be able to prioritise and juggle tasks and will have excellent oral, written, presentation, negotiation and decision-making skills. The post is likely to attract candidates who are computer literate, are ambitious, have established media contacts and enjoy UK travel.*

Event Co-ordinator (with a conference centre): *Acting as principal contact between the Centre and the client, devel-oping, organizing and managing events to ensure client requirements are carried out to the highest standard with the main objective of securing repeat and increased busi-ness. It is essential that the successful applicant has proven experience of organizing events where the focus is on high quality customer care/service, possesses excel-lent communication skills together with the ability to pro-duce detailed and accurate documentation. Applicants must be team players who are organized, thorough, able to work in a pressurised environment and possess a high level of motivation. This is a role for a dedicated and highly committed individual.*

Conference Organizers: *An international company, based in London, seeks two people to join its training and seminars office. We produce high-level seminars for ministers and senior officials of foreign governments. Skills required: an analytical mind, ability to work under pressure, attention to detail, experience of seminars or courses, interest in world affairs, knowledge of languages (especially Spanish, Russian, French), excellent written skills and ability to deal with senior people.*

Head of Convention Bureau: *... Convention Bureau seeks conference/meetings/exhibitions/incentive industry professional to drive the marketing and selling of this inter-national city as a business destination, working closely with – and providing benefit for – the range of hotels, venues and professional service suppliers in this market. Candidates will need 3–5 years' experience in at least one of these specialist sectors and will, ideally, have a wide network of UK and overseas contacts. A blend of* *marketing and sales skills will impress, but the prime requirement is the personal confidence to build positive and productive relationships with both prospective clients and the destination's suppliers.*

Conference Manager: *We are looking for a conference manager with a minimum of 3 years' experience to work for a specialist medical events company. Strong organizational and administrative skills are essential along with a flexible approach to work and the ability to work on your own initiative. You will be expected to manage all logistical aspects of your allocated conferences and manage their budgets accordingly. You will be liaising with suppliers, venues and clients and so excellent communication skills are key. This role is suitable for someone with an outgoing personality, strong work ethic and who is looking for a new challenge.*

Senior Manager – Convention Bureau: *Due to a promotion we have a vacancy in one of our key posts for a talented individual who will be a commercially oriented team player who understands the need for a high level of operational support to sustain a division within a highly competitive conference marketing and sales environment. Reporting to the Director for the successful co-ordination and implementation of a target-led marketing and sales programme, including production of print, development of operational systems, co-ordination of research, membership recruitment and the motivation and management of a sales and operational team of 8 people. Highly developed leadership, communications and excellent organizational skills plus computer literacy and a full appreciation of the conference industry are pre-requisites for this position.*

A number of skills and personal characteristics recur in this small selection of advertisements. Some also re-appear later in the chapter, identified by leading conference industry figures as important requirements when they outline their own career profiles. The industry is broad enough to accommodate people with various working backgrounds and educational qualifications, but the common thread is the ability to build productive relationships with a wide variety of people (colleagues, clients and customers, suppliers, the media, and others) and to enjoy doing so.

Research has consistently shown that, where conference organizers and meeting planners have problems with venues, it is not, for the most part, with the facilities and equipment but with staff service, specifically a lack of professionalism and friendliness. As the physical attributes of conference venues become more standardized and of a generally acceptable level, it is likely to be the quality of the staff which will differentiate one from another. This point was expressed very lucidly in a report published in the UK by the Department of National Heritage (DNH – now Department for Culture, Media and Sport) in 1996. Entitled 'Tourism: Competing with the Best – People Working in Tourism and Hospitality', the report said that:

> The quality of personal service is perhaps more important to tourism and hospitality than to any other industry. Consumers who buy one of this industry's products will often have made a significant financial investment, but also an emotional investment and an investment of time. Of course the physical product – the facilities of the holiday village, the distinctiveness of the tourist attraction, the appointments of the hotel, the quality of the restaurant's food – is very important to them. But during the period customers are in the establishment, they will have many interactions with people: some indirect, with the management and chefs and cleaners; and many direct, with the front-line staff. The quality of those interactions is an integral part of the experience and has the potential to delight or disappoint the consumer. We do not believe that this potential is there to the same extent in any other employing sector.

The DNH report rightly claims that:

> Excellent service at a competitive price can only be provided by competent, well-managed and well-motivated people. This means recruiting the right people in the first place, equipping them with the skills they need, managing staff well to create motivation, job satisfaction, and high productivity.

The report analyses some of the tourism industry's shortcomings in respect of these objectives (and their analysis, sadly, is as accurate in the first decade of the new millennium as it was in the mid-1990s), specifically:

> The threat of a self-perpetuating vicious circle that is harmful to profitability and competitiveness. In some parts of the industry a number of characteristics reinforce each other: recruitment difficulties, shortages of skilled and qualified staff, relatively low pay, high staff turnover and a relatively unattractive image as an employing sector.

The report then gives examples of good practice, and makes some proposals for future improvements to overall standards, through better dissemination of good practice, a greater understanding of customer needs and improving quality, improving the image of the industry, and improving the supply of skills to the industry.

The conference sector of the tourism and hospitality industry is not immune from these criticisms. While they apply specifically to the supply side of the industry, it is undoubtedly the case that there is also scope to improve the training and professionalism of those on the industry's buying side. Perhaps there is a need for a 'Code of Practice' for buyers, in the same way that conference venues now offer quality-assured branded products delivered with customer guarantees. In the author's experience, familiar failings on the part of buyers include:

- ludicrously short lead times for planning events and booking venues and services
- 'no shows' or last-minute cancellations from buyer familiarization trips, when flights have been paid for and hotel rooms booked
- a failure to evaluate events. Research regularly shows that around one third of organizers do not obtain delegate feedback and evaluate the effectiveness of their meetings
- a failure to provide fully comprehensive technical and organizational specifications
- a tendency to assume too much about a venue's capabilities and responsibilities
- failing to inform bureaux and agencies which have provided them with a venue finding service of bookings made, and then complaining when they get follow-up calls.

The conference industry is a wonderful, dynamic, seductive industry but one which still fails to command the recognition it deserves. For it to achieve its full potential and be appreciated as a major benefactor to national economies, both sides of the industry must embrace and maintain the same high standards of integrity and professionalism. The status of the conference organizer must be raised to that of a real profession, of equal standing with solicitors, accountants, scientists or engineers.

There is a need to invest in education and training programmes for buyers (a few are now available and others are coming on stream, but there is still a long way to go), to develop career structures so that experience and expertise are retained within the meetings industry, to ensure that the rapidly growing number of college and university courses on conference/events management and business tourism are in tune with the industry's needs, and to provide recognized qualifications in line with other professions.

Buyers and suppliers are inter-dependent, neither can succeed without the other. Effective collaboration and partnerships should be born of respect for the skills and knowledge of each other, built on mutual trust and confidence.

To translate such needs and aspirations into reality will depend to a great extent upon developments to education and learning, training and CPD (Continuing Professional Development) programmes. As described in earlier chapters of this book, the profession is certainly more established as a true profession in the USA than in most, if not all, other countries and high quality education programmes are in place – there must be scope to tailor and develop further such programmes so that they are relevant to other cultures and educational systems, as well as for individual countries to initiate their own.

The next section looks at the opportunities for education and learning, training and CPD currently available within the conference industry, some of which are appropriate to those looking to make a career in the industry, others are for those already employed within it.

EDUCATION AND LEARNING, TRAINING AND CPD OPPORTUNITIES

This section looks firstly at the provision of opportunities at an international level. It then focuses on the current situation in the UK as an example of one country's response to perceived education and training needs. It is the author's impression that educational provision in the UK is at least on a par with that in other European countries and may be more advanced than many, but as yet no research exists which fully documents the range of meetings industry education on a European or global scale.

International courses and qualifications

IAPCO courses • • •

The International Association of Professional Congress Organizers (IAPCO) runs courses at several levels through its Training Academy. The best known is the annual IAPCO Seminar on Professional Congress Organization, popularly known as the Wolfsberg Seminar, first staged in 1975. This is a week-long seminar held in Switzerland in late January and provides a comprehensive training programme for those at all levels involved in conference organization, international conference destination promotion or ancillary services. In-depth topics covered include: introduction to the industry, association/corporate/government meetings, congress promotion, scientific programme and abstract handling, bids and promotion of a destination, registration, marketing strategies of a PCO company, accommodation management, finance, information technology, social programme and protocol, venue management, sponsorship and exhibitions, contracts/insurance/security, presentation skills, and more. IAPCO also runs regional and national seminars, in co-operation with governments, tourist authorities or destination hosts, which typically cover two and a half days of concentrated sessions similar to those presented at the Wolfsberg Seminar. Advanced Management Courses for executives covering managerial subjects such as risk assessment, event accountability, business excellence and inspired leadership, financial planning and marketing strategies for one's own organization are also offered both on a regional and international basis.

Full details on all IAPCO courses are available from: International Association of Professional Congress Organizers. Tel/Fax: +44 (0)1983 755546; E-mail: *info@iapco.org*; Web site: www.iapco.org.

'Certification in Meetings Management' and 'Certified Meeting Professional' Programmes • • •

The Certification in Meetings Management (CMM) programme has been developed by Meeting Professionals International (MPI) as an advanced level professional designation for meeting and event professionals. The CMM focuses on strategic issues and executive decision-making. Applicants for CMM have ideally ten or more years' experience in the industry. If accepted onto the CMM programme and registered for a course, participants are required to:

a) Attend a 5-day residency (or residential) programme, with sessions covering 'Strategic Thinking', 'Leadership', 'Strategic Financial Management', 'Contingency Planning and Business Continuity', 'Negotiation', 'Strategic Marketing', and 'Writing a Strategic Business Plan'.
b) Complete successfully an on-line exam.
c) Undertake a post-residency (post-residential) business plan project (which requires participants to produce a business plan based on what they have learned during the programme).

The CMM is held annually in North America and in Europe. Approximately 50 participants are registered for each programme to encourage networking and interaction. The costs include an application fee of US$75 for MPI members and of US$125 for non-members, and registration fees of US$1800 for MPI members and US$2200 for non-members (as at December 2006).

The CMM qualification does not affect the status of the Certified Meeting Professional (CMP) designation (CMP is also a largely North American designation currently). In fact, the CMM is structured to complement, rather than compete with, the CMP designation: the former is more strategic in approach, the latter more tactical. Meeting professionals can apply for the CMP designation if they have:

- at least 3 years of meeting management experience
- current employment in meeting management
- responsibility and accountability for the successful completion of meetings

and fees payable are approximately $US600 (December 2006).

Further details on the CMM are available from: Meeting Professionals International, 3030 LBJ Freeway, Suite 1700, Dallas, Texas 75234, USA. Tel: +1-972-702-3000; Fax: +1-972-702-3070; E-mail: information@mpiweb.org; Web site: www.mpiweb.org/education/ cmm.

MPI European Office, 22 Route de Grundhof, L-6315 Beaufort, Grand Duchy of Luxembourg. Tel: 352-2687-6141; Fax: 352-2687-6343; E-mail: dscaillet@mpiweb.org.

Further details on the CMP are available from: Convention Industry Council, 1620 I Street, NW, 6th Floor, Washington, DC 20006, USA. Tel:+1-202-429-8634; Fax: +1-202-463-8498; Web site: www.conventionindustry.org.

'Certified Destination Management Executive' and 'Professional in Destination Management' Programmes • • •

The Certified Destination Management Executive (CDME) and Professional in Destination Management (PDM) programmes have been developed by Destination Marketing Association International (DMAI) and are relevant to those working in the convention and visitors bureau (CVB) and destination management/marketing side of the conference and tourism industry.

The CDME programme is an advanced educational programme for experienced and career-minded CVB executives looking for senior-level professional development courses. Its focus is on vision, leadership, productivity and the implementation of business strategies. Demonstrating the value of a destination team and improving personal performance through effective organizational and industry leadership are the expected outcomes. Those completing the programme successfully are entitled to use the CDME credential.

The course has three 'core' courses:

- Strategic issues in destination management
- Destination marketing planning
- Destination leadership.

Each of these courses lasts for $2\frac{1}{2}$ days and involves a 'take-home' assignment to be undertaken by the participant with a subsequent report of findings and conclusions returned for final evaluation.

Participants must also take a minimum of two 'elective' courses, chosen from the following options:

- Agritourism destination management
- Communications and technology in destination management
- Culinary tourism management
- Cultural tourism in destination management
- Destination information and research
- Destination positioning and branding
- Destination product development
- Destination Marketing Accreditation Program (DMAP) and performance management
- Sports in destination marketing and management
- Convention/tradeshow marketing and sales management
- International tourism and convention marketing
- Destination financial management
- Rural and small community destination management
- Destination community relations planning
- Sustainable destination development and marketing
- Human resources in destination management
- Festivals and events tourism
- Communications and technology in destination management
- Resort destination management
- Destination promotion planning
- Wine destination marketing and management
- Gaming and destination management
- Visitor servicing in destination management
- Destination partnership development
- Destination product development.

The costs (as at December 2006) are US$1275 per core course for DMAI member bureau staff, and US$1750 for non-member bureau staff. The elective courses are US$750 each for DMAI member bureau staff and US$1050 for non-member bureau staff.

The PDM programme leads to the PDM certificate (but, unlike CDME, is not a professional credential) and is geared towards CVB professionals seeking the knowledge and skills that will help to ensure successful careers in destination management. The PDM Certificate requires completion of 40 credits within a 5-year period. Since 2001 credits have only been tracked for those with an individual DMAI membership. As well as its 'Fundamentals of Destination Management Course' (1.5 credits), there are four required courses which must be completed:

- Essentials of CVB Management (1 credit)
- Communications in Destination Management (1 credit)
- Information Technology for Destination Management (1 credit)
- Destination Marketing (1 credit).

All of these required courses are also available on-line in partnership with the George Washington University Institute of Tourism Studies. The 36 additional credits are earned through a variety of courses offered at DMAI's annual events. Online fees per core course are US$125 for member bureau staff and US$175 for non-member bureau staff.

Further details on the CDME and PDM programmes are available from: Manager of Meetings & Events, Destination Marketing Association International, 2025 M Street NW, Suite 500, Washington, DC, 20036 USA; Tel: +1-202-296-7888; Fax: +1-202-296-7889; E-mail: info@destinationmarketing.org; Web site: www.destinationmarketing.org.

European Cities Marketing summer school and senior educational forum • • •

European Cities Marketing (ECM) (until 2006 known, in part, as the European Federation of Conference Towns (EFCT)) has been running an annual Summer School since 1987, held in a different country each year (normally end of August/early September). The 2006 and 2007 Summer Schools took place in Berlin (Germany) and Tallin (Estonia) respectively.

The Summer School is open to meetings industry professionals from all over the world. This intensive 3-day event is for people working in all sectors of the conference marketplace (convention bureaux, tourist offices, congress and convention centres, airlines, hotels, DMCs, PCOs and meeting planners). The aim is to equip attendees with the latest marketing tools and help them develop the knowledge and skills required for a successful career in conference, meeting and event management. The Summer School is driven by highly experienced teachers from many professional backgrounds and countries. The faculty includes senior ECM personalities and keynote speakers from the meetings industry sector. Speakers address topics such as:

- The Meetings Industry Scene – Competing in the Global Marketplace
- The World of Meetings Statistics
- Marketing a Destination or a Congress Centre
- Working with the Press
- How to Bid Successfully.

Practical and imaginative sessions are complemented by hands-on demonstrations and site inspections. The programme also allows time for networking with colleagues from different cultures and backgrounds.

As well as the Summer School, ECM holds an annual Senior Educational Forum which takes the form of a 2-day conference where speakers discuss matters of interest and members exchange business. The 2006 Forum was held in Madeira in March.

Further details from: European Cities Marketing, 99 rue de Talant, F-21000 Dijon, France. Tel: +33 380 56 02 04; Fax: +33 380 56 02 05; E-mail: service-centre@europeancitiesmarketing.com; Web site: www.europeancitiesmarketing.com.

Professional Convention Management Association • • •

The Professional Convention Management Association (PCMA) provides educational programmes for meeting managers, hotels, convention and visitor bureaux, and others in the meetings industry. PCMA views lifelong learning as the key to a satisfying job and continued career advancement. Educational opportunities are delivered through seminars, self-study courses, reference materials and distance learning programmes. They include: the PCMA Annual Meeting which takes place each January and is one of the industry's premier educational events; a Leadership Conference; a Certified Meeting Professional (CMP) Online Programme (the 'only online course specifically designed to prepare for the CMP examination'), and the CASE (Certified Association Sales Executive) Program (designed to help meetings industry suppliers better understand the needs of their association customers).

In 2006–2007 PCMA developed and launched its 'Principles of Professional Performance' (PoPP). PoPP is a framework for bringing relevant and effective education to PCMA members, but also impacting students, institutions, and the entire meetings industry. PoPP is not an accreditation or certification programme, as PCMA will continue to support other organizations involved with these. Rather it is designed as a framework for the 'knowledge domains' and 'core competencies' essential to successful careers in the convention and meetings industry.

Professional Meeting Management®, fifth edition, was published in 2006 and is a comprehensive collection of information for the industry. The Instructor Resource Center was also launched in 2006 and provides classroom learning resources including test items, activities discussion questions and more. Checklists and case studies were due to be added in 2007. Further details from the PCMA web site or direct from Kendall/Hunt Publishers.

Further information: PCMA, 2301 South Lake Shore Drive, Suite 1001, Chicago, IL 60616-1419, USA. Tel: 001-312-423-7262; Fax: 001-312-423-7222; Web site: www.pcma.org/education/.

UK university and college courses

As will be made clear later in this chapter in the section on careers, it is not essential for those looking to make a career in the conference industry to have pursued a particular educational course, although certain courses can provide skills and knowledge which are readily applicable to the industry. For those wishing to study a course which is directly relevant to a future career, the best options are probably conference and event management courses or courses in destination marketing and management. Other disciplines such as hotel and catering, tourism and tourism management are also relevant. This section looks specifically at the range of provision in the UK, as an example of one country's current offering – other countries may offer similar courses and programmes, but these are unlikely to be identical.

Comprehensive details of the current provision of UK courses at higher education level (i.e. full-time and sandwich first degree courses) can be accessed via the Universities and Colleges Admissions Service web site: www.ucas.co.uk. Some examples of the dedicated conference/event management and business tourism courses follow.

The UK Centre for Events Management at **Leeds Metropolitan University** offers a BA/BA (Hons) Conference & Exhibition Management. This is a 1-year full-time degree or 2-year part-time programme for students in employment who have gained an HND or Foundation Degree in a related discipline or have relevant experience. The programme is sensitively timetabled on 2 days to allow for event professionals, in employment, to attend on a part-time basis. Modules studied include strategic marketing, the strategy process, conference and exhibition production, developing and optimising the event space, managing partners and clients, the venue environment and a dissertation. The UK Centre for Events Management also offers a 3-year HND and 4-year BA (Hons) Events Management which includes a 12-month work placement in the second year, providing a learning experience for students to develop their skills while working in the event industry.

Further details are available from: Ruth Chambers, Course Administrator, UK Centre for Events Management, The Leslie Silver International Faculty, Leeds Metropolitan University, Civic Quarter, Calverley Street, Leeds LS1 3HE (Tel: +44 (0)113-283-3447; Fax: +44 (0)113-283-3111; E-mail: events@lmu.ac.uk; Web site: www.worldofevents.net).

The University of Central England (UCE), Birmingham. The University launched in September 2006 a Postgraduate Diploma/MA Event and Exhibition Management. The programme is run in conjunction with the National Exhibition Centre and the Events Industry Alliance. To achieve the Masters in Event and Exhibition Management, a cumulative total of 180 credits needs to be achieved. This can be done through either a full-time (1 year) or a part-time (2 year) study programme. Keynote industry speakers, practical assessments, a 5-week internship and a master research project are features of the course. Both recent graduates and people already working in the industry can apply for a place on the programme.

Further details are available from: Mathilde Stein, Course Director, UCE, Units 2&3 Progress Works, Bromley Street, Digbeth, Birmingham B9 4AN; Tel: +44 (0)121 204 9882; E-mail: mathilde.stein@uce.ac.uk; course details can be accessed at www.mediacourses.com.

The University of Gloucestershire offers a single honours undergraduate degree in Events Management, in which the MICE module (meetings, incentives, conferences and exhibitions) is to be made compulsory.

Further details are available from: Tracy Jones, Course Leader Events Management, University of Gloucestershire, The Business School, The Park, Cheltenham, Gloucestershire GL50 2RH. (Tel: +44 (0)1242 543210; E-mail: tjones@glos.ac.uk). Further details of the module content can be accessed via: www.glos.ac.uk/subjectsandcourses/undergraduatefields/ew/maps/index.cfm.

Sheffield Hallam University offers a BSc (Honours) Hospitality Business Management with Conference and Events/International Hospitality Business Management with Conference and Events course (UCAS code N225), on a 4-year full time (including one year's work placement) or 3-year full-time basis. The course is designed for those wanting a career in the hospitality industry with an emphasis on managing conferences and events. Study topics include: business management; food and drink management; facilities management; conference and events management. Further information is available from Jenny Wade or Jenny Cockill (address below) or visit the university web site: www.shu.ac.uk.

Sheffield Hallam University also offers an MSc (or Postgraduate Diploma or Postgraduate Certificate) in International Conference Management on both a full-time and part-time basis. Entry requirements are an honours degree or at least 5 years' industry experience. The course involves study of general management and special modules. These include: critical thinking; conference management; destination marketing; innovation in conference and meetings management; leisure leadership and entrepreneurship in hospitality and tourism. Students submit a dissertation in order to gain an MSc.

Further details from: Jenny Wade or Kate Morse, Faculty of Organisation & Management, Stoddart Building, Sheffield Hallam University, City Campus, Howard Street, Sheffield S1 1WB – Tel: +44 (0)114 225 5555; E-mail: ominfo@shu.ac.uk.

Thames Valley University, Ealing, provides a full-time and part-time BA(Hons)/DipHE in Event Management. The degree is built around a central theme of event management principles and practices that include the chance to manage and run a live event of your own.

Further details are available from e: *thl@tvu.ac.uk* or to arrange a visit day contact: Ray Brown on t: 0208-231-2771; f: 0208-231-2744; e: *ray.brown@tvu.ac.uk*.

The same university also runs at its London School of Tourism, Hospitality and Leisure three further courses: Certificate of Higher Education in Business Travel and Tourism (1 year), Higher National Diploma in Business Travel & Tourism (2 years) and BA (Hons) in Business Travel & Tourism (3 years). Opportunities exist for full-time, part-time and flexible study. These courses specialise in meetings, exhibition & conference planning and developing skills in compiling incentives. There are student intakes in September and February.

Further details are available from: Programme Leader Paul Fidgeon, t: 0208-231-2317; f: 0208-566-1353, e: *paul.fidgeon@tvu.ac.uk*; **w:** www.tvu.ac.uk.

The University of Westminster provides an MA in Conference and Events Management on a full-time (1 year) or part-time (2 years) basis. The degree is specifically designed for people wishing to enter careers at management level in the conference and events–related industries including conference and events planning, venue management and employment in convention bureaux. It is appropriate for those aiming for careers in both the private and public sectors in Britain or internationally.

Further details are available from: University of Westminster, Course Enquiries Office, 35 Marylebone Road, London NW1 5LS, t: +44 (0)20 7915 5511 or +44 (0)20 7911 5000 ext. 3076; E-mail: davidsr@westminster.ac.uk or www.wmin.ac.uk.

Other institutions offering courses in conference/event management (at various levels including Foundation Degree, Honours Degree, Higher National Certificate/Diploma) include:

- Birmingham College of Food, Tourism & Creative Studies (e.g. Marketing with Events Management)
- Bournemouth University (e.g. Events Management)
- University of Brighton (e.g. Hospitality & Event Management)
- Brockenhurst College (e.g. Event Management)
- Buckinghamshire Chilterns University College (e.g. Events with Conference Management)
- University of Wales Institute, Cardiff (e.g. Events Management)
- University of Central Lancashire (e.g. Event Management)
- City College Manchester (e.g. Event Management)
- City of Westminster College (e.g. Business Studies specialising in Conference Management)
- University of Derby (e.g. Events Management)
- University of East London (e.g. Events Management)
- Farnborough College of Technology (e.g. Business & Event Management)
- University of Greenwich (e.g. Events Management)
- The University of Huddersfield (e.g. Events Management)

- London Metropolitan University (e.g. Business & Events Management)
- The Manchester Metropolitan University (e.g. Events Management)
- University of Paisley (e.g. Events Management)
- University of Plymouth (e.g. Events Management)
- Queen Margaret University College, Edinburgh (e.g. Events Management)
- Sheffield College (e.g. Tourism & Event Management)
- Southampton Solent University (e.g. Event Management with Tourism)
- Suffolk College (University of East Anglia) (e.g. Event Management)
- University of Wolverhampton (e.g. Event & Venue Management and Business).

For further details on these and all other courses, refer to the UCAS web site and/or to the individual university web site.

CAREERS IN THE CONFERENCE INDUSTRY

Unlike many other professions, the conference industry does not yet have clear entry routes or easily identified career progression paths. It is one of the facets which illustrate its relative immaturity as an industry. This lack of structure may be somewhat frustrating and confusing for those, both within and outside the industry, who have set their sights on reaching a particular career goal but are uncertain about how best to get there. At the same time, however, this lack of precedent and structure can encourage a greater fluidity and freedom of movement between jobs. There is often no set requirement to progress in a particular way, or to have obtained specific qualifications before being able to move on.

Many of those now working in the industry have come to it as a second or third career. This is not surprising in view of the need to be at ease in dealing with a wide range of people, or in coping with a last-minute crisis in the build-up to a high-profile conference – situations which require a reasonable maturity and some experience of life.

Previous experience in hotel and catering, sales and marketing, business administration, secretarial work, financial management, local government administration, training, travel and transport, or leisure and tourism could be advantageous, depending upon the position being considered. But many other backgrounds and disciplines can also give very relevant skills and knowledge, provided that these are combined with a natural affinity for working with people.

For those looking to find employment straight from university or college, vacancies do arise in conference agencies (e.g. administrative posts, assisting in venue finding, computer work) and in conference venues (as assistant conference and banqueting co-ordinators, or in venue sales and marketing). It can also be possible for new graduates to obtain posts in conference offices and convention bureaux, although some previous experience in sales and marketing or local government administration may be desirable.

Relatively few conference organizers, especially within the corporate sector, are full-time conference organizers and meeting planners. They are first and foremost secretaries/PAs, marketing assistants/managers, training managers, or public relations executives, who find themselves asked to organize events on behalf of their department or company. Their role in conference organizing may, of course, develop if they prove to have the right talents and enthusiasm and if this meets the company's own development needs.

Other openings arise, from time to time, in conference industry trade associations and, for those with an interest in publishing, in the industry's trade magazines (either in advertising sales or, for those with some journalistic background, as part of the editorial team).

Before beginning a career within conferencing, it is probably helpful to know whether one's interest is primarily in the buying or supply side of the industry, although it is quite possible at a later stage to switch from one side to the other, and an understanding of how both buyers and suppliers operate is obviously important and beneficial. It is a moot point whether intermediary agencies are best described as buyers or suppliers. Their activities certainly revolve around venue finding and event management, but they do this by supplying a service to their clients, the actual buyers.

It should be stressed that most companies and organizations operating within the conference industry are small, employing limited numbers of people. This is true of most corporate and association event departments, convention bureaux, conference venues, agencies, and trade associations. They cannot offer multiple career opportunities and endless possibilities for progression. But their smallness does often ensure that there is a great variety of work with considerable responsibility and lots of scope to display initiative. It does also mean that it is possible, quite quickly, to get to know many of the players in the industry, building friendships and networks of colleagues nationally and, indeed, across the world.

SALARY LEVELS

Perusal of vacancies in trade magazines or on web sites is one good way to obtain information on salary or compensation levels for different types of positions within the industry. Another useful indicator are surveys undertaken by industry magazines, recruitment agencies and trade associations. The figures quoted below are taken from two such surveys.

i) The UK trade magazine *Event*, in association with specialist events sector recruitment consultancy, ESP Recruitment, carries out an annual 'Event Industry Salary Survey'. The results are collated by research company Vivid Interface. The survey questionnaire is emailed to the readers of *Event* and *Conference & Incentive Travel* magazines, typically generating around 2000 responses (in a ratio of 70% from women, 30% from men, clearly reflecting the prominent role that women play in the twenty-first century conference industry). A sample of the findings from the 2006 survey is reproduced in Table 7.1.

In addition to collecting salary data, the survey asks questions about promotion opportunities, staff motivation factors, benefits, male/female salary differentials, training and hours of work. The full survey findings are available online at www. esprecruitment.co.uk.

Job Title/Sector	Average Salary 2005 £	Minimum Salary 2006 £	Maximum Salary 2006 £	Average Salary 2006 £
1. Event Director				
Exhibitions	45 250	35 000	58 000	45 750
Agency events management	36 000	29 000	50 000	37 000
Hotels	40 500	30 000	49 000	42 000
Production company: production	45 000	35 500	65 000	52 000
Production company: logistics	46 250	34 000	62 000	48 000
Venues	41 750	39 000	65 000	47 500
Event services	40 500	32 000	60 000	43 000
Commercial conferences	42 000	36 500	60 000	45 000
Charity/public sector	37 500	33 000	42 750	40 000
Corporate in-house	70 000	41 500	96 000	65 000
Conference & incentive travel agency	37 500	33 750	45 000	36 500

Table 7.1
UK Event Industry Salary Survey 2006 – 'Event' Magazine in association with ESP Recruitment

Job Title/Sector	Average Salary 2005 £	Minimum Salary 2006 £	Maximum Salary 2006 £	Average Salary 2006 £
Commercial conferences: producer	28 000	18 000	34 000	28 500
Commercial conferences: senior producer	32 000	28 500	40 000	32 500
2. Event Manager				
Exhibitions	30 000	25 750	36 000	31 000
Agency events management	28 000	25 000	33 750	28 500
Hotels	26 000	23 950	40 000	29 000
Production company: production	33 000	25 500	43 000	35 000
Production company: logistics	30 000	26 000	46 000	30 250
Production company: technical	41 500	33 000	58 000	42 000
Venues	29 000	19 000	39 000	26 000
Event services	29 500	24 975	34 000	30 000
Commercial conferences	28 500	25 000	33 000	30 250
Charity/public sector	28 750	26 250	34 000	29 250
Corporate in-house	36 000	28 000	47 500	35 000
Conference & incentive travel agency	30 000	25 000	32 000	28 000
Not for profit	28 375	25 000	43 300	30 000
3. Event Co-ordinator				
Exhibitions	22 500	21 600	24 650	23 125
Production company	21 500	16 000	24 500	20 300
Agency events management	18 500	16 250	22 000	19 250
Hotels	18 750	16 000	22 000	19 000
Commercial conferences	21 500	19 750	25 000	22 000
Charity/public sector	22 150	21 900	23 900	22 500
Corporate in-house	23 000	21 700	26 625	24 165
Venues	21 000	17 000	24 000	20 341
Not for profit	-	19 570	23 300	22 141

Source: 'Event' Magazine in association with ESP Recruitment (reproduced with permission)

Table 7.1
Continued

ii) MPI Salary Survey 2005 – Meeting Professionals International (MPI) is developing its 'Member Solutions' as a suite of online and offline personalized products and resources in response to meeting professionals' career growth and resource needs. As part of this process, MPI conducted research in 2005 to assess North American planners' professional skill levels and career pathways, as well as salaries and career-related trends. The Survey provides a detailed breakdown by location, job title, educational level, experience, and type of organization. A few of the key findings are listed below (the full Survey is available for purchase from MPI):

- The average base salary for US meeting planners was $65 613 but there were differences between male planners (earning an average of $73 833) and female planners (an average of $57 394)
- Planners working for corporations in a management capacity earned an average of $65 758 while those working for associations at a similar level of responsibility earned, on average, $52 229
- Total compensation (ie. including salary, overtime, commissions and bonuses) ranged from an average $110 258 for a CEO/President to £45 677 for a Coordinator.

Other findings were:

- 39 per cent of respondents were full-time meeting planners (this compares with 29 per cent in a Survey undertaken in 2002) – a further 32 per cent stated that meeting planning accounted for over three-quarters of their role
- 25 per cent had less than 5 years' experience of meeting planning, but 46 per cent had up to 14 years and 29 per cent 15 years or more
- 40 per cent reported that their largest meeting had between 101 to 500 delegates, easily the largest category. However, 23 per cent organized meetings of 1001 to 5000 delegates, and a further 8 per cent of more than 5000 delegates
- Perhaps not surprisingly, 58 per cent of respondents felt that their salary/compensation package did not adequately reflect their responsibilities and their contribution to their employer.

CAREER PROFILES

The last section of this chapter contains a series of career profiles written by personalities within the international conference industry. They each describe their current jobs and those aspects of their work which they find rewarding and fulfilling. Some also outline the parts of their work which they find less enjoyable. And previous career experiences, including education and training, are touched on. It is hoped that these profiles will be instructive and maybe inspirational, encouraging some of the readers of this book to want to follow in their footsteps and forge their own careers in the infinitely varied and endlessly stimulating conference industry. Their specific experience, in the order in which they appear, is as:

- a destination marketer/convention and visitor bureau chief executive – Rick Antonson
- a writer, consultant and trainer – Tony Carey
- a convention centre sales and marketing director – Jenny Salsbury
- an exhibition director and company chairman – Ray Bloom
- an industry academic, lecturer and writer – Rob Davidson
- a conference and incentive agency managing director – Patrick Delaney
- a chief executive officer of an international conference industry trade association – Martin Sirk
- an events and marketing executive with a national conference industry trade association, as an example of a recent entrant to the industry – Lucy Watkins
- a managing editor of a conference and incentive industry trade magazine – Martin Lewis.

Rick Antonson

President & CEO of Tourism Vancouver. Tourism Vancouver represents over 1000 member businesses and is responsible for the market development of Greater Vancouver as a convention, incentive, and

Figure 7.1
Rick Antonson.

leisure travel destination. Rick is a former travel writer, book publisher, and train company executive.

Ours is a peculiar industry. We sell dreams, really. And trust. People often agree with us to hold a convention in a hotel which isn't constructed yet, flying there on a plane that is still being designed, and on a date that is six or more years away. The name of our industry? It's called Destination Marketing, and it's always about the future.

What is more peculiar is what brings people to choose this field to spend their career; a career of setting high expectations in the minds of others, and then striving to exceed those expectations by delivering experiences that are better than the ones before.

The only way to succeed in Destination Marketing is by continuous improvement: improvement of one's organization, of oneself, and of one's industry's reputation.

Nowadays it's common to identify various educational options to prepare to become a 'destination marketer' but, not so long ago, those options did not exist. The range of university courses, credible books (you hold a prominent one in your hands right now), ongoing educational programmes, and mentors that we today take for granted, were once notably absent (well, perhaps save for the mentors – which I'll get to in a moment).

My own entry into the field of destination marketing was quite by accident. I actually went to apply for a summer job during a university break, got the address wrong, went in the wrong door, and ended up at the counter filling out an application, before I realized I was next door to my intended place. Not to be deterred, I stuck with the process, the subsequent interview, received a job offer that day, and began as *Membership Sales Representative* for the Greater Vancouver Convention & Visitors Bureau. I did not have a clue what a CVB, let alone a DMO, was. That role lasted a year and a half, and 20 years later I returned to the same organization, rebranded by that time as Tourism Vancouver. My new (and current) job was *President & CEO*.

Most destination marketing organizations (DMOs to much of the world, often CVBs or convention & visitors bureaus in North America), are an alloy of sorts – like a manufactured metal that is stronger because it is composed of many elements. Among the elements that form a DMO are the following:

It is one part 'association' which may mean a not-for-profit (or, at the least, a not-for-loss!) structure. The lessons I have learned in preparation for my current role have relied heavily on the need to develop relationships, on the paramount importance of 'the opinions of members' and the overriding need for an association to have a good, clear, agreed 'governance structure'.

Another part of this amalgam is the line-of-sight between the organization's structure and the marketplace. If you ever lose sight of the customer, you are doomed.

I would venture that my time on the job is quartered: one for my colleagues on staff (prime importance); one for the board and their representation of the membership; one for the customers; one for the community. Are all quarters created equal? No, of course not, but you must shift that balance carefully, and by the time of year, or the selling/buying process, or the election cycle, or the shifting marketplace – and by the end of the year, they are at least in equilibrium, if not equal.

It is therefore true that, as a CEO or managing director for a DMO, you need to have life's experiences teach you a lesson or two before you hold this position (and a primary lesson is to learn how little you really know; a secondary lesson is to find people who know what you don't know, and listen to them).

I can outline a few lessons which I've learned along the way, thanks to patient advisors or inadvertent mentors. There are several endearing phrases which should be carved on the hallway walls in every DMO office. They came my way through mentors who knew not that they were my mentors, and the admonitions include:

'Don't walk too tall, nor talk too wise . . . ' (would Kipling maybe allow the addition of 'Despite the temptation . . . '?) This quote was given to me by a colleague, much the wiser, who wanted to save me from the comfort of a recent accomplishment and guide me towards humility (before someone in the industry did so unceremoniously);

'Happy is the day that what the members want is also what the customer wants.' And this one is re-learned in every DMO, every day. Often, if they are membership-based set-ups, DMOs juggle the needs, expectations and tolerance of their members (whose views are often short-term) with those of the clients (who often are years away from an actual booking, let alone the conference being held in your city). If you have to choose, choose the customer's needs – it's the only way to ensure you'll get their business and keep your members happy!

'The biggest problem in tourism is that most people in it, don't know they're in it.' The actions of a DMO must involve destination development as well to ensure the product they take to the marketplace is solid, reputable and desired. You owe it to the client that the characteristics you use for 'luring' their business, are the same ones you deliver when they come years later to consume the experience. Yet many of the service providers whose business base overlaps between local residents and visitors/delegates, do not realize they are in the business of providing an integral part of their destination's experience, and thus creating the destination's reputation.

'Many people in destination marketing confuse their partners as their competitors.' A valuable lesson for all: perhaps hotels are the best example. Until a convention has chosen our destination for its future conference, there really isn't anything for local businesses to fight over. If the meeting planner chooses another destination, it really doesn't matter who *would have been* the headquarters hotel.

None of these, nor other management-inducing factors, came my way through formal education. That was not something I was privileged to have after 'dropping out' of university. It is better, I have since concluded, to gain the solid foundation of the formal education. Yet that, too, is but a starting point. The world of associations is indeed the biggest provider, worldwide, of ongoing adult education. Membership and participation in such organizations as ICCA, BACD, DMAI (formerly IACVB), MPI, ABPCO, PCMA, PATA, WTTC and others will make the difference between one having achievements or near-misses; between finishers and also-rans; between old information and current knowledge. And if you really want to hone your intuition, benefit from candour, and contribute to the industry, then accept the nomination to serve on a board or executive. During the year I served as chair of IACVB, I left every board meeting with two pages of ideas or cautions or information willingly shared by those around the table; given by them to help me, without the ask of anything in return.

It has been my great good fortune that others have let me share in their ideas and visions. That is true whether one thinks of the subtle nudge, 'why don't you do something about the taxi industry and professional training?' which led to my chairing the 'taxi partnership' that created the TaxiHost Program, which has since had over 7000 graduates.

Or when a colleague said, 'I have an idea. Tourism Vancouver should launch a bid to host the 2010 Winter Olympic Games in Vancouver and Whistler' and it led to my being a member of the board for both the Domestic Bid Committee and then the International Bid Committee, where I observed the depth of planning required, the attention to reputation management and the sophistication of international competition.

Or when our area's senior politician pronounced that the plan to expand the convention centre was 'officially dead' and our DMO, within days, initiated the Convention Centre Expansion Task Force, on which I served, and from which I learned much about the building of coalitions, aligning of interests and badgering of bureaucrats.

It was true when the challenge passed over to a few of us: 'Vancouver is so beautiful that you must protect your environment and your natural image, and your reputation for caring.' It led to the creation of the Oceans Blue Foundation, my role as one of the co-founders and initially as Chair where I participated in the setting of objectives, watched the floundering of cohesion, and became a bystander to the beaching of a once beautiful vision.

Always, though, in every experience, there were others. And that is a cornerstone to being a destination marketer. NOTHING that you do is ever done alone. There are always partners. Sometimes you lead. Sometimes you follow. Of all the accomplishments I've been privileged to see come about at Tourism Vancouver, not one was ever done by us alone. Without partners, without shared visions, without accomplices, we'd be irrelevant.

DMO CEOs are rare, which is not to say they are anything special. But the only person who has a similar job lives in another city, another jurisdiction. Think of this in the context of a hotel general manager's role. There's another one across the street, and dozens more in the city with very similar structures and expectations and marketplace dynamics. Yet for a DMO, the most comparable compatriot may be a thousand miles away, and in a different country.

And if I had a closing piece of advice for those considering their future careers in destination marketing, it might be this: don't be afraid to walk in the wrong door.

Tony carey
Writer, consultant, trainer for the meetings industry

After 20 years of global travel (at the expense of the taxpayer), I mothballed my uniform and sought more home-based employment than the British Infantry could offer. Apparently unqualified for anything other than killing people, I threw myself at the mercy of the readers of the classified ads in my local Guernsey paper and was delighted to receive a number of offers. One of

Figure 7.2
Tony Carey.

which was to become General Manager of a newly established events management agency.

Setting up a trading company (albeit for someone else) when you are unfamiliar with the word 'Profit' proved a daunting challenge, but within 2 years the agency had expanded from 3 to 9 staff and my boss was pocketing well-deserved dividends on his investment.

Observing his returns on my success, I decided to branch out on my own and, in 1981, created a small (just me) company specialising in marketing and events.

Many people harbour the ambition to be self-employed but I wonder if I would have taken the leap had I known what hazards lay ahead.

A sole trader needs back up – or at least health insurance – and a coronary with complications is not a great commercial start. **Lesson One: Go into business with a friend.**

Slowly, the company began to attract business and show a profit. Clients who originally wanted a DMC to handle local arrangements, gave me longer term contracts to organise their events in the UK and Europe. I found myself graduating from DMC to PCO. It seemed that what I had to offer was popular.

Referrals, and a growing reputation, brought us both corporate and association meetings ranging in size from 20 to 2000. And to fill those lean months, we staged our own events. **Lesson two. Never complain about a lack of business. If you can't attract it – create it.**

For example, in the 1980s there were no formal training courses in the UK for aspiring meeting planners. You 'learned on the job'. So, rather arrogantly, I decided to plug this educational gap – with the help of industry friends. The first 5-day course: 'An Introduction To Conference Management' attracted industry novices from all over Europe. 20 years later, when the series ended, a more concentrated, 3 day, programme was still attracting international attendees.

After a few years, the body of knowledge built up for the course cried out to be compiled into a book so, in 1997, 'Crisis or Conference' was born. This slim volume was the first manual to reduce meeting management to a series of check lists. It proved popular – not least because it slipped easily into a pocket. **Lesson three: Recycle your knowledge.**

A commission to write a similar guide for the German Convention Bureau followed, as did the task of editing a new publication: 'Professional Meeting Management – A European Handbook' which was published by Meeting Professionals International (MPI) with support from the European Commission. (See lesson three!)

Research for all these publications added significantly to my knowledge both of the international convention industry and of the practice of event management. It also signposted the direction in which I should go for career number three.

Both the Army and the event management business require a certain expertise in speaking, confidently, to an audience. It is something that I have always enjoyed and, following the publication of the books and various articles for trade magazines, I found myself in demand as a presenter. **Lesson four: Speaking is a necessary skill.**

At an early stage I realised that, more than in many industries, we are in the people business. The ability to make friends easily across cultures and classes is fundamental to success. Fortunately, I am a social animal so what we now term 'networking' comes naturally. **Lesson five: Relationships matter**.

Related to that is the importance of getting involved. The MICE industry (because we are all so 'clubbable') is awash with acronymous professional associations which purport to bring their members business. Many do, but only if one contributes to their aims and becomes an active member.

I was fortunate to be elected chairman of the UK's first association for meeting professionals. The Association of Conference Executives (ACE) had 1000 members in its heyday and introduced me to many of the major players in the British events industry at that time.

Shortly after joining MPI in 1988, I helped to create the UK Chapter of what is now a 20 000 strong international association with 300 British members. This involvement brought me into contact with the leadership and staff in Dallas, Texas, and, before long, I was serving on international committees and had been elected to the main Board of Directors for a 3-year term; one of the first Europeans to be so honoured.

These volunteering experiences not only proved useful, interesting and educational, but helped to improve my communication, negotiation and leadership skills. Not least, they have given me an international network of friends, for life. **Lesson six: Join in.**

As a young industry, the possibility of gaining professional qualifications is a recent development. The Certified Meeting Professional (CMP) award has been available in North America for over 20 years but only recently extended internationally. The university-backed: Certificate in Meeting Management (CMM), sponsored by MPI, was launched in 1995.

Both exams were an ordeal for me at the time and required considerable homework, but the qualifications have proved helpful – if only as a badge of professional commitment. Today, having edited one of the set books for the CMP exam, I derive great pleasure from coaching applicants! **Lesson seven: Get qualified.**

So, after almost 30 years in the conference industry, I am putting to profitable use my experience in the Army and my experience as an event organiser. I have sold my company in order to concentrate on sharing my accumulated knowledge through speaking and writing.

I find my latest career as a commentator extremely rewarding on several levels:

- I am able to pass on my accumulated knowledge to those who want it, especially in countries where the MICE business is relatively new.
- I am able to lobby influential people about the economic and social importance of the international MICE industry.
- In my travels as an itinerant presenter (36 cities in 2006), I continue to learn about this fascinating industry – and the places where it is conducted.
- The dozens of events which I attend every year (an education in itself) provide me with material and colour for my monthly magazine columns.
- I am continually expanding my global network of friends and colleagues in the business.
- I thoroughly enjoy my very minor role in this dynamic industry. **Lesson eight: If you don't enjoy it – get out, fast!**

Although I would like to claim that success, such as it is, has been the result of long term, strategic planning, I can't. My career in the meetings business seems to have naturally evolved. Now I can't wait to see what happens next!

Jenny Salsbury
Director of Marketing and Sales, Kuala Lumpur Convention Centre, Malaysia

This industry is a hidden and very understated revenue earner. Like most people working in conferences, I discovered it pretty much by accident, loved it, got addicted and here I am twenty-odd years later still loving it – my family, however, are still none the wiser and have a slight mumble about what I do when talking to their friends!

The reality of our role in selling convention centres is that we are little more than grown-up space sales people – and some of us feel slightly less grown up than others. I have specialised somewhat in the field of association conferences, in particular the international congresses which are really fascinating to negotiate for, but not for those who want the constant fix of a sale. There is a need to be an exceptionally good listener, to have a good memory to make the links that all go together to build the case and to remember who you've met before, plus having a talent for spotting an opportunity where the particular person you are with can see a link with your 'product' and also a gain towards their own goals, thus producing the ideal 'win win' situation. The rest is common sense.

Figure 7.3
Jenny Salsbury.

Other people actually put the event on and it's really up to us to spark the imagination and act as a kind of catalyst putting together the elements. In order to do this, I have always felt it necessary to understand what the organization is trying to achieve – hurrah for my bright idea to do a shorthand and typing course as when I started out I could just get the client talking and take down exactly what they said, since I could always figure out exactly what they wanted later on.

It is surprising to me that so many organizers have not yet realised the revenue potential from their exhibition alongside their regular conference and still talk in terms of charity work done by not-for-profit organizations. These opportunities have, of course, increased with technology developments with webcasting and recording providing even more revenue streams. The more sponsorship of an event can be encouraged, the more erudite aims and worthy causes can be achieved – thankfully most of the main organizers today have realised this potential and are working really well with growing their conferences – it's great to work with them as you can then see ways in which your venue services can assist with an even bigger, better show or smarter, smoother presentations. The older style Secretary General has pretty much retired by now but they do still pop up, usually as a fam. trip luvvy.

People in convention centres do have a huge range of experience in many different types of events and it is surprising to me that organizers are sometimes hesitant to trawl through the mental files to help their own event, transferring their experience from a totally different venue they have used before. Gaining this experience as a sales person can be a long and very frustrating road – try asking an operations person how many people can be fed in a certain room – the response depends on a seemingly endless list of factors that will cover the worst-case scenario in terms of health and safety issues. Sales people are always, therefore, talking second hand. The important thing is to take a situation or a perceived problem and work together to sort out how it can be managed, and have an open mind ready to consider all approaches. The solutions are not always about spending more money and are usually about the design of 'traffic flow' of people through an event or the placement of food of varying types at strategic points and times.

There will, however, be certain battles a venue sales person is not going to win and knowing when to walk away from a situation, put a different face onto the particular case and move on is key to minimising stress levels. My training in the industry has really come from on-the-job experience working in a convention bureau, where I was in an overseas office selling a high value destination (Hong Kong). We had to talk big whilst being quite small, the fact that I was selling my home town and I loved it was a huge help. I would spend hours researching and finding out details for people – and this was before the web, electronic databases and PCs on the desktop. There are really many things I would have liked to have learnt from some kind of study but there really were no courses beyond the one run every year by IAPCO (see earlier in this chapter for details), which I persuaded my boss in 1987 would be an exceptionally good investment for the company to send me on. I am continuously learning from the network of friends in the industry who all have a like-minded approach.

I also learnt from attending seminars alongside trade exhibitions and from endless discussions at the bar at the end of the day. The gatherings at convention industry trade associations are always great fun and one of the best I used to attend was the annual conference of the European Federation of Conference Towns. Just what Hong Kong had to do with European Conference Towns was totally beside the point: I was being introduced by Geoffrey Smith who had been taken on as a consultant to a complete novice.

Having done 10 years at the Hong Kong Tourist Association, I felt it was time to move and wanted to take the next step in developing a lead rather than passing it on once it got interesting. The problem was I had the best job in the industry and it took me quite a while to find something that matched up. Eventually I moved into sales in the Hong Kong Convention & Exhibition Centre.

Moving from a bureau to a venue is a culture shock and the relationship between the two disciplines is traditionally fraught with potential dispute, not to say angst. I am a great believer in trying my utmost to keep a happy balance but it is hard to explain to a salesperson who has just won a contract that it was a team effort and also hard to explain to a local authority-funded organization which needs to justify its return to the community that the venue (i.e. the commercial world) played a part in winning.

The clients I love are the ones who have really become friends and with whom we develop new ways of doing things. Moving into the Scottish Exhibition and Conference Centre (SECC) in Glasgow, Scotland in 1996 opened me up to the way the British conference industry works and I have to say it is very satisfying working with repeat clients where we see annual conferences come back and how they have moved into new technology etc. I do think Britain is way ahead of other countries in the field of presentation technology. International PCOs, too, bring more of their clients back to us and I love the openness with which we talk/negotiate where they know we have to make something to continue the level of service and where we are given enough space with this to pull out all the stops to deliver a great event to the client.

It is quite unusual for a convention centre person to move countries. There are a few in the industry who have moved between many centres, however, actually opening a centre from a plan proved to be the next step for me after 8 years in the UK. I had moved into becoming increasingly active in the ICCA organization, ending up running the UK & Ireland Chapter and working on a series of workshops, seminars and various information exchange projects. This, of course, had to go out of the window as I moved into a role that was all-consuming – working as one of the very early recruits in the pre-opening team for the Kuala Lumpur Convention Centre. Again, another culture shock not so much another country but different working styles mean that assumptions and regular expectations all had to be completely re-evaluated. The volume of tasks that had to be achieved meant that we didn't often have the luxury of much discussion, it was all hands to the pumps. Added to this was a different business mix with more emphasis on the Food & Beverage aspect which was new to me in this degree of detail. Two and a half years later and the company has completed its first year of operation and is well into the second. There is a sense of achievement but new stresses come into play, maintaining the pace and motivating the team to reach the new levels set, having outstripped the original forecasts set in the preliminary studies. Being back in Asia is fun and working with people here, learning and understanding their different, less confrontational ways of doing things can be challenging. Probably the major challenge is the short lead time mentality – we can regularly have a week's notice for major functions of 1000-plus or find attendees double up with those attending who have not RSVP'd and are suddenly free at the last minute – with a couple of friends. This attitude is a major hurdle in getting local associations to understand that 2011 is really only just round the corner – it can be a major test in persistence. However, every now and then something really surprises you and the idea takes off. All of a sudden you have a bunch of highly enthusiastic local professionals totally 'gung ho' swinging into action commandeering all sorts of civic services, including acrobatic traffic police motorbike outriders, to ensure a site visit goes with a convincing swing. It's hard to not get caught up in the excitement with pitches like this. In Malaysia one of the most satisfying things is the fact that relationships matter above all else and I found this so fascinating that I started a workshop to introduce international organizers to some of the layers of cultures that could be so easily missed – protocol was definitely something that was taken to a new level in this country and, whilst one could quite easily organize successful international events, how nice to be aware and 'get it right' – it brings a new type of communication.

Another aspect of not being in Europe is that not many of the clients have visited our country and are even less aware of it. We joined forces with sister property Cairns Convention Centre (our company is managed by a joint venture with local owners and an Australian venue management company) and a few other key venues in less obvious cities to promote as 'All Corners of the World' (see also Chapter 4) offering clients an opportunity to be introduced to prospects for working on an event in one of the countries – Asia is fast growing in interest for organizations looking for partnerships to get into China, ASEAN and India. It hasn't been an easy transition from an established venue to starting a new one and if anyone had told me what 'opening' a property meant I don't think I would have done it – even with the move back to Asia but now, 2 years on, I am so glad of the experience. I wouldn't hurry to do it again and I look forward to a time when there is a possibility of a level of working hours that are accepted in Europe, but I don't think that's going to be too soon!

Sometimes I think I would like a different job, one where you could spend more time with the family – especially now that I'm a granny – and know when you could book holidays and not be too tired to travel for short breaks with pals, but then something exciting comes along and I just get my teeth into the next presentation – hope we can convince them!

Ray Bloom
Chairman of IMEX, theWorldwide Exhibition for Incentive Travel, Meetings and Events (Frankfurt)

I suppose you could say that I fell into this industry by chance. My early career certainly gave me no indication that I would fall in love with the world of Incentive Travel and Meetings.

Figure 7.4
Ray Bloom.

I left school at 17 to enter the family motor business – we were Volkswagen-Audi dealers and little did I realise that being the recipient of Incentive Travel Rewards and International Product Launches would be of such benefit later on! Having sold the business (giving me my first taste of the negotiating table) we entered the world of two-star hotels. With only 150 rooms between the two hotels we found that our main business came from the residential meetings sector.

At this rather more naïve stage of my career, I felt that my learning curve was extremely steep and looked forward to the day when I would be able to sit back with experience and 'level off'. Over the years I've begun to understand that it is at the point of 'levelling off' that you may as well stop. It is at this point that innovation ceases to exist and business can become stale. The mistakes never stop, but what I have learnt is how to use these mistakes to drive my various ventures forward, and how to accept when I've made one and change my course accordingly.

So how did I eventually get into the business? A childhood friend of mine, Ian Allchild, was the sales manager of an Incentive Marketing Exhibition held at the Metropole Exhibition Halls in Brighton; our home town. He was one of our hotels' best customers, booking numerous room allocations for exhibitors. One day in 1983, we just got talking and decided to join up and launch an Incentive Show at the Barbican in London. It started as an 1800 sq m show and ended up 6 years later as a 10 000 sq m show held at Olympia. Trials and tribulations were of course involved, but my overriding memory of the period was one of great satisfaction and delight at finally having found 'my' industry. It is, of course, the people that make it – you will hear that a lot over these few pages – that's because it is true. This industry is all about partnerships and relationships and making friends around the world. What could be better than that?

In 1986 I launched EIBTM. As I said earlier, the learning curve never stops and after a while you begin to thrive on it. Launching an Incentive Travel Show was another steep one! We selected Geneva for a number of reasons – a great geographical location, together with the fact that my mother-in-law was there to feed and look after me were great incentives! The development of such an ambitious project proved to me the importance of inner conviction and positive attitude – values passed on to me through my family businesses. It really is true that, as long as you work hard enough to find it, the appropriate solution will manifest itself.

This was proved with the development of the now well-known 'Hosted Buyer Programme'. About seven months before the first show, having invested heavily in database and tele-research to pin-point decision makers in key European markets, I was a little uneasy about where exactly our buyers would come from and how many there would be. This was not a mistake I was willing to make. I decided to 'Host or Fail'. We got in touch with trade publications from around the world and invited them to bring groups of top buyers to the show – hosted and paid for by us. Some would say it was an expensive gamble, I would say that it is one that paid off. Sometimes in business you may feel that you are playing a roulette wheel, but calculated risks are usually worth it.

As I said earlier, relationships are paramount in this business. We established close partnerships with major international associations by ensuring that the relationship was always mutually beneficial – not always financially – but invariably supportive of each other's aims. These partnerships have now been proved to have stood the test of time and, once again, I am proud to be working closely which such prestigious and important associations as SITE, MPI, ICCA, DMAI, AIPC, IAPCO and more. Additionally, we worked hard to develop relationships with strong Swiss institutions, from the National Airline – SwissAir – to City Government. It was with our partners' support that we made our show a success.

Now I am entering a new 'phase' – a whole new learning curve in fact. Having dabbled in a completely different industry (the espresso bar market), I am now firmly back where I belong, having launched and established IMEX (The Worldwide Exhibition for Incentive Travel, Meetings and Events) in Frankfurt, Germany. Using my experience (at last!), using my prior steep curves and jumping on another in order to innovate and create a new show for a new era. When I re-entered the industry in 2001 I did so with a fresh perspective, one which only a few years' break can give; and saw that innovation and creativity were once more needed in our market place. IMEX, in just 5 years, is now established as the leading exhibition in our market place. It is unique in combining an enormous hosted buyer programme of 3500 key decision makers who travel to the show from almost 60 world markets; together with the major German outbound market. It welcomes over 3000 exhibitors annually, who represent more than 150 countries.

Additionally, a dozen 'new vision' initiatives ensure that the innovative nature of the show continues – focussing on future industry growth and development and pushing the boundaries of industry thinking. Our Future Leaders' Forum has educated over 1000 students worldwide and encouraged them to enter the industry; the Politicians' Forum has brought together our industry's top leaders with politicians from around Europe; the Wild Card initiative introduces four new destinations a year to the meetings industry and our focus on the environment is leading the way in changing industry thinking on this issue. In addition, our innovative use of new technology and continued partnerships with international associations have created a global meetings and incentive travel exhibition 'for the industry, by the industry'.

There are no right or wrong ways to develop a career, nor develop a business, although it's important to keep a few things in mind. Firstly, have the courage of your convictions and take responsibility for the mistakes as well as the successes. Secondly, remember to try to keep a positive and balanced attitude towards your work and career. Thirdly, remember always that goodwill takes years to cultivate and grow, but can be lost in a minute of thoughtlessness; and finally be assured that the incentive travel and meetings market is one of the most welcoming, gracious and sociable industries to work in. Enjoy it.

Rob Davidson
Senior Lecturer in Business Travel and Tourism – University of Westminster, London

My professional activities are primarily concerned with the human resources element of the conference industry – specifically, the education and training of the next generation of professional staff. I passionately believe that success for conference destinations, conference venues and conference planners depends, first and foremost, on the quality of the skills and knowledge of the men and women who are working in this vibrant, expanding industry. The worldwide professionalisation of the conference industry over the past few decades has been one of the most exciting developments in the history of this sector, and I am delighted to be involved in work that allows me to make a contribution to that vitally important process.

Figure 7.5
Rob Davidson.

For most of my professional career, I have been focusing on cities and countries as destinations, and how they are marketed to people who are on the move, for business or for leisure. After studying English Literature and Language at the University of Aberdeen, I moved to London, where I worked as Education and Training Manager for VisitBritain, the organization responsible for marketing the UK as a destination for holidaymakers, business travellers and people attending conferences and trade shows in this country. Part of my mission in that job was to introduce Tourism as a subject in UK universities. It seems strange now to recall that, in the 1980s, Tourism was hardly present as a subject for study in universities in the UK, but that was indeed the situation two decades ago. One of the barriers to teaching Tourism in universities was the lack of suitable teaching materials and so, in 1989, I wrote my first textbook (simply entitled Tourism) to contribute towards the lifting of this barrier.

Just after the publication of that book, I decided to move overseas to work for a few years, to broaden my horizons, culturally and professionally. For the following 9 years, I lived in the city of Montpellier in the south of France, where I worked as a freelance travel journalist and writer, and where I made my first move, part-time, into teaching. I taught Tourism Management in the University of Montpellier and in the ESSEC-Cornell Management School in Paris, and thoroughly enjoyed the experience. In 1990, Le Corum, Montpellier's flagship conference centre opened its doors, and that city became a popular destination for international meetings events. That was the real origin of my interest in the conference industry, as I saw how, in the space of a few years, Montpellier's economy and image were transformed as a direct result of the opening of the city's conference centre.

In 1994, I wrote the first university-level textbook ever to be published on the subject of conferences and trade shows – 'Business Travel' – and it was adopted as required reading by many universities throughout Europe and beyond, where Tourism was being offered as a subject of study. As the call of Academia became stronger, I returned to the UK in 1998, to join the University of Westminster in London, as a Senior Lecturer, and I added undergraduate courses in Business Travel & Tourism and Conference Planning to the range of courses already on offer. In 2003, the University of Westminster added a unique Masters-level course in Conference Management to its portfolio of tourism-related courses, and this course continues to attract students from all over the world.

Researching and writing about the conference industry have always enriched my teaching of this subject. In 2003, I was employed as business tourism Industry Analyst by Reed Travel Exhibitions, for whom I carry out ongoing research. At Reed Travel Exhibitions' 'EIBTM' show in Barcelona each year, my annual report on current and future developments in the conference and incentive industry worldwide is launched and then posted on to the EIBTM web site. In addition, I often conduct practical research projects for conference-related organizations such as convention bureaux, and this gives me further useful and up-to-date information to use in my teaching.

I have continued to write about the conference industry and, in 2005, I collaborated in a writing project with Tony Rogers of the British Association of Conference Destinations. As a result, our book, *Marketing Destinations and Venues for Conferences, Conventions and Business Events*, was published by Elsevier Butterworth-Heinemann the following year. In addition, I regularly write articles for the professional business tourism press, including *Conference News*.

Anyone who meets me quickly understands that I am passionate about the conference industry and its vital contribution to economic prosperity, to regeneration and to communication and cooperation between professionals as well as between different countries and cultures. I also try to make it clear that I believe that education and training are essential to the continuing successful expansion of this industry.

I have good reason to believe that my message is being heard: in February 2005, only 2 days before my 50th birthday, I was nominated Meetings and Incentive Personality of the Year, at the 'Meetings & Incentive Travel' Awards ceremony in London, in the presence of Her Royal Highness Princess Anne. And the following year, I was nominated as one of *Conference & Incentive Travel* magazine's 'Power 50' – the 50 most influential people in the UK conference industry. I hope that, for many more years, I will be able to continue to inspire young people to make their careers in the conference industry and to help prepare the next generation of managers of conference centres, convention bureaux and conference planning agencies.

Patrick M Delaney
CITE, CMM, Managing Director, Ovation Group (now MCI Dublin and MCI Belfast)

I've been playing parts in and around this industry for more than 30 years now and I can honestly say it's an industry that continues to delight, excite and motivate me. I am constantly delighted by the cast of wonderful, fully developed personalities that constitute the *dramatis personae* of this very dramatic industry; I am excited by the constantly changing scenery that obligates you to alter your strategic viewpoint all the time; I am motivated by the breadth of new opportunity that materialises on stage every hour of every day.

I wandered into Hotel Management following a steady but unremarkable career at secondary school where I was the only male to take 'Domestic Economy' as a Leaving Certificate Subject (Ireland's equivalent to 'A' levels). At college I met wonderful people and made life-transforming friendships. During my degree I gained practical hotel experience in Italy, France and Canada but, following many failed soufflés, soon realised that my skill base would never extend to work in the kitchen.

Figure 7.6
Patrick Delaney.

Following graduation I joined the excellent management training programme operated by Jury's Hotel and cut my management teeth as 'Coffee Dock' Manager – a late night eatery which attracted the good and the great of Dublin, usually in a state euphemistically referred to as 'tired and emotional'. There I learned that public order was best maintained by leaving it to the 'real professionals' – the hard boiled but big hearted Coffee Dock waitresses – and I exercised, developed and sharpened my management skills as custodian of a rather large bunch of keys.

Following three years opening and closing important doors at Jury's, I handed in my bunch of keys and received a clip board from the Irish Tourist Board whom I joined as Hotel Inspector with responsibility for grading accommodation providers, mainly in the South West of the country. I didn't allow the minor detail of my non-possession of the job-specific, essential valid driving licence to stand in the way of accepting what I regarded as the perfect job for me. If I didn't have the licence when asked about it at the interview, well this was merely a chronological anomaly and, by the time I commenced work, I had obtained the required document!

How my impressive sales and marketing qualifications came to the attention of the powers-that-be at the Irish Tourist Board I will never know as, in truth, I didn't have any. However, I was soon dispatched to St Louis, Missouri as the new Irish Tourist Board Officer for the Mid-West Region. Being in St Louis allowed me gradually to get up to speed with the requirements of my job without being the under the watchful scrutiny of my superiors. After all, they were all in New York City while I was many miles away!

In the early 1980s the Irish Tourist Board was continuing its focus on the 'incentive' segment as one which could produce excellent revenue yields for Ireland while not being limited either by seasonality or regionality. I was mandated to assist in the development of this market and my efforts quickly brought me in contact with the Society of Incentive & Travel Executives (SITE), an organization that was to play a seminal role in my professional development. I learned how a corporate group travel experience, when marketed cleverly and operated flawlessly, could stimulate best-in-class executive performance and assist corporations in their achievement of strategic objectives.

During my time at the Irish Tourist Board I developed the rather quixotic 'Delaney Letters', an award-winning marketing campaign which generated very welcome increased levels of interest in Ireland as an incentive destination and very unwelcome new interest in me and in what I was doing on the part of my superiors at the Tourist Board. My campaign concept pivoted on two 'Patrick Delaneys' who promoted diverse, but complementary aspects of Ireland as a destination – its classic elegance versus its casual informality etc. I feel privileged to have played a role in helping to put Ireland on the map for organizers of incentive travel experiences and to have been there in the early years when it was all so new and exciting. And there are folk out there who still remember the 'Delaney Letters'!

After more than 10 years in the United States it was time to move back to Ireland and Tom Kane, an Irish American businessman, offered me a wonderful challenge – to launch a classical musical festival in the grounds of his newly acquired Adare Manor, a stunning example of Ireland's architectural heritage located close to Shannon Airport and recently converted by Kane into a 5-star hotel.

I could see the potential of Adare as a new resort destination for Ireland. Based in Dublin, I enthusiastically applied myself to my new role of Sales and Marketing Director targeting the full gamut of potential channels for this stunning property, including the lucrative agency and corporate sector in the US.

In 1993 I teamed up with Pádraic Gilligan, a friend since the early 70s whose career had brought him, by circuitous means, into this industry, and formed Delaney Marketing Consultants (DMC), a DMC operation aimed, initially, at offering DMC services to Incentive Houses based in the US. We expected to gain immediate market share out of the US but how wrong I was!!! I realised that 'knowing people' wasn't enough. They had to be convinced that you could actually deliver for them and this would only happen gradually, once you had proven your credentials.

Delaney Marketing gradually developed and increased its product offering to include event and conference management. In 2002 we acquired another company with specific expertise in these sectors and re-branded as Ovation Group. Today we employ over 60 people and have been designated among the 'Top 50 companies to work for in Ireland'.

So here I am, at the helm of a company which offers a livelihood to over 60 people and generates significant financial activity within the Irish economy. It's been a rollercoaster, full of unexpected peaks and troughs. But the people I have met along the way have delighted me. They have influenced and shaped my attitude not only to business, but to life. The challenges along the way have excited me. They have generated sleepless nights but also led to euphoric victories. And, overall, this industry has motivated me to get up every morning and get out there and make it happen!

Martin Sirk
Chief Executive Officer, ICCA

Like many of my generation who are working in the international meetings industry, I fell into the business almost by accident. I originally wanted to work for a UK outbound tour operator but

Figure 7.7
Martin Sirk.

was fifth candidate in a year when only four graduate trainees were taken on, and so I went for 'interview practice' for a job I thought I had no chance of getting at the British Tourist Authority (BTA – now VisitBritain). This led to a 7 year stint with the BTA in the USA, Hong Kong and London Head Office, before spotting an opening as Conference Sales & Marketing Manager for the city of Brighton and their 5000 capacity convention centre.

Taking over this role despite having no direct meetings business experience, I rapidly became involved in the industry's trade associations. It was a great way to make contacts and learn about the business from my most experienced colleagues and competitors, as well as raising the profile of my destination and venue. I was at various times a Board member of BACD, Chairperson of the British Conference & Exhibition Centres Export Council, and Chairperson of the UK Chapters of MPI and ICCA, as well as sitting on numerous committees and working groups looking at strategic issues in the UK meetings industry.

After 9 years with Brighton in various roles, finally controlling all sales and marketing of tourism and conferences, as well as directing the Brighton Centre and two other major venues in the city, I found myself being headhunted by Stakis Hotels to plan and direct the sales and marketing launch of the London Metropole, which was to become Europe's biggest meetings hotel with the opening of its new West Wing. That was an interesting time. Within a few weeks of joining the company, Hilton launched a takeover of Stakis, so every piece of new collateral and branding material had to be thrown out and the whole process started over again! I launched the new facility and was then promoted to direct Hilton's 'big events' team in the UK.

I took over as ICCA Chief Executive Officer in July 2002. This was a job I had always coveted. I'd been an enormous fan of ICCA ever since I attended my first ICCA client-supplier workshop in Barcelona in 1989, primarily because of the open business culture that is driven by the exchange of information on international association meetings that ICCA members regularly undertake. ICCA covers all the major supplier sectors in the industry, and so my career path meant that I'd actually worked in most of these different business environments. During my first 4 years in charge, the organization has grown by over 25 per cent, and now has almost 800 member companies and organizations in 80 countries worldwide. I have overseen major structural and cultural changes and have organized annual ICCA congresses in countries as varied as Korea, Denmark, South Africa, Uruguay, and most recently in Rhodes, Greece. ICCA is a genuinely global organization, with offices in four continents, and our Head Office team has a dozen nationalities amongst 25 staff members. We're building a business-focused culture rather than one which concentrates on administrative matters, and one which aims for high quality membership and excellent retention rates rather than growth at any price. We're definitely regarded along with MPI and SITE as one of the leading associations worldwide.

I live in the centre of Amsterdam with my American wife and 12-year old son, cycle a great deal more than I did before but less than I probably ought to do. I travel extensively but still turn down far more invitations to speak at meetings industry events than I'm able to accept!

I'm always tremendously thankful that I fell into the meetings industry. It offers an enormous variety of challenges, and is so central to the Information Revolution which we are all living through. It's also an incredibly friendly and open industry, and once someone's hooked on it there's no going back. Now, of course, there are university degrees and clearly signalled career paths for young professionals, but the industry is still wide open to individuals with widely varying backgrounds, personalities and skills.

Lucy Watkins
Marketing and Events Executive – British Association of Conference Destinations

I always knew I wanted to work in tourism and, after completing my degree, I embarked on my goal of finding a job that would enable me to travel the world. But these things aren't always easy and so I joined a recruitment agency and started temp work. It was while I was temping that I was offered an interview at a nearby stately home for the position of Conference

Figure 7.8
Lucy Watkins.

and Banqueting Co-ordinator. Although I hadn't previously considered working in event organization, the job sounded like a challenge and an interesting place to work.

Hagley Hall, in Worcestershire, is the ancestral home of the Lyttelton family and, during the 2 years I worked there, I was given a great introduction to the world of conferencing. At just 21 years of age, I was responsible for organizing a whole array of events from conferences, meetings, private dinners, team building and weddings to an outdoor concert for over 4000 people. With just four permanent office staff, I had a steep learning curve and needed to quickly develop many skills, from sales and marketing to budgeting and managing an events team. Being a working estate, there was also the challenge of dealing with estate workers, housekeeping, farmers and not forgetting that this venue was also a private family home.

Always eager to learn more, I felt after a couple of years that it was time to move on and so I found a job in the Tourism Unit at Worcestershire County Council. The position of Assistant Economic Development Officer had two functions: inward investment and promoting business tourism within the county. Through my education and employment experience, I quickly established a preference for the business tourism aspect of the role.

Marketing a relatively unknown destination is a challenge but nonetheless one I was prepared to take on. Starting with pretty much a blank piece of paper, I established a membership scheme for the conference desk, brought in additional funding through commission charging and increased general awareness of the destination and our service both locally and nationally.

The difference between public sector and private sector working soon became evident. Resources and funding, whilst limited, were still greater than those at Hagley Hall. But I didn't just have my line manager to answer to. Councillors, conference desk members, event organizers and, of course, the taxpayer all have to be satisfied and this means that any project undertaken needs to be comprehensively thought through from start to finish, carefully budgeted and done with the best interests of the county's residents and businesses in mind.

Working closely with other destination marketing organizations, it has become apparent to me that a passion for the product you are promoting is essential. Visiting the venues within the county and travelling around made me develop an appreciation for the county and indeed the country in which I live and work. Without this enthusiasm it is difficult for event organizers to buy into the dream as well. Stating that a destination is easily accessible with a great location and variety of venues is all very well, but so are the hundreds of other destinations in the world. But knowing your product inside out and enthusing its unique selling points enables you to paint a picture for the client of how successful their event will be.

Forging good relationships with conference bureaux and meetings industry professionals is the first thing a newcomer to the industry should do. Networking is never easy but such relationships have been invaluable to me. Just being able to pick up the phone and talk through a particular problem or share an idea is, I believe, unique to our industry. I don't know of any other where your nearest competitor can also become your closest ally.

And it was through such relationships that I found myself moving to the British Association of Conference Destinations (BACD), to join the team in Birmingham as Events and Marketing Executive.

The bureaucracy of public sector life was taking its toll and I missed the challenge and excitement of organizing events. BACD, I knew, was a leading organization in the conference industry and so this was a great opportunity to continue in the field of destination marketing, but this time on a national scale.

Using my experiences of running a conference desk, I have been able to turn around the decline in venue location enquiries from event organizers. I have also been successful in organizing a number of training courses and seminars for BACD members and for non-members.

In June 2006, I organized my first BACD annual convention in Leeds. This was a daunting task as I had been to the previous year's event in Troon as a delegate and member of the association. Not only was the Leeds event thoroughly enjoyable and educational, but other delegates commented that it was the best BACD convention they had ever been to. But with the support of the conference team in Leeds (as the host destination) and the BACD team, the conference was a success.

It is this element of my job at BACD that gives me the greatest satisfaction. After a long hard day, when my feet are hurting, hearing from a delegate that it was the best conference they've ever been to, makes it all worthwhile.

Tony Rogers asked me, in writing this personal profile, not only to detail my career path so far, but to also consider what it is I like about working in the conference and event industry, what the challenges are and what advice I could give to those looking for a job in this sector.

So, in conclusion, what I enjoy about my work is that every week I'm doing something different, be it travelling around UK destinations, organizing an event, producing some marketing literature or just spending some time in the office catching up on my e-mails.

But as with most things in life, there are the good points and the bad. Although I wouldn't say that there is anything in my work that is bad – just a testing, for example, dealing with demanding delegates, balancing a busy workload and spending time away from home.

Finally, tips for those just starting out in event management:

1) Be prepared to start from the bottom and work your way up – it's the best way to get experience in all aspects of managing events.
2) Take on every opportunity that comes your way because you never know where it might lead.
3) Be prepared for hard work and you'll reap the rewards – not necessarily financially but certainly personally.
4) Don't be afraid to ask for help.

Martin Lewis
Managing Editor, Meetings & Incentive Travel magazine

Diversity of activities, products and services. That's what has made this industry fascinating for me.

After all, how do you produce a magazine to interest as eclectic a group of people as a personnel manager for a tyre company, a brand manager for a confectionery company, the chairman of a computer company, an hotelier, an audio-visual producer, a travel agent, an after-dinner speaker, the secretary of the National

Figure 7.9
Martin Lewis.

Union of Teachers, a professional conference organizer . . . need I go on?

It's more like producing a consumer magazine than trade publishing – the only common denominator is that all our readers are involved in the events business as a part of their lives. Some are involved for every working minute of their professional lives in organizing meetings or incentive travel programmes, product launches, training programmes and the like. Others do it as just a small part of a wider professional brief – personnel management, marketing and association managers, for example, are the part-time professionals. But all need to know how, where, when and why they should do things to be efficient and successful.

That's our brief – to produce a magazine to interest men and women, from chairman to secretary, from full-timer to part-timer, from corporate man to association woman. It's an interesting challenge and one which I often think can only result in degrees of failure. After all, *any* subject can alienate *part* of the target audience so we start from that position. My aim has always been modest: to persuade readers there is at least *one* item in the magazine that will interest, inform and/or entertain them. If they happen to find more than one, we have reduced the degree of failure still further.

If the diverse nature of the readership is the challenge, it is the diverse nature of the business that is the reward. When I left newspapers where I had worked as a reporter and sub-editor on news and sport for the apparently lush and cushier pastures of travel trade newspapers, I was initially attracted by the travel opportunities but then bored by the mind-numbing sameness of it all.

When I then joined a magazine called 'Conference & Exhibitions' 26 years ago, it was because I was out of work and needed a job rather than out of any sense of professional calling. I joined my old mate Rob Spalding and, having done so, immediately wondered what on earth I was doing up this particular career cul-de-sac. But gradually the conference business wooed me and won me over. Yes, I liked the people and, yes, I liked the business – the idea of a business dedicated to better communication between people appealed to my naïve and romantic view of a worthwhile industry. But the real reason I have stayed in it is because of the diversity – and it is constantly changing and totally international.

Even I, with the attention span of a 2 year-old and the concentration level of a squirrel, cannot be bored in this business.

In 'Meetings & Incentive Travel' we cover venues and destinations at home and abroad, technical equipment from simultaneous interpretation to back-screen projection, marketing methods from exhibitions to the Internet, event management methods from sponsorship funding to event software, staff movement from agencies to hotels, case histories of actual events from a BT roadshow to a conference of the Multiple Sclerosis Society, price surveys of hotels and conference centres, legal requirements at home and abroad, government policy at home and overseas and the trading results of the leading agencies.

We talk to tourist offices, airline people, conference producers, video designers, graphic artists, hoteliers, travel agents, interpreters, motivators, trainers, corporate entertainers, after-dinner speakers – the list is endless. We meet people of every nationality and every cultural background.

How could I be bored?

It is interesting to see how many others stay in the business and how many of those who leave, then return and are delighted to be back. Rob Spalding once called it a 'global village hall' and the phrase has stayed with me. The meetings and incentive travel business is bigger and more international than ever but still it is a tight community of old friends.

It has meant we have published things that some of my friends (I mean contacts) haven't liked and some of them are no longer friends. But, on the whole, a fairly 'shoot-from-the-hip' editorial style has won more friends than it has lost.

My first ever editor told me on my first day's work as a reporter: 'Martin, don't get too close to your contacts'. I didn't understand the advice then, but I do now and he was right. Unfortunately, in this business I have not been able to follow his words. I'm afraid it just isn't possible.

The meetings and incentive travel business is just too social, just too darned friendly and just too much fun.

Summary

- excellent inter-personal skills are essential to anyone looking to make a career in the conference industry. A range of other qualities will also be needed, including organizational ability, computer literacy, a facility for working well under pressure, and oral and written communication skills.
- as the quality of the physical conference product (venues, equipment, infrastructure) reaches a generally acceptable standard, it will be the quality of service delivered by the industry's employees which will distinguish one venue or destination or supplier from another.
- the conference industry and the education sector were initially slow to develop appropriate education and training opportunities for the industry's current workforce and for potential new entrants. This situation is now changing as educational institutions and professional associations begin to develop full-time, part-time, and short course programmes.
- there is a lack of professional qualifications specific to the conference industry, although initiatives are under way to address this need, both at national and international levels.
- the industry is broad enough to welcome into its ranks people from diverse employment backgrounds and disciplines. The lack of clear career structures and progression routes can be confusing and frustrating, but also stimulates greater fluidity and freedom of movement between jobs.
- the conference industry offers a rich diversity of employment opportunities. Few people will become millionaires, but the rewards in terms of job satisfaction, fun, creativity, and building friendships around the world are rich indeed.

Review and discussion questions

1. Re-read the job advertisements and career profiles in this chapter and use these to write a 'person specification' for three vacancies which are about to be advertised: i) a conference organizer (with a company or association), ii) a conference sales manager (with a venue), iii) a destination marketer (working for a conference desk or convention bureau).
2. The hotel sector has a reputation for high staff turnover, with insufficiently-trained staff and limited career opportunities. To what extent is this an accurate description of the hotel sector in your country? What measures should be taken to

change perceptions of the sector and ensure that it really does attract, and retain, the highest calibre of personnel?

3. What image does the conference industry have among the general public? Design a questionnaire and carry out a survey among friends, family, colleagues to establish their understanding of what the industry is like, whether it is important and why, their experience of attending conferences, and to clarify their overall impressions of the industry. Use the findings to make recommendations for changes which could lead to greater recognition for the industry and for the people it employs.

4. The Department of National Heritage report quoted in this chapter says that: 'The quality of personal service is perhaps more important to tourism and hospitality than to any other industry. The quality of interactions (with industry employees) is an integral part of the experience and has the potential to delight or disappoint the consumer. We do not believe that this potential is there to the same extent in any other employing sector.' Compare tourism and hospitality with another service industry and give reasons why you would agree or disagree with the DNH report.

Notes and references

1. *Tourism: Competing with the Best No.3 'People Working in Tourism and Hospitality'*, Department of National Heritage (now (UK) Department for Culture, Media and Sport) (1996).

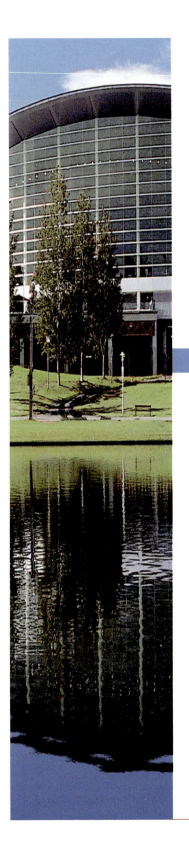

8

Leading industry organizations

Introduction

The conference industry has been described, or more accurately criticised, as being 'fragmented', because of its multiplicity of representative bodies and organizational structures. Even those working full-time within the industry are frequently confused by the bewildering array of abbreviations and acronyms in use. Within the British Isles alone, widely differing public and private sector structures for the 'management' of the industry are to be found, whether at national, regional or local level. At an international level, an ever-growing number of professional and trade associations and industry forums, almost all established since 1950, seek to raise standards, increase recognition for the economic importance of conferences and business events, and develop a clear vision for the evolution of the industry into the twenty-first century. This chapter attempts to identify the key players and explain their current roles. It looks at:

- the activities of international organizations and associations
- the roles of selected national trade and professional associations.

and includes an assessment of the conference industry's fragmentation.

On completion of this chapter, you should be able to:

- Understand the roles of the major trade and professional organizations in the conference industry
- Discuss the areas of complementarity and duplication between the different bodies.

THE ACTIVITIES OF INTERNATIONAL ORGANIZATIONS AND ASSOCIATIONS

American Society of Association Executives (ASAE) and the Center for Association Leadership

Although not directly a conference industry trade association, the American Society of Association Executives (ASAE) is, nonetheless, a very important body for the international convention industry because of the scale of convention activity undertaken by its members.

ASAE is an individual membership organization of more than 22 000 association executives and industry partners representing nearly 11 000 organizations. Its members manage leading trade associations, individual membership societies, and voluntary organizations across the United States and in 50 countries around the globe. ASAE members also provide products and services to the association community. ASAE is also a leading voice for the not-for-profit sector, promoting and representing voluntary organizations so that they may continue to improve the quality of life in the USA.

The Center for Association Leadership claims to be the 'premier provider of learning, knowledge, and future-oriented research for the association profession'. The Center delivers innovative learning experiences, performance-enhancing resources, new thinking and models for the profession, opportunities for peer-to-peer collaboration, and strategic tools and data designed to advance the association profession. Offerings include nearly 100 professional development programmes through Center University, environmental scanning and other future-focused research, a peer-reviewed journal, and more than 5000 on-line articles, models and case studies.

ASAE and The Center for Association Leadership are two organizations linked together by a common belief and passion namely, the belief that associations have the power to transform society for the better, and the passion to help associations and association professionals to achieve previously unimaginable levels of performance and reach even higher goals. Together, ASAE and The Center for Association Leadership provide resources, education, ideas and advocacy to enhance the power and performance of the association community.

Contact details: ASAE and The Center for Association Leadership, 1575 I Street NW, Washington, D.C. 20005, USA. Tel: +1-202-371-0940; Fax: +1-202-371-8315; E-mail: ASAEservices @asaecenter.org; Web site: www.asaecenter.org.

ASAE has a sister organization in Europe, the **European Society of Association Executives (ESAE)**, whose Secretariat is based at: 1 Queen Anne's Gate, Westminster, London, SW1H 9BT, UK. Tel: +44-(0)20-7227-3590; E-mail: info@esae.org; Web site: www.esae.org.

Association Internationale Des Villes Francophones De Congrès (AIVFC) (International Association of French-Speaking Congress Cities)

Formed in 1975, the Association Internationale des Villes Francophones de Congrès (AIVFC) now has over 50 members spread across the main French-speaking countries of Europe, America and Africa. Its principal objectives can be summarized as 'exchange, act, promote, innovate, communicate and anticipate':

- exchanging experiences by organizing regular seminars and continuous training
- acting by being present in international trade exhibitions, and by sharing information on congresses that might potentially interest other members
- promoting the French language by encouraging clients to use simultaneous translation for their congresses, and by creating and distributing a glossary of French congress terms
- innovating as a constant and continuous state for members
- communicating through PR activity and the AIVFC web site
- anticipating and observing the evolution of occupations and professions in the field of congresses and related events.

Contact details: Association Internationale des Villes Francophones de Congrès, Palais des Congrès-Expositions, Dijon-Bourgogne – Centre Clémenceau, 3 boulevard de Champagne, BP 67827, 21078 Dijon Cedex, France. Tel: +33 (0) 3 80 77 39 00; Fax: +33 (0) 3 80 77 39 39; E-mail: *contact@dijon-congrexpo.com*; Web site: www.aivfc-congres.com.

Confederation of Latin American Congress Organizing Entities and Related Activities (COCAL)

Established in 1985, COCAL is a civil, not-for-profit body of Latin American Professional Conference Organizers specialising in congresses and events. The Confederation aims to unite the efforts of the region's countries to improve the performance of the Latin American meetings industry. COCAL has an important educational role in the training and continuing professional development of its members. This role is fulfilled by the staging of an annual seminar and congress for members, both held in March. 14 associations, one per country, were members (as at December 2006): Argentina, Brazil, Chile, Colombia, Costa Rica, Cuba, Guatemala, Mexico, Paraguay, Peru, Puerto Rico, Spain, Uruguay, and Venezuela, with Bolivia and Panama as 'observers'.

Contact details: Confederation of Latin American Congress Organizing Entities and Related Activities. E-mail: info @cocalonline.com; Web site: www.cocalonline.com.

Convention Industry Council (CIC)

The Convention Industry Council's 32 member organizations represent more than 103 500 individuals as well as 17 300 firms and properties involved in the meetings, conventions and exhibitions industry. Formed in 1949 to provide a forum for member organizations seeking to enhance the industry, CIC facilitates the exchange of information and develops programmes to promote professionalism within the industry and educates the public on its profound economic impact. CIC is well known for its Certified Meeting Professional (CMP) Program (see Chapter 7). CIC is also responsible for the Hall of Leaders Program (which seeks to recognise industry leadership) and the Accepted Practices Exchange (APEX). APEX is working to unite the entire meeting, convention and exhibition industry in the development and eventual implementation of voluntary standards, which will be called accepted practices (see also Chapter 1).

Contact details: Convention Industry Council, 1620 I Street, NW, 6th Floor, Washington, DC 20006, USA. Tel: +1-202-429-8634; Fax: +1-202-463-8498; Web site: www.conventionindustry.org.

Destination Marketing Association International (DMAI)

The Destination Marketing Association International (DMAI) is the world's largest and most reliable resource for official destination marketing organizations (DMOs). Called the International Association of Convention & Visitor Bureaus until August 2005, the association has worked to enhance the professionalism, effectiveness and image of more than 1300 professionals from 600 destination marketing organizations in 25 countries since 1914.

The association offers cutting-edge educational and professional development programmes for destination marketing professionals and provides a voluntary accreditation program for DMOs called the Destination Marketing Accrediation Program.

DMAI maintains a premier convention and meetings database, the Meetings Information Network (MINT), that contains data on over 34 000 association and corporate meetings from more than 17 000 organizations (mainly headquartered in North America). DMAI also sponsors two annual *Destinations Showcase* tradeshow events in Washington, DC and Chicago, highlighting exhibiting destinations to thousands of qualified meeting professionals.

The DMAI Foundation was established in 1993 to enhance and complement the association and the destination management profession through research, education, visioning and developing resources and partnerships for those efforts.

Further information is available from: Destination Marketing Association International, 2025 M Street NW, Suite 500, Washington, DC, 20036 USA; Tel: +1-202-296-7888; Fax: +1-202-296-7889; E-mail: info@destinationmarketing.org; Web site: www.destinationmarketing.org.

European Association of Event Centres (EVVC)

The European Association of Event Centres (EVVC), founded in 1955, is a leading umbrella organization for event and convention centres, arenas, and other multi-purpose halls in Europe. It represents about 300 facilities in Germany, Austria, Switzerland and other European countries. The EVVC acts as a platform for the active exchange of experiences and information between its members and offers various services, seminars and consultation services.

The main activities of EVVC include communication and exchange with the industry and with other associations, support for technical developments, market research, and lobbying. For its members EVVC provides agreements with partners from different industry sectors (hotels, technology, software, etc.), support in marketing activities, the organization of workshops and seminars, and information exchange and consultancy on tax and legal issues.

Further information is available from: European Association of Event Centres, Ludwigstrasse 3, D-61348 Bad Homburg, Germany. Tel: +49 61 72 27 96 900; Fax: +49 61 72 27 96 909; E-mail: info@evvc.org; Web site: www.evvc.org.

European Cities Marketing (ECM)

European Cities Marketing is a joint initiative between the former European Cities Tourism (ECT) and the European Federation of Conference Towns (EFCT) to form the leading tourism organization in Europe, with effect from January 2007.

The new organization is a professional network promoting and linking the interests of European cities in the leisure and convention sectors. The network connects more than 130 major cities from 30 countries. It aims to strengthen city tourism by giving sales and marketing opportunities, by communicating information, sharing knowledge and expertise, educating and working together on an operational level.

It seeks to be the focal point for Europe's meetings industry and for international clients willing to organize events in Europe. Today Europe is still at the forefront as a leading leisure and meeting destination but, to be successful in the future, Europe will have to promote itself as a unified destination, and the mission of European Cities Marketing is to play this essential role.

Member benefits include an intranet: a virtual network giving access to online discussions, a library, news, projects and more. Seminars and conferences are organized three times a year in different member cities.

The Conventions division is a key resource for clients searching for destinations in Europe, and its 'Meet Europe' event (held several times a year) offers face-to-face meetings between buyers and suppliers. The Conventions division also arranges a Senior Educational Forum and Summer School (see Chapter 7), while its Politicians' Forum aims to educate and inform local politicians about the economic importance of the meetings industry, as well as providing the opportunity to debate current issues.

EMC's Leisure division provides a range of services for those of its members focused on the leisure tourism sector.

Further information is available from: European Cities Marketing, 99 rue de Talant, F-21000 Dijon, France. Tel: +33 380 56 02 04; Fax: +33 380 56 02 05; E-mail: service-centre@europeancities marketing.com; Web site: www. europeancitiesmarketing.com.

European Federation of the Associations of Professional Congress Organisers (EFAPCO)

EFAPCO was formed in 2004 to complement the national activities of its members and to ensure a single and strong voice across Europe. Its specific objectives are to:

- increase the recognition of professional congress organizers within the European Union
- promote the interests of European professional congress organizers and their suppliers
- raise and maintain high professional standards across the meetings industry through the provision of education and training opportunities
- increase business for professional congress organizers in Europe
- monitor, propose and advise on European Union laws affecting the meetings industry
- assess problems faced by professional congress organizers and promote relevant solutions

- provide opportunities for networking and exchanging ideas and experiences
- further and encourage the commercial relationships between its members and with clients
- provide relevant information to international public authorities.

As at December 2006, full membership comprised national PCO associations from Belgium, Germany, Greece, Hungary, Italy, Poland, Portugal, Spain and the United Kingdom.

Contact details: EFAPCO Executive Office, 1 Plaza de Mariano de Cavia, 28007 Madrid, Spain. Tel: +34 91 552 7745; Fax: +34 91 377 4669. Web sites: www.efapco.eu and www.europe meetings.org.

Eventia

In 2006 a trade body, Eventia, was created from the fusion of two complementary associations: the Incentive Travel and Meetings Association (ITMA) and the Corporate Events Association (CEA). The resulting body represents organizations that provide business solutions through the use of events.

Eventia provides a central hub for live communication agencies, conference and incentive travel specialists, producers of experiential marketing activity, performance improvement companies and corporate entertainment agencies – as well as suppliers of services to these event management companies.

It exists to deliver value to its members and their corporate clients by providing:

- a conduit for the exchange of ideas and expertise in event management – through training, education and events
- a centre of information, providing news, guidance and advice on all legal and other regulatory issues affecting members' business
- a point of contact for corporate event planners seeking impartial guidance on supplier selection
- a marketing channel for the promotion of the events industry
- a unified voice with which to communicate to government departments and agencies, Parliament, the European Commission and Parliament and other relevant organizations
- networking opportunities and introductions between members
- recognition of excellence through two industry award programmes.

Eventia offers three principal categories of membership:

Event Organizer Members – these are professional event management agencies. The category is sub-divided into companies that organize UK-based events and those that produce events both in the UK and overseas.

Partner Members – these are companies and tourism organizations whose services support and provide services to event organizers. This category is also sub-divided, into those members that trade from the UK and those that trade from addresses outside the UK.

Freelance Members – these are self-employed individuals providing freelance services to event organizers.

Eventia also offers **Affiliate Membership** to organizations, bodies, associations or academic institutions whose activities are complementary to its own objectives.

Contact details: Eventia, 1 Queen Anne's Gate, London SW1H 9BT, UK. Tel: +44-(0)870 112 6970; Fax: +44-(0)870 403 0256; E-mail: info@eventia.org.uk; Web site: www.eventia.org.uk.

International Association of Congress Centres (AIPC – Association Internationale Des Palais De Congrès)

Founded in 1958, AIPC is as a not-for-profit trade association of international congress, convention and exhibition centres devoted to the promotion and recognition of excellence in facility management. With a global network of 150 of the world's leading centres in over 50 countries, its mission is to help members enhance management expertise in the areas of operations, finance, technology, staff development, marketing, client relations and environment.

AIPC addresses this mission with a variety of activities including:

- industry research, analysis and technical publications
- training, educational and professional development activities, including the launch in 2007 of the AIPC Academy as a week-long professional education programme. The Academy is designed to: a) provide a broad overview of the meetings industry and the management, operation and marketing of congress centres for staff who are new to the industry, and b) provide a skills and knowledge upgrade for staff who are moving from a specific operational area into a broader management role
- global marketing and communications for the industry
- member networking and information exchange forums
- performance standards and recognition programmes
- the annual AIPC Apex Award for 'World's Best Congress Centre'.

AIPC focuses specifically on the issues, opportunities and challenges facing convention and exhibition centres and maintains close working links with related industry organizations to ensure members are well connected to overall industry issues.

Contact details: Marianne de Raay, Secretary General, AIPC, 55 rue de l'Amazone, B-1060 Brussels, Belgium. Tel: +32 496 235 327; Fax: +32 2 534 6338; E-mail: Marianne.de.raay@aipc.org; Web site: www.aipc.org.

International Association of Exhibitions and Events (IAEE)

The International Association of Exhibitions and Events (IAEE) was born in 1928 as the National Association for Exposition Managers (and subsequently traded as the International Association for Exhibition Management, until November 2006). Today IAEE is the largest international association for individuals with business interests in the exhibition and event industry, representing over 5700 member representatives and 1500 companies who organize and support exhibitions around the world.

The mission of IAEE is to promote the unique value of exhibitions and events that bring buyers and suppliers together, such as roadshows, conferences with an exhibition component, and proprietary corporate exhibitions, and IAEE is the principal resource for those who plan, produce and service the industry.

It oversees the 'Certified in Exhibition Management' (CEM) programme and awards the designation of CEM to those who complete the programme successfully. The CEM was created to raise professional standards and provide a vehicle for certification in the exhibition industry.

Further information from: International Association of Exhibitions and Events, 8111 LBJ Freeway, Suite 750, Dallas, Texas 75251-1313, USA (Mailing address: PO Box 802425, Dallas, Texas 75380-2425, USA). Tel: +1-972-458-8002; Fax: +1-972-458-8119; E-mail: iaem@iaem.org; Web site: www.iaem.org.

International Association of Professional Congress Organizers (IAPCO)

Helping the world to meet • • •

The International Association of Professional Congress Organizers (IAPCO) is the international association for professional congress organizers (PCOs), serving the needs of PCOs and international meeting planners all over the world. It is exclusively for organizers of international meetings and special events and has 99 members in 37 countries around the world including intergovernmental organizations (European Parliament; IMF/World Bank; Asian, African and European Development Banks).

IAPCO Aims are:

• to further the recognition of the profession of the congress organizer
• to further and maintain a high professional standard in the organization and administration of congresses, conferences and other international and national meetings or special events

- to undertake and promote the study of theoretical and practical aspects of international congresses
- to undertake research work concerning all problems confronting professional organizers of international meetings to seek and promote relevant solutions
- to establish and maintain effective relations with other organizations concerned in any way with international meetings
- to develop a programme of educational courses through its Training Academy
- to offer a forum for PCOs
- to encourage meetings' convenors to seek the assistance of reputable PCOs
- to provide members with opportunities to exchange ideas and experiences.

Quality assurance • • •

Since the founding members met in 1968 to establish this international association, IAPCO has set standards for an industry which has grown dramatically in terms of service and economic impact. The IAPCO logo is a global quality branding for professional meeting planners and managers specialising in international events whose membership is universally recognised as a sign of excellence by clients and other suppliers within the conference industry. Prospective members are required to provide evidence of their experience, competence, client references and quality procedures for consideration by the IAPCO Council before membership applications are considered. There is an on-going quality maintenance programme to ensure that existing members retain the exacting standards required for IAPCO membership.

IAPCO training academy • • •

IAPCO has an unparalleled record in conference education. The annual IAPCO Seminar on Professional Congress Organization, popularly known as the Wolfsberg Seminar, was first staged in 1975. Since then over 1800 participants from more than seventy countries have completed the week-long Seminar, entitling them to an IAPCO Seminar Certificate (see chapter 7 for further details). This is one of the world's most comprehensive training programmes for executives involved in conference organization, international conference-destination promotion or ancillary activities. In addition, IAPCO National and Regional Seminars are staged at the invitation of local hosts, normally in countries outside Europe such as Asia, Africa and the Middle East.

IAPCO internationally • • •

IAPCO is a founder member of the Joint Meetings Industry Council (JMIC), a world-wide council of international associations whose representatives meet on a regular basis to report on new initiatives and explore ways in which they can co-operate in conference education, publications and research.

IAPCO is actively involved in initiatives with other meeting industry partners and organizations such as the International Pharmaceutical Congress Advisory Association (IPCCA) and the Healthcare Convention & Exhibitors Association (HCEA), founding the Healthcare Congress Alliance to develop a better understanding of specific needs and interests as well as common guidelines between the different industry players involved in conference organization.

IAPCO publications • • •

In addition to the international biennial newsletter, The PCO, IAPCO also publishes a range of useful conference guidelines for PCOs, planners and suppliers, such as:

- Bidding for a Congress
- How to Choose the Right PCO
- Guidelines for Co-operation between the International Association, the National Organising Committee and the PCO
- Guidelines for the International Scientific Programme Committee
- Meetings Industry Terminology – the conference industry's leading dictionary and glossary of over 900 words in 12 languages
- Meetings Industry Terminology Supplement – incorporating Chinese, simplified and traditional
- First Steps for the Chairman in the Preparation of an International Meeting.

The following guidelines are produced in association with the Healthcare Congress Alliance:

- Sponsorship Prospectus template
- Housing Guidelines
- First Steps in the Preparation of an International Medical Meeting for the Chairman of the Meeting
- Security and Safety at Healthcare Congresses
- Accountability Issues in Healthcare Congress Management.

Contact details: International Association of Professional Congress Organizers. Tel/Fax: +44 (0)1983 755546; E-mail: info@iapco.org; Web site: www.iapco.org.

International Congress and Convention Association (ICCA)

The International Congress and Convention Association (ICCA) was founded in 1963 and is the most global of all the international meetings industry trade associations. Its membership (numbering 800 companies and organizations in 80 countries) is organized in eleven Chapters (by regions of the world) for networking. Traditionally members were also categorized by type of business but, in 2007, the original seven Categories were replaced by a broader Sector structure comprising Meetings Management, Transport, Destination Marketing, Venues, and Meetings Support.

ICCA's mission statement says: ICCA is the global community for the meetings industry, enabling its members to generate and maintain significant competitive advantage. ICCA membership benefits and services include:

- Business opportunities
  - online associations database
  - provision of hot leads on association events
  - client/supplier business workshops
  - business leads exchange at ICCA member events
  - information on the international corporate meetings market.
- Promotion
  - ICCA pavilions for members to exhibit at international trade shows
  - listing/advertising in a widely distributed membership directory
  - listing/advertising in a wide range of educational publications aimed at international meeting planners
  - ICCA Intelligence – an online resource published four times a year and distributed to over 2500 international association clients.
- Education
  - ICCA Congress and Exhibition
  - ICCA Research, Sales and Marketing Programme
  - ICCA Forum for Young Professionals/Youth Forum
  - Association Expert Seminar.
- Networking
  - ICCA Congress & Exhibition
  - Client/Member networking evenings at major trade shows such as IMEX and EIBTM
  - Members Update online.

ICCA is a member of the Joint Meetings Industry Council and the Convention Industry Council, and is an Associate Member of the United Nations World Tourism Organization.

Contact details: International Congress and Convention Association, Toren A, De Entrée 57, 1101 BH Amsterdam, The Netherlands. Tel: +31-20-398-1919; Fax: +31-20-699-0781; E-mail: icca@icca.nl; Web site: www.iccaworld.com.

ICCA also maintains regional offices in Malaysia, Uruguay and the USA, which run their own regional events and business opportunities for members.

International Pharmaceutical Congress Advisory Association (IPCAA)

Membership of the International Pharmaceutical Congress Advisory Association (IPCAA) is open to internationally active healthcare companies engaged in medical congresses. All member companies must maintain a permanent healthcare-oriented research programme. IPCAA's mission is to 'ensure the most beneficial outcome for all parties involved in medical congresses, through the development of common and consistent congress policies and through recognised partnerships with medical societies'. IPCAA's main objectives are to:

- promote the highest possible standards at medical congresses
- establish a common and consistent congress policy through recognised partnership with medical societies
- ensure optimum benefit for all parties involved in medical congresses
- exchange experience, data and documentation on medical congresses
- organize meetings of members to exchange knowledge and information about medical congresses
- organize training courses and seminars for those involved in medical congress management
- maintain a Code of Conduct and Guidelines on the organization of, and participation in, medical congresses.

Contact details: International Pharmaceutical Congress Advisory Association, PO Box 182, CH-4013 Basel, Switzerland. Tel: +44-(0)1625-890035; Fax: +44-(0)1625-890112; E-mail: secretariat @ipcaa.org; Web site: www.ipcaa.org.

Joint Meetings Industry Council (JMIC)

The Joint Meetings Industry Council (JMIC) was founded in 1978 as a forum for the exchange of information and perspectives among international associations engaged in various aspects of the Meetings Industry. Today the JMIC has three primary objectives:

- to create a forum for the exchange of information and expertise among organizations that represent the various sectors of the Meetings industry
- to recognize formally the achievements of individuals who have successfully advanced the positioning and professionalism of the industry on an international basis

291

- to support and carry out activities that promote the profile and positioning of the Meetings industry as a distinct and important part of the global economy.

Its members consist of a number of international organizations who share a common interest and involvement in the meetings industry. The active member associations which comprised JMIC in 2006 were: International Association of Congress Centres (AIPC), International Association of Professional Congress Organizers (IAPCO), International Congress and Convention Association (ICCA), COCAL (the Latin American Confederation of PCO and Related Companies), European Federation of Conference Towns (EFCT/ECT), Meeting Professionals International (MPI), Society of Incentive and Travel Executives (SITE), European Association of Event Centres (EVVC).

In 2002 JMIC members recognized that the Meetings industry was at a disadvantage relative to other industries because of a low level of awareness of its purpose, activities and benefits. In order to address this, the Council commissioned the development of a strategy to raise the profile of the industry worldwide. The result was a report entitled 'Profile and Power' which recommended a 'bottom-up' strategy based on individual community initiatives which JMIC could support by providing materials and recognition while acting as a vehicle for sharing the experiences and successes of participants. Further details of the 'Profile and Power' initiative are accessible on the JMIC web site (see below).

The JMIC Profile and Power Award was established by the Council as a way of recognizing individuals who have made significant contributions to advancing the awareness and influence of the Meetings industry in their respective communities. It is presented annually at a major industry event.

JMIC has also established a Unity Award as a way of recognizing individuals who have made significant contributions to the advancement of the Meetings industry and the level of professionalism it represents. The Award is made each year based on criteria which evaluate industry leadership and initiative.

Contact details are those for whichever member body is currently acting as JMIC President. Since 2004 this has been the International Association of Congress Centres (AIPC). Further details: www.themeetingsindustry.org/jmic_home.html.

Meeting Professionals International (MPI)

Meeting Professionals International (MPI) is one of the leading associations for the global meetings industry and is committed to delivering success for its 21 000 worldwide members by providing innovative professional development, generating industry awareness and creating business development opportunities.

Founded in 1972, the Dallas-based organization delivers success through its 68 chapters and clubs in 20 countries around the world.

Membership benefits and services include:

- education: three major conferences (the World Education Congress (WEC), the Professional Education Conference – North America (PEC-NA) and Europe (PEC-E)), Institutes in Meeting Management, the Certificate in Meeting Management programme (see Chapter 7), regular network evenings, other educational programmes
- publications: a monthly magazine, MPI Global Membership Directory plus a European Membership Directory, 'Meeting Europe' (European newsletter), Chapter newsletters
- information: MPI Foundation (research and development arm), Resource Centre (library), MPINet (global on-line communications network)
- professional recognition: Meeting Professional Awards.

Further information is available from: Meeting Professionals International, 3030 LBJ Freeway, Suite 1700, Dallas, Texas 75234, USA. Tel: +1-972-702-3000; Fax: +1-972-702-3070; E-mail: information@mpiweb.org; Web site: www.mpinet.org.

MPI European Office, 22 Route de Grundhof, L-6315 Beaufort, Grand Duchy of Luxembourg. Tel: 352-2687-6141; Fax: 352-2687-6343; E-mail: dscaillet@mpiweb.org.

Professional Convention Management Association (PCMA)

Founded in 1957, the mission of the Professional Convention Management Association (PCMA) is to deliver breakthrough education and promote the value of professional convention management. Membership of PCMA was initially restricted to meeting managers in the medical and healthcare fields. In 1990 the Association opened its membership to chief executives and meeting professionals from not-for-profit associations in all sectors. And, in 1998 PCMA further opened its membership by removing the requirement that meeting professionals be employed by (statute) 501(c)3 (i.e. not-for-profit) organizations. PCMA has 16 chapters located across North America. In addition to large conventions and exhibitions, PCMA members plan an estimated 250 000 smaller meetings each year.

In 1985 PCMA created an Education Foundation, designed to support college and self-study courses, professional training and book publishing. The Foundation recently published the fourth edition of *Professional Meeting Management*, widely recognised in North America as the 'bible' of the industry. PCMA publishes its own magazine, *Convene*, one of the leading industry magazines. In 1994 PCMA initiated the 'Space Verification Program', designed to help meeting managers and hotels validate meeting room specifications.

Contact details: Professional Convention Management Association, 2301 South Lake Shore Drive, Suite 1001, Chicago, Illinois 60616-1419, USA. Tel: +1-312-423-7262; Fax: +1-312-423-7222; E-mail: communications@pcma.org; Web site: www.pcma.org.

Society of Incentive and Travel Executives (SITE)

Founded in 1973, the Society of Incentive and Travel Executives (SITE) is a worldwide organization of business professionals dedicated to the recognition and development of motivational and performance improvement strategies of which travel is a key component.

Membership, which numbers just over 2000 in 87 countries, is open to qualified individuals who 'subscribe to the highest standards of professionalism and ethical behaviour'. Members are drawn from airlines, cruise lines, corporate users, destination management companies, ground transportation companies, hotels and resorts, incentive houses, official tourist organizations, travel agencies and supporting organizations such as restaurants and visitor attractions. As representatives of every discipline in the incentive travel industry, SITE members design, develop, promote, sell, administer and operate motivational programmes as an incentive to increase productivity in business.

SITE has 33 national and regional Chapters around the world. Among the membership benefits and services offered are:

- participation in the only worldwide society devoted to excellence in incentive travel
- access to over 2000 SITE member contacts in 87 countries, representing every discipline in the incentive travel industry
- a copy of, and listing in, the SITE Resource Directory (Directory of Members) and its on-line membership directory, including free hyperlink to the member's own web site
- a subscription to 'In-SITE', a quarterly member newsletter covering issues affecting incentive travel worldwide and organizational activities
- discounted rates to attend the annual International Conference which brings together experts from around the world to examine business trends and the application of business products that apply to them. Discounted rates to attend ESNEP, SITE's European event. Both of these events are a mix of educational sessions and networking, and are an excellent way of interacting with SITE members from around the world
- e-learning modules
- a special programme for Young Leaders

- an Annual Executive Summit to bring education to destinations new to incentive travel
- access to Chapter activities and education programmes around the world
- a listing in the SITE Finder Service
- access to the SITE logo for use on personal business cards and letterheads
- access to SITE membership display material for members' booths or stands at the incentive industry's major trade shows: IMEX, IT&ME/The Motivation Show and EIBTM
- eligibility to seek designation as a Certified Incentive Travel Executive (CITE), the field's highest professional designation for individuals
- eligibility to enter the prestigious SITE Crystal Awards competition
- discounts on SITE publications, mailing lists and SITE research papers, as well as free access to several new research publications.

Contact details: Society of Incentive and Travel Executives, 401 North Michigan Avenue, Chicago, Illinois 60611, USA. Tel: +1-312-644-6610; Fax: +1-312-527-6783; E-mail: hq@site-intl.org; Web site: www.site-intl.org.

and

Society of Incentive and Travel Executives, Europe Office, 15 Learmonth Gardens, Edinburgh EH4 1HB, Scotland. Tel: +44 (0)7717 827457; Fax: +44 (0)131 332 3325.

Union of International Associations (UIA)

The Union of International Associations (UIA) was formed in 1907 as the Central Office of International Associations, becoming the UIA in 1910. It was created in an endeavour to co-ordinate international organization initiatives, with emphasis on documentation, including a very extensive library and museum function. Gradually the focus has shifted to promoting internationality, as well as to a role in representing the collective views of international bodies where possible, especially on technical issues.

The UIA is an independent, non-governmental, not-for-profit body that undertakes and promotes study and research into international organizations. Of particular importance to the conference industry is the UIA's production of statistics on international congresses and conventions, statistics which have been collected annually since 1949. The meetings taken into consideration are those organized or sponsored by international organizations appearing in the UIA publications *Yearbook of International Organizations* and *International Congress Calendar*. The UIA publishes its 'International Meeting Statistics' on an annual basis (some of its 2005 conference statistics are reproduced in Chapter 1). UIA publications are available in printed, cd-rom and on-line formats.

Contact details: Union of International Associations, Congress Department, Rue Washington 40, B-1050 Brussels, Belgium Tel: +32-2-640-4109; Fax: +32-2-643-6199; E-mail: uia@uia.be; Web site: www.uia.org.

THE ROLES OF SELECTED NATIONAL TRADE ASSOCIATIONS

In addition to the international industry associations described above, there is a much larger number of trade bodies operating at a national level. This section provides brief profiles of a small selection of these as examples of the types of organizations to be found within individual countries.

Association of Australian Convention Bureaux Inc. (AACB)

The Association of Australian Convention Bureaux Inc. (AACB) consists of 14 city and regional bureaux dedicated to marketing their specific region as a premier business events destination. The mission of the Association is 'to represent the collective interests of Australian convention bureaux'. While recognizing the specific destinational marketing role of individual bureaux, the AACB plays a role in promoting Australia internationally through major publicity campaigns launched in conjunction with the Australian Tourist Commission. As an incentive for individual bureaux to promote their city/area internationally, the AACB holds approved body status for eligible bureaux to receive a rebate on international marketing expenditure through the Export Market Development Grant scheme.

In addition to its promotional role, the AACB has several key focus areas:

- *Information and Research*: the AACB Bureaux Comparison Survey generates relevant and timely statistical reports for effective lobbying, planning and performance review.

  Each year updated information from bureaux is provided to the Australian Tourist Commission (ATC) for compilation of the ATC Conventions, Trade Shows and Exhibitions Calendar. This Calendar lists details for confirmed events and is aimed at assisting with delegate boosting to conventions, trade shows and exhibitions. The AACB is also involved with the joint National Business Events Survey (NBES) in partnership with the Cooperative Research Centre for Sustainable Tourism (CRC) and the business events industry. The Survey measures the size, scope and value of the segment (see Chapter 3)

- *Education*: an annual staff conference is held for members to develop sound professional practices, educate members and provide networking opportunities. In addition, a Staff Scholarship and Staff Prize (for newcomers to bureaus) are offered annually to encourage excellence, in partnership with ATC and Qantas
- *Lobbying and Government Liaison*: as a representative body, the AACB communicates a co-ordinated industry view and voice to the Governments of Australia and to the public, thus strengthening industry influence on policy formulation. It also seeks to further industry liaison through its involvement with two organizations: the National Tourism Alliance and the Business Events Council of Australia.

Contact details: Association of Australian Convention Bureaux Inc., Level 13, 80 William Street, Woolloomooloo 2011, New South Wales, Australia. Tel: +61-(0)2-9326-9133; Fax: +61-(0)2-9326-9676; E-mail: mike.cannon@aacb.org.au; Web site: www.aacb.org.au.

Association of British Professional Conference Organisers (ABPCO)

ABPCO was founded in 1981 and is the only association in the UK whose members are exclusively professional conference organizers (PCOs). Membership of ABPCO is subject to eligibility, based on experience and professionalism, and is limited to individuals who have a proven record of achievement nationally and (in many cases) internationally. Membership is on an individual not a company basis, is open not only to conference and event organizers from independent conference organizing businesses, but also to in-house organizers working within associations, educational/official bodies and corporate organizations.

Members are required to uphold an agreed Code of Practice. ABPCO's main aims are to:

- Position ABPCO as the leading body representing the interests of professional conference organisers and increase its profile and recognition
- Constantly develop and enhance the benefits it provides to ABPCO members by creating opportunities for networking and by encouraging its members to achieve the highest possible standards of excellence
- Raise standards of professionalism across the meetings industry through the provision of education, training and personal development opportunities
- Increase the volume and value of business being won by ABPCO members through a range of marketing activities.

The benefits of ABPCO Membership include:

- *Recognition and accreditation:* as a leading professional conference organizer – membership requires a high level of experience and proven competence. The status of ABPCO membership confers a clear commercial advantage when bidding for contracts or when applying for new positions within the industry
- *Networking:* sharing ideas, issues, best practice with a peer group of event organizers. This includes access to a members' intranet enabling e-mail communications with all other members
- *Continuing professional development:* regular meetings and seminars are held where relevant hot topics are addressed by guest speakers. These meetings are complemented by an annual conference featuring presentations by high profile industry speakers
- *Marketing:* members and member services are promoted via the ABPCO web site www.abpco.org, attendance at trade shows, PR, an annual Directory, and a range of other promotional channels. Full members also receive business leads from a variety of potential clients
- *Information:* regular distribution of information and intelligence on the conference industry ensures members are kept abreast of the latest research, business opportunities, articles and reports
- *Representation and advocacy:* ABPCO represents the interests of the PCO profession to government, business and commerce, and academia.

Contact details: Association of British Professional Conference Organisers, 6th Floor Charles House, 148–149 Great Charles Street, Birmingham B3 3HT, UK. Tel: +44 (0)121 212 1400; Fax: +44 (0)121 212 3131; E-mail: information@abpco.org; Web site: www.abpco.org.

British Association of Conference Destinations (BACD)

The British Association of Conference Destinations (BACD) was founded in 1969 and represents some 65 destinations throughout the British Isles, from the north of Scotland to the Channel Islands. Its members are conference offices (of local authorities) and convention and visitor bureaux, through which it represents around 3000 conference venues. BACD also has as members the four national tourist boards: VisitBritain, VisitScotland, Visit Wales and the Northern Ireland Tourist Board (see Chapter 4 for further details of these organizations). BACD's mission is to support, promote and represent British conference destinations. Its principal activities include:

- *Marketing*: publication of an annual members' directory, promotion of BACD web site, PR activity, participation in industry exhibitions, organization of BACD's own 'Destinations Showcase', administration of a venue finding service known as 'More Than A Venue' (www.morethanavenue.co.uk).
- *Research and Consultancy*: management of annual 'British Conference Venues Survey' research project, support for other industry research, provision of consultancy services to destinations; maintenance of several industry databases (buyers, venues, destinations, universities and colleges).
- *Representation and Advocacy*: representing and promoting the interests of BACD members and the wider conference industry to government (local and national), business and the media; forging links and alliances with other key industry bodies. BACD is a founder member of the UK's Business Tourism Partnership (www.businesstourismpartnership.org).
- *Education, Training and Continuing Professional Development*: provision of seminars, courses, an annual conference, and the development of close working links with educational institutions offering programmes in destination marketing, business tourism, conference and event management.
- *Quality Standards*: supporting initiatives which develop quality assurance and accreditation for destination marketing organizations.

BACD also has an Affiliate membership open to venues, consultants, suppliers, educational bodies and others and, from 2007, a Student membership open to students on conference industry-related courses at either undergraduate or postgraduate levels.

Contact details: British Association of Conference Destinations, 6th Floor Charles House, 148–149 Great Charles Street, Birmingham B3 3HT Tel: 44-(0)121-212-1400; Fax: 44-(0)121-212-3131; E-mail: info@bacd.org.uk; Web site: www.bacd.org.uk and www.bacd.biz.

Hellenic Association of Professional Congress Organizers (HAPCO)

The Hellenic Association of Professional Congress Organizers (HAPCO) was established in 1996 to represent congress tourism professionals and to promote the congress industry throughout Greece by implementing actions that contribute both to its prestige and its effectiveness. HAPCO's activities focus on the continuing improvement of Greek congress tourism, aiming to turn Greece into an attractive destination in the international congress market. Its intention is to forge a distinct conference culture and shape a competitive profile that support both its members and

Greek tourism overall. Since its establishment, HAPCO has been developed into one of the principal institutions in the Greek tourism sector and has been acknowledged as an official partner of the Greek State on issues relating to congress tourism.

HAPCO represents 98 members (as at December 2006), which include PCOs, conference centres, conference centres with resort hotels, hotels with conference facilities, audio-visual companies, as well as a number of companies offering services related to congress organization and support.

As part of its efforts to develop and establish itself in the congress sector, HAPCO seeks to:

- promote the services of its members in the national and inter-national meetings market
- contribute to the diversity and competitiveness of the Greek meetings industry
- promote its views and proposals to public and private national stakeholders, contributing to the systematic development of Greek congress tourism
- provide specialized education and training to executives in the tourism sector on matters relating to congress tourism
- promote quality specifications and raise standards of profes-sionalism that enhance the prestige and image of the Greek meetings industry.

Contact details: Hellenic Association of Professional Congress Organizers, 2–4 Alkmeonidon Street, 16121 Athens, Greece Tel. No: +30 210 72 58 486: Fax No: +30 210 72 58 487; E-mail: hapco@hapco.gr; Web site: www.hapco.gr.

Meetings Industry Association (MIA)

The Meetings Industry Association (MIA) is a leading associa-tion for the meetings industry reflecting the needs of the buyer, improving the standards of the supplier. It was established in 1990 and has over 400 organizations in membership, drawn from the supply side of the conference industry in the UK and Ireland. The MIA aims to improve the quality of service and facilities offered by its members, encouraging the highest possible stan-dards. It seeks to strengthen the position of its members' busi-nesses in an increasingly competitive marketplace and raise the profile of the United Kingdom as an international conference destination. Specific member services and benefits include:

- marketing opportunities via the MIA web site, publications, exhibition representation, and media relations
- sales opportunities
- networking at MIA national and regional events (an Annual General Meeting, Annual Conference, Annual Summer and Winter Golf Challenges and regional events)

- training courses, including a 5-module programme entitled the 'MIA Certificate in Management Development'
- research and information
- consultancy and arbitration services
- management of the quality accreditation scheme for venues 'Accreditation in Meetings' (AIM)
- the unique MIA tracker system, Meetings Intelligence, for measuring Customer Satisfaction with Expectation, providing a benchmarking tool for industry suppliers.

Contact details: Meetings Industry Association, PO Box 515, Kelmarsh, Northampton NN6 9XW; Tel: 44-(0)845-230-5508; Fax: 44-(0)84-230-7708; E-mail: info@mia-uk.org; Web site: www.mia-uk.org.

Meetings & Events Australia (MEA)

Meetings & Events Australia (MEA), formerly known as the Meetings Industry Association of Australia (MIAA), is a national, independent not-for-profit organization dedicated to fostering professionalism and excellence in all aspects of meetings management. It also promotes the value and effectiveness of meetings as an important high-yield sector of business travel and tourism. MEA offers professional development programmes and accreditation. It also disseminates information, provides a forum for its members to discuss current issues, and represents the industry to government.

In order to achieve these broad aims, it has set for itself a number of 'key result areas', which include:

- creating business opportunities and facilitating business-to-business relationships
- encouraging better business practice
- promoting professional development
- providing information, forums and advice that lead to improved business performance
- promoting the value of meetings and the industry
- acting in an advocacy capacity in respect of pertinent industry issues
- managing a sustainable association.

Members of MEA comprise meetings management companies, special event organizers, venues, staging/AV service providers, convention/visitors/tourist organizations and bureaux, and a range of meetings and events industry suppliers and services.

Contact details: Meetings & Events Australia, Level 1, Suites 5 & 6, 1 McLaren Street, North Sydney, New South Wales 2060, Australia. Tel: +61-2-9929-5400; Fax: +61-2-9929-5600; E-mail: mea@mea.org.au; Web site: www.meetingsevents.com.au.

Southern African Association for the Conference Industry (SAACI)

The South African Association for the Conference Industry (SAACI) was formally established in 1987. There are three separate Chapters within the association: Conference and Events, Venues and Services. These deal with the specific interests of these groups. The Southern African conference industry is being recognized internationally as a dynamic growth area and SAACI is dedicated to maintaining and improving the standards of efficiency and professionalism of the conference industry as a whole, and its members in particular. SAACI is the central professional forum and communication centre for the conference industry in Southern Africa. Now in its 20th year, it is recognized by government as the voice of the industry. SAACI gives its members the opportunity to meet others in the industry and to keep up-to-date with new services and developments. It is a vibrant, active association with 800 members in branches in the four main centres of South Africa. It also offers quick and easy access to industry members to those located outside the country's borders.

Membership benefits and services include:

- the official SAACI journal, the definitive 'Southern Africa Conference, Exhibition & Events Guide', which is produced on a monthly basis as well as a Yearbook, in which members have an entry
- a membership database
- distribution of the SAACI catalogue at trade shows
- generation of business enquiries
- international exposure via the SAACI web site
- attendance at the annual SAACI conference and regional events.

Contact details: Southern African Association for the Conference Industry, National Secretariat, PO Box 155, Durban 4000, South Africa. Tel: +27-31-360-1282; Fax: +27-31-360-1001; E-mail: sec@saaci.co.za; Web site: www.saaci.co.za.

AN ASSESSMENT OF THE CONFERENCE INDUSTRY'S FRAGMENTATION

It cannot be denied that the tourism industry as a whole is fragmented. It is composed of thousands of mainly small operators and businesses, providing accommodation, restaurants, attractions, coach and taxi services, and so forth. The conference sector shares this same infrastructure, but also encompasses conference venues and other suppliers specific to the industry. With the exception of chain hotels, conference venues are, for the most part, run as discrete business units, independent of any centralised management or structure.

The sense of fragmentation is reinforced by the apparent proliferation of trade associations and similar bodies representing segments of the conference industry. In comparison with many other professions and industries, such as the oil/petroleum and aviation industries or the legal profession, the conference industry can be said to lack a single, cohesive voice.

At another level, however, the industry enjoys a very real sense of unity across the world. It is characterised by an openness and sharing, by friendships and networking between colleagues, which are immensely attractive and create almost a sense of family. Martin Lewis pays eloquent testimony to this aspect of the industry in his career profile in Chapter 7, quoting another colleague who described the industry as a 'global village hall'.

There is undoubtedly scope to bring some greater harmonisation to the industry, and there would also be benefits arising from a rationalisation of the industry's representative bodies, but it is to be hoped that these can be achieved without damaging the international friendship and collaboration which are such an important, and winsome, feature of the conference and conventions sector today.

Summary

There are many trade associations and similar bodies operating within the conference sector, at national, continental and international levels. Some have clearly defined roles and a niche membership which is not being served by other associations. Some, however, appear to duplicate the activities of other associations, suggesting that rationalisations and mergers may become necessary both to ensure their own survival and for the wider health of the industry.

Review and discussion questions

1. To what extent is the description of the conference sector as 'fragmented' justified? Is there a greater degree of fragmentation within the conference and business tourism sector than in the leisure tourism sector?

2. Read through the descriptions of the various international and national trade bodies described in this chapter. Identify those characteristics that are common to a number of the bodies and comment on why these seem to be important. Then make a list of some of the key unique features that

differentiate one from another. What features and services would you expect to be crucial to the future survival and prosperity of these associations?

3. 'There should just be one conference industry association per country.' Discuss the pros and cons of such a development.

9

Trends, issues and future developments

Introduction

Satellite technology now gives us instant communications across our planet. The internet provides access to an ever-expanding encyclopaedia of information and knowledge. Both phenomena enable us to understand and evaluate more effectively the opportunities and threats facing us in many aspects of our daily lives. What insights can we glean into the trends, issues, opportunities and threats affecting the twenty-first century conference and conventions industry, and how will they shape its future development? This chapter looks at a number of these, in particular:

- Global trends and forecasts
- Events and the marketing mix
- Virtual versus face-to-face conferencing
- Sustainable meetings
- Corporate social responsibility (CSR)
- Accessibility not disability
- Procurement
- Return on investment (ROI).

On completion of this chapter, you should be able to:

- Discuss the current and potential future growth of the conference industry
- Identify key trends impacting that growth and the ways in which people confer, both face-to-face and virtually
- Understand some of the key societal and environmental pressures now affecting the industry
- Appreciate the importance of conferences providing effective returns, and the ways in which these can be measured.

GLOBAL TRENDS AND FORECASTS

Unsurprisingly, many people both within and outside the conference industry frequently ask whether the industry is still growing, and whether in the years ahead it will experience growth or decline. Investors, for example, need answers to such questions to inform their investment decisions; students need to know if the conventions industry can offer long-term career opportunities; politicians demand to know whether the sector justifies their interest and support; those of us working in the industry wish to understand how we are faring compared with other sectors, and what the projections are for the medium to long term.

There is, however, no simple answer to this very big question. Many factors impact the current health and future development of the sector: trends in national and global economies; environmental issues and concerns; technological developments and the opportunities to 'meet' electronically or virtually; threats from terrorism and epidemics such as 'SARS'; sociological factors and priorities; and many more. Some of these have been explored in earlier chapters of this book; some are examined in more depth later in this chapter. The very dynamism of the industry means that change is a constant feature, and it becomes increasingly difficult to measure one characteristic against another because the characteristics themselves change substantially within a relatively short timeframe.

Despite these caveats, there is, in the author's view, some evidence to suggest that the industry may have reached a plateau. Within the international association congress and conventions sector (see Chapter 2), for example, the number of international meetings monitored by both ICCA and the UIA has ceased to show the rapid growth of the 1980s and 1990s. Whereas the UIA reported on 4864 international meetings in 1983, a number which had grown to 8871 by 1993, the total had only reached 9259 by 2001 and, by 2005, had fallen to 8953 (although account does need to be taken of changes in the method of analysis introduced in 2003).

Within the UK, the actual number of conferences increased in 2005 compared with 2004, but their economic value fell because of their shorter duration and the fact that fewer were residential events. Does this constitute a growing market or one in decline? Is this a temporary phenonemon or part of a longer-term trend? In reality it is too soon to tell and an accurate assessment will require a period of years.

From a supply-side perspective, it is now the case that most of the developed countries are active players (218 countries were monitored in the 2006 UIA survey, for example), and there would seem to be only limited growth opportunities. Countries such as China and India are investing heavily in conference and business event facilities, and their own burgeoning economies will generate substantial demand for meetings space. At an international level, however, they will only add to the already fierce competition that exists and their success seems likely to be at the price of a lower market share for some of the more established players.

One piece of research which attempts to monitor trends in the 'global business of meetings' is the annual *FutureWatch* survey undertaken by Meeting Professionals International. The 2007 survey (based on feedback from 1443 respondents (441 client-side planners, 180 intermediaries and 814 suppliers)) shows a robust market with optimistic trends and forecasts. For example, it reveals:

- Overall the market was expected to show further growth in 2007 compared with 2006 with client-side planners (also known as corporate and association organizers or buyers) predicting increases of 7 per cent (corporations) and 18 per cent (associations) in the number of meetings held by their organizations, with expenditure also increasing by 6 per cent overall. They also expected larger meetings but not longer events – this latter finding mirrors the trend for shorter meetings noted in the UK
- The growth of international meetings travel, however, has flattened or even reduced as US planners project that they will use fewer meeting destinations outside North America, and European planners forecast that fewer events will be held outside Europe.

The full Survey findings can be accessed online at www.mpiweb.org.

Global client management companies

One area of the international conference and conventions industry that has shown undoubted growth in recent years has been the rise, consolidation and influence of global client management companies. For example:

Conferon: with reservations for nearly four million room nights annually, and a commitment to being the leading provider of meeting and related services in the hospitality industry.

Helms Briscoe: based in the USA and serving 8000 client organizations. It provides site selection services to corporate, government and association clients on a no charge basis.

Maritz: headquartered in the USA but merged with a UK-based client management group, Grass Roots, making it arguably the largest client management group in the meetings, events and incentives sector in the world.

MCI Group: headquartered in Switzerland and with claims to be Europe's pre-eminent association, communications and event management company. It has partnered with Smith Bucklin, based in the USA, to deliver 'seamless' association and event management services worldwide. MCI Group booked over 400 000 hotel rooms in 2006 (see also MCI Group case study in Chapter 2).

Smith Bucklin: also claims to be the world's largest association management company providing services to over 200 trade and professional associations.

What these organizations have in common, according to Jon Hutchison, Managing Director of Sydney Convention and Visitors Bureau (speaking at the 2006 BACD Convention), is that:

> *their focus has moved away from supply to demand. They seek to own the consumer and, because of this, to be the hoop that suppliers must jump through to sell their products. Previously meetings and event management companies relied heavily on convention and visitor bureaux and their link to consumers and suppliers. This has declined because it is no longer about suppliers, it is about consumers.*

Such global client and event management companies have established preferred vendor agreements with blue chip corporations, at either a national, regional (i.e. continental) or worldwide level. As these corporations have outsourced specialist services, such as conference and event management, these intermediary organizations have stepped in to secure this business.

The trends for international associations to appoint a core PCO (see Chapter 2) and to outsource the management of the association to a specialist association/client management company have also created opportunities for these global event management companies, upon which they have seized eagerly.

Hutchison commented:

> *Through massive buying power due to customer reach, third party intermediaries (i.e. global client management companies) secure very competitive pricing and instant confirmation.*

He added that their global reach, allowing them to represent thousands of destinations, poses a threat to the traditional role of convention and visitor bureaux (CVBs), who can only represent one destination (or at most just a few). He argued that CVBs would need to play to different strengths if they were to survive, strengths such as: destination co-ordination and promotion; being the official and unbiased point of access to destinations; providing destination leadership; focusing on consumers rather than stakeholders; and ensuring high quality visitor experiences.

In reality, there is no simple answer to the question posed at the beginning of this section: is the conference industry growing or declining? There will always be variations by industry sector and by geographical region. What is perhaps key, however, is access to robust and reliable data that will enable accurate assessments and measurements to be made in response to the specific perspectives of the enquirer.

EVENTS AND THE MARKETING MIX

Earlier chapters of this book have looked at the marketing mix and the ways in which different marketing tools can be used in the promotion of destinations and venues (Chapter 4), and at event marketing and how this is used to maximize delegate and/or media participation in a conference or convention (Chapter 5). Of equal importance is the role that events can play in the marketing of a company product or service, an area that is regularly researched and monitored by, among others, The George P. Johnson Company (www.gpjco.com). Their annual research into event marketing and its role in the marketing mix is made available through the MPI Foundation web site (www.mpifoundation.org). Their 2006 research (entitled 'EventView'), conducted among almost 900 individuals in marketing management positions from North America, Europe and Asia Pacific in sectors including automotive, high technology, healthcare, and financial services, noted the following findings and trends:

- Meetings and events can play a strategic role in driving business value in every organization ... as corporate executives now see the benefits that face-to-face interactions can provide to their bottom line
- Current customers and prospects can benefit from meetings and events as they provide the greatest opportunity to learn about a company's brand, value proposition and (new)

products/services. Companies can derive business value from events to strengthen product or brand awareness; differentiate from the competition; educate or train employees and ultimately increase sales

- A slight reduction in the importance of event marketing was found in 2006 compared with 2005, but this should *not* be:

    > *taken as a downward trend within the event marketing industry. In fact, there are clear signs of an industry that is stabilizing and showing signs of maturation*

- Almost one in four of respondents believe that event marketing provides the greatest ROI (return on investment) in marketing. The main reasons for event marketing's high returns on investment are that it provides:
    - the greatest opportunity for direct, in-person, face-to-face contact
    - the best opportunity to reach a targeted audience
    - one of the only opportunities to reach a large and engaged audience in one venue.
- Senior marketing professionals are looking beyond traditional event marketing tactics for an integrated campaign that offers the opportunity for an audience to interact with a company's product/service and its brand before, during and after event(s) through the combination of advertising, direct, interactive and traditional event marketing. Over half of survey respondents (55 per cent) gave this definition to the term 'experience marketing'. Almost 80 per cent of respondents said they were adding experience marketing in some form or another to their marketing mix, because they saw it as a better method to convey persuasive difference between their brand and the competition's. It was also seen as more effective in levering marketing spend across all of a company's marketing disciplines.

VIRTUAL VERSUS FACE-TO-FACE CONFERENCING

The technology for virtual conferencing continues to evolve and improve at a rapid rate. Chapter 5 examined the key technologies available and their applications. This chapter looks at whether virtual conferences and meetings will, in time, replace the need for face-to-face events.

Campbell (2000) contends that:

> *the weight of argument and evidence suggests that precisely because technology is invading our lives, then so is there an increased requirement for human contact and inter-personal chemistry. In other words, touchy-feely events will always matter, and perhaps even more so.*

Some suggest that motivational and morale-boosting get-togethers will, in fact, grow in importance, for precisely the reason that technology exacerbates the sense of working in isolation.

Corbin Ball, conference technology expert and professional speaker (www.corbinball.com), shares his experiences of both types of conference in an article 'Face-to-Face Vs. Web Conferencing – What Should I Use When?' He suggests that face-to-face (F2F) meetings have:

Focus: F2F can accomplish many goals including: information exchange (learning), collaboration, commerce, interaction and more.

Strengths: F2F has many strong points – as the saying goes 'There is no such thing as a virtual beer'.

- Richer experience: there is no better way of getting to know a person than by meeting them in person. There are so many nuances we tune into instinctively when we are meeting someone, or see them on the platform, that simply cannot be transmitted on the web. These subtleties in communication in a speaking/training situation assist in learning. As a speaker, to be able to see the whites of people's eyes, to hear their questions, to observe how attentive they are is invaluable in adjusting my presentation to keep them with me and enhance the learning process
- Networking, brainstorming, interactivity: F2F has other strengths as well. There is the opportunity to network, brainstorm, to break people into small groups, and much more that will enhance learning and increase the fun. Often much of the learning at a meeting happens in the hallways outside the room or during the social functions. Virtual meetings simply can't compete in this realm
- More conducive learning environment: as people are away from the distractions of their office (except for the mobile or cell phone), they can focus better on the learning environment.

Length: presentations can last for 10 minutes or workshops for 2 days or longer. As long as you keep people engaged, and keep them fed and happy, people will stick to the tasks in hand.

Weaknesses: time and travel costs/hassle are two of the biggest weaknesses of live meetings.

Ball then assesses virtual meetings in the same way, with particular reference to web conferences:

Focus: virtual meetings focus primarily on one issue: information exchange – the ability to collaborate, brainstorm, etc is significantly limited.

Strengths: the major strengths are the opposite of weaknesses of F2F – they are cheap, easy to set up, and easy to get to as they happen at your computer:

- **Less travel hassle**
- **Lower cost**: up to 90 per cent less expensive if the total costs of F2F are considered (travel costs, time out of the office, room/AV rental, catering, marketing)
- **Shorter time to market**: web conferencing can have a much shorter time to market. Web conferences can be set up to happen almost instantly
- **Global access**: people can meet immediately from around the world – all that is needed is a computer and a good connection to the internet
- **Interactivity tools**: several interactive tools are built into many of the web conferencing products: the ability to ask questions, annotate slides, create ad hoc surveys/polls with the results appearing immediately on the screen are just some of the options. Desktop sharing, application sharing, audience chat, audience feedback to ask the speaker to speed up or slow down are others. The tools are needed to keep the audience's attention
- **Archive capabilities**: these allow the conference to be recorded and played back at a later time
- **More structure**: more likely to follow a structure (i.e. follow the slides) and less likely to overrun time-wise.

Time: virtual meetings should almost never last more than 45 minutes. After that, you will lose people. There are simply too many distractions at the desktop. Viewers may be reading their e-mail, people are walking by, and a host of other disruptions – and the speaker never knows. It is imperative for the speaker, even to keep attention for 45 minutes, to be well organized, enthusiastic, articulate, and he must use the interactivity tools.

Weaknesses: the flip side of F2F meetings: they are less interactive and with a less sensory-rich learning experience.

Ball concludes his article:

> *When television and VCRs came out, pundits predicted the end of the movie industry. They were wrong – the film industry is as strong as ever as people like to get together in groups and they like the rich sensory environment. We are gregarious animals and grouping is what we tend to do. Very similarly, when videoconferencing and web conferencing emerged, some predicted the end of F2F meetings. This will never happen for the same reason. We like to get together and there are social exchanges*

that just can't be replicated over the web. Planners should think of virtual meeting tools not as a threat but as additional tools in their toolbox, to be used effectively to bring people together.

Tony Carey, industry writer and trainer, makes a similar point (in an article entitled 'The Personal Touch', Meetings & Incentive Travel magazine, July/August 1999) that:

the internet and the telephone, the CD-Rom and the video recording can give us voices and pictures but they can't give us 'presence', that intensely individual aura that is both intellectual and chemical. You can't share a glass of wine over the internet or enjoy the same walk in the park. You can't see deep into someone's eyes when you ask them a question, nor banter in the company of friends. So people arrange to meet. It's pretty obvious really.

It is to be hoped, for the sake of society, that the benefits of face-to-face meetings do, indeed, continue to be accepted and embraced by the next generation and generations beyond. There are some suggestions, mainly anecdotal and experiential at this stage, that future generations may lack the skills and the desire for F2F communications. Reared on computer games and playstations, text messaging and e-mail correspondence, is there a possibility that electronic communications will predominate and that events will, in the main, be only virtual? Davidson and Rogers (2006 – page 256) outline some of the challenges in attracting 'Generations X and Y' (i.e. those born between 1964 and 1994) to attend conferences in the future. They argue that:

time spent now in convincing them of the rewards of attending face-to-face events will reap rewards in the future.

SUSTAINABLE MEETINGS

Few news broadcasts today are completed without some reference to environmental issues such as global warming, carbon emissions, and the very sustainability of our planet. These same issues are now becoming mainstream concerns and challenges within the conference and conventions industry. Barbara Maple, President of the International Association of Congress Centres (AIPC), President of the Vancouver Convention and Exhibition Centre, President of the Joint Meetings Industry Council and Chairman of the World Council for Venue Management, lists four reasons for this in an article entitled 'Green Meetings: does anyone really care?' (Conference + Meetings World magazine, January 2007):

1. Our communities will increasingly expect it of us. We and our activities are highly visible wherever we operate, and attract a lot of attention from the local community: this means people expect that we will take a leadership role in implementing more programmes where the good of the community is at stake. At the same time, we are often government-owned and operated, which means we are under pressure to set an example in this regard.
2. The second reason is that our clients will increasingly want it because their own members will want it. Environmental concern has gone from being a 'cause' to simply an expectation; people today just assume that environmental concerns are being addressed because they have become a fact of life in most parts of the world. For this reason, the people who make up the membership of the organizations whose events we host will be applying more pressure on organizers to address the role environmental and sustainability considerations can play in their events. This, in turn, will make sustainability issues and the record of a centre in this regard more of a decision factor for meeting planners.
3. The third reason sustainability will become a bigger factor is that it will contribute to cost-effective operations, particularly in key areas like energy. One of the big points of the sustainability concept is that industries must manage long term costs if they are to be successful in an ongoing way, and the costs of energy and waste management are among the largest and least predictable we face as facility managers. Like so many other aspects of environmental management, it is often only when there are significant cost implications that action gets taken.
4. Finally, this whole area will increasingly be a matter of law, as communities and governments in many parts of the world strengthen their regulations around how businesses manage their environmental and social impacts. Just as issues like smoking have moved from the encouragement stage to outright prohibition, so we can expect that what are today seen as being good practices will likely become legal requirements as community expectations evolve.

She concludes that:

The results of all this will affect many different areas of facility management: everything from building operations and environmental control measures to how new facilities are designed and constructed, and even how we market and sell our facilities. We will, for example, likely have to get more involved with our clients to make sure that they comply with community sustainability expectations when they hold their events in our cities. This is now simply a 'good thing to do', but will increasingly be a requirement for being allowed to operate at all.

An MPI Foundation Canada White Paper entitled 'The Economic Impact of Meetings and Events' (2006) describes the opportunity to 'green' meetings and events and improve the eco-efficiency of the facilities that host them as an *'important trend with significant economic potential for the meetings industry'*. It goes on to say:

Increasingly, meeting professionals are recognizing that green practices like recycling and re-use can translate into lower onsite costs. On the facilities side of the industry, a handful of trendsetters have achieved dollar savings by reducing the energy and water they consume and the waste they generate – and have gained a distinct marketing advantage by positioning themselves as green venues.

When the Canadian government was hosting the Eleventh Conference of the Parties to the Framework Convention on Climate Change, also known as the Kyoto Protocol, in Montreal in 2005, it committed to organizing an environmentally friendly, carbon-neutral conference. The plans included:

- Reducing greenhouse gas emissions, in partnership with the provincial electrical utility, Hydro-Québec
- Distributing 4750 free transit passes to attendees and conference volunteers
- Using hybrid, ethanol, and biodiesel vehicles for conference shuttles
- Minimizing the need for shuttles, by locating 19 of 50 conference hotels within walking distance of the convention centre
- Introducing a catering plan that included fair trade coffee service, composting of food waste, and a strong commitment to recycling
- Turning off all non-essential electrical equipment at night, and specifying EnergyStar standards for rented equipment
- Using canvas delegate bags and functional gifts to minimize waste
- Reducing the volume and environmental impact of the printing process through double-sided production on EcoLogo™ paper, on-demand printing, wireless internet access for attendees, and the use of vegetable-based inks.

The White Paper concluded that:

> Although some of the conference's green initiatives led to higher costs, others were revenue-neutral or actually saved money. More important, the green character of the event drew the attention of media and sponsors while reinforcing Canada's international reputation for environmentally friendly practices. The green plan ultimately saved energy, paper, and waste, demonstrated the benefits of a participatory approach to green meetings management, generated tangible support for Canadian technology and expertise, reduced costs and stress for delegates, and increased the capacity of the local meetings industry to host future green events.

Meeting venues are being designed with a view to reducing the environmental impact of meetings and events. For example, the David L. Lawrence Convention Center, Pittsburgh, Pennsylvania (USA) lays claim to be the first 'green' convention center and the world's largest 'green' building. Opened in 2003 and located on the banks of the Allegheny River, the Center states that

> green is glorious, both from an environmental – and marketing – perspective. No other convention center in the country boasts so many green technologies. The use of natural ventilation, daylight sensors and carbon monoxide sensors, a water reclamation system that reduces potable water use by 60 per cent, along with substantial use of recycled and non-toxic materials makes this Convention Center unique. Roof skylights and walls of glass produce diffused light and uniform temperature, admitting natural daylight into the exhibit(ion) space and pre-function areas. Seventy five per cent of the Center's exhibition space is naturally lit. Blackout shades are available for exhibitors who require a low-light environment. The shape of the building captures natural airflow from the Allegheny River to help ventilate and cool the building. This, combined with other features to minimize energy usage, such as occupancy and daylight sensors, creates annual energy savings of about 35 per cent. The Center also maximizes the use of non-toxic materials, such as paint and carpets that do not emit harmful fumes, thereby establishing a more wholesome indoor environment for meeting attendees. It was awarded a Gold LEED certification for its excellence in building environmental performance (LEED stands for Leadership in Energy and Environmental Design and is a rating system developed

Figure 9.1
The David L. Lawrence
Convention Center, Pittsburgh,
USA. (Source: The David
L. Lawrence Convention
Center.)

Figure 9.2
The roof of The David L.
Lawrence Convention Center.
(Source: The David L.
Lawrence Convention Center.)

by the Green Building Council – Oregon Convention Center in Portland was the only other US convention centre to be LEED-certified as at September 2006).

For more information: www.pittsburghcc.com.

Figure 9.3
Harrogate International Centre,
England. (Source: Harrogate
International Centre.)

In Harrogate (England), the Harrogate International Centre (HIC) has introduced training programmes for front line staff, covering such issues as waste reduction, recycling and offering free advice to exhibition contractors and exhibitors. The Centre has also teamed up with a local waste management company to explore re-cycling of waste. As a result, the volume of waste has been reduced and the Centre claims that now 95 per cent is sent for re-cycling. A large amount of cardboard and paper is compacted on-site and then sent to Scotland for use in the manufacture of plasterboards. In November 2003 HIC received an accreditation award from The Institute of Energy for achievements in Energy Efficiency. The award recognises the excellent work undertaken by HIC staff in reducing energy consumption and the introduction of energy efficient systems.

The Riviera International Conference Centre in Torquay became the first conference and leisure venue in England to gain silver status through The Green Tourism Business Scheme, which encourages the adoption of green policies and practices. The scheme criteria can be viewed at www.green-business.co.uk.

The Travelodge hotel chain estimates that it can save 250 000 cubic metres of water simply by fitting aerated shower heads in its bathrooms, and will help the company to reduce carbon dioxide emissions by 272 tonnes (*The Times* newspaper, 22 November 2006).

The (UK) Events Industry Alliance has worked with engineering consultancy Arup and the British Standards Institute to develop a new industry-wide British Standard for Sustainable Event Management Systems. The standard, to be called BS8901, was due to be finalised by Summer 2007.

CORPORATE SOCIAL RESPONSIBILITY

There is a strong link between green and sustainable events and the rapidly growing interest in corporate social responsibility (CSR). For many years there have been minority pressure groups attempting to focus the world's attention on the ethical, commercial and environmental practices of major corporations, particularly when such practices have been shown to cause harm to developing countries. The promotion of baby milk products in place of breast feeding in West Africa, the decimation of the rainforest causing flooding and irretrievable damage to fragile ecologies, the use of child labour in Asian countries to manufacture sports goods for western countries, investments in corrupt regimes and exploitative businesses, are just a few examples of issues highlighted by these pressure groups. But, until the last few years, the work of these groups has caused little more than occasional embarrassment to the offending corporations.

Now this is changing as companies begin to appreciate the commercial and employment benefits of adopting socially responsible policies and practices. Davidson and Rogers (2006) suggest that companies are increasingly seeking to:

> *engage with their stakeholders and deal with potentially contentious issues proactively, instead of waiting until campaigners' accusations lead to disastrous press coverage. Now, more companies than ever are engaged in integrating CSR into all aspects of their business, encouraged by a growing body of evidence that CSR has a positive impact on businesses' economic performance.*

Companies are realizing that all areas of their operations are under the microscope and that they are increasingly required to demonstrate their credentials as good corporate citizens. In addition to corporate citizenship, Davidson and Rogers (2006) list a variety of terms relating to CSR including business ethics, corporate accountability and sustainability. They quote a definition for CSR used by the US-based organization Business for Social Responsibility as:

> *achieving commercial success in ways that honour ethical values and respect people, communities, and the natural environment.*

They describe how:

> *in Europe, CSR has moved to a prominent place in both the business and policy agenda. The European Commission has placed CSR at the core of Europe's competition strategy, and has issued a Green Paper on CSR*

and a subsequent communication outlining the Commission's definition of CSR and steps that companies, governments, and civil society can undertake to refine their commitments to it.

The United Nations World Tourism Organization (UNWTO) has launched, in partnership with the exhibition *World Travel Market*, 'World Responsible Tourism Day', to be celebrated each year during *World Travel Market* in November. The aim of the Day is to stimulate actions by tourism companies, tourists and public tourism stakeholders to promote tourism in terms of its economic, social and environmental sustainability.

The conference industry itself is beginning to acknowledge the importance of CSR, and this will intensify in future years. Davidson and Rogers (2006) claim that:

> *As the drive for greater transparency grows, all industries and organizations, public as well as private, will be increasingly obliged to demonstrate their ethical, environmental and social credentials. All stakeholders in the conference industry, from airlines, hotels and venues to intermediaries and the delegates themselves, will need to examine their own commitment to CSR.*

An attempt to expedite the adoption of CSR within the conference and conventions sector was spearheaded by *Conference & Incentive Travel* magazine with the launch of its 'Campaign for Change' in September 2006. Ray Bloom, chairman of IMEX, wrote the following in support of the magazine's initiative:

> *The C&I sector, with the help of vehicles such as the C&IT 'Campaign for Change', is becoming more aware of the need to embrace environmental and socially responsible practices. This is the first step to change, but ultimately the sector needs to embrace basic good practices as a part of its overall culture; ensuring that green-minded programmes are always pitched at agency level, focusing on potential cost savings that such practices afford and using charity initiatives as motivational tools for staff and clients – an already proven formula. Building good practice within our way of working and proving that such practice helps, rather than hinders, will help the industry to embrace social responsibility to all our benefit.*

Iain Palfreman, head of sourcing at PricewaterhouseCoopers, speaking to the UK Hotel Booking Agents Association in 2006, said that if conference agencies and venues do not know their CSR 'footprint', they could be dropped by a socially responsible corporate client. He suggested that the footprint covers the marketplace, workplace, environment and community and that agencies should adopt CSR practices for the good of the company's reputation, in order to have a pleasant place in which to work, and to exceed customers' expectations. Agencies and venues who fail to demonstrate good CSR policies may well find themselves losing business with key clients. The leading agencies are actively taking steps to becoming carbon neutral and to offering neutrality to their clients.

Some of the practical suggestions for encouraging CSR and sustainable policies listed in *Conference & Incentive Travel* magazine's first CSR supplement, entitled 'Without a Trace' (September/October 2006), included:

- Read the Green Meetings Report of the Convention Industry Council (www.conventionindustry.org). This details 'minimum' and 'strongly recommended' best practices for key services including accommodation, event venues, transport providers, exhibition service suppliers and destinations. Note also the 'conference greening' recommendations made by www.meetingstrategiesworldwide.com and the Green Meeting Industry Council's tips (www.greenmeetings.info)
- Use recyclable products throughout an event: delegate bags for such things as conference agendas, programmes and hand-outs can be made from 100 per cent-recycled material. Alternatively, use cotton bags that are re-usable and biodegradable
- Offset your flight emissions: aircraft produce large volumes of CO_2, so www.myclimate.org provides a climate-protection opportunity by inviting delegates to offset their flight emissions
- Serve food that takes into account considerations such as sustainability, ethical trade, cruelty-free farming and local sourcing
- Give your preferred meetings venue tips to consider: The Oceans Blue Foundation (www.bluegreenmeetings.org) makes reference to such issues as recycling, energy management, re-usable linens and dishes, the use of eco-friendly cleaning agents and responsible procurement
- Introduce a legacy initiative for the event: a successful business event can be marked with a 'legacy' initiative, for example with a corporate donation to a sustainable project, or by fundraising among delegates, possibly with top-ups by the venue, agency and other suppliers.

CSR is certainly here to stay and both sides of the conference industry need to understand its implications and seize the opportunities it offers.

ACCESSIBILITY NOT DISABILITY

Another important development in society over the past few decades has been a change in the way that people with disabilities are viewed and treated. The focus has moved away from emphasizing disability (and hence people's limitations) to the positive promotion of accessibility. It means promoting inclusion and not exclusion, and working to overcome the principal barriers faced by disabled people: inaccessible environments, lack of appropriate information, and lack of awareness or negative attitudes. In the UK, for example, this has led to the implementation of the Disability Discrimination Act (DDA) giving disabled people rights of access to buildings, transport, work, services, decision-making and all the cultural, commercial and social activities of a modern and civilised society (the USA has its Americans with Disability Act or ADA). The DDA provides the legislative framework to a growing movement which seeks to ensure that disabled people can play the fullest possible part in society, including participation in meetings and conferences.

The Act itself continues to be adjusted and strengthened in order to cover a wider range of individuals and their needs, demanding that all delegates should be well provided for and that all venues and facilities should be 'reasonably accessible'. The principles of the DDA and their recommended practical outworking should be applied equally in all countries around the world.

There is a growing international trend towards the protection of individual and group rights for disabled employees and customers through anti-discrimination and human rights legislation. Around 75 countries already have some form of disability discrimination legislation and the number is steadily rising. European Directive 2000/78/EC required European states to introduce protection for their disabled citizens by 2006. International stakeholders are in the process of developing a new convention on disability.

One city that has adopted a destination approach to the business opportunities and ethical requirements of accessibility is Perth in Western Australia. The Perth Convention Bureau and the State's Disability Services Commission, together with a local university, have pioneered a programme entitled 'Beyond Compliance' which aims to bring about social change by rewarding tourism industry operators who are proactive in improving their accessibility. It also aims to secure or create disability sector conferences to be held in Western Australia. Davidson and Rogers (2006) describe in detail the 'Beyond Compliance' programme, which serves as a model for other cities to emulate.

For conference venues, an accessible approach means that facilities should be designed in a way that takes full account of the needs of people with disabilities. These include wheelchair users, those with hearing and visual impairments, but also many others such as people with cerebral palsy or facial disfigurements and those with learning difficulties. All will be delegates at some time, all with differing losses but also with differing gifts, and all at different stages of coming to terms with their particular disabilities.

The charity Tourism for All UK (www.tourismforall.org.uk) provides consultancy to venues on the needs of disabled people. Their advice to conference venues and destinations includes the following:

- in general terms, extend the same positive approach to disabled clients as you would to others. In other words, do not treat disabled clients differently
- have a copy of destination information available in large print, Braille or on audio tape. Or, if you use a promotional video, ensure, for example, that it has commentary and text description. It should also describe facilities that have been designed to be accessible
- if you book accommodation for wheelchair users, ensure that it has been inspected under the 'National Accessible Scheme', and that it has an access category and facilities appropriate to your clients' needs
- where an induction loop/inductive coupler system has been fitted for hard-of-hearing delegates, the appropriate symbols should be prominently on display – for example, at the reception desk, in the conference room and beside the public telephones. A public 'phone should be placed at desk height 700 to 800 mm
- venues should try to place posters/display/merchandise that specifically express a welcome to people who use a wheelchair at a height of 900 mm, for example at registration points. At this height it also remains accessible for delegates who can stand up. Print styles should be large and clear for delegate packs and signage
- where practical, venues should allow 800 mm minimum aisle width for people using wheelchairs, with a turning circle at the end of the aisle of 1500 mm minimum. Is there a ramp available up to the stage?
- venues should avoid placing items where they may be a danger to, or become easily dislodged by, delegates who are blind or partially sighted
- try to put yourself in a disabled person's position. How 'user friendly' would your destination or venue appear if you were seated at a height of 400 to 500 mm, or if you had your eyes closed?

Other useful resources include a 64-page guide 'Organising Accessible Events' published by the UK Disability Rights Commission which is available for download at www.drc-gb.org/pdf/SP13.pdf, and advice about 'Creating Accessible Destinations' is available from www.tourismforall.org.uk.

Catering professionally and in a caring way for the needs of disabled delegates is not only good from an ethical standpoint. It also makes sound business sense. There is a huge potential market for venues which can provide the correct combination of well-designed facilities and well-trained staff. Training in disability awareness is a sensible investment for destination managers and venue operators.

PROCUREMENT

'Procurement' is a term now commonly heard in the conference, meetings and business events industry. It is essentially the same as 'purchasing', but it has come to represent a more structured and systematic approach, especially among larger corporations, to the ways in which contracts are made with those supplying goods and services. One of the objectives of procurement is to maximize a company's bulk purchasing power and its ability to negotiate the best possible deals, ensuring that cost savings can be made, wherever possible, and that it is receiving value for money from its various suppliers.

One practical outworking of procurement within the conference sector has been for some companies to introduce much tighter controls on how they source venues and manage their events. Historically it has been the case, referenced in earlier chapters of this book (especially Chapter 2), that people with a myriad of job titles across a number of company departments have had the freedom to organize their own events, book their own venues, outsource the management of an event to a PCO, for example, with only minimal involvement or interference from a centralised purchasing department. These staff have been allocated a budget but then allowed to decide how that budget is spent. Procurement departments are now introducing much tighter controls and looking for efficiencies and savings in the ways that budgets are spent. For example, by deciding to place all of their conferences and meetings with one hotel chain, they expect to negotiate a more favourable deal through discussions with the chain's senior management, than might be possible by allowing individual budget holders to negotiate their own deals at a local level with individual hotels in that chain. Staff freedom is reduced and their ability to organize successful events may be threatened through the necessity of conforming with policies laid down from 'on high' by the procurement department. Conference organizers may be required to use a particular venue or type of venue to conform with a company's procurement policy, even though in their judgement it is not the most appropriate venue for their event.

Many in the meetings industry are wary of these changes, arguing that it is very difficult to quantify the provision of a service such as conference or event management. The constraints imposed by procurement limit the scope for creativity and impact adversely on the delivery of successful events. For a number of years there has been a perception, especially among event agencies, that procurement is only interested in price: relationships and added value are irrelevant. The counter argument is that, as the global business environment evolves, it is inevitable that there will be a renewed emphasis on accountability, cost consciousness, and consolidation, and so meeting planners and suppliers must employ broader business strategies in order to excel. For planners, it is no longer acceptable to focus solely on logistics or fail to measure adequately a meeting's success. For suppliers, it is not good enough simply to provide a product or to do business based on relationships alone. Procurement officers represent just some of the many senior stakeholders that meeting professionals must convince of the value of meetings.

In an article entitled 'In defence of procurement' ('Conference + Meetings World' magazine, July/August 2006), Mike Ford, Managing Director of event management company Universal CIT, says:

> The process of procurement has moved the more traditional 'relationship' driven way of doing business, one that frankly had little strategy or transparency in budget or cost management, into something more solid; a far more level and honest playing field which guarantees business and cuts down on the practice of buying events in on an ad-hoc basis. There's a lot of fear and worry that procurement is only interested in the price tag but that's simply not the case. Procurement wants value for money, a different thing entirely. And if you look at the industry as a whole, this way of doing business at last gives us the platform to stand up and prove that we provide a professional service and finally bury the perception that we are merely glorified hotel bookers and travel agents providing a service that anyone can cobble together.

Research into procurement in the business events industry undertaken by the MPI Foundation Europe includes the following description of procurement from the European Institute of Purchasing Management:

> Yesterday, procurement was buying a product or a service for the best price. The only objective was to negotiate a discount! Today, procurement is buying a solution for a cost. The objective is no longer the discount, but better service. Better quality for a total cost that includes the cost of definition of requirements, buying price, administration and cost of utilisation. Tomorrow, procurement will be buying a client's satisfaction for a value: it will be possible

to agree to pay more for increasing satisfaction, whether for an internal or external client. Event planners and event agencies have to be ready to adapt to these changes to become more proactive and more professional.

The MPI research (published in 2005) contains a number of key findings, including:

- 82 per cent of procurement professionals and 86 per cent of event planners operate a preferred supplier list
- 100 per cent of procurement professionals, 83 per cent of event planners and 73 per cent of event agencies said that preferred supplier lists made their jobs easier
- Cost, professionalism and experience are the three most popular factors that event planners and procurement professionals look for when appointing a supplier. The same qualities were identified by event agencies as those they assume clients look for when appointing a supplier
- Procurement professionals cited a number of frustrations including lack of adequate lead time and overselling when dealing with event planners and event agencies
- Event planners cited a number of frustrations including lengthy processes and poor communication when dealing with procurement professionals and event agencies
- Event agencies cited a number of frustrations including a lack of information about the brief and lack of understanding of their role when dealing with procurement professionals and event planners.

The report concludes by recommending:

improved communications all round and a conscious effort to understand and respect each contribution. Procurement professionals can be much more than just the enforcer of the lowest price solution and event planners could learn to mediate far more. Event agencies and event planners must work together to better understand the context of what they do. They must devise better, SMART measures and become more strategic in their approach. More event agencies need to recognize real selection criteria and smaller agencies will need to specialize to survive (The full research is available from the MPI European Office – see Chapter 8).

RETURN ON INVESTMENT (ROI)

Another complementary trend to the growing influence of procurement professionals is the increasing need for conferences and business events to demonstrate that they are providing appropriate returns on the investments that companies and organizations are making in them. Such events are required to show that they have led to greater productivity, higher sales, enhanced performance by the individuals who have attended them. The ROI Institute defines return on investment (ROI) as the net meeting benefits achieved when set against the total costs of a meeting.

This means that it is no longer sufficient to carry out evaluations after an event in the form of reaction and satisfaction surveys among delegates. Companies now demand to know how effective their meetings and events have been. As budgets come under closer scrutiny, more companies are now asking questions such as: 'Why are we holding this meeting?' 'Could we achieve our objectives more effectively?' – the kind of questions it was suggested earlier in this book (Chapter 5) that event organizers should always be asking.

The challenge for conference organizers and meeting planners is to find a consistent way of measuring the effectiveness of their events, one that will convince the procurement department and chief financial officer of the return on their investment.

Peter Haigh, a performance improvement consultant, writing in 'Meetings & Incentive Travel' magazine (September 2006) in an article entitled 'Happy Returns', describes work being done jointly by MPI and the ROI Institute to promote the Phillips ROI Methodology as a robust and logical approach to ROI measurement. He emphasizes the importance of setting objectives for a return on investment before the meeting takes place so that, post event, an assessment can be made of the extent to which the objectives were met. He outlines an ROI methodology split into five levels:

1-2. The first two levels relate to the end-of-meeting evaluations that meeting planners have been using for many years to measure the reaction and satisfaction of attendees and to determine the relevance of the content to the attendees' development. Level 2 deals with learning objectives i.e. meeting planners clarifying what new skills or knowledge the attendees should gain from attending the meeting

3. Application and implementation: after the meeting the attendees should apply what they have learnt back at their place of work, and so objectives need to be set which can then be measured

4. Business impact: at this level evaluation is made of the business impact objectives, measuring how what has been learnt has led to changes in performance e.g. is a salesperson selling more? or has productivity improved?

5. Once the first four levels have been completed, the meeting planner can calculate a return on investment by comparing the monetary benefits to the cost of the meeting. An example of the calculation made would be as follows, for a meeting

costing £80 000 and with the benefits of the meeting being valued at £240 000:

$$\text{Benefits/Cost Ratio} = \frac{\text{Meeting Benefits}}{\text{Meeting Costs}} \quad \text{i.e.} \quad \frac{£240\,000}{£80\,000} = 3$$

$$\text{ROI} = \frac{\text{Net Meeting Benefits}}{\text{Meeting Costs}} \quad \frac{£160\,000}{£80\,000} = 200\%$$

Haigh concludes his article by saying that:

> Conducting a full ROI analysis can be a costly and time-consuming exercise so not all meetings would be evaluated in this way. Typically, the larger and more expensive meetings would warrant such an evaluation. It is important to ensure that the meeting planner is involved at the objective planning stage so that the appropriate measurement tools can be introduced at each level.

Davidson (2006) contends that the logical conclusion of focusing on ROI is for companies to take steps to introduce cost-saving measures where possible. He states that:

> There is ample evidence of this trend intensifying. In a recent survey, US businesses reported to consultants Randall Travel Marketing that their focus was firmly on cost-containment of business travel costs. This translates to using more new technologies for individual business travel (web and video conferencing); consolidating meetings, negotiating lower prices for holding multiple-year meetings at the same destination, and other cost-containment measures.

Davidson also suggests that:

> More ROI is also being sought in the way that meetings are planned, and the buzz-word is 'extendibility' – extending the life of the event, before and after. For example, letting delegates interact with each other as soon as they register (chatrooms, online special interest groups, blogging, etc.); and putting more information online after the event, in order to extend its reach globally.

In addition to ROI, there is growing interest in measuring Return on Objectives (ROO) as another measurement model for capturing the organizational contribution of meetings, one that is not just using financial criteria to evaluate their effectiveness but also looks at whether an event has added genuine value to a business.

IN CONCLUSION

An optimistic forecast

The author makes no claim to have covered all of the topical issues facing the conference industry in this chapter or even in this book. Reference has been made to a number of important issues elsewhere in this book – the need to continue improving the industry's statistical base, the desirability of rationalising the number of trade associations, the importance of enhancing education and training programmes, the need to attract and retain staff with the right personal qualities and skills, for example – but space has precluded adequate coverage of other key issues.

Readers must, and will, draw their own conclusions on whether this great conference industry faces future expansion or contraction. In the author's view, and in the opinion of many leading figures in the industry, the importance of face-to-face contact and personal networking will continue to sustain the conference and meetings industry. People are social, gregarious creatures by nature, and conferences and conventions are a wonderful way of bringing people together in beneficial interaction, and for communicating and sharing experiences through inspirational presentations, educational workshops and memorable social programmes.

To those working in this dynamic industry, buyers and suppliers, it offers variety, stimulation, scope for creativity and imagination, travel, fulfilment, excitement, enjoyment, constant challenges, the chance to build friendships around the world, and so much more. Few other industries can offer as much. Surely, none can offer more. Industry journalist Rob Spalding, writing in 'Association Meetings International' magazine (September 2002), sums it up well when he writes about the.

> *sense of warmth, the heart, and the personality of the meetings phenomenon.*

He refers to the

> *skill and devotion, the generosity of sharing and the loyalty of service of those who make meetings that makes the profession so unique. Oh yes, and that meetings have saved the world from self-destruction once or twice.*

The Congress of Vienna marked the beginning of a long period of peace and stability for Europe in the nineteeth century. Conferences and conventions have the potential for ensuring a permanent peace for the world throughout the 21st century and beyond, as they provide the framework for discussion rather than conflict, for uniting rather than dividing communities and nations, and for encouraging the sharing of ideas and information for the benefit of all mankind. Whether 'conference' will still be the most appropriate word to describe what the industry will become in this millennium is another matter, and perhaps a keynote topic for a 21st century congress!

Summary

- the conference market is resilient and still remains generally buoyant, despite the impacts of economic downturns, political instability, security and terrorism threats, and new technology. Live events are still viewed as vital marketing tools
- the application of new multi-media technologies is revolutionising communication systems and learning methods, but not impacting significantly the need for delegates to confer on a face-to-face basis. Technologies such as video-conferencing and web conferencing offer additional tools for the conference organizer, and provide the potential for the global distribution of an event over an extended period of time
- in responding positively and promptly to other contemporary issues, such as the needs of disabled delegates or the concerns for environmental conservation, the industry can demonstrate its growing maturity and sense of social responsibility. It should also see that there are good business reasons for adopting an ethical approach to these issues
- greater accountability, more professional procurement systems and the need to demonstrate effective and measurable returns through the staging of a conference will continue to feature strongly
- the conference industry faces an exciting future at the beginning of the 21st century. The potential is huge, the competition is immense, the rewards in terms of enjoyment and job satisfaction are incalculable.

Review and discussion questions

1. Television, computers and the internet have had a dramatic effect on society and on the lives of individual people. Television, in particular, has been accused of creating a generation of 'couch potatoes'. Texting and e-mail have reduced the need to speak to other human beings. Computer games have replaced the outdoor games and 'playtime' familiar to previous generations. Is the home, therefore, likely to become

the conference venue of the future as we all become 'virtual' delegates? Or are people's social and gregarious instincts strong enough to ensure that face-to-face communication remains the pre-eminent form of human interaction. Outline the arguments for and against both scenarios, and attempt an assessment of where future growth will lie.

2. Summarize the key issues driving the growth in sustainable and eco-friendly conferences and conventions. To what extent are these being driven by buyers (event organizers) as opposed to suppliers (event venues)? How should the industry best mitigate the harmful impacts of live meetings?

3. Arrange to visit two conference venues and assess the degree to which they meet the principles of accessibility described in this chapter. Do the staff demonstrate a genuine commitment to making their venue fully accessible and understand the business opportunities that such best practice offers?

Notes and references

1. Ball, C, *Face-to-Face Vs. Web Conferencing – What Should I Use When?*, an article accessible via www.corbinball.com.
2. *Campaign for Change* special supplement, Conference & Incentive Travel magazine (September 2006).
3. Campbell, D, *Market-driven venues adapt to meetings needs*, an article in Catering magazine, Issue 15 (December 2000), Croner CCH Group Ltd.
4. Carey, T, *The Personal Touch*, an article in Meetings & Incentive Travel magazine (July/August 1999).
5. Davidson, R and Rogers, T, *Marketing Destinations and Venues for Conferences, Conventions and Business Events*, Elsevier (2006).
6. Davidson, R, *EIBTM 2006 Industry Trends & Market Share Report*, Reed Travel Exhibitions.
7. *EventView 2006*, MPI Foundation.
8. *FutureWatch 2007*, published by Meeting Professionals International and American Express.
9. *Happy Returns*, article by Peter Haigh in Meetings & Incentive Travel magazine (September 2006).
10. *In Defence of Procurement* article, Conference+Meetings World magazine (July/August 2006).
11. Maple, B, *Green Meetings: does anyone really care?*, an article in Conference+Meetings World magazine (January 2007).

12. *Research into Procurement in the Events Industry and The Relationship between Procurement Professionals, Event Planners and Event Agencies*, MPI Foundation Europe (2005).
13. Spalding, R, editorial article entitled *Packaged At Last!* in Association Meetings International magazine (September 2002 issue), published by CAT Publications.
14. *The Economic Impact of Meetings and Events*, MPI Foundation Canada White Paper (2006).

Further reading

1. Phillips, J, Myhill, M and McDonaugh, J, *Proving the Value of Meetings and Events*, Meeting Professionals International (2007) (available via MPI Store on www.mpiweb.org).

Case Studies

Introduction and background

Located in the State of Victoria, in the south-east corner of Australia's mainland, Melbourne is a modern, cosmopolitan city set around the shores of beautiful Port Philip Bay. With a population of more than 3.5 million people, Melbourne is the country's second largest city and has twice been voted the world's most liveable city (in 2002 and 2004) by the London-based Economist Intelligence Unit.

The city's wealth was founded on the gold rushes of the nineteenth century with Victoria contributing more than one third of the world's gold output in the 1850s. The gold frenzy also had a major effect on Melbourne's development as a multi-cultural city with more than 370 000 immigrants arriving in one year alone.

With residents speaking 200 languages from more than 150 different nations now living side by side, Melbourne is the home of one of the world's most harmonious and culturally diverse communities.

Melbourne's future rests firmly as a major centre for research and development. It is recognised worldwide for its work in medicine, science, technology, business and finance, making it a very appropriate location for business and scientific conferences.

As one of the top five agri-biotech centres in the world, Victoria's biotechnology credentials are also significant, with the State responsible for more than 40 per cent of Australia's biotechnology research and development. Victoria is also the nation's largest exporter of food and fibre products.

Locals and visitors alike love the city's vibrant energy that stems from the massive range of major events that are held each year such as the Spring Racing Carnival, Melbourne International Arts

Festival, Australian Open Tennis Championships, the Formula 1 Australian Grand Prix and Australian International Airshow.

Melbourne's expertise in staging major events was highlighted through its successful hosting of the 2006 Commonwealth Games, which attracted 90 000 international and interstate visitors.

As a destination, Melbourne offers conference delegates a wealth of options outside the meeting room. There are beautiful parks and gardens, fine art galleries and museums, fascinating historic sites, a variety of shopping experiences from boutiques to markets and over 4500 restaurants, bistros and bars. Getting out of the city for the day is also easy with spectacular wineries, beaches, golf courses and wildlife sanctuaries all situated just a short drive from the city.

Melbourne as an international conference destination

When Melbourne's first convention centre opened in 1990, its impact on the city was immediate and significant: advancing the city's profile in international business, scientific and medical circles. Conference organizers embraced not only the versatility and technical expertise of the centre but the city itself and Melbourne quickly became a popular destination for international conventions and business meetings.

Over subsequent years, delegate and visitor numbers increased steadily and the city developed its infrastructure to keep up with demand: opening new hotels and tourist attractions. In 1996, Australia's largest and most flexible exhibition centre was built adjacent to the convention centre and a unique convention precinct evolved along Melbourne's picturesque Yarra River supporting a range of convention hotels, speciality venues and attractions.

Melbourne now has Australia's highest concentration of convention facilities located in a city centre including 20 000 accommodation rooms within a 15-km radius and 12 000 in the greater city area.

Beginning in 2005, Melbourne's airport embarked on the most ambitious development programme ever seen at an Australian airport including a major expansion of the international arrivals hall, a widened runway, a new third level to the international terminal and dual-level A380-capable aerobridges.

For more than three decades, the work of the Melbourne Convention and Visitors Bureau (see below) has been integral in helping the city grow as an international convention destination and has been extremely successful in promoting and developing the industry.

Melbourne's business events product

Melbourne offers superb event facilities including five major convention hotels within close proximity to a diverse range of multi-purpose venues and the acclaimed Melbourne Exhibition and Convention Centre (MECC).

As the demands on the existing infrastructure have again increased, plans were announced in 2006 to commence construction of a new 5000-seat convention centre to be built adjacent to the existing centre. When complete in 2009, Melbourne will boast the largest exhibition and convention centre in Australia. The new six-star energy-rated centre will feature a ballroom; an 18-metre high glass wall fronting the Yarra River; a gala seating system in the Plenary Hall; 32 meeting rooms; and a ground foyer for 11 000 guests. The development includes a 5-star Hilton Hotel and a riverfront promenade of retail outlets.

Sitting adjacent to the MECC, the Crown Entertainment Complex, hosting two world-class hotels with a combined inventory of more than 900 rooms, announced plans in 2006 to build a third convention hotel next to the Melbourne Exhibition and Convention Centre.

The development of Melbourne's latest iconic landmark, Federation Square, has provided Melbourne with a new contemporary dimension to its tourism and convention appeal. With its bold architecture and diverse cultural offerings, Federation Square is a central and unifying public space, bringing together open spaces and innovative architecture. Filling an entire city block, Federation Square's creative mix of attractions embodies Melbourne's best features: fine art, hospitality, bold design and vibrant events.

Sports-mad Melburnians

It is no secret that Australians love sport. Proudly wearing the mantle of the nation's sports capital, Melburnians take great pleasure in their role as spectators ensuring that every major sporting event is well supported.

Home of the world-famous Melbourne Cricket Ground, Melbourne lives by the motto 'build it and they will come'. The only city in the world with three retractable roof stadiums, Melbourne is set to add to this with another new sporting stadium to seat 20 000 people.

The new stadium, to be built at a cost of AU$190 million, will be situated in the Olympic Park precinct and will be used for rugby and soccer. It will include a sports campus, an elite training centre and accommodation for a number of sporting organizations.

Melbourne Convention and Visitors Bureau

The Melbourne Convention and Visitors Bureau (MCVB) has a vision:

to make Melbourne one of the world's most successful business events destinations

It already has a successful track record in promoting and developing business events for Melbourne and Victoria.

The foresight of the MCVB led to the founding of the AsiaPacific Incentives and Meetings Expo (AIME) in 1992, making Melbourne the only city in the world to own and host one of the largest meetings and convention trade shows in the world – and the benefits are substantial.

As a not-for-profit company, MCVB operates in partnership with the Victorian Government and private enterprise and relies on these two groups for funding. In particular, the MCVB enjoys a unique relationship with the MECC: combining resources with the centre to work in the highly competitive international market.

The MCVB tailors its services to assist in every aspect of bidding, planning advice and support for meetings, conventions, incentive programmes and special events in order to meet clients' needs.

With a dedicated team of over 30 people working in marketing, corporate services and sales, as well as representatives in Sydney, New York, London, Singapore and Hong Kong, the MCVB works to ensure that Melbourne is recognised nationally and internationally as one of the world's best cities for business events.

Marketing Melbourne

International marketing activities are largely centred around attracting business for the new convention centre: the MCVB and the MECC work collaboratively in the international arena. The MCVB, together with the State Government and City of

Melbourne, is also supporting the MECC's new marketing venture, Club Melbourne.

The innovative Club Melbourne strategy has established a network of influential people including 62 leading Victorian scientists to help attract international business events to the city. The programme has already delivered 12 convention wins for 2006 to 2010, collectively bringing 13 500 visitors to the city and worth AU$62 million to Victoria's economy.

The MCVB is also one of the founder members of the strategic alliance BestCities, a global alliance of convention bureaux that develops best practices through innovation and knowledge exchange, professional development and client servicing within the meetings industry. Member cities include Copenhagen, Cape Town, Dubai, Edinburgh, Melbourne, San Juan, Singapore and Vancouver. (See Davidson & Rogers (2006) for a case study on the BestCities Global Alliance.)

MCVB provides a range of products and services for members and clients. They include convention bidding; Planners Guide; Planners Guide Online; VenueMenu; MCVB web site; publications; AIME – AsiaPacific Incentives & Meetings Expo.

Issues and challenges faced

The main challenge faced by Melbourne as a business events destination in recent years was its inability to bid for large-scale international events due to the size of its existing convention facilities. The ongoing investment by governments and the private sector in new centres both in Australia and especially the Asia Pacific region also had an impact on Melbourne's competitiveness in the international arena.

The announcement by the Victorian Government of plans to build a new Convention Centre in Melbourne will help to address these issues. The new facility will generate significant benefits for the State and strengthen Melbourne's position as one of the top destinations in the world for the business events industry. These benefits are already being realised with 10 events for the new centre already secured worth over AU$100 million.

Further information: www.mcvb.com.au.

Case Study 1.2   The Queen Elizabeth II Conference Centre, London

The Queen Elizabeth II Conference Centre (QEIICC) is one of London's purpose-built venues, situated in the heart of Westminster, with stunning views of Westminster Abbey and the Houses of Parliament. It was opened by Queen Elizabeth II in 1986 as a venue specifically for government conferences, but not long after it was also made available for events organised by the private sector.

The QEIICC is government-owned, established as an executive agency of the Department for Communities and Local Government. As an executive agency, the QEIICC's objective is to achieve best value for money in operating the conference centre as a high quality facility, on a commercial basis, for government and private sector customers organising both national and international events. It pays a dividend on its profits to government which may be seen as the equivalent of paying dividends to shareholders by listed companies.

Facilities and client services

The facilities extend over six floors, comprising of four main auditoria, seven conference rooms and over 20 smaller meeting rooms, catering for events from 40 to 1000 delegates in plenary session and 3000 in total capacity. The four main auditoria, all with full audio-visual and projection facities, are the Churchill Auditorium, the Whittle Room, the Fleming Room and the Westminster Suite. The Churchill Auditorium is located on the ground floor and can be used in a variety of formats, hosting up to 700 people theatre-style, 328 classroom-style and 280-cabaret style. The Whittle Room is on the third floor, and is particularly suited to groups of between 100 and 375. The Fleming Room (also on the third floor) has 725 square metres of flexible meeting space which can accommodate 700 theatre-style, 320 classroom-style, 259 cabaret-style or alternatively it can be used in conjunction with the rest of the third floor for a large exhibition or conference space (up to 1000 capacity theatre-style). The Westminster Suite is located on the fourth floor of the Centre, offering a capacity of 140 theatre-style, 66 for classroom, or 63 cabaret-style.

As well as the wide range of facilities provided, clients also benefit from the large team of experienced staff. A truly international team, employees of the QEIICC range in nationality from British, Brazilian, Portuguese and Italian, to Hispanic and Nigerian. In total the Centre employs 53 permanent staff, along with numerous contract staff at any one time. Clients holding an event at the QEIICC are offered expert advice throughout the planning process, with a dedicated event manager from the in-house team to guide them. The Centre employs seven event managers, and an event operations manager. This team will offer specialist advice on all aspects of planning and, if required, offer creative contributions to an event. On hand from beginning to end, the event manager is able to suggest ways in which to make each event both successful and unique, as well as ensuring that the event runs smoothly.

Facilities and access for the disabled throughout ensure that all visitors to the Centre enjoy their surroundings and clients also benefit from using one of the most IT-intelligent buildings in the UK. A built-in wireless network, in-house audio-visual services and webcasting, as well as an on-line conference service, are all provided at the Centre by the in-house AV team, Interface. Interface staff are employed by the QEIICC and offer a complete AV/production service for clients of the Centre. With a branded name, Interface, it is easier to distinguish and identify the AV service in line with the other services provided in-house by the Centre, such as the catering from Leith's. The combination of permanent installations and a flexible AV team means that Interface is able to provide unusually quick quotations for potential clients as well as to assist in the creative aspect of event management.

Catering is provided by in-house caterers, Leith's, who are on hand to provide a range of quality food and refreshments to suit all requirements, ranging from finger buffets and snacks to sit-down banquets. As a result of a competitive tendering process, Leith's was appointed as the QEIICC's in-house caterers in 1997 and the contract will run over a 15-year period. When the current contract ends in 2012, the contract will go to competitive tender again.

Figure 1.2
The Queen Elizabeth II
Conference Centre, London.
(Source: The Queen Elizabeth II
Conference Centre)

The QEIICC's hotel accommodation agency, Expotel, is key to providing residential conferences. Fully licensed with both the Association of British Travel Agents (ABTA) and the Air Travel Organiser's Licence (ATOL) agencies, Expotel handles the booking of appropriate and discounted accommodation for clients and organises travel solutions for event attendees. Residential conferences are an important part of the work at the Centre.

Business Mix

Although designed originally for government conferences, the majority of the QEIICC's business is now private sector, whether corporate or association business, and only around 25 per cent of the Centre's business is now government or public sector-related. The QEIICC is a venue for large conferences, annual general meetings and gatherings of international organisations, both with or without exhibition space. As well as having the facilities to cater for these large events, it also continues to host smaller events, award ceremonies and banquets. Events hosted by the Centre include the announcement for the route of the Grand Départ for the Tour de France 2007, the World Maritime Technology Conference 2006 and Ford Motor Company's press conference announcing their £1 billion investment in CO_2-reducing technologies in the UK.

The QEIICC generated record turnover figures for the financial year 2005–2006 totalling £10.845 million, a rise of three per cent on the previous year and representing their third consecutive year of strong financial growth. It also exceeded all performance targets and paid an increased contribution of £1.45 million back to the government – exceeding the annual target of £1.40 million.

The Centre was the venue for some 415 events during 2005–6, with clients benefiting from a high security service, and cutting-edge technology. A full 'airport style' client-led security service is available, ensuring that security is at the forefront of any event held at the Centre. It is also in tune with the Disability Discrimination Act legislation, having implemented all the necessary changes ahead of time.

The QEIICC's marketing strategy involves a range of media. Exhibitions, promotional materials, advertising, public relations, web site, client events, and key partnerships all form part of the core marketing for the Centre. The Centre is an affiliate of the International Congress & Convention Association, Meetings Industry Association, Association Internationale des Palais de Congrès, the Association of Exhibition Organisers, VisitLondon and London First.

Investments and Future Plans

From 1st October 2006 the Centre became a no smoking venue following the enforcement of a ban on all staff and contractors smoking in the building from May 2006. The move to a 'smoke free' environment ensures that the Centre is compliant with the much anticipated Health Bill, due to come into force in England in the Summer of 2007.

The QEIICC has made substantial investment in refurbishments over the past few years. The total spend is in excess of £6 million and has included a refurbished foyer and upgrade to the air conditioning system. The plans for the future include more capital projects and investment in the building with a bias towards technological innovation.

Concludes Stephen Norcliffe, commercial director/chief operating officer at the QEIICC, commenting on how he sees the future of the industry:

> I see continually increasing competition from new conference centres and hotels and an even greater professional environment. New-build facilities have incorporated within them all the lessons learned from older properties and will continue to do so.
>
> The QEIICC is one of a select band of properties that isn't judged on its contribution to the local economy. It must trade at a profit and use its reserves to finance repair, maintenance and improvement projects. A much more difficult feat, but one that it must do in order to stay ahead of the competition. The continual investment is its way of giving back to customers who use the Centre on a frequent basis as well as keeping the building fresh in order to attract new business.
>
> Just as important to the Centre are its people and to remain competitive in the future it will continue to put great emphasis on recruitment and retention excellence.

Further Information: www.qeiicc.co.uk

Case Study 1.3   Hyderabad International Convention Centre, India

Background

Hyderabad, the fifth largest metropolis in India with a population of over six million, is the state capital of Andhra Pradesh. It is known for its rich history and culture with monuments, mosques, temples, and a varied heritage in arts, crafts and dance. The city is nearly 400 years old and is noted for its natural beauty, mosques and minarets, bazaars and bridges, hills and lakes. It is perched

Figure 1.3
Hyderabad International
Convention Centre. (Source:
Hyderabad International
Convention Centre)

on the top of the Deccan Plateau, 1776 feet above sea level, and covers an area of 100 square miles. A multitude of influences has shaped the character of the city. Its palaces and buildings, houses and tenements, gardens and streets have a history and an architectural individuality of their own, making Hyderabad, nicknamed the 'Pearl City', a place of enchantment.

With its burgeoning economy boosted by the IT, pharmaceutical, biotechnology and finance industries, Hyderabad is poised to become a major business tourism or MICE hub for South Asia. Microsoft, Infosys and other IT multinationals are establishing impressive research and development centres, and the city's homegrown pharmaceutical and biotechnology companies are already earning themselves a global reputation.

The new international airport, scheduled to open in 2008, with an initial capacity of ten million passengers per annum in phase I increasing to 40 million in the second phase, and also being purpose-built for the new Airbus A380 aircraft, will contribute significantly to the overall growth in business tourism in the state and in India overall. Investment in the road network is also underway with a 144-kilometre ring road under construction. Additional world class facilities such as new hotels, golf courses, and theme parks are also planned for Andra Pradesh. Hyderabad itself expects to have more than 3500 new hotel rooms by 2009.

Genesis of Hyderabad International Convention Centre

Following the successful bid by the Andhra Pradesh State Government to host the Asian Development Bank's 39th AGM, there was an invitation for tenders to build a world-class convention facility in Hyderabad. Emaar Properties PJSC, Dubai – one of the world's leading real estate companies (in the process of building the world's tallest building in Dubai) partnered with Andhra Pradesh Industrial Infrastructure Corporation to secure the contract. The next step was to identify a construction company – L&T, India's largest engineering and construction conglomerate, proved to be the natural choice. Construction work commenced in November 2004. Accor, the Paris-based hospitality and hotels group, was awarded the management contract, based on its success in managing the Dubai Convention Centre.

Datelines

Development Application	–	Sept'04
Land work	–	Nov'04
Slab work	–	Mar'05
Roof & major beams	–	June'05
Interiors	–	Sept'05
Commissioning	–	Dec'05
Soft opening (Pravasi Bharatiya Divas)	–	Jan 6'06
Full operations	–	Mar'06

Although the convention centre was being specifically built to host the Asian Development Bank's meeting in May 2006, the Government of India and the State Government of Andra Pradesh recognised a huge opportunity for staging the Pravasi Bharatiya Divas (an annual event for successful Indians domiciled and working outside India), scheduled to be held in Hyderabad in January 2006, much earlier than the planned April opening. The owners, operators and builders were re-briefed on the revised deadlines accordingly in September 2005. Sleepless nights, countless numbers of additional construction workers, and close supervision from the owners defined the course of action for the next few weeks. It is interesting to note here that the architect, interior designer, developer and operator all worked in parallel to ensure that the centre opened on time in January 2006.

Philip Logan, general manager, Hyderabad International Convention Centre, recalls:

> *We were a team of three on December 20 and had a mammoth event just a fortnight away. There were so many concerns jeopardizing our efforts: what if the coffee machine malfunctions? what if the client complains of no water in the toilets? or simply what happens if the lights don't work or the audio fails! The whole nation was watching us and we did not have a second chance with an event of this magnitude. The Who's Who? of the country, including the President and the Prime Minister, would walk down this floor in a few days from now and the floors were not even polished and the carpets were still in the cargo area awaiting customs clearance!*

343

The Pravasi Bharatiya Divas event proved to be highly successful. In the period from January to September 2006, the Centre went on to host over 50 events, including two international events, with a total of 28 000 delegates. Future confirmed events include the Asia Pacific Congress of Endoscopic and Laparoscopic Surgeons of Asia 2007, the International Astronautical Congress in September 2007, and the International Leprosy Conference in 2008.

Key Features of the Hyderabad International Convention Centre

Hyderabad International Convention Centre (HICC) is India's first purpose-built convention facility. Developed by the Cyberabad Convention Centre Private Limited, a joint venture between Emaar Properties (PJSC) of Dubai and Andhra Pradesh Investment Infrastructure Corporation (APIIC), this convention facility is managed by Accor, one of the world's leading hospitality and tourism management companies.

Built across a 15-acre landscaped environment, and located at a 30 minutes' drive from the international airport, HICC has a pillar-free internal hall of 6480 square metres net which can be partitioned into six smaller halls, using mobile operable walls which are soundproofed and covered in teak and silk. In open formation the main hall can seat up to 7000 theatre-style, or accommodate up to 400 tables for a banquet. The six smaller halls have a combined capacity of 5000. The foyer area also exceeds 6500 square metres.

The main hall has an in-built rear projection screen measuring 18×16 feet, together with the latest sound systems built into the roof to provide a complete concert-like experience at the flick of a switch. The roof has been constructed in such a way that it includes the following:

- Dimmable halogen lights across the entire facility
- North, South, East and West cat-walking facility at 6 metres and 18 metres
- Three levels with a fixed seating of 650 on level 1 and eight interpreter/corporate lounges and two audio-visual control systems overlooking the main stage
- Catwalks and truss to hold heavy weights when suspending large physical items.

To facilitate the staging of exhibitions in the main hall, the floor has been provided with pits to carry power, water, outflow/waste, cables and phone lines across the entire 6400 square metres.

HICC meeting rooms

Located at ground-floor level is a 500-person reception area with 16 terminals for registration. An additional reception area at the entrance to the convention centre has eight further terminals to cater for foreign currency transactions, travel administration, PCO services, a concierge facility or any other front desk operational requirements. The main reception has a back-office with 16 workstations with adjacent kitchen, pantry, two additional meeting rooms, plus an all-purpose space for organizers. Each office has a suite of four rooms, which includes an arrival lounge area for the organizer's guests. There is also a cloakroom facility with phone and Internet for delegates on the ground-floor level. Also located on the ground-floor level is a business centre with Internet facility, where security, event organizers and the operations team can overlook the facility through 34 closed circuit televisions with displays on dual plasma screens for easy venue viewing.

HICC has six more boardrooms and meeting rooms with four separate speaker preparation rooms as well as breakout rooms on level 2.

Other Points of Interest

1. State-of-the-art IT infrastructure, technology, telecommunications, AV and other facilities
2. Cutting edge design features including environmentally sustainable practices
3. A Novotel Hotel adjacent to HICC will be Hyderabad's finest purpose-built business hotel specifically designed for the international business traveller. In total Hyderabad has more than 1250 hotel rooms (as at December 2006), many in 5-star quality hotels.
4. In-built power back-up generation capability
5. 1000 + car parking base
6. Loading decks
7. 24/7 security with CCTVs

HICC's In-built Audio-Visual Capability

- Sound reinforcement system for the entire hall suitable for speech/light music, seminars, lectures, presentations etc.
- Rear projection screens & LCD projector for detailed presentations of all formats of video from presentations to motion pictures
- Auto dome CCD cameras for capturing live video of the stage proceedings and projecting onto the main screen display
- Video distribution of the proceedings of the hall to the entire convention centre through various plasma screens & TVs placed at selected locations
- State-of-the-art Digital Congress Network, equipped with chairman & delegate microphone units, facilitates conference and seminar discussions

- Up to six language interpretation booths with thousands of wireless infrared receivers with headphones for reception of simultaneous language interpretation
- DVD recorders enable recording and storage of all the interpreted languages or floor language, along with video, directly onto the DVD recorders.

Future opportunities

India as a destination is enticing to many travellers because of its varied cultures, spiritual teachings, mystical tourist locations and eventful history. The recent economic growth has made the country appear more approachable and viable for business as well. Most multinational corporations are considering setting up a base in the country, or have already done so. All this translates into great business tourism/MICE potential for India.

Traditionally, Delhi and Mumbai have been the principal business centres in India, followed by cities like Chennai, Bangalore, Hyderabad and Kolkata. However, Hyderabad, assisted by the strength of its economy, is now forging ahead of the other cities. Appropriate marketing is a pre-requisite to identify and target key audiences, not least those in the lucrative business tourism/MICE sector, in order to build further on this success. The pharmaceutical, medical and finance segments, already key to Hyderabad's economic growth, will be priorities for the city and for HICC, working in close partnership with the Andhra Pradesh Tourism Board.

Further information: www.hicc.com

Case Study 1.4   Abu Dhabi, United Arab Emirates

Background

Abu Dhabi is one of the seven emirates of the United Arab Emirates (UAE), a federation formed in 1971, following British withdrawal from the Persian Gulf, for 'mutual defence, security, prosperity and law and order'. The other six emirates are Ajman, Dubai, Fujairah, Ras Al Khaimah, Sharjah and Umm al Quwain.

Abu Dhabi is the capital of the UAE and, with its population of 1 600 000, is the wealthiest of the seven emirates. In 2005 it had the highest per capita income in the world at US$46 147. Yet, less than 50 years ago, the emirate of Abu Dhabi was little more than an empty desert inhabited by nomadic Bedouin tribes. Today, the ultra-modern cities of Abu Dhabi and Al Ain underline the remarkable transformation that has occurred in the intervening years. The population is expected to grow at 6.8 per cent per annum over the next decade to a total of 3.4 million by 2015.

This transformation has been based on wealth created by the oil industry. Huge reserves of oil were discovered offshore in 1958, and it is now estimated that Abu Dhabi possesses 10 per cent of the world's known oil reserves, which should last for another 150 years. The emirate produces 3.5 million barrels of oil per day generating an excess of US$90 billion annually.

Abu Dhabi the Destination

The emirate is steeped in the ancient culture and heritage of Arabia with the strong tradition of desert hospitality apparent in the genuine warmth of welcome shown to all visitors. According to the Abu Dhabi Tourism Authority, Abu Dhabi 'combines old world charm and cosmopolitan sophistication in a spotlessly clean and safe environment. The distinct blend of east and west offers immense diversity and variety. Visitors will be spoilt for choice with experiences that appeal to travellers seeking adventure, culture or just simple relaxation.' It is considered a priority to safeguard the unique traditions, crafts, artefacts and architecture that define the emirate's culture.

Much of the emirate is made up of the Rub Al Khali (the empty quarter), a vast arid desert area famous for its spectacular dunes. This is in total contrast with the Manhattan skyline and lush parks of the island city of Abu Dhabi. Al Ain, known as the garden city, is situated 150 kilometres inland from the capital, close to the Oman border and overshadowed by the rugged Jebel Hafeet, the UAE's highest mountain. Lying to the south of the emirate, the Liwa oasis, gateway to the empty quarter, is set amidst towering red

Figure 1.4
Abu Dhabi city-scape. (Source: Abu Dhabi Tourism Authority)

dunes offering the visitor another spectacular scenic experience. The Gulf coast of Abu Dhabi's Western Province is lined with endless unspoilt beaches with some 200 natural islands off the coast, several of them earmarked for future tourism development.

MICE and Tourism infrastructure development

The Abu Dhabi Tourism Authority was formed as recently as September 2004, symbolising a commitment by the government not only to promote the emirate but also to develop its tourism facilities and attractions. Great attention is being paid to ensuring that this development is in complete harmony with the environmental goals and management of Abu Dhabi's sustainable resources.

Plans have been announced to add 25 000 hotel rooms to the current inventory of approximately 10 000, with 4000 of these to be completed by the end of 2009, in a bid to increase tourism to the emirate from under one million visitors in 2004 to more than three million by 2015. Table 1.9 gives a more detailed analysis

Source Market	Hotel Visitors in 2005	Share (%) in 2005	Visitor Nights in 2005	Share (%) in 2005
Arab Countries	558,085	53	1,179,589	43
AGCC* (including UAE)	410,666	39	835,308	30
Asia	166,841	16	418,487	15
Europe	240,778	23	895,747	33
United Kingdom	73,750	7	252,766	9
Germany	50,475	5	210,878	8
France	28,911	3	103,854	4
Americas	61,218	6	194,825	7
USA	44,407	4	143,611	5
Other	25,920	2	62,747	2
TOTAL	1,052,842	100	2,751,395	100
Growth compared with 2004	9.8%	10.2%		
TOURISM TARGETS 2015				
Purpose of Visit	2003	Share (%)	2015	Share (%)
Leisure Visitors	167,000	20	1,215,000	41
MICE Visitors	40,000	5	236,000	8
Business	627,000	75	1,554,000	51
TOTAL	834,000	100	3,005,000	100

Source: Abu Dhabi Ministry of Planning
*AGCC = Arab Gulf Cooperation Council

Table 1.9
Abu Dhabi Visitor Statistics and Future Targets

of visitor numbers by geographic market and by purpose of visit, including projections to 2015.

The major conference venue in Abu Dhabi is the opulent Emirates Palace Hotel, which has a 1000-seat auditorium and a ballroom able to accommodate 2400 delegates. Among the more unusual venues is The Armed Forces Officers' Club, a substantial self-contained complex offering 600 bedrooms, a theatre and other conference and meetings facilities, plus the capacity to handle banquets for up to 15 000 people. There are plans to expand this venue by adding a further 1000 bedrooms and a new banqueting hall for 5000 people, due for completion by 2009.

The Abu Dhabi International Airport is undergoing a huge US$6.8 billion redevelopment and expansion project to serve the fast-growing tourism industry. The national airline, Etihad Airways, has a new fleet of aircraft and US$8 billion worth of aircraft on order. Some 50 airlines fly to Abu Dhabi from around the world. Flight times to continental Europe, for example, are six hours and to the UK, seven hours.

Other major development projects planned include:

Abu Dhabi National Exhibition Centre

The first phase of the new state-of-the-art Abu Dhabi National Exhibition Centre (ADNEC) opened in December 2006. When completed, the complex will have 57 000 square metres of exhibition floorspace, a 21 000 square metre visitor concourse and 7500 square metres of multi-purpose halls. The centre will also feature dedicated conference facilities for 1200 people, banqueting areas and more than 30 high-specification meeting rooms.

Among the prestigious events to be held at the new centre is 'GIBTM, the Gulf Incentive, Business Travel and Meetings Exhibition', organized by Reed Travel Exhibitions. The first annual GIBTM is scheduled for March 2007.

This commitment by Reed Travel Exhibitions makes Reed one of four 'Foundation Partners', each of which has undertaken to organize a number of events in Abu Dhabi. The other three partners are CMP, IIR (Middle East) and Dmg World Media. The Foundation Partnership concept is designed to guarantee that some 30 new exhibitions and events will be staged in the emirate over the next few years, underpinning the growth of the business tourism sector.

ADNEC is one part of the Capital Centre development which, when completed, will be a micro-city in its own right with shops, residential areas, a marina, and more.

Saadiyat Island Project

The Saadiyat Island (which in Arabic means Island of Happiness) project will see the transformation of a 27-square kilometre natural island, located 500 metres offshore from the city of Abu Dhabi, into a strategic international tourism destination, which will be the largest single mixed-use development in the Arabian Gulf. The island, which has 30 kilometres of water frontage and many natural eco-features including mangrove forests, will be developed in three phases with total completion by 2018. The master plan envisages six highly individual districts and includes 29 hotels (including an iconic 7-star property), three marinas with combined berths for around 1000 boats, museums and cultural centres, two golf courses, civic and leisure facilities, sea-view apartments and elite villas.

The Emirates Pearl

The Emirates Pearl is a 5-star hotel and serviced apartment resort, featuring a 240-metre high tower, to be built at a cost of US$136 million on the capital's Khalidiya coast, opposite the prestigious 5-star Emirates Palace Hotel. The business and leisure resort is to be centred around a 47-storey tower which will contain 352 spacious rooms and suites and 104 luxuriously furnished apartments. The complex will include meeting rooms and a business centre, plus a range of other facilities.

Shangri-La Hotel

Shangri-La, one of the world's leading hotel groups, opens its first property in Abu Dhabi in March 2007. Situated amongst landscaped gardens and canal waterways, Shangri-La Hotel Abu Dhabi will have 220 guest rooms and 228 serviced apartments, together with extensive meeting and banqueting facilities.

Ferrari Museum

Expected to boost further Abu Dhabi's appeal to incentive groups, the Ferrari Museum due to open in 2008, will comprise a race track, numerous rides and attractions, virtual simulations, and visitors/delegates will be able to take test drives and races. The venue will also cater for private functions such as receptions and dinners.

Guggenheim Museum

Abu Dhabi has formalised plans with the New York-based Guggenheim Foundation to establish a world class museum devoted to modern and contemporary art. To be called the Guggenheim Abu Dhabi, the museum will position the emirate as a leading international cultural destination. At 30 000 square metres, the museum will be larger than any existing Guggenheim worldwide. Construction is expected to be finished by 2011, and will form part of the Saadiyat Island development.

MICE Sector Marketing Activity

The ambitious targets for growth in MICE sector visitors set out in Table 1.9 depend on effective implementation of a range of marketing activities if they are to be realised. Angela Bates, Abu Dhabi Tourism Authority's Marketing and Sales Account Manager, comments:

The MICE market is one of the key areas for development and opportunity in Abu Dhabi and we aim to increase the number of MICE travellers to Abu Dhabi to over 230 000 by 2015. In order to achieve this, the Abu Dhabi Tourism Authority (ADTA) is committed to showcasing the excellent facilities that we have to offer by maintaining a strong presence at international exhibitions such as EIBTM, GIBTM and IMEX and at smaller forums such as 'Confec' and Conference & Incentive Travel's agency events. ADTA is also planning a series of familiarisation trips which will give corporate buyers and agents the opportunity to see the potential of Abu Dhabi as a MICE destination at first hand. The fam. trips will showcase the professionalism, high standard of service and creativity that Abu Dhabi has to offer, against the destination's backdrop of enthralling culture and heritage combined with its modern infrastructure.

Further Information

Head Office:
   Abu Dhabi Tourism Authority, PO Box 94000, Abu Dhabi, United Arab Emirates. Tel: +971 (0)2 444 0444; Fax: +971 (0)2 444 0400; E-mail: info@abudhabitourism.ae; Web site: www.exploreabudhabi.ae.

London Office:
   Abu Dhabi Tourism Authority, No. 1 Knightsbridge, London SW1X 7LY. Tel: +44 (0)20 7201 6400; Fax: +44 (0)20 7201 6426; E-mail: info@abudhabitourism.co.uk; Web site: www.exploreabudhabi.ae.

Case Study 1.5   Coral Beach Hotel & Resort, Paphos, Cyprus

The Coral Beach Hotel & Resort is a part of the Leptos Calypso Hotels Public Ltd., a leading hotel chain based in Cyprus and Greece, focusing on the operation and management of various tourism projects such as hotels, hotel apartments and restaurants.

The company portfolio currently comprises of a 5-star resort hotel, a deluxe boutique hotel, two 3-star hotels with self catering apartments and tourist villas, all situated in Paphos, Cyprus, and a 5-star hotel in Chania, Crete. The company aims to bring together the elegance and charm of resort hotels and hospitality services while preserving links with local architecture and cuisine.

Coral Beach Hotel & Resort

The 5-star Coral Beach Hotel & Resort opened its doors in 1993, establishing itself as the largest hotel in Cyprus with over 300 rooms and just under 4000 square metres of meeting space. Overnight this created opportunities for Paphos to target the conference and incentive market, a segment which till that date was only enjoyed by other towns on the island. In the winter of 2000 the hotel completed its second phase of expansion, bringing the total number of rooms to 424 and increasing its meeting space to 7500 square metres.

The hotel's other facilities include a gym, health and beauty spa, six restaurants, four bars, an arts and crafts centre, children's club and play area, four tennis courts, squash court, indoor swimming pool, two outdoor swimming pools and its own private pleasure harbour and boat.

Figure 1.5
Coral Beach Hotel & Resort, Paphos, Cyprus.

In 2004, with the Olympic Games being held just across the waters in Athens, the hotel saw great opportunities for sports tourism and thus expanded its facilities by building, on land adjoining the resort, an Olympic size swimming pool with top of the range electronic equipment. The Olympic pool complemented other sporting facilities available in the stadium of the neighbouring village of Peyia, which are suitable for teams training for archery, fencing, and a range of other sports. Construction of the Olympic pool enabled the Leptos Calypso group to secure a 10-year contract with the British Olympic Association, which will use the hotel and facilities for warm weather training in winter months.

Thalassa Boutique Hotel & Resort

The newest addition to the Leptos Calypso portfolio is the Thalassa Boutique & Spa. Thalassa is situated on a peninsula adjoining the Coral Beach Hotel & Resort, overlooking Coral Bay and the Mycenaean excavations of Maa Palaiokastro. It is uniquely surrounded by sea on three sides allowing its guests to choose between either a sunset or sunrise view. This deluxe 58-bedroom hotel opened in July 2004 and has redefined service standards in the Eastern Mediterranean. All rooms from a Superior Suite upwards have a personal butler as standard, and all other rooms offer this service on request. A member of the Small Luxury Hotels of the World marketing consortium, Thalassa is the first boutique hotel in Cyprus and provides the ideal venue for private company meetings, small board meetings or it may be taken over exclusively by a top incentive group. Its bedrooms can also be used by high-level executives attending a conference at the Coral Beach Hotel & Resort. Thalassa welcomes guests of 12 years of age and above.

Akamas International Conference Centre

The Coral Beach Hotel & Resort still has the largest, and arguably most flexible, meeting space in Cyprus, totalling 7500 square metres and incorporating twenty purpose-built syndicate rooms. The pivotal hub is the Akamas International Conference Centre, with a capacity of 1000 theatre-style, a flexible, column-free, multi-purpose room with a clear ceiling height of over 5 metres. The Akamas can be divided quickly into three sound-proof rooms with independent air-conditioning, lighting, communications and simultaneous translation booths which can double up as technical galleries. Each of these three smaller rooms has its own separate entrance from the extensive foyer and conference reception. In addition there are three fully equipped offices suitable for organizers adjoining the Akamas foyer. The Akamas has adjacent kitchens, should it be used for a gala dinner.

Target markets

Being a resort hotel the Coral Beach Hotel & Resort has the ability to cater for a variety of markets simultaneously, these markets being mainly:

- Conference and Incentive
- Leisure/Family Market
- Weddings & Honeymoons
- Sports Groups.

The resort is able to cater for each of the above segments without one interfering with the other. For instance, all meeting rooms have nearby areas for coffee breaks which are set away from areas looking after families and holidaymakers. There is also a wing of the hotel which only welcomes guests of 13 years of age and above, making it ideal for couples or guests who do not have children.

Conference & Incentive Market

With over 7000 sq metres of meeting space, the Coral Beach Hotel & Resort has invested strongly in the conference, meetings and incentives market. With 424 rooms to fill, a large percentage of group business must be secured in order to reach the required occupancy levels, especially during the months of November to April. Conference and incentive business accounts for between 10–20 per cent of the hotel's overall turnover.

The main conference and incentive market is the United Kingdom, generating approximately 60 per cent of the hotel's business. The second most important market is the local (Cypriot) market which provides about 20 per cent. It is estimated that Cyprus attracts around 600 business events a year.

The principal marketing activities undertaken to generate conferences and incentive groups are:

- Participation in specialist exhibitions
- Some advertising in trade magazines
- A growing concentration on specialist web sites, including the hotel's own web site
- Mailings to existing clients
- Organization of educational visits and sales calls.

Although the resort has superb facilities and the flexibility to meet the majority of demands and requirements set by groups, it faces some challenges that are not within its control. The number of flights, and particularly direct flights, into the island are not as frequent as they are to destinations in mainland Europe, especially during the winter months when group business is most important.

Sports Tourism

Cyprus, and especially Paphos, has become a centre for high quality sport since it was used as a training base for many National Olympic teams in the lead-up to the 2004 Athens Olympic Games, and today Paphos hosts sporting clubs from all over Europe for their warm weather training. Paphos' sweeping coastline, its proximity to the Troodos Mountains, and the facilities at Coral Beach and Peyia, provide terrain and water suitable for sports such as mountain biking, cycling, the triathlon, swimming and archery. In addition to these, Paphos has three 18-hole championship golf courses placing Paphos and Cyprus on the map as an official golf destination. All three courses are 20 minutes' drive from the Coral Beach Hotel & Resort.

Scale of investment and return

The total cost of construction of the Akamas International Conference Centre and associated syndicate rooms was two million Cyprus Pounds, and the estimated return is approximately 35 per cent per year. Construction of the Olympic swimming pool was approximately eight hundred thousand Cyprus Pounds, and the estimated return is 35 per cent per year. There were no loans or assistance from any government bodies towards either of these developments.

Quality systems

The Coral Beach Hotel & Resort has successfully achieved the European accreditations of ISO 1400 (environmental) and HACCAP – Hazzard Analysis Critical Control Points. ISO and HACCAP ensure consistent standards throughout all departments, operations and procedures, furthermore, with the combination of both these accreditations Food Hygiene and Safety is guaranteed together with an overall cleaner and healthier environment.

Further Information: www.coral.com.cy.

Case Study 2.2 International Federation of Library Associations and Institutions (IFLA)

This case study describes the IFLA World Library and Information Congress, the annual conference and council meeting of the International Federation of Library Associations and Institutions (IFLA), an international association which was founded in Edinburgh in 1927 and now has its headquarters in The Hague,

Netherlands. The IFLA is a membership organization with just over 1700 members in 150 countries. Members comprise national library associations, national libraries, large university and public libraries, and other kinds of libraries as well as 'personal affiliates' and 'student affiliates'.

Key Features of the IFLA World Library and Information Congress

- It attracts 3500 to 4500 participants
- They come from up to 150 countries
- The associated exhibition draws up to 175 exhibitors
- The Congress lasts for up to 5 days (with business meetings held outside those 5 days)
- It includes some 200 conference sessions.

The Locations of IFLA World Library and Information Congresses

- 2000 – Jerusalem
- 2001 – Boston
- 2002 – Glasgow
- 2003 – Berlin
- 2004 – Buenos Aires
- 2005 – Oslo
- 2006 – Seoul
- 2007 – Durban
- 2008 – Quebec City
- 2009 – Milan.

The Selection Process

- Four years ahead of time the IFLA Governing Board decides which world region will be the target area for the next open year
- IFLA's professional conference organizer (PCO), Congrex Holland, is commissioned to prepare a shortlist of suitable convention centres. (Congrex Holland was appointed on a 5-year contract for the period 2005–2009, and acts as a Core PCO with responsibility for organizing the Congress in whichever region of the world it is being held)
- The PCO asks conference centres, convention bureaux and tourist agencies in that region to respond to a questionnaire which reflects IFLA's criteria for conference centres and host cities
- All IFLA national association members are informed of this and are given the opportunity to send the IFLA HQ an Expression of Interest in hosting the IFLA World Library and Information Congress
- Based on a report after this phase, the IFLA Governing Board decides on a shortlist of three to five cities
- The shortlisted convention centres are then invited to make a presentation to IFLA headquarters

- Based on these presentations, another selection (two or three cities in one or more countries) is made
- Site visits are planned to the selected cities. These site visits are organized by the convention bureau/conference centre
- Discussions are held with the national association members in the countries concerned to gauge the level of interest and support from the profession and government authorities of the countries under consideration
- A final report is drafted by the PCO
- IFLA headquarters makes a recommendation to the Governing Board
- The Governing Board takes a decision ranking the venues in principle
- Negotiations take place with the ranked venues on the major cost elements
- The final decision is made and is ratified by the Governing Board
- The decision is announced during the closing ceremony of the Congress taking place 3 years before the Congress in question.

IFLA Selection Criteria

- Geographic spread, ensuring that the conference takes place in different parts of the world in order to maximise its accessibility for all members. IFLA wishes to hold meetings regularly outside Europe and North America, and to include a range of geography over any 5-year period
- The venue must be capable of accommodating plenary sessions of up to 3500 people, and have good, spacious registration areas
- The venue must also have the rooms to handle eight simultaneous sessions
- There must be sufficient office accommodation for IFLA headquarters staff, IFLA officers, editors, translators and interpreters
- It should be all under one roof, have sound-proof rooms and be able to provide good audio-visual services
- It must also be able to provide simultaneous interpretation facilities for conference sessions in 5 to 7 languages
- There needs to be an exhibition/exposition hall nearby with 3000 square metres of space, located so as to ensure a steady flow of delegates
- The destination must offer a wide range of hotels. There should be sufficient supply of hotel rooms in each category. Alternatives to hotels (homestays, dormitories, hostels, etc) are also considered
- There should be an efficient transport system. Transportation is assessed against its speed, cost, frequency, hours of service, and safety

- Details of meals and food services are assessed against both quality and variety-of-price criteria. Availability of different kinds of food to suit a range of cultures/religions is important
- Support from national government/local city administration/ sponsors. The convention centres and/or national association members must be able to provide evidence of financial support from local and national governments. Typical evidence will include: letters, money already raised/promised, or a reasonable strategy for raising money. There should also be an assurance that participants from all over the world will be able to enter the country
- The quality and availability of local professional support
- The availability of local libraries for study visits, and interesting professional activities occurring in the region/area. Support for the IFLA conference from local libraries is also assessed.

Other Desirable Facilities

- An internet café open all hours
- All facilities within easy walking distance
- A bank and post office nearby
- Plenty of places for delegates/attendees to meet and sit down
- Air conditioning within the conference venue
- Cheap and enjoyable post-conference tours
- Social events that capture culture
- A souvenir shop
- And, finally, a safe and welcoming environment.

Further information on IFLA can be accessed via its web site: www.ifla.org.

Case Study 2.3   MCI Group

Introduction and Background

MCI was established by Roger Tondeur and his wife, Ursula, in 1987. Roger had begun his career in Paris organizing concerts until, in 1979, he moved back to his home country of Switzerland where he worked for Wagonlit Travel in Geneva and was promoted to Managing Director in 1982. During his 5 years in this role, Wagonlit Travel took over the management of TELECOM, the world's largest telecommunications exhibition with over 250 000 visitors.

From its launch in 1987, MCI grew in size and reputation over the next 12 years to become the leading event management company in Geneva. In 1999, the second MCI office opened in Zurich and since then, expansion has been swift. By the end of 2006, MCI had 16 offices across Europe, the Middle East and Asia. They are located in: Brussels (Belgium), Petersfield/London (UK), Geneva, Zurich (Switzerland), Paris and Lyon (France), Berlin and Stuttgart (Germany), Barcelona and Madrid (Spain), Prague (Czech Republic), Stockholm (Sweden), Vienna (Austria), Dubai, Shanghai (China), and Singapore. In addition it has partnerships in North America and Asia Pacific.

In 2005 MCI was ranked 138th on the list of the fastest growing European companies, an annual ranking of the top 500 companies in Europe published by Europe's 500 Entrepreneurs for Growth. It now claims to be 'the foremost pan-European association, communications and event management group'. In 2006, MCI Group had a turnover of 150 million euros, employed over 500 permanent staff and organized 850 events around the world. It has ambitious targets to increase turnover to 260 million euros by 2010 and employ 750 staff.

This case study looks in more detail at the role and activities of the MCI Group. The impact that companies such as MCI will have on the conference and conventions industry in the future is examined further in Chapter 9.

Company Structure

The company is structured in two divisions: a Corporate Division and an Institutional Division.

a) Corporate Division

The Corporate Division was launched in 2004 to co-ordinate experience and expertise in supporting the activities of its corporate clients across Europe. The purpose of the Corporate Division underlines MCI's belief that face-to-face meetings are an extremely powerful way of informing, educating, training, motivating, stimulating and enthusing all stakeholders (employees, customers, distributors, partners, investors, suppliers) and to support companies in achieving their strategic objectives. MCI perceives the following as key issues and factors driving the corporate market:

- Regulation: in all countries in which MCI operates, governments and other regulatory bodies are introducing more regulations. These include financial regulations and the increased tightening and policing of the code governing the pharmaceutical industry
- Technology: increasingly technology is expected to provide greater automation of meetings and events and increase their business value

- Client Priorities: clients are seen to be looking for four key things when outsourcing their event management:
  - the 'Big Idea'
  - location
  - price
  - value.

The future of the Corporate Division is expected to see a movement away from key relationships with event management and procurement departments to a greater involvement with senior sales and marketing personnel, providing an opportunity for MCI to influence at a higher level and to be recognised for its contribution to a company's overall strategy.

The areas anticipated to show particularly strong growth are: trade show and press events; B2C experiential marketing; outsourcing of event departments; and integrated marketing.

In 2004, MCI Group initiated a Global Key Account Management structure. This has led to the development of partnerships and a consultative approach with its key accounts. Centralised purchasing continues to gain momentum among clients and MCI's 'think global, act local' approach has meant that it can help companies to increase value, and sometimes reduce the cost, of their face-to-face marketing communications. The Global Key Account Management structure has also allowed MCI to gain a better understanding of clients' businesses, their brands, internal processes and markets, thus enabling MCI to improve the value of the services it can offer. In other words, it can marry the needs of its global accounts with the benefits and assurance of local delivery.

b) Institutional Division

The Institutional Division oversees the provision of association management services (AMC) and PCO services to a wide range of non-corporate entities: national and international associations, institutions, and governmental bodies. Long-term clients include 26 healthcare associations and 20 associations in other industries.

In its AMC services, MCI's approach is based around the principles of long-term relationships, flexibility and trust. It seeks to work closely with association leaders in their business and strategic planning. By providing a permanent base with flexible staffing, it works closely with associations to support their key objectives in areas such as membership development, marketing and communications, industry and government relations, fundraising, certification and other activities. AMC services are offered through MCI's offices in Petersfield (England), Geneva and Paris.

A congress or convention is seen as playing an integral role in the development, overall growth and raison-d'être of an association. By working closely with associations' organizing and scientific committees, MCI's PCO services involve all aspects of the conference, including management of abstracts, sponsorship, exhibition and delegates, financial planning and marketing. As a core PCO (see Chapter 2), MCI provides a long-term partnership to secure maximum financial results and a consistent level of quality. The congresses organized by the Institutional Division attract more than 93 000 professionals as delegates.

MCI claims to be unique in being able to service its clients on a national basis, or on a pan-European basis, or on a global basis through its partnership with SmithBucklin (see below) and through its offices in Asia Pacific and Latin America.

The partnership with SmithBucklin was announced in February 2006 and is designed to deliver seamless association and event management services worldwide. US-based SmithBucklin is the world's largest association management company. Founded in 1949, SmithBucklin now employs 630 staff in all areas of association activity, including executive management, member and chapter administration, convention and trade show management, marketing and branding, web services, education programmes, government relations and financial management. It manages more than US$200 million in annual client budgets from offices in four US cities. The press release announcing the partnership between MCI Group and SmithBucklin stated that it 'created the world's largest network of association and event management resources. In addition to providing clients with immediate access to leading expertise and resources around the globe, it also affords unmatched purchasing and negotiation power in the hospitality industry.'

Conclusion

The rapid growth of the MCI Group illustrates very clearly the key role that such global client management companies are playing in the conference and convention sector. There are other companies, such as Congrex, Helms Briscoe, Maritz, Conferon, offering similar client management services.

Roger Tondeur, founder and now President of MCI Group, portrays the future of companies such as his in the following terms:

> We see tremendous growth opportunities as the events industry follows the outsourcing trends apparent in other sectors: companies are outsourcing specialist services and establishing preferred vendor agreements with a small number of key suppliers. In the association conference market, associations will increasingly look to appoint core PCOs and association management companies on a long-term contract basis. MCI is structured and resourced to capitalize on both types of opportunity.

Further information: www.mci-group.com.

Case Study 3.1   The Scottish Exhibition + Conference Centre, Glasgow

The Scottish Exhibition + Conference Centre (SECC) was built in Queens Dock on the River Clyde in the early 1980s, an area where 'decline was all too visibly giving way to dereliction', in the words of former Chairman Edward Cunningham who, as Director, Industry and Enterprise Development with the Scottish Development Agency, was responsible for promulgating the concept of the SECC and for its construction. The total cost of the project was £36 million, including £11.5 million for infilling of the former dock, ground stabilisation and road infrastructure, and £24.5 million for the building itself. Construction work began in June 1983 and was completed in August 1985.

Funding was derived from one of the industry's first public-private sector partnerships, with public contributions accruing from Strathclyde Regional Council, Glasgow District Council, the Scottish Development Agency and the European Regional Development Fund. Despite the 90 per cent public sector shareholding, an important consequence of the public-private sector partnership was to ensure that the Centre managed its business under commercial disciplines. Many similar types of venue are owned entirely by local authorities and their remit is to generate benefits for the local community through expenditure by visitors, exhibitors and organizers. The SECC also had, and still has, the responsibility to generate economic benefits for the City and for Scotland,

Figure 3.5
The Clyde Auditorium, SECC, Glasgow. (Source: The Scottish Exhibition + Conference Centre)

but to do so whilst making a profit. In 2007 the shareholding was 90.87 per cent Glasgow City Council, 9.13 per cent private sector.

Originally designed as a national exhibition centre, changes were made during construction to incorporate conference facilities when it became apparent that demand was growing for large conferences and conventions to have associated exhibition space. There were, at the time, very few venues in the UK that could simultaneously accommodate conferences and exhibitions. The decision was, therefore, taken to convert one of the proposed exhibition halls into a conference auditorium seating 2000 delegates. This was achieved within the original budget for the building. The name was changed from Scottish Exhibition Centre to Scottish Exhibition + Conference Centre, and it opened in 1985 with the conference auditorium plus five purpose-built exhibition halls totalling 17 260m^2 – over 95 per cent of which was clear-span exhibition space.

Within 5 years, however, it became clear that, if the SECC was to exploit properly the emerging market of conferences with associated exhibitions, purpose-built conference facilities would be required. This conclusion led directly to the construction, beginning in 1995, of the Conference Centre, named the Clyde Auditorium (and known locally as 'The Armadillo'), a most distinctive landmark building for Glasgow, along with a new exhibition hall and the development of the original auditorium into a smaller auditorium and a series of breakout rooms essential for staging international conferences – total project cost £39 million. With 3000 seats in the Clyde Auditorium, the SECC became one of the largest conference venues in the UK and, at the time of opening in 1997, one of only five venues in Europe capable of accommodating large conferences with concurrent exhibitions.

Specific objectives for the new Conference Centre were to:

- increase the level of conference business staged at the SECC threefold – from around 50 000 delegate days each year to 150 000 by the year 2003
- increase the annual economic benefit to the local economy accruing from the conferences staged from £8.6 million in 1993 to £25 million by 2003
- break into the corporate conference market.

In the financial year 1998–1999 these business and economic targets were met – 4 years ahead of schedule. In that year, the SECC secured 57 conferences generating 150 248 delegate days ('*delegate days' are calculated by multiplying the duration of a conference in days by the number of delegates attending e.g. a 300-delegate conference lasting for 2 days would generate 600 delegate days*) and an economic benefit to the City of Glasgow of £26.5 million. Corporate conferences were staged with clients ranging from multinational corporations (Microsoft, IBM, Pfizer) to local companies.

The conference sector has continued to grow. In 2005–2006, a new record performance was achieved, with 50 conferences generating 236 785 delegate days, creating an economic benefit of £58.3 million. In the same year the SECC as a whole:

- staged 230 different events
- attracted over 1.5 million visitors
- injected just over £127 million into the local economy
- supported more than 3500 jobs in the community
- made a profit of £2.4 million before tax.

In October 2003 the SECC unveiled a 'master plan' with its vision for the future of its 64-acre site. The development is being called 'QD2' because it marks the second redevelopment of Queens Dock. Whilst the SECC is already the UK's largest integrated conference and exhibition centre, the SECC site, which is predominantly surface car parking, can now be redeveloped to create capital receipts that will contribute towards the building of new facilities, dramatically transforming both the SECC's business and the surrounding area. QD2 is a £622 million development that will create a complete exhibition, conference and entertainments complex, expanding and enhancing the range and number of the SECC's core activities through the addition of new facilities. These will include:

- The Arena: a 12 500-seat purpose-built Arena costing £66 million, to be marketed as a National Arena for Scotland
- A 5-star hotel with restaurants, leisure facilities, car parking for 1600 vehicles and commercial office space
- Public/Arrival Square: hard and soft landscaping will be used to create both a sense of arrival at the SECC and to harmonise the existing buildings with the Arena
- A new sustainable village will be built to provide a range of housing from starter flats to townhouses along the river's edge, creating a mixed residential community of over 3000 people.

Work is expected to start on the Arena phase in 2008 but it is not yet possible to give precise projections for the completion of the overall QD2 project.

Research undertaken by management consultants KPMG in 2006 to 2007 found that the SECC had an annual economic impact on the Glasgow economy of £347 million. At the same time it generated net additional expenditure in the rest of Scotland of some £216 million, and around £109 million in the UK as a whole. It was responsible for sustaining over 6700 jobs in Glasgow, approximately 4200 in Scotland and a further 2200 in the UK.

Edward Cunningham became Chairman of the SECC in 1992 and on his retirement he wrote:

> The vision for the SECC has been realized. It has been making a profit since 1993 – over £900 000 in 2001 and, in the same year, injected almost £84 million into the economy of Greater Glasgow and £53 million into the economy of Scotland as a whole. Since opening in 1985, Glasgow's economy has benefited by almost £1 billion and the SECC has been the catalyst for the surge in investment in hotels and other business tourism-related enterprises in the City. The changes that have been made to the Clyde in the intervening years have been spectacular. The decline has halted; dereliction has given way to development. The City has turned to the river for growth and regeneration. From the outset, the SECC was the precursor for the renaissance of the Clyde. The Garden Festival in 1988 could not have been held without the availability of the SECC. That Festival boosted the image of Glasgow and Scotland and led on to other major events. Disappointingly, the recession of the early 1990s deferred developments. But the Conference Centre set off a new signal and now there is a great sense of momentum all along the Clyde. We can now be sure that the Clyde will indeed become the focus of a vibrant, dynamic city, albeit in a very different form from when Glasgow was the industrial hub of the (British) Empire.

Case Study 4.2   Edinburgh Convention Bureau

Origins of Edinburgh Convention Bureau

Edinburgh Convention Bureau (ECB) was established in 1996 under the Local Government Act (Scotland) 1994 which created a network of 14 Area Tourist Boards in Scotland. ECB was initially a separate Directorate within the Edinburgh & Lothians Tourist Board (ELTB) but as a result of financial retrenchment and restructuring, it was absorbed into the ELTB Marketing Division in 1991.

However, following the introduction of a new integrated Scottish tourism industry network in April 2005, the Edinburgh Convention Bureau Ltd, a new company limited by guarantee, was formed to serve the needs of the business tourism sector in the city.

Figure 4.3
Edinburgh Castle and Skyline.
(Source: Edinburgh Convention
Bureau Ltd.)

Governance

A membership organisation, the Edinburgh Convention Bureau Ltd represents over 130 members including hotels, venues, conference facilities, destination management companies and conference and event organisers. Its Board is made up of The City of Edinburgh Council, VisitScotland, Scottish Enterprise Edinburgh and Lothian and private sector representatives.

Structure

ECB has 12 full-time equivalent staff involved in a number of activities including:

- Sales Team
- Convention Services team
- IT Support
- CEO Office
- CABS operation (Conference Accommodation Booking Service).

Role of ECB

Edinburgh Convention Bureau Ltd is now the lead organization responsible for marketing and organizing Scotland's capital city as a premier conference, incentive and event destination.

In 2005–2006, ECB recorded over £37 million of business tourism expenditure for the local economy through the meetings and conferences won for the city. It also operates the Edinburgh Ambassadors Programme, which currently includes over

1400 ambassadors representing all the major academic and commercial fields in which Edinburgh has an international reputation. Since 1996, the Edinburgh Ambassador Programme, which is supported by Scottish Enterprise Edinburgh & Lothian, has attracted over 200 major conferences to Edinburgh, creating over £87 million in revenue to the area (see Davidson and Rogers (2006) for a detailed description of the Edinburgh Ambassadors Programme).

Financial performance of ECB

Table 4.5 presents the budget available for the operation of the ECB between 2000 and 2006, and shows the proportion of expenditure on staffing and office running costs (corporate costs) against expenditure on promoting Edinburgh as a conference and incentive destination.

A small increase in budget was reported in real terms in 2003 to 2004 and from that point onwards the budget continued to increase. Figure 4.4 depicts the budget against the level of business secured by the ECB during the same period. The term 'discounted gross value', used in Figure 4.4, describes the difference in economic value of an event between the time that it is won and when it actually takes place. For example, a conference may be won for Edinburgh in 2007 but not take place until 2010. In 2007 it would only be possible to estimate the conference's value to the city based on 2007 prices. Looking ahead to 2010, the diminishing effect of the time value of money (assumed to be 2.5 per cent per annum) would mean that the value of that conference would be less to the local area when it takes place than it would be in 2007. Inflation means that £1 million will purchase less in 3 years' time than it would in 2007. It is possible that, using current day expenditure values to estimate the future

TOTAL ANNUAL COSTS			
Year	Estimated costs £	Staff & Corporate costs £	Promotional costs £	Promotional costs as % of total
2000–2001	569 219	220 757	348 462	61
2001–2002	583 496	391 867	191 630	33
2002–2003	553 038	404 621	148 417	27
2003–2004	569 072	430 734	138 337	24
2004–2005	675 555	336 197	182 857	27
2005–2006	741 600	350 000	391 600	53

Table 4.5
Edinburgh Convention Bureau budget 2000–2006

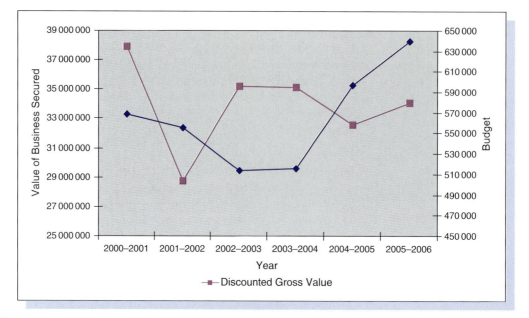

Figure 4.4 Impact of budget changes on business secured.

value of an event, convention bureaux may be reporting values that are artificially higher than they will be at the time the event takes place. Applying a 'discounting' figure over the time period between the event being secured and actually taking place may provide a better estimate of what the conference would actually yield in value terms at that future date.

During periods of low promotional budgets, a gradual reduction in value secured is apparent and vice versa. Increases in ECB promotional budget in recent years have been followed by an upturn in the value of business secured.

Membership numbers and income

In 2005–2006 revenue generated from membership fees totalled £171 300, an average of £1232 per member. Basic membership benefits include:

- Business entry in 'Blueprint', the official guide to meeting spaces and services distributed to 7000 businesses and used by decision makers who book conferences and conventions
- Listing on www.meetingedinburgh.com, which includes an online request for proposal form and opportunities to advertise
- Listing on the Conference Accommodation Bookings Service which provides a service to delegates attending conferences in the city.

The membership charge varies depending on the scale of the business and the sector within which they compete. In general, professional conference organisers (PCOs) are charged the highest membership fee as it is anticipated that they will achieve the greatest direct financial return from their membership.

Return on public sector investment in ECB

ECB receives core funding from both the City of Edinburgh Council and VisitScotland (the national tourist board). In 2005–2006 public sector contributions amounted to £360 000 out of a total operating budget of £741 600. Overall, for every £ of public sector support made towards the ECB budget, the organization has generated between £80 and £105 in economic benefit for the city during the period 2000–2005.

Public sector funding is also received from Scottish Enterprise Edinburgh & Lothians (SEEL) in support of the Edinburgh Ambassadors Programme. Table 4.6 and Figure 4.5 demonstrate the success which the Programme has had in generating conference business for Edinburgh.

The importance of the Ambassador Programme is illustrated by its contribution to the overall value of business generated by ECB, shown in Figure 4.6.

In terms of overall contribution of Ambassadors' events to the totality of ECB business, the programme generates around 30 per cent of total value and around 20 per cent of all delegates. In terms of overall importance, the programme declined from a peak in 2003 but in 2005 once again began to contribute an increasing proportion of all business.

Against this background, it seems that whilst the Ambassadors Programme has been successful in generating business, the

AMBASSADOR PROGRAMME IMPACT

Year	Number of Ambassadors	Number of events secured*	Number of delegates	Delegates per event secured	Value of events secured £	Value per event £	Value per delegate £
2000	1373	47	17 510	373	14 562 930	309 850	832
2001	1433	44	15 722	357	11 224 658	255 106	714
2002	1535	45	16 098	358	13 073 850	290 530	812
2003	1615	51	17 965	352	12 777 405	250 537	711
2004	1685	32	12 327	385	8 277 594	258 675	672
2005	1792	31	13 170	425	12 406 680	400 215	942

Table 4.6
Ambassador programme impact

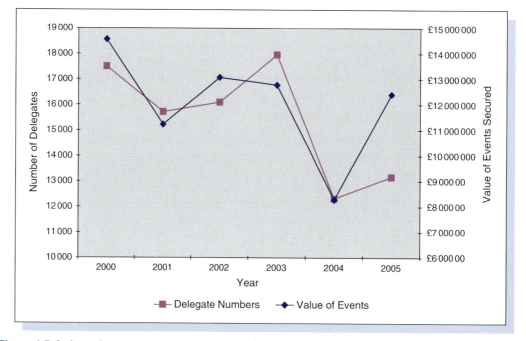

Figure 4.5 Ambassador programme – value of secured events.

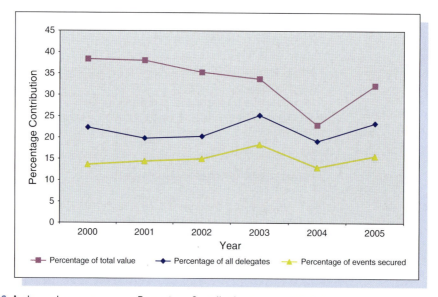

Figure 4.6 Ambassador programme – Percentage Contribution to overall ECB Business.

greater number of Ambassadors have not actively generated new business. The programme may be entering a phase of diminishing returns and although still showing positive trends, it may require a focus on generating more business from a smaller number of existing and active Ambassadors rather than recruiting and servicing the needs of up to 100 new, potentially 'sleeping' Ambassadors per year.

Clearly, however, the programme has generated business which would not have otherwise come to the city. In that context, it is essential that the programme continues to act in matching the expertise in the city to the available market opportunities.

Economic impact assessment

Multiplier effects of ECB activities

As described in Chapter 3, true economic impact assessments need to include direct, indirect and induced effects. The indirect and induced impacts can be calculated using multiplier analysis. The multipliers adopted by ECB are taken from the Scottish Tourism Multiplier Study (STMS) completed in 1992. This study generated a range of multiplier values representative of economic profile and visitor market profile across a range of locations in Scotland. Table 4.7 summarises the value of the indirect and induced impacts of participant and visitor expenditure, and provides a gross total impact. The multiplier analysis applies different multipliers depending on the nature of the direct expenditure.

Given the preponderance of expenditure on accommodation, it was considered reasonable to apply the multiplier which relates to the large hotels sector within Edinburgh. From the 1992 STMS report, the published value of this multiplier is 1.4989. This means that for every £1 spent in the city by conference delegates, there will be around £1.50 generated within the overall economy through indirect and induced expenditure.

It is estimated, therefore, that the gross value of all of the conference activity generated by ECB since the year 2000 was in the region of £306 million.

MULTIPLIER EFFECT OF CONFERENCE SPENDING			
Year	Total direct expenditure*	Output Multiplier Value	Total D+I+I Expenditure
2000	37 926 900	1.4989	£56 848 630
2001	28 770 380	1.4989	£43 123 923
2002	35 254 219	1.4989	£52 842 549
2003	35 166 036	1.4989	£52 710 371
2004	32 638 800	1.4989	£48 922 297
2005	34 076 420	1.4989	£51 077 146
Total	£203 832 755	1.4989	£305 524 916

Table 4.7
Multiplier effect of conference spending

CUMULATIVE EMPLOYMENT IMPACT				
	Total Discounted D+I+I Expenditure £	TOTAL FTE	ECB Budget £	Cost per Job £
2000	56 848 630	1 675	569 219	340
2001	43 123 923	1 271	583 496	459
2002	52 842 549	1 557	553 038	355
2003	52 710 371	1 553	569 072	366
2004	48 922 297	1 441	675 555	469
2005	51 077 146	1 505	741 600	493
Total	**305 524 916**	**9 001**		

Table 4.8
Cumulative employment
impact

Employment generation

The estimated net expenditure impact generated by visitor spend can be converted into an employment impact using employment multipliers from the Scottish Tourism Multiplier Study. In 1992, STMS estimated that expenditure of £24 331 created or safeguarded one full-time equivalent (FTE) job. At 2005 prices, this value was £33 942.

Applying these figures to the net direct, indirect, and induced expenditures produces the estimates in Table 4.8.

Overall ECB's activities created or safeguarded around 9000 full-time equivalent jobs during the period, helping to create or safeguard around 1500 full-time equivalent jobs per year in the Edinburgh economy.

Further information: www.conventionedinburgh.com.

Case Study 4.3   Team San José

The City of San José, California, was once a largely agrarian community set in a valley dotted with orchards of apricots, walnuts, cherries and plums, giving it the nickname of the 'Prune Capital of the World'. Today its economy has been transformed and it is probably best known as the 'Capital of Silicon Valley', an area with a global reputation and which claims the largest concentration of technology expertise in the world, with more than 6600 technology companies employing over 254 000 people. San José is now the tenth largest city in the USA with a population of 954 000, and has the highest median household income of all US cities.

This case study examines an innovative approach adopted by the City for the management and marketing of its convention centre and theatres through the creation of a company, Team San José, set up specifically for this purpose.

Background

In March 2003 the Mayor of San José requested the City Administration to report on opportunities to save costs and improve efficiencies at the City's San José McEnery Convention Center by revising the operations structure. At that time, the Conventions, Arts and Entertainment Department (CAE) was responsible for the management and operation of the Convention and Cultural Facilities, specifically overseeing event co-ordination, technical services, sales and marketing, facility set-up, security, and maintenance of the Facilities. In 2003 to 2004 CAE operated the Convention Facilities with a budget of US$11.3 million and 93 staff.

The Facilities include three Convention Facilities and three Cultural Facilities. The Convention Facilities are:

1. **San José Convention Center:** The Convention Center provides over 425 000 square feet of exhibition and general assembly space. This includes space for a number of large, concurrent exhibitions, up to 30 meeting rooms seating up to 2400, and banquets for up to 5000.
2. **Civic Auditorium:** The Civic Auditorium includes 3060 seats and four meeting rooms designed for performing arts, general assembly, community and sporting events.
3. **Parkside Hall:** The Parkside Hall includes 30 000 square feet of exhibition and general assembly space with capacity for banquets up to 1800.

Figure 4.7
Downtown San José. (Source: Team San José)

The Cultural Facilities are the Center for the Performing Arts, Montgomery Theater, and California Theater.

A Request for Proposal (RFP) was issued by the City Administration in December 2003 for the management of the Convention and Cultural Facilities, generating four responses. TSJ were successful and were awarded a 5-year contract commencing July 2004. The Management Agreement provided a first year subsidy from the Transient Occupancy Tax amounting to US$3.7 million.

Team San José

Team San José (TSJ) is a private, public benefit (or 'not for profit') corporation formed in December 2003 for the exclusive purpose of ensuring that San José's convention and theatre facilities are managed with the goal of reducing costs, improving the local economy, and adding value for the residents, workers, and businesses in the city. It is composed of San José's hospitality industry stakeholders including: local businesses, organized labour, cultural arts groups, hoteliers, convention and visitors bureau representatives, and community leaders.

TSJ is comprised of staff from TSJ (10 staff), the San José Convention & Visitors Bureau (SJCVB) (34 positions), Centerplate (the exclusive catering company providing all food and beverage in the facilities)(4 positions), and 85 City employee positions. It has a Chief Executive Officer, an Executive Committee, and a 27-member Board of Directors. The Board is represented by four distinct stakeholder groups: 1) local hoteliers, 2) organized labour, 3) the arts, 4) the Convention and Visitors Bureau. The Board elects officers (Chairman, Vice Chairman, Secretary, and Treasurer), establishes policy, and approves annual operating budgets. The members of each stakeholder group elect a representative to sit on the Executive Committee, which is responsible for the day-to-day decisions of TSJ.

The SJCVB, formerly a division of the San José Chamber of Commerce, became a separate entity in 1984. The City entered into an Agreement with the SJCVB in 2000 for a 10-year period. The SJCVB's mission is to enhance the image and economic well-being of San José by taking the leadership role in marketing San José as a globally-recognized destination. The SJCVB provides a comprehensive marketing programme to promote the City in order to achieve, as the City's first priority, the goal of booking conventions, trade shows, conferences, and other events at the Convention Center and area hotels. The SJCVB staff working for TSJ operate from the TSJ office which is located in the San José McEnery Convention Center.

While the SJCVB was formerly able to book business into the San José facilities, it had no control over the delivery of a quality experience for the facilities' customers. It was intended and expected that the direct involvement by SJCVB in TSJ would remedy this situation.

Objectives

In making its submission for the contract to manage the Facilities, TSJ put forward the following objectives:

- To reduce the City's costs for Convention Center and Cultural Facilities' operations. By year 5 a profit of US$28 635 will be generated
- To increase hotel usage and Transient Occupancy Tax revenues by US$17.3 million over 5 years
- To assist local arts groups to expand and thrive
- To provide quality employment for civil service workers and sustain a constructive labour/management relationship through partnerships with local labour
- To generate more customers and more revenue for local businesses with an economic impact of over US$173 million over the 5 years
- To expand cultural and economic opportunities for the diverse ethnic communities in San José
- To build a vibrant, exciting, growing Downtown that will attract larger numbers of visitors
- To provide US$1.4 million immediately in investments for facility upgrades
- To play a vital and constructive role in supporting the City's economic development strategy
- To implement a unified and aggressive sales and marketing effort
- To offer a seamless guest experience through its unique 'One Stop Shopping' in event services
- To rally all employees with an aim to provide the 'Best Event Experience in the Nation'
- To protect the City's assets with a detailed preventative maintenance and housekeeping plan.

Outcomes

An audited review of the TSJ performance at the end of its first year of operation found that, while not all performance measures were met, revenues generated by the Facilities were higher and the City's subsidy was reduced compared with the previous management by the CAE Department. The auditors reported that the Management Agreement had identified 59 specific requirements to be addressed by TSJ. Of these, 49 had been implemented by TSJ and progress had been made in implementing the remaining

10 requirements. The auditors concluded that TSJ would be able to meet fully the requirements set out in the Management Agreement. The preliminary audit of the fiscal year 2005–2006 showed continued improvement.

A survey of event planners found that most considered that TSJ had met or exceeded their expectations in all of the service and product areas. 92 per cent stated that they would host another event in San José.

The initial success of TSJ has been due, primarily, to collaboration by the many TSJ stakeholders. Having hotels, labour and arts organizations, the SJCVB and the local community and business leaders all working together has energized the whole process of meeting TSJ's goals and objectives. On a practical level, more efficient cost management for the facilities has been achieved, from staffing levels to energy usage controls, while improved marketing has secured more events for the city generating additional revenues.

Looking to the future, further efficiencies are being sought through servicing client needs in a more streamlined manner.

Dan Fenton, TSJ's Chief Executive Officer (and also President and CEO of SJCVB), commented:

> Having a clear plan, communicating goals and achieving consensus on the overall mission are the most important components in the success of a model such as Team San José. It is our view that the people who are on the 'front line' of customer service must understand the necessity of an excellent experience, and we expect delivery of that level of service to every client and each event in our facilities.

A number of other US cities are currently investigating whether the partnership model adopted in San José is one which they should replicate.

Further information: www.sanjose.org.

Case Study 5.1 British Educational Research Association's 'Invitation to Tender'

This Invitation to Tender (sometimes referred to as a Request for Proposal or RFP) was compiled by the British Educational Research Association in May 2006 when seeking to appoint a professional conference organizer (PCO) to manage its annual conference. It illustrates the tendering process and also provides details of the kinds of services to be provided to an academic conference by a PCO on an outsourced, contracted basis. Guidelines on the drafting of an Invitation to Tender and the tendering process are included on the web site of the Association of British Professional Conference Organisers: www.abpco.org.

Tender for the management of the British Educational Research Association annual conference and student conference 2008–2010

Tenders are invited for the management of the 2008, 2009 and 2010 British Educational Research Association (BERA) annual conferences.

BERA conferences are held in universities across the UK and, during the contract period, venues are provisionally booked for Heriott Watt University (10–13 September 2008) and the University of Manchester (9–12 September 2009) – the 2010 venue is not yet confirmed. The annual event comprises a 1-day student conference with about 150 delegates followed by a main conference, duration 3 days, attended by 1000+ delegates. The structure of a typical conference programme comprises four keynote presentations and eight parallel sessions of academic papers (each comprising 25 parallel sessions), plus a smaller number of posters. This extensive academic programme customarily includes 600 individual papers and 70 symposia (which generally comprise about four papers) giving a grand total of about 900 papers. Short abstracts are submitted for each paper and these are subjected to peer review. The successful applicant will be expected to create on-line systems to manage and monitor the submission and review processes. A hard copy of the conference programme is sent to all delegates, together with a CD containing the paper abstracts. The successful applicant would also be expected to provide an on-line registration system. A detailed tender document outlining the areas of service required is provided below. It is anticipated that a proportion of the fee will be performance-related and linked to deliverables and deadlines.

Further information on the BERA organization and its SIGs (Special Interest Groups) can be found on the web site www.bera.ac.uk. Applicants may approach the current Chair of the Conference Committee (contact details supplied) for points of clarification up to and including 26th June.

Bids should be sent to (contact details supplied) before noon on 26th June 2006. E-mail applications are preferred and should be sent to (contact details supplied). Interviews for shortlisted applicants will be held on 17th July in London. Intention to bid should be communicated to (contact details supplied) by e-mail by 12th June.

Event management requirements

1. *Event Planning and Reporting.*
   - Negotiating deadlines with the BERA conference team and producing a conference planner
   - Attending planning meetings as agreed
   - Producing minutes from the meetings documenting action points
   - Reporting updates on attendee and sponsorship/exhibition figures, accommodation and social event bookings
   - Providing updates on the budget and current anticipated income
   - Ensuring the project runs to schedule and that key deadlines are met.

2. *Financial Arrangements.*
   - Drafting a detailed budget, monitoring and reporting on expenditure
   - Acting as agents for BERA in all matters relating to procurement of goods and services
   - Collecting and banking all registration and exhibition fees on behalf of BERA
   - Producing accounts no later than four months after the end of the conference
   - Arranging monthly stage payments of income over expenditure.

3. *Publicity and Promotion.*
   - Producing and mailing 1st Announcement and Call for Papers to BERA members
   - Arranging for the production of posters and advertisements as required
   - Managing the setting up and maintaining/updating of the conference web site which will be linked from the home page of the existing BERA web site
   - Recruiting and liaising with sponsors etc.
   - Collecting promotional items and packing the information into delegate bags.

4. *Registration.*
   - Setting up an on-line registration and accommodation booking system
   - Sending confirmations and invoices/receipts
   - Banking delegate fees and balancing delegate income
   - Dealing with delegate queries
   - Providing facilities to collect outstanding fees at conference registration.

5. *On-line Abstract Submission and Review.*
   - Co-ordinating the abstract submission process for the student and main conferences
   - Corresponding with and briefing reviewers
   - Co-ordinating the main conference review process.

6. *Conference Programme Construction.*
   - Co-ordinating the programming of the conference
   - Organizing poster display boards
   - Distributing accepted abstracts to convenors of Special Interest Groups (SIGs) for grouping
   - Informing authors of the acceptance, date and time of their presentation and audio-visual arrangements
   - Creating on-line and CD versions of the programme with hyperlinks to abstracts
   - Co-ordinating the SIG participation at the conference including posters and meeting attendance.

7. *Programme Documents.*
   - Producing copy, arranging for design and production of the Call for Papers, Final Programme and conference CD
   - Mailing the Call for Papers, the Final Programme and CD of abstracts to registered delegates
   - Ensuring an updated copy of programme documents is available on the web site.

8. *Keynote Speakers.*
   - Contacting the keynote speakers to ascertain their audio-visual requirements
   - Organizing speakers' accommodation and liaising with them on travel arrangements.

9. *Conference Sessions.*
   - Ensuring Chairs receive the 'Instructions for Chairing' in advance of the conference
   - Ensuring that agreed audio-visual equipment is ordered and set up in the auditorium and in all breakout rooms
   - Ensuring adequate on-site audio-visual support
   - Ensuring instructions, timekeeping cards and evaluations are available in all breakout rooms.

10. *The Venue/On-site Arrangements.*
    - Handling arrangements with the venue and maintaining regular contact
    - Ensuring adequate directional signage and local stewards to assist delegates
    - Planning all catering with the venue team
    - Organizing the appropriate audio-visual equipment for the various meeting rooms and sufficient audio-visual support staff to service conference sessions
    - Securing sufficient access to the Internet for conference delegates
    - Organizing the design, print and packaging of delegate bags
    - Providing name badges and attendee lists
    - Providing the required personnel for on-site registration management and exhibition build-up.

11. *Social Programme.*
    - Advising on suitable venues and costing proposals for the evening and social events
    - Handling arrangements with the venue and maintaining regular contact
    - Managing the transportation of delegates to and from the conference functions
    - Providing staff to assist delegates at the event.

12. *Exhibition and Sponsorship.*
    - Compiling and distributing a sponsorship opportunities package
    - Liaising closely with all exhibitors and sponsors, collecting fees and producing a floorplan
    - Producing exhibitor information outlining all venue details and technical information
    - Ensuring company logos from exhibitors and sponsors are in the final programme.

13. *Accommodation.*
    - Handling accommodation management, signing hotel and university contracts
    - Providing information on off-site accommodation for delegates.

Case Study 5.2   A PCO Philosophy in a Changing World

This Case Study has been written by PCOs Peter Mainprice and Rebecca Lawrence Bristol of Index Communications Meeting Services, Hampshire, England (email: icms@indexcommunications.com), *and describes the ways in which PCOs help their clients and bring added value to clients' events.*

Of the millions of conferences and meetings that take place every year, a large number of them are supported by a professional conference organizer (PCO). Since research has proved that many people believe that they have the necessary skills to organize a conference, the inevitable question is asked: what does a PCO contribute to a conference and what extra is achieved for a client who contracts a PCO?

Take a look at a job advert for a PCO and the essential skills are outlined: methodical administration, attention to detail, impeccable customer care, commercially-orientated approach, etc etc – all very predictable attributes for anyone providing any kind of administrative service interfacing with clients. However, for conferencing, this is just the pencil sketch of a picture on to which the rich hues of organizing an excellent conference are added. These skills represent the basic starting points of someone taking on a conference and while this outline could still, in the end, constitute an effective result, a real masterpiece requires a different level of operation, organization, determination and awareness.

While an amateur or inexperienced conferencer has a vision in mind, a PCO has knowledge and experience balanced with a healthy cynicism, paranoia and 'worst ways' mentality, contributing a realistic idea of how a conference is really going to turn out, and what level of resources will be required to complete the journey successfully. PCOs have 'been there, done that' in most cases and can steer (overtly or otherwise!) the client and the conference away from danger – be it the inappropriate (e.g. location), the vulnerable (e.g. budget) or the practical (e.g. a programme that goes on too long), effectively contributing to an event that will meet more completely the needs of the client, delegate and exhibitor. PCOs should act as consultants, advisors in all aspects of conference development from marketing to taxation issues, and sometimes as decision-makers. Reliance upon the PCO is often overlooked and underestimated by the more confident client at the outset of a project, only to change later in the life of the conference.

The advantages of having a PCO involved are well documented in PCOs' marketing material, but these are sometimes flouted by PCOs themselves. Lists of promises, generated to reassure potential clients of impeccable service while pointing out the possible 'Bermuda Triangles' within non-PCO conferences, are common. But, however over-the-top these claims and warnings seem, they flow from both the positive and negative experiences of a PCO. With conferences there is always, always the need to be careful, to pay close attention to all the details and to use all potential problem analysis skills available. Only through meticulous attention to these will an excellent event be staged.

PCOs frequently promise to relieve the stress involved with conference organization. A former slogan of ABPCO (The Association of British Professional Conference Organisers) – *Sleep easy with a PCO* – typifies this. Most clients who set out to organize a conference are specialists at something else and organizing a conference can place them outside this 'comfort' zone and known skill set. This does not mean that their competence to organize a conference is in question, but it is very obvious that if the administrative planning, logistical management and routine processing aspects are taken away from them, they will have more time and more 'brain space' to concentrate on their vision of the meeting, which is more likely to be within their comfort zone and skill set. Some clients find conferencing stressful simply contemplating how they will be judged by their peers and superiors after the conference is over. ABPCO's view is that to cash-in on a PCO's experience, tried and tested resources and ready-made systems means to have fewer sleepless nights. The views of ABPCO members' clients would seem very much to support this.

Leading on from relieving stress, PCOs are also able to make up for a client's skill deficit in terms of the professional skills and tricks which can be crucial to a conference's welfare – for example, budget generation and control. Even a small conference of 100 people can represent very significant expenditure by a client organization or very large liability carried by an underwriter. *Realistic* budget models should be produced early on to flag up some very major key elements – e.g. can sufficient sponsorship be obtained? What is the target number of registrants and is the level of uptake assured? Can the venue really be afforded or does the programme need to change to work in line with the budget? (Budgets are addressed in more detail elsewhere is this book). Budgets can often be a bête noire to an amateur organizer. The responsibility can weigh heavily because of the potential conse-quences of a failure and this is often the area where the client obtains the most comfort from the involvement of a PCO who can manage the changing situation wisely and also contribute a cautionary (but realistic) approach to the potential popularity of an event.

The fact that conferences are commercial entities (or should be regarded as such) is also frequently overlooked by the client. While to the client the event is educational, an auditing accountant sees a conference as a very long list of transactions with the need to keep all costs tight, negotiate wherever possible and keep a constant eye (not just a periodical glance) on the accounts as also being key to its success. Where a client may lack the confidence to negotiate, not only in terms of cost but also securing the required performance from a supplier, it quickly becomes part of everyday life, even for a junior PCO, within a conference management company.

Because conferences can regularly make a profit, many orga-nizations ambitiously set about launching a conference or even a series of conferences in order to contribute financially to the organization, hand in hand with the provision of education and networking opportunities. This seems a logical step but this plan can often be blighted by over-optimism, lack of business planning and minimal commercial strategy. Many PCOs are involved with a series of meetings by the same client, run over a period of many years. The result of this involvement is that they are able to see conferencing in the context of real growth and development year on year and this knowledge can be invaluable, a constant factor to a client about to embark on a set of meetings, and helps in setting appropriate objectives against the backdrop of a world where numerous meetings are staged.

A PCO can also enlighten a client as to the market value of his product. A good PCO can create sponsorship opportunities and marketing outlets for any event. Often wearing a more commercial hat than the client, the PCO takes an objective view of the mutual benefits to client and sponsor and it is frequent for a PCO new to a project to identify and locate new streams of financial support simply by using objectivity, relevant contacts and previous conferencing experience.

Logistically, having a PCO involved in the running of a conference is an option second-to-none. While many venues provide exemplary support to conferences, many don't and, in the final lead-in particularly, a conferencing expert on hand to spot potential problems, provide motivation and directives and iron out ambiguities can be invaluable. Most PCOs have used hundreds of venues and they come to the table of each conference organizing team with one objective in mind: to ensure an excellent event. This remains their focus, whatever effort (within reason) it takes, adding creativity where there are philosophies such as 'we always do it like that' and cross-fertilizing good ideas from previous experience of other conferences and other venues, to best effect. PCOs have experience of industry standards, pricing, catering, people flow, queue management, efficient conference registration practice and speaker liaison and management, and these skills click in at each event. To envisage several hundred people collecting together and moving effectively and safely around a building without utilising some professional knowledge and careful planning is to turn down an opportunity for improving the experience of all participants at a meeting. You could say that PCOs enjoy the bits that other people, frequently the clients, do not want to be bogged down with, or even do not consider.

Q: So, if a PCO can achieve all this: enable a host to sleep better, ensure that participants have the optimal experience at the conference etc etc, what is the astronomical cost associated with their service?

A: The good news is that good PCOs should pay for themselves in terms of generating extra income and avoiding expensive options. PCOs should help to construct a conference budget which means that their fees are included without additional expenditure by the client, because the cost is covered by the income to the project e.g. via registrations or sponsorship. PCOs construct their fees in different ways depending upon the size of the conference. Sometimes there is a fixed management fee covering all aspects – including management of the venue, speakers, delegates, sponsors, marketing, print etc etc, and sometimes the fixed fee is lower, being subsidised by a per unit fee for processing delegate registrations or simply charging a percentage of the turnover of the conference. It should be said that because of the nature of conferencing and the potential for repeat business, PCOs often fix their rates to reflect their interest in a long-term relationship, working to establish themselves and illustrate their value over the medium to long term, unlike other kinds of agencies who charge 'for the moment'.

Conclusion

Conferences are like paintings. They can be very similar, but never exactly the same. There can be variances within the basic design of the picture or the way in which the paint has been applied. Sometimes the originator has the whole idea complete before beginning and sometimes the picture takes shape over a period of time. Some artists are able to paint without first mapping out the plan, while others are more laborious and careful.

To refer back to the basic skills required of a PCO, these are really just the start of what is behind an impressive conference – like a sketch behind a painting. Building on these basics, the colours of the meeting get added and the design of the end product evolves and is influenced by all of those behind the project, shaped by their vision and previous experience of what works and what doesn't. It is almost impossible to ascertain at the beginning of a project exactly what the role of all of those involved will end up being and the extent of their involvement, but in the end a PCO can act as a more experienced artist working with the other painters, used for reference and expertise where they seek advice, comfort and experience.

A good PCO is there to advise, manage, juggle, pre-empt, test, negotiate, steer, process, buffer and liaise. To balance these things: to make a conference a client's pride, a delegate's pleasure, a sponsor's benefit and an organization's financial success, while managing the personal stress of responsibility and protecting the well-being of your conference management company, is the art of being a PCO. For any client to turn down this potentially pivotal and crucial addition to a conference organizing team would be like an amateur artist choosing to ignore an Old Master.

Case Study 5.4 Technology and Virtual Meetings and Conferences

Technology in the conference and meetings industry is developing at an ever-faster pace, with new applications coming onto the market on a very regular basis. Understanding and keeping pace with these developments is a continuous challenge, but is an essential part of the conference organizer's role. The need to maximize the opportunities afforded by these new technologies is vital to remain competitive. They may help to reduce costs, generate new income streams, improve the efficiency and effectiveness of meetings, enhance the delegate experience, extend the life and spread of a conference.

Figure 5.5
A videoconference.
(Source: Elsevier
Butterworth-Heinemann)

In an article entitled 'Selecting the Right Meeting Planning Technology – A Step-by-Step Guide', Corbin Ball, a well-known speaker, writer and consultant focusing on the meetings, events and tradeshow industries (www.corbinball.com), lists the following areas where meetings technology tools can help:

- Abstract and educational content management
- Association and membership tracking
- Attendee/delegate matchmaking and networking
- Auctions and fundraising
- Audience polling
- Badge making
- Banquet seating
- Contact management
- Customer relationship management
- Event web sites and portal management
- Exhibition sales and floorplan management
- Incentive tracking
- Lead retrieval
- Marketing, communication and attendance building
- Meeting specification
- Meetings consolidation, procurement and request for proposal (RFP) management
- Onsite technology (registration, cyber cafes, product directories, internet access)
- Registration
- Room diagramming
- Scheduling

- Site/venue selection
- Speaker management
- Surveys
- Travel and ground transportation management
- Virtual meetings and shows.

This brief guide will focus on this last area of virtual meetings and conferences, in itself a huge and growing topic. It will attempt to explain how the key technologies operate and summarize their specific applications. Readers interested in technology tools for the other areas listed above will find Corbin's web site a valuable resource, together with publications such as 'The Ultimate Meeting Professionals Technology Guide' available as a free download from the MPI Foundation (www.mpifoundation.org) – this contains detailed, categorized listings for more than 1300 software products in 28 categories.

Selecting the right virtual technology

Susan Friedmann (www.thetradeshowcoach.com) says (in an article entitled 'Using Teleconferencing for Meeting Success' (2004)) that:

> selecting the right technology requires you to analyze your goals for the meeting you're planning, and determine what resources you can put into it. From there, you'll decide which method can best help you reach those goals in a cost effective manner. If speed and immediacy are important, and you don't want to spend a lot of money, teleconferencing is a good option. If you want to impress a large audience with a high quality video presentation of a speech, and you have the money to spend, satellite videoconferencing is the way to go. To demonstrate a computer application, you'll probably want to use web conferencing.

She lists seven questions which, she advises, need to be considered and ranked in terms of their importance:

1. **How many locations will be involved in the meeting?**
   Depending on the type of meeting you choose to host, you might have to set up facilities at each of these sites. For example, a videoconference would require you to either create or rent a room with the necessary equipment at each location. If you're only going to have one or two people at each of ten sites, it might not be worth the cost of setting up videoconferencing equipment at each. A desktop conference or a teleconference might be more suitable.

2. **How many people will be involved in the total meeting and at each specific location?**
   Some methods are more suited for small audiences, while others are perfect for large broadcasts. Knowing how many people will be involved at each location will also factor into the cost effectiveness of setting up facilities at each site.

3. **How important is it to impress meeting participants?**
   This will help to determine the quality of the broadcast that you want to invest in. If it's simply an internal meeting between employees who you don't particularly need to impress, a high quality videoconference might not be worth the price. If, however, you need your audience to be awed, then go for the best!

4. **What resources do you have available?**
   This includes financial resources, facilities, equipment, staff, and so on. The prices of the systems differ substantially, and the investment you are willing to make will guide your decision. You can save costs if you already have in-house technical staff that can help set up the event.

5. **How much time do you have available to plan the meeting?**
   Some methods, such as videoconferencing, can take a great deal of preparation, particularly when being done for the first time.

6. **What do you hope to accomplish with the meeting?**
   Are you looking for a quick decision on a time-sensitive topic? Do you want to demonstrate a process or show samples to a client? Do you want a one-way transfer of information from a single source to a large audience? Is it important that participants are able to interact with one another? These are some of the major questions you need answered to help with your selection.

7. **What special needs do you have for the meeting?**
   Do you want the ability to work on a document collaboratively? Would you like to show 'PowerPoint' presentations? Or do you have other specifics for the meeting?

Susan Friedmann concludes by saying that:

> depending on your answers to these questions, one of the technologies might clearly appear the best fit. It's also possible, however, to combine different technologies to create the ideal environment for your meeting. Consider a web broadcast partnered with a conference call, an interactive whiteboard used during a teleconference, or any number of these combinations.

Teleconferencing

Teleconferencing, or the act of meeting via the telephone, is one of the simplest and most cost effective forms of meeting. It requires a telephone at each location and a long distance service provider. In the same article referred to above, Susan Friedmann lists what she sees as the pros and cons of teleconferencing:

Pros:

- Decisions can be made quickly, and problems can be handled immediately, without wasting time on extensive planning and travel. This allows participants to address client needs and changing markets faster
- Teleconferencing is one of the simplest and most cost-effective forms of meeting. There is little or no capital investment, and the price is relatively low. The only additional cost (assuming that participants already have access to a phone) is the fee to the service provider and any long distance charges that accrue
- Contacts can participate from anywhere, as long as they are near a phone.

Cons:

- Meeting without visual communication can sometimes be difficult. There is no way to read facial expressions or body language over the phone
- Some people are easily distracted from phone conversations. A well-planned teleconference can minimize the risk of this, however
- Some people find it hard talking in a vacuum and might refrain from participating, whereas face-to-face they might be more chatty.

However, the traditional teleconference is changing driven, in part, by the impact of new conference furniture. For example, interactive screens and virtual flip charts allow information from laptops, scanned images and video to be input onto flip charts (and/or participants can write by hand onto the flipcharts), with the images being transmitted simultaneously to a flip chart or computer in a remote location. Participants can share their laptop screen, actively add content and annotate just as if they were physically present in the room with the initiator of the original message. One example of this product is the Thunder Virtual Flipchart System (www.harrisonltd.co.uk or www.polyvision.com/products/thunder.asp).

Videoconferencing

Videoconferencing is a set of interactive telecommunication technologies which allows two or more locations to interact via two-way video and audio transmissions simultaneously. Videoconferencing first appeared in the 1980s, but did not attract wide usage because of high costs, unreliable and incompatible technologies, and poor quality images. However, over the past couple of decades, major improvements have been made to the technology and the costs have fallen substantially. Some venues have invested in videoconferencing suites designed to replicate the appearance and feel of face-to-face meetings. Research in the UK found that, while only 11 per cent of companies used videoconferencing in 1997, this had grown to an estimated 63 per cent by 2005 ('UK Conference Market Survey 2006').

The core technology used in a videoteleconference (VTC) system, according to Wikipedia (*http://en.wikipedia.org/wiki/Video_conferencing*) is digital compression of audio and video streams in real time. The hardware or software that performs compression is called a codec (coder/decoder). Wikipedia describes the two basic kinds of VTC systems as:

1. **Dedicated systems** have all the required components packaged into a single piece of equipment, usually a console with a high quality remote-controlled video camera. These cameras can be controlled at a distance to pan left and right, tilt up and down, and zoom. The console contains all electrical interfaces, the control computer, and the software or hardware-based codec. Omnidirectional microphones are connected to the console, as well as a TV monitor with loudspeakers and/or a video projector. There are several types of dedicated VTC devices:
   a) Large group VTC are non-portable, large, more expensive devices used for large rooms and auditoria.
   b) Small group VTC are non-portable or portable, smaller, less expensive devices used for small meeting rooms.
   c) Individual VTC are usually portable devices, meant for single users, have fixed cameras, microphones and loudspeakers integrated into the console.
2. **Desktop systems** are add-ons (hardware boards, usually) to normal PCs, transforming them into VTC devices. A range of different cameras and microphones can be used with the board, which contains the necessary codec and transmission interfaces. Videoconferences carried out via dispersed PCs are also known as **e-meetings**.

Wikipedia summarizes two outstanding issues which are preventing videoconferencing from becoming a standard form of communication, despite the ubiquity of videoconferencing-capable systems, as:

- **Eye Contact**: it is known that eye contact plays a large role in conversational turn-taking, perceived attention and intent, and other aspects of group communication. While traditional telephone conversations give no eye contact cues, videoconferencing systems are arguably worse in that they provide an incorrect impression that the remote interlocutor is avoiding eye contact.

- **Appearance Consciousness**: a second problem with videoconferencing is that participants are literally on camera, with the video stream possibly even being recorded. The burden of presenting an acceptable on-screen appearance is not present in audio-only communication. Early studies found that the addition of video actually impaired communication, possibly because of the consciousness of being on camera.

High speed internet connectivity has become more widely available at a reasonable cost and the cost of video capture and display technology has decreased. Consequently personal video teleconference systems based on a webcam, personal computer system, software compression and broadband internet connectivity have become affordable for the general public. The hardware used for this technology has continued to improve in quality, and prices have dropped dramatically. The availability of free software (often as part of chat programmes) has made software-based videoconferencing accessible to many. For many years, futurists have envisaged a future where telephone conversations will take place as actual face-to-face encounters with video as well as audio. Desktop PC videoconferencing promised to make this a reality, although it remains to be seen whether there is widespread enthusiasm for video calling.

Videoconferencing provides students with the opportunity to learn by participating in a 2-way communication platform. Furthermore, teachers and lecturers from all over the world can be brought to classes in remote or otherwise isolated places. Students from diverse communities and backgrounds can come together to learn about one another. Students are able to explore, communicate, analyze and share information and ideas about one another. Through videoconferencing students can visit another part of the world to speak to others, visit a zoo, a museum and so on, as 'virtual field trips'.

Videoconferencing can enable individuals in faraway places to have meetings at short notice. Time and money that used to be spent on travelling can be used to have short meetings. Technology such as VoIP (voice over internet protocol – the internet protocol is the internationally agreed standard for communicating data across and between networks; VOIP is also known as IP telephony or IPT) can be used in conjunction with desktop videoconferencing to enable face-to-face business meetings to take place without leaving the desktop. The technology is also used for telecommuting, in which employees work from home.

An article in *The Times* newspaper (5th December 2006) described new videoconferencing technology in the following terms:

> *The arrival of internet protocol communications and the plummeting cost of big TV screens have ushered in a new generation of videoconferencing systems – a technology dubbed 'telepresence'. A telepresence suite looks much like a boardroom, except that the table has very large flat screens along one side. When the screens are switched on, the images show a similar boardroom, as if a mirror was mounted across the table. The others taking part are shown in full size, as realistically as possible. Instead of having a single microphone over each screen, microphones are placed around the room to pick up the direction in which a person is speaking. Participants in the virtual "boardroom" then turn to look at them, as if they were all in the same room. Both boardrooms have the same whiteboard showing the same presentations, and documents can even be "passed" across the table by inserting them into a scanner in one room and printing them out in the other. Telepresence is a big corporate system, each room costing at least £200 000 to equip, but prices are likely to fall dramatically over the next 10 years.*

Podcasting

Corbin Ball defines podcasting ('Meetings & Incentive Travel' magazine, October 2006) as a 'method of distributing audio or video programs over the internet to be played on portable digital players or personal computers'. He explains that it is possible to subscribe to podcasts in a manner similar to e-newsletters, or by searching through the podcast offerings of iTunes (www.itunes.com) and RSS (really simple syndication) sites; or by simply clicking on a web link and listening to on-demand internet radio programmes. As the cost of MP3 players (the generic name for an iPod) and related technology continues to fall, Corbin predicts that they will be found in mobile phones and personal digital assistants (PDAs). He says that the cost of producing and globally distributing audio or video podcasts is nearly always less than traditional print, radio, CD video/audio, DVDs, and even other electronic media such as web sites.

Other benefits include a large listener base, as tens of millions of MP3 players have been sold and nearly every computer made since 2001 can play MP3 (audio) and MP4 (video) files. Podcasting is also convenient as listeners can access 24/7 at their own convenience. Low production and distribution costs mean a highly targeted listening base can be addressed affordably, known as narrow casting.

Corbin's article lists a number of applications for podcasting in the conventions and meetings industry. They include:

- Meetings and events can be podcast (either audio or video) as a service to members unable to attend or as a promotion for those wishing to attend in the future
- Podcasts can be an alternative or an addition to blast e-mails on important event announcements
- Podcast interviews with key presenters posted at a conference web site can create interest in an event
- MP3 and MP4 files promoting events or providing content can easily be added to web sites to add 'punch' or provide an alternative communication method
- MP3 players (pre-loaded with conference or promotional content) will become cheap enough to be conference 'giveaways' or even promotional merchandise for tradeshows
- Convention and visitor bureaux can send out promotional videos customized to each group – all by simply adding a link to a targeted blast email.

Further information can be found at: http://en.wikipedia.org/wiki/Podcasting.

Web conferencing and Web casting

Web Conferencing

Holding conferences over the web has become increasingly popular since the advent of broadband technology which enables the simultaneous transfer of one or two-way voice, video and data over IP to take place. The technology allows unlimited on-line viewers or participants sharing a common computer screen interface, with added tools including chat rooms, polling, on-line Q & A and resources downloads including presentations, PDFs, case studies, research and other relevant items. The conference can be integrated with a live event for both face-to-face and on-line audiences, be it an on-line archive of a previous event, or a stand-alone live web conference with an on-line audience only.

A variation on the theme of web conferencing is known as 'webinars', short for virtual web seminars. Often pre-recorded, they present the user with a streamed video of a conference, additional key information like text or statistics to support a 'PowerPoint' presentation, or images used during the conference, and links to related web sites. Events can either be joined live for interactivity or viewed afterwards on demand at a time that suits.

Web casting

Web casting is broadcasting over the internet. It is the electronic distribution of audio and video over IP. Conference sessions and presentations can be broadcast in this way, either in real time as a live event or recorded and made available after the conference, either as free access or on a paid-for basis. Registration systems capture relevant information about viewers as well as preventing unauthorized access to content by requiring viewers to enter a password to view the content. The technology, therefore, extends the life of the conference and extends its reach, with the potential to attract a worldwide audience.

Examples of web conferences and web-cast events can be seen at www.frederation.com – search through the Digital Media Services section of the site.

There is clear evidence of a growing use of web casting. The 'UK Conference Market Survey 2006', for example, found that 19 per cent of corporate respondents used web casting in 2005, compared with just 9 per cent in 2004.

Wi-Fi

Wi-Fi is an abbreviation for 'wireless fidelity', although this full term is rarely used these days. Wi-Fi refers to the technology of *wireless* local area networks. A person with a Wi-Fi-enabled device such as a computer, mobile (or cell) phone, or PDA can connect to the internet when in proximity to an access point. The region covered by one or several access points is called a hotspot. Hotspots can range from a single room to many square miles of overlapping hotspots (e.g. Wireless Philadelphia – www.phila.gov/wireless, and other cities such as Amsterdam, Manchester, Seattle, San Francisco, which provide free internet access across large urban areas).

When the technology was first commercialized there were many problems because consumers could not be sure that products from different suppliers would work together. The Wi-Fi Alliance began as a community to solve this issue and address the needs of the end user, and allow the technology to mature. The Alliance created the branding *Wi-Fi CERTIFIED* to show consumers that products are interoperable with other products displaying the same branding.

Conference venues and hotels are increasingly offering Wi-Fi facilities, although many currently charge a fee for this service provision. Wi-Fi has a range of applications in formal business meetings but is also a benefit for conference delegates during refreshment breaks or outside the conference sessions, enabling them to access the internet and their e-mail messages.

The disadvantages of Wi-Fi include its potential for interruption by other devices, such as 2.4 Ghz cordless phones. Wi-Fi 'pollution', interference by other open access points in an area, can also be a problem in high-density areas such as office buildings with many Wi-Fi access points.

Conclusion

The scale of the development of new conference industry technologies, and the speed with which they are coming on 'stream', mean that a number of the products described above may already have been superceded by the time this book is being read. One useful way of keeping abreast of the many new developments is by subscribing to technology expert, Corbin Ball's e-newsletter by emailing corbin@corbinball.com (subscription is free). Corbin's web site (www.corbinball.com) is also an invaluable source of articles and information.

The issue of whether and how these technologies will reduce the demand for face-to-face meetings is discussed in Chapter 9.

Appendix A

List of Conference Industry Trade Magazines

The list below provides details of some of the international conference industry's leading trade magazines.

Title	Contact Details
Association Meetings	10 Fawcett St., Suite 500 Cambridge, MA 02138, USA *www.meetingsnet.com/associationmeetings*
Association Meetings International	CAT Publications Ltd, Kings House Cantelupe Road, East Grinstead, West Sussex, RH19 3BE *www.meetpie.com*
Conference & Incentive Management	CIM Verlag GmbH & Co KG, Postfach 10 07 51, D-64207 Darmstadt, Germany *www.cim-publications.de*
Conference & Incentive Travel	Haymarket Marketing Publications Ltd, 174 Hammersmith Road, London W6 7JP *www.citmagazine.com*
Conference + Meetings World	Mash Media, Faraday House, 39 Thornton Road, Wimbledon, London, SW19 4NQ *www.mashmedia.net*
Conference News	Mash Media, Faraday House, 39 Thornton Road, Wimbledon, London, SW19 4NQ *www.mashmedia.net*
Congresos, Convenciones e Incentivos	Meetings & Incentive SL, Plaza de España 18, 28008 Madrid, Spain *www.cci@cciweb.info*
Convegni	Via Ezio Biondi 1, 20154 Milano, Italy *www.convegni.it*

Title	Contact Details
Convene	Professional Convention Management Association, 2301 South Lake Shore Drive, Suite 1001, Chicago, IL60616-1419, USA *www.pcma.org*
Conventions & Incentives Marketing	Rank Publishing Co Pty Ltd, Box 189 St Leonards PO, NSW 1590, Australia *www.cimmagazine.com*
Incentive Travel & Corporate Meetings	Market House, 19-21 Market Place, Wokingham, Berkshire RG40 1AP *www.incentivetravel.co.uk*
International Association Executive	PO Box 7804, Bishop's Stortford Herts, CM23 1XY *www.association-executive.co.uk*
L'Evénementiel	2 allée de Longchamp, 92281 Suresnes Cedex, France *www.evenementiel.fr*
Meeting & Congressi	Ediman srl, Via Ripamonti, 89 - 20139 Milan, Italy *www.mconline.it*
Meetings & Incentive Media	Mechelseplein 23, B-2000 Antwerp, Belgium *www.meetingmedia.be*
Meetings & Conventions	Northstar Travel Media, 500 Plaza Drive, Secaucus, NJ 07094-3626, USA *www.meetings-conventions.com*
Meetings & Incentive Travel	CAT Publications Ltd, Kings House Cantelupe Road, East Grinstead West Sussex, RH19 3BE *www.meetpie.com*
Meetings & Incentive Travel	Meeting & Travel Group, One Mount Pleasant Road, 7th Floor Toronto, Ontario, Canada M4Y 2Y5 *www.meetingscanada.com*
Quality in Meetings	Postbus 341, 1700 AH Heerhugowaard, The Netherlands ***www.qualityinmeetings.nl***
Quality Travel	Promos Edizioni SRL, via Giacomo Watt 37, 20143 Milan, Italy *www.qualitytravel.it*
Spain Travel & Business Meetings	General Yague 10-3 1. 28020 Madrid, Spain
Successful Meetings	770 Broadway, New York, NY10003, USA *www.mimegasite.com*
TW Tagungs Wirtschaft	Mainzer Landstrasse 251, D-60326, Frankfurt-am-Main, Germany *www.tw-media.com*

The author wishes to acknowledge the assistance given by Friday's Media Group (*www.fridays-group.co.uk*) in the compilation of this list.

Index